The Seamless Garment

THE
SEAMLESS GARMENT

Writings on the Consistent Ethic of Life

CARDINAL JOSEPH BERNARDIN

THOMAS A. NAIRN
EDITOR

THE BERNARDIN CENTER
CATHOLIC THEOLOGICAL UNION, CHICAGO

ORBIS BOOKS
Maryknoll, New York 10545

Founded in 1970, Orbis Books endeavors to publish works that enlighten the mind, nourish the spirit, and challenge the conscience. The publishing arm of the Maryknoll Fathers and Brothers, Orbis seeks to explore the global dimensions of the Christian faith and mission, to invite dialogue with diverse cultures and religious traditions, and to serve the cause of reconciliation and peace. The books published reflect the opinions of their authors and are not meant to represent the official position of the Maryknoll Society. To obtain more information about Maryknoll and Orbis Books, please visit our website at www.maryknoll.org.

Cardinal Bernardin's text copyright © 2008 by the Archdiocese of Chicago. Introduction, foreword and arrangement copyright © 2008 by the Bernardin Center, Catholic Theological Union, Chicago.

Published by Orbis Books, Maryknoll, New York, U.S.A. All rights reserved.

No part of this publication may be reproduced or transmitted in any form or by any means, electronic or mechanical, including photocopying, recording, or any information storage or retrieval system, without prior permission in writing from the publishers. For permissions, write to Orbis Books, P. O. Box 308, Maryknoll NY 10545-0308, U.S.A.

Manufactured in the United States of America.

Library of Congress Cataloging-in-Publication Data

Bernardin, Joseph, 1928-1996.
    The seamless garment : writings on the consistent ethic of life / Cardinal Joseph Bernardin ; Thomas A. Nairn, editor.
        p. cm.
    Includes index.
    ISBN-13: 978-1-57075-764-8
1. Christian ethic—Catholic authors. 2. Christian ethics. 3. Ethics. 4. Catholic Church and philosophy. I. Nairn, Thomas A., 1948- II. Title.
    BJ1249.B47 2008
    241'.697—dc22
                                        2007037216

CONTENTS

FOREWORD

December of 2008 marks the twenty-fifth anniversary of Cardinal Joseph Bernardin's Gannon Lecture at Fordham University in which he first described his consistent ethic of life. The Cardinal had just completed his work on the bishops' pastoral letter, "The Challenge of Peace: God's Promise and Our Response," and had also become the chair of the then National Conference of Catholic Bishops' Pro-Life Committee. Having been asked to address the drafting of the peace pastoral, he used the lecture to link both of these areas of concern. The following day a description of his talk appeared on the front page of the *New York Times* and triggered a debate among Catholics and others regarding the possibility of such a consistent ethic linking life issues and justice issues. In responding to this debate, the Cardinal would eventually devote almost three dozen lectures to the consistent ethic of life, continuing the task until shortly before his death in 1996. Under his influence, the National Conference of Catholic Bishops would also make the consistent ethic of life the basis for a variety of statements on life issues and on issues of political responsibility. Whether people agreed or disagreed with Cardinal Bernardin's analysis, the consistent ethic of life became a much-discussed element of the Catholic moral vision in the United States during the Cardinal's life time.

Shortly before Cardinal Bernardin's death, the Catholic Theological Union (CTU) asked him for permission to found the Bernardin Center for Theology and Ministry in order to carry on the Cardinal's legacy in a variety of areas of Church life. In a letter to the President of CTU giving his permission, the Cardinal recommended that "the prospectus of the Bernardin Center make explicit mention of the Consistent Ethic of Life." He added: "It would be a source of great consolation to me to know that theologians will continue to develop the concept and continue that dimension of my legacy."

When the Erica and Harry John Family Chair of Catholic Ethics was established at CTU in 2002, part of the task of the holder of the Chair was to continue this development of Cardinal Bernardin's consistent ethic of life. Respecting the Cardinal's wishes, the Bernardin Center established a scholars' seminar, inviting ten moral theologians from around the United States to spend three years investigating the consistent ethic. Papers written for this seminar will comprise a companion volume to this work and serve not only as a commentary for Cardinal Bernardin's lectures but also a constructive work analyzing the consistent ethic twenty-five years after its inception and questioning how it might respond to issues that were not yet envisioned by the Cardinal.

As the seminar progressed, the participants articulated the need that all of the lectures devoted to the consistent ethic of life be made more easily available to the public. This present volume is the first compilation of all thirty-five of the lectures dealing with this theme. Previously, these lectures could be accessed only by culling through a variety of books and journals. Some have never been previously published.

Reading through the lectures in the order of their delivery is a useful exercise. On the one hand, one realizes that, like similar enterprises, there is a great deal of repetition among the lectures. Nevertheless, it is also instructive to discover what elements of the lectures are repeated and when they are repeated. Some themes are developed and others are not. Some themes seem to disappear without an apparent reason, only to re-appear months or even years later. It is also enlightening to see often subtle changes in nuance of even familiar themes as the Cardinal continues to develop his understanding of the consistent ethic of life.

The Consistent Ethic of Life Scholars' Seminar at the Bernardin Center was able to begin its work because of grants from the Catholic Health Association, from its then President, Rev. Michael Place, and from the Menard Family Foundation. Further grants from the Menard Family Foundation and the ongoing interest of Barbara Menard allowed the seminar to continue and this volume to be printed. The Scholars' Seminar is especially grateful to her. At the same time, the Bernardin Center is indebted to the Archdiocese of Chicago and the Joseph Cardinal Bernardin Archives and Records Center for the permission to publish these lectures.

Thomas A. Nairn, O.F.M.
Erica and Harry John Family Professor of Catholic Ethics,
Catholic Theological Union

INTRODUCTION

*An Overview of the Key Ideas
in the Consistent Ethic of Life*

THOMAS A. SHANNON

General Themes of the Consistent Ethic of Life

Coherence

There is one principle with diverse applications. Consistency and coherence need to be present in resolving social and public policy questions. The viability of the principle of the sacredness of life depends on consistency of application across a broad range of diverse questions and problems, but questions and problems that are linked by their relation to the value of life. This desire for consistency is grounded on the identification of "a single principle with diverse applications" (p. 18). This coherence then is to help "build a bridge of common interest and common insight on a range of social and moral questions . . . to highlight common interest and reciprocal need which exist among groups interested in specific issues" (p. 25). Finally, "consistency does rule out contradictory moral positions about the unique value of human life" (p. 17).

Diversity

The Consistent Ethic of Life ("CEL" in the rest of this introduction) is not to be a type of moral Procrustean bed in which all moral problems are cut to size by one principle. Cardinal Bernardin is careful to stress "the distinction among cases rather than their similarities. We need different principles to apply to diverse cases" (p. 18). Later the Cardinal notes that the CEL "rejects collapsing all issues into one, and it rejects isolating our moral vision and insulating our social concern on one issue" (p. 104). This diversity will ground the vigorous debate within the Church, which is an affirmation that the CEL is to help generate a public vision even while recognizing that "the consistent ethic [is] not a finished product but a framework in need of development" (p. 108). Thus even though Bernardin affirms strongly that all the life issues are linked or related, nonetheless he recognizes that "Admittedly, these are all *distinct* problems, enormously complex. Each deserves individual treatment. Each requires its own moral analysis. No single answer or solution applies to all" (p. 126).

1

Public Policy

The core of the CEL's relevance to public policy is the recognition that "Catholic social doctrine is based on two truths about the human person: life is both sacred and social" (p. 42). The CEL grounds the right of the Church to speak to public policy issues and provides a framework in which to do it. For example, the CEL gives us a "standard to test public policy, party platforms, and the posture of candidates for office" (p. 108). Bernardin uses a framework consisting of five key elements, developed by John Courtney Murray, to discuss the Church's involvement in these issues: the recognition of religious pluralism, the legitimate secularity of the political process, the complexity of the issues, the relation between civil law and morality, and the determination of public morality through a determination of whether the issues affect the public order of society. The tests for whether or not an issue is one of public order are three goods: public peace, essential protection of human rights, and commonly accepted standards of moral behavior in a community (p. 122). There is an important qualification, though, of the public policy debates: "Although the premises or foundations for public policy and civil law ought to be rooted in an ethical perspective, the scope of law and public policy is limited, and its purpose is not the moralization of society" (p. 155).

Bernardin argues that there are three ways in which religion can contribute to policy debates in civil society: the sharing of one's religious vision and discourse, an example of which would be the CEL; the ministry of various religious institutions to society, e.g. through religiously supported social service agencies; and the participation in society by citizens who are fully informed and shaped by their religious traditions. This orientation is to lead to an engagement with society, taking the form of advocacy and/or restraint; the civic virtue of civility; and "a spirit of fairness, respect, restraint and a search for common ground among contending positions" (p. 292).

The Foundation of the Consistent Ethic of Life

Though the foundation of the CEL is the value and dignity of the human person, this value is expressed in a variety of ways; this section will present several of those articulations. In the first CEL lecture at Fordham, Bernardin articulates the principle this way: "The central idea in the letter [*The Challenge of Peace*] is the sacredness of human life and the responsibility we have, personally and socially, to protect and preserve the sanctity of life." Thus "every human life has transcendent value [and this] has led a whole stream of the Christian tradition to argue that life may never be taken" (p. 10). In this same lecture, the Cardinal, in linking war and abortion, stated that "The more explicit connection is based on the principle which prohibits the directly intended taking of innocent human life" (p. 12). An alternative statement occurred in his address to Amnesty International: "The person is the clearest reflection of the presence of God among us. To lay violent hands on the person . . . is to come as close as we can to laying violent hands on God . . . The person, then, is the key to the entire social presence and outreach of the Church" (p. 27).

The Cardinal also articulated several different framings of this foundation of the CEL. In an address on euthanasia, he describes the basis for the ethic this way: "In this religious tradition, the meaning of human life is grounded in the fact that it is sacred because God is its origin and its destiny. Many other people of good will also accept the basic premise that human life has a distinctive dignity and meaning or purpose, that innocent human life must not be directly attacked, threatened, or diminished" (p. 159). Later in this same address, he notes that "euthanasia is wrong because it involves a direct attack on innocent human life . . . [I]t involves a violation of a basic human good" (p. 174). In another address, Bernardin affirms Vatican II's declaration that "from the moment of conception life must be guarded with the greatest care" (p. 193). Because "the right to life is the fundamental human right," what happens when "protection of the right to life is selective," when the "right to life is denied to inherently vulnerable and dependent unborn life" (p. 193)? Thus in abortion there is a double moral failure: "a human life is taken, and society allows or supports the killing" (p. 194). Here Bernardin joins several issues: "we present our views in terms of the dignity and the quality of human life, the bond between human dignity and human rights, and the conviction that the right to life is the fundamental human right" (p. 195).

Another articulation, from the context of a discussion of euthanasia, is: "In this religious tradition [Judeo-Christian], human life is considered *sacred* because God is its origin and its destiny. Consequently, innocent human life must not be directly attacked, threatened, or diminished. Many other people of good will—not of this tradition—also accept the basic premise that human life has a distinctive dignity and meaning or purpose. They, too, argue that because of the privileged meaning of human life, we have the responsibility for preserving, protecting, and nurturing it" (p. 234).

What Cardinal Bernardin presents as the foundation for the CEL is the traditional framework for understanding the value of life within the Catholic tradition. His language is the customary language of expression, he is clear in his articulation of it, and he sets it within a larger ecclesial context, mainly with references to Vatican II and only a few direct quotes from the papal magisterium. The one addition of Bernardin to this is in the discussion of capital punishment: the focus is not so much on the dignity of the life of the prisoner to be executed, though that is clearly part of the argument. Rather the argument against capital punishment is based on its negative social consequences and a rejection of the revenge motive.

Evaluating the Consistent Ethic of Life

General Comments

One of the issues with respect to the CEL is to determine how it functions. That is, is it a method, a perspective, a stance, an orientation? Bernardin himself is not too helpful in resolving this question, because he frequently claimed he was speaking as a pastor, as a concerned citizen bringing his religious perspective to bear on public policy, and that since he was not a theologian, his was not the job of the theologian. He seems to have left it to others to figure out how the method works.

But what Bernardin clearly was about, first of all, was making linkages among a variety of issues, such as the frequently mentioned ones of abortion, euthanasia, war, capital punishment, poverty, and health care reform. His point is that all of these issues are life issues: each in its own unique way engages the question of the value of life and the dignity of the person, and each, therefore, should be thought of from the perspective of the value of life. Second, the CEL is a way to ensure that the social ethic of the Church is brought into a variety of questions and integrated into the work of the Church. Third, the CEL functions to help prevent single-issue politics within the Church. The CEL declares that the Church is on the side of life and that when insults to life occur, the Church will speak out and act.

However, the fact that the CEL seeks to address these questions in a systematic way does not necessarily mean that the CEL is an ethical method. Linkage claims are descriptive, but do not necessarily give a normative method or arrive at a conclusion. The point of the CEL is well taken: we cannot be schizophrenic in our moral approach to reality, nor can we simply address moral issues in an ad hoc fashion. But linkage of problems or concerns is neither methodology nor consistent analysis.

Specific Issues

Reading the corpus of the CEL texts also highlights differences in analysis that illustrate an oft-cited discrepancy in Catholic morality: there is a different methodology of analysis for social issues than for sexual issues or issues grouped under the pro-life heading. This difference is shown clearly in the arguments against abortion and the death penalty, war and euthanasia.

In arguing against abortion, the CEL appeals to the transcendent value of human life, the sacredness or sanctity of life, the prohibition on the taking of innocent life, the person's being the *imago Dei,* the argument that harming the person is as close to harming God as we can come, and the demonstrable humanness of fetal life because of its genetic character and development. These are essentially deontological appeals or appeals to the inherent dignity and/or value of the early embryo. Thus fetal life may never be directly ended under any circumstances. There are no exceptions.

In the first CEL lecture at Fordham, Bernardin notes, in speaking about *The Challenge of Peace,* that there is "a *presumption* against taking human life, but in a limited world marked by the effects of sin there are some narrowly defined *exceptions* where life can be taken" (p. 10). Here, set forth as an absolute principle, is the prohibition on direct attacks of civilians based on their innocence. The death of civilians as an indirect effect of a particular war strategy remains permitted, though subject to rigorous moral analysis. With respect to the death penalty, the CEL affirms the traditional position that the state has the right to use capital punishment, again an exception to the presumption against taking human life. In an address specifically on the death penalty, Bernardin approvingly cites the reasoning of the 1980 USCC statement, which argues that goods of punishment need not be obtained by using the death penalty. "The limits of punishment must be determined by moral objective which go beyond the mere infliction of injury on the guilty" (p. 87). Additional arguments against the use of the death penalty are derived from its lack of justification for "deterrence, retribution, reform, or protection of society," as well as the recognition of "God's boundless love for every person, regardless of human merit or worthiness" (p. 88). In another address, Bernardin continues to argue that such a right should not be exercised because "there are other ways—more appropriate and effective than capital punishment—for the state to defend its people" (p. 31). Additionally, the exercise of the right of capital punishment does not encourage an attitude of respect for life. Thus "means other than the death penalty are available and can be used to protect society," and "we recognize the need of society to move beyond mere justice in dealing with the victims of crime and their families" (p. 31).

The arguments against euthanasia begin with the affirmation of the sacredness of life, its dignity, and a defense of the life of the innocent, leading to the conclusion that euthanasia is a violation of a fundamental human good. But the social arguments are also important: we must not generate a class of humans who are described as no longer possessing human dignity; decisions about dying are not essentially private ones in which the state has no interest; and if the inviolability of life is diminished, "neither individual nor society can long survive" (p. 160). Additionally, euthanasia also presents a threat to the physician-patient relationship, and would present a variety of pressures on patients to make them vulnerable to euthanasia. Finally, once established, the practice of euthanasia might not be able to be controlled (p. 255).

The CEL is clearly vulnerable to the critique that in arguments about social issues a different methodology is in play and exceptions can be made, whereas in arguments about abortion, euthanasia, and sexual morality, no exceptions are permitted.[1] The way this argument is cast is that there is a

---

[1] See, for example, Christine Gudorf, "To Make a Seamless Garment, Use a Single Piece of Cloth." *Cross Currents* 34 (Winter 1984): 473-91, and Timothy A. Byrnes, "How 'Seamless' a Garment: The Catholic Bishops and the Politics of Abortion." *Journal of Church and State* 33 (Winter 1991): 17-35.

presumption against the taking of life and that, though arguments against this presumption are getting stronger, nonetheless this is still a presumption and exceptions can be made. And the basis for the exceptions is an analysis of the social context. Thus policies with respect to social and economic justice that do not fully respect human dignity and that in fact harm the innocent can be tolerated. The practice of using nuclear targeting strategies as part of deterrence policy can receive conditional approval. The acceptance of large numbers of civilian deaths, as a possible consequence of such policies, can also be tolerated.[2] The strong arguments against exercising the right of capital punishment acknowledge the dignity of the criminal but look more to social consequences. Core arguments against the death penalty are cast in terms of forgiveness and mercy, not the value of innocent human life, perhaps for the reason that the life of the criminal is not so innocent, though one must be careful of equivocations here.

---

[2] An early attempt to apply this principle to a practice of modern warfare—obliteration bombing—is "The Morality of Obliteration Bombing" by John Ford in *Theological Studies* 5 (1944): 261-309. The article is conspicuous in its attempt to take seriously the principle of civilian immunity during war. But Ford also clearly shows how the principle was simply disregarded as victory was given an ever higher priority.

1.

A CONSISTENT ETHIC OF LIFE

An American Catholic Dialogue

GANNON LECTURE, FORDHAM UNIVERSITY,
DECEMBER 6, 1983

It is a privilege to be invited to give the Gannon Lecture at Fordham University. Fr. Gannon's life as a priest, a Jesuit, and a scholar offers a standard of excellence which any Gannon lecturer should seek to imitate.

I was invited to address some aspect of the U. S. Catholic bishops' pastoral letter, *The Challenge of Peace: God's Promise and Our Response.* I am happy to do so, but I want to address the topic in a very specific manner. The setting of today's lecture has shaped its substance. The setting is a university, a community and an institution committed to the examination and testing of ideas. A university setting calls for an approach to the pastoral which does more than summarize its content; six months after its publication, it is necessary to examine the document's impact and to reflect upon the possibilities for development which are latent in its various themes.

More specifically, Fordham is an *American* Catholic university, an institution which has consistently fostered the work of enriching American culture through Catholic wisdom and has simultaneously sought to enhance our understanding of Catholic faith by drawing upon the American tradition.

Today I will discuss the pastoral letter in terms of the relationship of our Catholic moral vision and American culture. Specifically, I wish to use the letter as a starting point for shaping a consistent ethic of life in our culture. In keeping with the spirit of a university, I have cast the lecture in the style of an inquiry, an examination of the need for a consistent ethic of life and a probing of the problems and possibilities which exist within the Church and the wider society for developing such an ethic.

I do not underestimate the intrinsic intellectual difficulties of this exercise nor the delicacy of the question—ecclesially, ecumenically, and politically. But I believe the Catholic moral tradition has something valuable to say in the face of the multiple threats to the sacredness of life today, and I am convinced that the Church is in a position to make a significant defense of life in a comprehensive and consistent manner.

Such a defense of life will draw upon the Catholic moral position and

7

the public place the Church presently holds in the American civil debate. The pastoral letter links the questions of abortion and nuclear war. The letter does not argue the case for linkage; that is one of my purposes today. It is important to note that the way these two issues are joined in the pastoral places the American bishops in a unique position in the public policy discourse of the nation. No other major institution presently holds these two positions in the way the Catholic bishops have joined them. This is both a responsibility and an opportunity.

I am convinced that the pro-life position of the Church must be developed in terms of a comprehensive and consistent ethic of life. I have just been named the Chairman of the National Conference of Catholic Bishops' Pro-Life Committee; I am committed to shaping a position of linkage among the life issues. It is that topic I wish to develop today in three steps: (1) a reflection on the pastoral letter on war and peace; (2) an analysis of a consistent ethic of life; and (3) an examination of how such an ethic can be shaped in the American public debate.

The Church in Public Debate: The Pastoral in Perspective

The pastoral letter on war and peace can be examined from several perspectives. I wish to look at it today in ecclesiological terms, specifically as an example of the Church's role in helping to shape a public policy debate. Early in the letter the bishops say that they are writing in order to share the moral wisdom of the Catholic tradition with society. In stating this objective the American bishops were following the model of the Second Vatican Council which called dialogue with the world a sign of love for the world.

I believe the long-term ecclesiological significance of the pastoral rests with the lessons it offers about the Church's capacity to dialogue with the world in a way which helps to shape the public policy debate on key issues. During the drafting of the pastoral letter one commentator wrote in the editorial section of the *Washington Post*: "The Catholic bishops . . . are forcing a public debate on perhaps the most perplexing nuclear question of them all, the morality of nuclear deterrence . . . Their logic and passion have taken them to the very foundation of American security policy."

This commentary accurately captures the purpose of the pastoral letter. The bishops intended to raise fundamental questions about the dynamic of the arms race and the direction of American nuclear strategy. We intended to criticize the rhetoric of the nuclear age and to expose the moral and political futility of a nuclear war. We wanted to provide a moral assessment of existing policy which would both set limits to political action and provide direction for a policy designed to lead us out of the dilemma of deterrence.

It is the lessons we can learn from the policy impact of the pastoral which are valuable today. The principal conclusion is that the Church's social policy role is at least as important in *defining* key questions in the public debate as in *deciding* such questions. The impact of the pastoral was due in part to its specific positions and conclusions, but it was also due to the way it brought the entire nuclear debate under scrutiny.

The letter was written at a time it called a "new moment" in the nuclear age. The "new moment" is a mix of public perceptions and policy proposals. The public sense of the fragility of our security system is today a palpable reality. The interest in the TV showing of "The Day After" is an example of how the public is taken by the danger of our present condition. But the "new moment" is also a product of new ideas, or at least the shaking of the foundation under old ideas.

Another commentary generated during the drafting of the pastoral letter, this one from *The New Republic,* identified the policy characteristics of the "new moment": "The ground is not steady beneath the nuclear forces of the United States. The problem is not modes of basing but modes of thinking. The traditional strategy for our nuclear arsenal is shaken by a war of ideas about its purpose, perhaps the most decisive war of ideas in its history."

The significant fact to which this editorial points is that the "new moment" is an "open moment" in the strategic debate. Ideas are under scrutiny and established policies are open to criticism in a way we have not seen since the late 1950s. From the proposal of "no first use," through the debate about the MX, to the concept of a Nuclear Freeze, the nuclear policy question is open to reassessment and redirection. The potential contained in the "new moment" will not last forever; policies must be formulated, ideas will crystallize, and some consensus will be shaped. As yet, the content of the consensus is not clear.

The fundamental contribution of *The Challenge of Peace*, I believe, is that we have been part of a few central forces which have created the "new moment." We have helped to shape the debate; now we face the question of whether we can help to frame a new consensus concerning nuclear policy.

The "new moment" is filled with potential; it is also filled with danger. The dynamic of the nuclear relationship between the superpowers is not a stable one. It is urgent that a consensus be shaped which will move us beyond our present posture. The pastoral letter has opened space in the public debate for a consideration of the moral factor. How we use the moral questions, that is, how we relate them to the strategic and political elements, is the key to our contribution to the "new moment." I could spend the entire lecture on the moral dimension of the nuclear debate, but my purpose is rather to relate the experience we have had in dealing with the nuclear question to other issues. Without leaving the topic of the war and peace discussion, I will now try to show how our contribution to this issue is part of a larger potential which Catholic moral vision has in the public policy arena. This larger potential is to foster a consideration of a consistent ethic of life and its implications for us today.

A Consistent Ethic of Life: A Catholic Perspective

The Challenge of Peace provides a starting point for developing a consistent ethic of life but it does not provide a fully articulated framework. The central idea in the letter is the sacredness of human life and the responsibility we have, personally and socially, to protect and preserve the sanctity of life.

Precisely because life is sacred, the taking of even one human life is a momentous event. Indeed, the sense that every human life has transcendent value has led a whole stream of the Christian tradition to argue that life may never be taken. That position is held by an increasing number of Catholics and is reflected in the pastoral letter, but it has not been the dominant view in Catholic teaching and it is not the principal moral position found in the pastoral letter. What is found in the letter is the traditional Catholic teaching that there should always be a presumption against taking human life, but in a limited world marked by the effects of sin there are some narrowly defined exceptions where life can be taken. This is the moral logic which produced the "Just War" ethic in Catholic theology.

While this style of moral reasoning retains its validity as a method of resolving extreme cases of conflict when fundamental rights are at stake, there has been a perceptible shift of emphasis in the teaching and pastoral practice of the Church in the last 30 years. To summarize the shift succinctly, the presumption against taking human life has been strengthened and the exceptions made ever more restrictive. Two examples, one at the level of principle, the other at the level of pastoral practice, illustrate the shift.

First, in a path-breaking article in 1959 in *Theological Studies*, John Courtney Murray, S.J., demonstrated that Pope Pius XII had reduced the traditional threefold justification for going to war (defense, recovery of property, and punishment) to the single reason of defending the innocent and protecting those values required for decent human existence. Second, in the case of capital punishment, there has been a shift at the level of pastoral practice. While not denying the classical position, found in the writing of Thomas Aquinas and other authors, that the state has the *right* to employ capital punishment, the action of Catholic bishops and Popes Paul VI and John Paul II has been directed against the *exercise* of that right by the state. The argument has been that more humane methods of defending the society exist and should be used. Such humanitarian concern lies behind the policy position of the National Conference of Catholic Bishops against capital punishment, the opposition expressed by individual bishops in their home states against reinstating the death penalty, and the extraordinary interventions of Pope John Paul II and the Florida bishops seeking to prevent the execution in Florida last week.

Rather than extend the specific analysis of this shift of emphasis at the levels of both principle and practice in Catholic thought, I wish to probe the rationale behind the shift and indicate what it teaches us about the need for a consistent ethic of life. Fundamental to the shift is a more acute perception of the multiple ways in which life is threatened today. Obviously questions like war, aggression and capital punishment have been with us for centuries and are not new to us. What is new is the *context* in which these ancient questions arise, and the way in which a new context shapes the *content* of our ethic of life. Let me comment on the relationship of the context of our culture and the content of our ethic in terms of: 1) the *need* for a consistent ethic of life; 2) the *attitude* necessary to sustain it; and 3) the *principles* needed to shape it.

The dominant cultural fact, present in both modern warfare and modern medicine, which induces a sharper awareness of the fragility of human life is our technology. To live as we do in an age of careening development of technology is to face a qualitatively new range of moral problems. War has been a perennial threat to human life, but today the threat is qualitatively different due to nuclear weapons. We now threaten life on a scale previously unimaginable. As the pastoral letter put it, the dangers of nuclear war teach us to read the Book of Genesis with new eyes. From the inception of life to its decline, a rapidly expanding technology opens new opportunities for care but also poses new potential to threaten the sanctity of life.

The technological challenge is a pervasive concern of Pope John Paul II, expressed in his first encyclical, *Redemptor Hominis*, and continuing through his address to the Pontifical Academy of Science last month when he called scientists to direct their work toward the promotion of life, not the creation of instruments of death. The essential question in the technological challenge is this: in an age when we *can* do almost anything, how do we decide what we *ought* to do? The even more demanding question is: In a time when we can do anything technologically, how do we decide morally what *we never should do*?

Asking these questions along the spectrum of life from womb to tomb creates the need for a consistent ethic of life. For the spectrum of life cuts across the issues of genetics, abortion, capital punishment, modern warfare, and the care of the terminally ill. These are all distinct problems, enormously complicated, and deserving individual treatment. No single answer and no simple responses will solve them. My purpose, however, is to highlight the way in which we face new technological challenges in each one of these areas; this combination of challenges is what cries out for a consistent ethic of life.

Such an ethic will have to be finely honed and carefully structured on the basis of values, principles, rules and applications to specific cases. It is not my task today, nor within my competence as a bishop, to spell out all the details of such an ethic. It is to that task that philosophers and poets, theologians and technicians, scientists and strategists, political leaders and plain citizens are called. I would, however, highlight a basic issue: the need for an attitude or atmosphere in society which is the pre-condition for sustaining a consistent ethic of life. The development of such an atmosphere has been the primary concern of the "Respect Life" program of the

American bishops. We intend our opposition to abortion and our opposition to nuclear war to be seen as specific applications of this broader attitude. We have also opposed the death penalty because we do not think its use cultivates an attitude of respect for life in society. The purpose of proposing a consistent ethic of life is to argue that success on any one of the issues threatening life requires a concern for the broader attitude in society about respect for human life.

Attitude is the place to root an ethic of life, but ultimately ethics is about principles to guide the actions of individuals and institutions. It is therefore necessary to illustrate, at least by way of example, my proposition that an inner relationship does exist among several issues not only at the level of general attitude but at the more specific level of moral principles. Two examples will serve to indicate the point.

The first is contained in *The Challenge of Peace* in the connection drawn between Catholic teaching on war and Catholic teaching on abortion. Both, of course, must be seen in light of an attitude of respect for life. The more explicit connection is based on the principle which prohibits the directly intended taking of innocent human life. The principle is at the heart of Catholic teaching on abortion; it is because the fetus is judged to be both human and not an aggressor that Catholic teaching concludes that direct attack on fetal life is always wrong. This is also why we insist that legal protection be given to the unborn.

The same principle yields the most stringent, binding, and radical conclusion of the pastoral letter: that directly intended attacks on civilian centers are always wrong. The bishops seek to highlight the power of this conclusion by specifying its implications in two ways: first, such attacks would be wrong even if our cities had been hit first; second, anyone asked to execute such attacks should refuse orders. These two extensions of the principle cut directly into the policy debate on nuclear strategy and the personal decisions of citizens. James Reston referred to them as "an astonishing challenge to the power of the state."

The use of this principle exemplifies the meaning of a consistent ethic of life. The principle which structures both cases, war and abortion, needs to be upheld in both places. It cannot be successfully sustained on one count and simultaneously eroded in a similar situation. When one carries this principle into the public debate today, however, one meets significant opposition from very different places on the political and ideological spectrum. Some see clearly the application of the principle to abortion but contend that the bishops overstepped their bounds when they applied it to choices about national security. Others understand the power of the principle in the strategic debate, but find its application on abortion a violation of the realm of private choice. I contend that the viability of the principle depends upon the consistency of its application.

The issue of consistency is tested in a different way when we examine the relationship between the "right to life" and "quality of life" issues. I must confess that I think the relationship of these categories is inadequately understood in the Catholic community itself. My point is that the Catholic position on abortion demands of us and of society that we seek to influence an heroic social ethic.

If one contends, as we do, that the right of every fetus to be born should be protected by civil law and supported by civil consensus, then our moral, political, and economic responsibilities do not stop at the moment of birth. Those who defend the right to life of the weakest among us must be equally visible in support of the quality of life of the powerless among us: the old and the young, the hungry and the homeless, the undocumented immigrant and the unemployed worker. Such a quality-of-life posture translates into specific political and economic positions on tax policy, employment generation, welfare policy, nutrition and feeding programs, and health care. Consistency means we cannot have it both ways: we cannot urge a compassionate society and vigorous public policy to protect the rights of the unborn and then argue that compassion and significant public programs on behalf of the needy undermine the moral fiber of the society or are beyond the proper scope of governmental responsibility.

Right to life and quality of life complement each other in domestic social policy. They are also complementary in foreign policy. *The Challenge of Peace* joined the question of how we prevent nuclear war to the question of how we build peace in an interdependent world. Today those who are admirably concerned with reversing the nuclear arms race must also be those who stand for a positive U. S. policy of building the peace. It is this linkage which has led the U. S. bishops not only to oppose the drive of the nuclear arms race, but to stand against the dynamic of a Central American policy which relies predominantly on the threat and the use of force, which is increasingly distancing itself from a concern for human rights in El Salvador and which fails to grasp the opportunity of a diplomatic solution to the Central American conflict.

The relationship of the spectrum of life issues is far more intricate than I can even sketch here. I have made the case in the broad strokes of a lecturer; the detailed balancing, distinguishing, and connecting of different aspects of a consistent ethic of life is precisely what this address calls the university community to investigate. Even as I leave this challenge before you, let me add to it some reflections on the task of communicating a consistent ethic of life in a pluralistic society.

Catholic Ethics and the American Ethos: The Challenge and the Opportunity

A consistent ethic of life must be held by a constituency to be effective. The building of such a constituency is precisely the task before the Church and the nation. There are two distinct challenges but they are complementary.

We should begin with the honest recognition that the shaping of a consensus among Catholics on the spectrum of life issues is far from finished. We need the kind of dialogue on these issues which the pastoral letter generated on the nuclear question. We need the same searching intellectual exchange, the same degree of involvement of clergy, religious and laity, the same sustained attention in the Catholic press.

There is no better place to begin than by using the follow-through for the pastoral letter. Reversing the arms race, avoiding nuclear war and moving toward a world freed of the nuclear threat are profoundly "pro-life" issues. The Catholic Church is today seen as an institution and a community committed to these tasks. We should not lose this momentum; it provides a solid foundation to relate our concerns about war and peace to other "pro-life" questions. The agenda facing us involves our ideas and our institutions; it must be both educational and political; it requires attention to the way these several life issues are defined in the public debate and how they are decided in the policy process.

The shaping of a consensus in the Church must be joined to the larger task of sharing our vision with the wider society. Here two questions face us: the substance of our position and the style of our presence in the policy debate.

The substance of a Catholic position on a consistent ethic of life is rooted in a religious vision. But the citizenry of the United States is radically pluralistic in moral and religious conviction. So we face the challenge of stating our case, which is shaped in terms of our faith and our religious convictions, in non-religious terms which others of different faith convictions might find morally persuasive. Here again the war and peace debate should be a useful model. We have found support from individuals and groups who do not share our Catholic faith but who have found our moral analysis compelling.

In the public policy exchange, substance and style are closely related. The issues of war, abortion, and capital punishment are emotional and often divisive questions. As we seek to shape and share the vision of a consistent ethic of life, I suggest a style governed by the following rule: we should maintain and clearly articulate our religious convictions but also maintain our civil courtesy. We should be vigorous in stating a case and attentive in hearing another's case; we should test everyone's logic but not question his or her motives.

The proposal I have outlined today is a multi-dimensional challenge. It grows out of the experience I have had in the war and peace debate and the task I see ahead as Chairman of the Pro-Life Committee. But it also grows from a conviction that there is a new openness today in society to the role of moral argument and moral vision in our public affairs. I say this even though I find major aspects of our domestic and foreign policy in need of drastic change. Bringing about these changes is the challenge of a consistent ethic of life. The challenge is worth our energy, resources and commitment as a Church.

2.

A CONSISTENT ETHIC OF LIFE

Continuing the Dialogue

THE WILLIAM WADE LECTURE SERIES,
ST. LOUIS UNIVERSITY, MARCH 11, 1984

I first wish to express my appreciation to St. Louis University for the invitation to deliver the 1984 Wade Lecture. "The William Wade Lecture Series" is a fitting way to celebrate Father Wade's life as a priest, a philosopher, and a teacher. His interest in the moral issues confronting today's Church and society was an inspiration to all who knew him. I hope that my participation in this series will help to keep alive his memory and his ideals.

Three months ago I gave a lecture at Fordham University honoring another Jesuit educator, Father John Gannon, and I addressed the topic of a consistent ethic of life. That lecture has generated a substantial discussion both inside and outside the Church on the linkage of life issues, issues which, I am convinced, constitute a "seamless garment." This afternoon I would like to extend the discussion by expanding upon the idea of a consistent ethic of life.

The setting of a Catholic university is one deliberately chosen for these lectures. My purpose is to foster the kind of sustained intellectual analysis and debate which the Jesuit tradition has cultivated throughout its history. The discussion must go beyond the university but it will not occur without the involvement of Catholic universities. I seek to call attention to the resources in the Catholic tradition for shaping a viable public ethic. I hope to engage others in the Church and in the wider civil society in an examination of the challenges to human life which surround us today, and the potential of a consistent ethic of life. The Fordham lecture has catalyzed a vigorous debate; I seek to enlarge it, not to end it.

I will address three topics today: (1) the case for a consistent ethic of life; (2) the distinct levels of the problem; and (3) the contribution of a consistent ethic to the Church and society generally.

The Seamless Garment: The Logic of the Case

The invitation extended to me for both the Gannon Lecture at Fordham and the Wade Lecture today asked that I address some aspect of

15

the bishops' pastoral, *The Challenge of Peace: God's Promise and Our Response*. While I would gladly have spent each lecture on the question of war and peace, I decided that it was equally necessary to show how the pastoral is rooted in a wider moral vision. Understanding that vision can enhance the way we address specific questions like the arms race.

When I set forth the argument about this wider moral vision—a consistent ethic of life—it evoked favorable comments, often from individuals and groups who had supported the peace pastoral but found themselves at odds with other positions the Catholic Church has taken on issues touching human life. At the same time, the Fordham address also generated letters from people who fear that the case for a consistent ethic will smother the Catholic opposition to abortion or will weaken our stance against the arms race.

Precisely in response to these concerns, I wish to state the essence of the case for a consistent ethic of life, specifying why it is needed and what is actually being advocated in a call for such an ethic. There are, in my view, two reasons why we need to espouse a consistent ethic of life: (1) the dimensions of the threats to life today; and (2) the value of our moral vision.

The threat to human life posed by nuclear war is so tangible that it has captured the attention of the nation. Public opinion polls rank it as one of the leading issues in the 1984 election campaign; popular movements like the Nuclear Freeze and professional organizations of physicians and scientists have shaped the nuclear question in terms which engage citizens and experts alike. The Church is part of the process which has raised the nuclear issue to a new standing in our public life. I submit that the Church should be a leader in the dialogue which shows that the nuclear question itself is part of the larger cultural-political-moral drama. Pope John Paul II regularly situates his examination of the nuclear issue in the framework of the broader problem of technology, politics, and ethics.

When this broader canvas is analyzed, the concern for a specific issue does not recede, but the meaning of multiple threats to life today—the full dimension of the problems of politics and technology—becomes vividly clear. The case being made here is not a condemnation of either politics or technology, but a recognition with the Pope that, on a range of key issues, "it is only through a conscious choice and through a deliberate policy that humanity can be saved." That quote from the Holy Father has unique relevance to nuclear war, but it can be used creatively to address other threats to life.

The range of application is all too evident: nuclear war *threatens* life on a previously unimaginable scale; abortion *takes* life daily on a horrendous scale; public executions are fast becoming weekly events in the most advanced technological society in history; and euthanasia is now openly discussed and even advocated. Each of these assaults on life has its own meaning and morality; they cannot be collapsed into one problem, but they must be confronted as pieces of a larger pattern.

The reason I have placed such stress on the idea of a consistent ethic of life from the beginning of my term as chairman of the Pro-Life Committee of the National Conference of Catholic Bishops is twofold: I am persuaded by the interrelatedness of these diverse problems, and I am convinced that the Catholic moral vision has the scope, the strength, and the subtlety to address this wide range of issues in an effective fashion. It is precisely the potential of our moral vision that is often not recognized even within the community of the Church. The case for a consistent ethic of life—one which stands for the protection of the right to life and the promotion of the rights which enhance life from womb to tomb—manifests the positive potential of the Catholic moral and social tradition. It is both a complex and a demanding tradition; it joins the humanity of the unborn infant and the humanity of the hungry; it calls for positive legal action to prevent the killing of the unborn or the aged and positive societal action to provide shelter for the homeless and education for the illiterate. The potential of the moral and social vision is appreciated in a new way when the systemic vision of Catholic ethics is seen as the background for the specific positions we take on a range of issues.

In response to those who fear otherwise, I contend that the systemic vision of a consistent ethic of life will not erode our crucial public opposition to the direction of the arms race; neither will it smother our persistent and necessary public opposition to abortion. The systemic vision is rooted in the conviction that our opposition to these distinct problems has a common foundation and that both Church and society are served by making it evident.

A consistent ethic of life does not equate the problem of taking life (e.g. through abortion and in war) with the problem of promoting human dignity (through humane programs of nutrition, health care, and housing). But a consistent ethic identifies both the protection of life and its promotion as moral questions. It argues for a continuum of life which must be sustained in the face of diverse and distinct threats.

A consistent ethic does not say everyone in the Church must do all things, but it does say that as individuals and groups pursue one issue, whether it is opposing abortion or capital punishment, the way we oppose one threat should be related to support for a systemic vision of life. It is not necessary or possible for every person to engage in each issue, but it is both possible and necessary for the Church as a whole to cultivate a conscious explicit connection among the several issues. And it is very necessary for preserving a systemic vision that individuals and groups who seek to witness to life at one point of the spectrum of life not be seen as insensitive to or even opposed to other moral claims on the overall spectrum of life. Consistency does rule out contradictory moral positions about the unique value of human life. No one is called to do everything, but each of us can do something. And we can strive not to stand against each other when the protection and the promotion of life are at stake.

The Seamless Garment: The Levels of the Question

A consistent ethic of life should honor the complexity of the multiple issues it must address. It is necessary to distinguish several levels of the question. Without attempting to be comprehensive, allow me to explore four distinct dimensions of a consistent ethic.

First, at the level of general moral principles, it is possible to identify a single principle with diverse applications. In the Fordham address I used the prohibition against direct attacks on innocent life. This principle is both central to the Catholic moral vision and systematically related to a range of specific moral issues. It prohibits direct attacks on unborn life in the womb, direct attacks on civilians in warfare, and the direct killing of patients in nursing homes. Each of these topics has a constituency in society concerned with the morality of abortion, war, and care of the aged and dying. A consistent ethic of life encourages the specific concerns of each constituency, but also calls them to see the interrelatedness of their efforts. The need to defend the integrity of the moral principle in the full range of its application is a responsibility of each distinct constituency. If the principle is eroded in the public mind, all lose.

A second level of a consistent ethic stresses the distinction among cases rather than their similarities. We need different moral principles to apply to diverse cases. The classical distinction between ordinary and extraordinary means has applicability in the care of the dying but no relevance in the case of warfare. Not all moral principles have relevance across the whole range of life issues. Moreover, sometimes a systemic vision of the life issues requires a combination of moral insights to provide direction on one issue. At Fordham, I cited the classical teaching on capital punishment which gives the state the right to take life in defense of key social values. But I also pointed out how a concern for promoting a *public attitude* of respect for life has led the bishops of the United States to oppose the *exercise* of that right.

Some of the responses I have received on the Fordham address correctly say that abortion and capital punishment are not identical issues. The principle which protects *innocent* life distinguishes the unborn child from the convicted murderer. Other letters stress that while nuclear war is a *threat* to life, abortion involves the actual *taking* of a life, here and now. I accept both of these distinctions, of course, but I also find compelling the need to *relate* the cases while keeping them in distinct categories. Abortion is taking of life in ever-growing numbers in our society. Those concerned about it, I believe, will find their case enhanced by taking note of the rapidly expanding use of public execution. In a similar way, those who are particularly concerned about these executions, even if the accused has taken another life, should recognize the elementary truth that a society which can be indifferent to the innocent life of an unborn child will not be easily stirred to concern for a convicted criminal. There is, I maintain, a political and psychological linkage among the life issues—from war to welfare concerns—which we ignore at our own peril: a systemic vision of life seeks to expand the moral imagination of a society, not partition it into airtight categories.

A third level of the question before us involves how we relate a commitment to principles to our public witness of life. As I have said, no one can do everything. There are limits to both competency and energy; both point to the wisdom of setting priorities and defining distinct functions. The Church, however, must be credible across a wide range of issues; the very scope of our moral vision requires a commitment to a multiplicity of questions. In this way the teaching of the Church will sustain a variety of individual commitments. Neither the Fordham address nor this one is intended to constrain wise and vigorous efforts to protect and promote life through specific, precise forms of action. Both addresses do seek to cultivate a dialogue within the Church and in the wider society among individuals and groups who draw on common principles (e.g. the prohibition against killing the innocent) but seem convinced that they do not share common ground. The appeal here is not for anyone to do everything, but to recognize points of interdependence which should be stressed, not denied.

A fourth level, one where dialogue is sorely needed, is the relationship between moral principles and concrete political choices. The moral questions of abortion, the arms race, the fate of social programs for the poor, and the role of human rights in foreign policy are *public* moral issues. The arena in which they are ultimately decided is not the academy or the Church but the political process. A consistent ethic of life seeks to present a coherent linkage among a diverse set of issues. It can and should be used to test party platforms, public policies, and political candidates. The Church legitimately fulfills a public role by articulating a framework for political choices, by relating that framework to specific issues, and by calling for systematic moral analysis of all areas of public policy.

This is the role our Bishops' Conference has sought to fulfill by publishing a "Statement on Political Responsibility" during each of the presidential and congressional election years in the past decade. The purpose is surely not to tell citizens how to vote, but to help shape the public debate and form personal conscience so that every citizen will vote thoughtfully and responsibly. Our "Statement on Political Responsibility" has always been, like our "Respect Life Program," a multi-issue approach to public morality. The fact that this Statement sets forth a spectrum of issues of current concern to the Church and society should not be understood as implying that all issues are qualitatively equal from a moral perspective. As I indicated earlier, each of the life issues—while related to all the others—is distinct and calls for its own specific moral analysis. Both the Statement and the Respect Life Program have direct relevance to the political order, but they are applied concretely by the choice of citizens. This is as it should be. In the political order the Church is primarily a teacher; it possesses a carefully cultivated tradition of moral analysis of personal and public issues. It makes that tradition available in a special manner for the community of the Church, but it offers it also to all who find meaning and guidance in its moral teaching.

The Seamless Garment: A Pastoral and Public Contribution

The moral teaching of the Church has both pastoral and public significance. Pastorally, a consistent ethic of life is a contribution to the witness of the Church's defense of the human person. Publicly, a consistent ethic fills a void in our public policy debate today.

Pastorally, I submit that a Church standing forth on the entire range of issues which the logic of our moral vision bids us to confront will be a Church in the style of both Vatican II's *Gaudium et spes* and Pope John Paul II's consistent witness to life. The pastoral life of the Church should not be guided by a simplistic criterion of relevance. But the capacity of faith to shed light on the concrete questions of personal and public life today is one way in which the value of the Gospel is assessed. Certainly the serious, sustained interest manifested throughout American society in the bishops' letter on war and peace provides a unique pastoral opportunity for the Church. Demonstrating how the teaching on war and peace is supported by a wider concern for all of life may bring others to see for the first time what our tradition has affirmed for a very long time: the linkage among the life issues.

The public value of a consistent ethic of life is connected directly to its pastoral role. In the public arena we should always speak and act like a Church. But the unique public possibility for a consistent ethic is provided precisely by the unstructured character of the public debate on the life questions. Each of the issues I have identified today—abortion, war, hunger and human rights, euthanasia, and capital punishment—is treated as a separate, self-contained topic in our public life. Each is distinct, but an ad hoc approach to each one fails to illustrate how our choices in one area can affect our decisions in other areas. There must be a public attitude of respect for all of life if public actions are to respect it in concrete cases.

The pastoral on war and peace speaks of a "new moment" in the nuclear age. The pastoral has been widely studied and applauded because it caught the spirit of the "new moment" and spoke with moral substance to the issues of the "new moment." I am convinced there is an "open moment" before us on the agenda of life issues. It is a significant opportunity for the Church to demonstrate the strength of a sustained moral vision. I submit that a clear witness to a consistent ethic of life will allow us to grasp the opportunity of this "open moment" and serve both the sacredness of every human life and the God of Life who is the origin and support of our common humanity.

3.
LINKAGE AND THE LOGIC OF THE ABORTION DEBATE

Address for the Right-to-Life Convention

KANSAS CITY, JUNE 7, 1984

I first wish to express my appreciation for the opportunity to address this Convention of the National Right-to-Life Committee. I take the chairmanship of the National Conference of Catholic Bishops Committee for Pro-life Activities as a very serious responsibility and a significant opportunity for service. I am convinced of the total personal commitment of each of our bishops to the philosophy and program of the pro-life movement. I am also equally convinced that the heart and soul of the movement is the personal dedication of all those who are represented at this meeting.

I thought it might be most useful for me to set forth in this address a general perspective of where we stand in the struggle against abortion, the struggle to protect the life of the unborn. It is now eleven years since the Supreme Court decisions which legalized abortion on request; there are lessons to be learned from this decade. In light of this experience, we can also examine our present choices and establish our future direction.

The Past: Witness for Life

An examination of the past decade generates both sadness and pride. Sadness—perhaps moral dismay is a better phrase—is a product of evaluating the abortion policy set in place by the 1973 Supreme Court decisions. Pride is the justifiable product of evaluating the efforts of thousands of volunteers who are committed to reversing the present national policy and re-establishing respect for the right to life as a national policy and practice.

First, the implications of *Roe v. Wade* bear examination. In order to grasp the dimensions of the present challenge we face, it is necessary to describe the depth of the problem created by the 1973 Supreme Court decisions. The decisions were radical in nature and systemic in their consequences. They were radical since they overturned in one stroke an existing political and legal structure which treated any form of abortion as an exception to normal practice. The end product of *Roe v. Wade* was to establish a political and legal framework with no restraint on abortion. Many of us sensed then, and all of us can be sure now, that public opinion was not at all in favor of a policy opening the floodgates to 1.5 million abortions a year. Some radical decisions are justified morally and they are necessary politically, but the Court decisions in 1973 were neither justified, necessary, nor acceptable to large segments of the American public.

The Court's decisions were systemic in the sense that they changed not only a given law, but they established operating presumptions in medical practice, social service agencies, and administrative policy which legitimated and facilitated access to abortion. The result of the decisions was to change the structure of this society's approach to abortion. What the decisions did *not* change was the substantial, broad-based, and solidly grounded view of American citizens across the land that abortion on request is not a satisfactory way to address the real problems individuals and families face in this delicate area of respecting unborn life.

It was this deeply felt personal opposition to abortion which crystallized the public policy position of the pro-life movement. There has undoubtedly been a strong Catholic core to this movement, but it has cut across religious and political lines, as is evidenced by the participants in this convention. It is this pro-life constituency which is an authentic source of pride for anyone associated with it. At a time when grassroots coalitions are often talked about, the pro-life constituency has a claim second to none in demonstrating local support. At a time when citizen apathy is a serious public problem, the pro-life movement has mobilized men and women personally, professionally, and politically in opposition to abortion. At a time when the moral dimension of public policy on a variety of issues is in need of a clear statement, the pro-life movement has cast the political issue in decisively moral terms. Finally, the movement has been not only political but pastoral. It has joined its public advocacy with practical efforts to provide alternatives to abortion.

For all these reasons, I maintain that the witness to life in the past decade has been a cause for hope and pride. The lessons learned in the decade of the 1970s prepare us to analyze our choices in the 1980s.

The Present: Shaping Public Choices for Life

The effect of the pro-life movement has not been limited to its inspirational quality; there has been a specific political impact. Eleven years after the Supreme Court decisions, and after a string of other legal actions reaffirming the *Roe v. Wade* philosophy, the pro-abortion philosophy has not been accepted by millions of Americans. In brief, the legal status of abortion still lacks public legitimacy. The political debate which ensued shows the nation radically divided on the state of public policy on abortion.

Normally, the force of existing law provides legitimacy for policy. Keeping the question open for reform and reversal of existing policy is a significant political victory. It is a tactical success. It should not, however, be mistaken for total success. Nonetheless, it provides space to move the nation toward a different future on abortion.

Creating space to change law and policy is a pre-condition for what must be accomplished. It is imperative in the 1980s to use the space creatively. In working to change national policy on abortion, I submit that we must cast our case in broadly defined terms, in a way which elicits support from others. We need to shape our position consciously in a way designed to generate interest in the abortion question from individuals who thus far have not been touched by our witness or our arguments.

Casting our perspectives broadly does not mean diluting its content. Quite the opposite. It involves a process of demonstrating how our position on abortion is deeply rooted in our religious tradition and, at the same time, is protective of fundamental ideas in our constitutional tradition.

Speaking from my perspective as a Roman Catholic bishop, I wish to affirm that the basis of our opposition to abortion is established by themes which should be compelling for the Catholic conscience because they are so centrally located in Catholic moral and social teaching. The basic moral principle that the direct killing of the innocent is always wrong is so fundamental in Catholic theology that the need to defend it in the multiple cases of abortion, warfare, and care of the handicapped and the terminally ill is self-evident. This is why one cannot, with consistency, claim to be truly pro-life if one applies the principle of the sanctity of life to other issues but rejects it in the case of abortion. By the same token, one cannot, with consistency, claim to be truly pro-life if one applies the principle to other issues but holds that the direct killing of innocent non-combatants in warfare is morally justified. To fail to stand for this principle is to make a fundamental error in Catholic moral thought. But the moral principle does not stand alone; it is related to other dimensions of Catholic social teaching.

The opposition to abortion is rooted in the conviction that civil law and social policy must always be subject to ongoing moral analysis. Simply because a civil law is in place does not mean that it should be blindly supported. To encourage reflective, informed assessment of civil law and policy is to keep alive the capacity for moral criticism in society. In addition, the Catholic position opposing abortion is rooted in our understanding of the role of the state in society. The state has positive moral responsibilities; it is not simply a neutral umpire; neither is its role limited to restraining evil. The responsibilities of the state include both the protection of innocent life from attack and enhancement of human life at every stage of its development. The fact of 1.5 million abortions a year in the United States erodes the moral character of the state; if the civil law can be neutral when innocent life is under attack, the implications for law and morality in our society are frightening.

These themes drawn from Catholic theology are not restricted in their application to the community of faith. These are truths of the moral and political order which are also fundamental to the Western constitutional heritage. The opposition to abortion, properly stated, is not a sectarian claim but a reflective, rational position which any person of good will may be invited to consider. Examples can be used to illustrate the convergence of our concerns about abortion with other key social questions in American society.

The appeal to a higher moral law to reform and refashion existing civil law was the central idea that Dr. Martin Luther King, Jr,. brought to the civil rights movement of the 1960s. The pro-life movement of the 1980s is based on the same appeal. Pro-life today should be seen as an extension of the spirit of the civil rights movement. Similarly, the Baby Doe case has proved to be a meeting ground of principle and practice between civil rights and pro-life advocates. The common ground is as yet not sufficiently explored, but there is significant potential for development in this area.

Civil rights are the domestic application of the broader human rights tradition. The right to life is a fundamental basis of this tradition. By standing for the right to life in our society, we stand with all who argue for a strong national commitment to human rights in our domestic and foreign policy.

A final example of convergence is pertinent to your program today. Father Bruce Ritter has caught the imagination and interest of broad sectors of American society with his defense of human dignity in the face of sexual exploitation. The themes of the pro-life movement, promoting a sacred vision of sexuality and support for the family, coincide with Father Ritter's courageous and compassionate witness to life.

The Future: A Strategy for Witness to Life

It is precisely because I am convinced that demonstrating the linkage between abortion and other issues is both morally correct and tactically necessary for the pro-life position that I have been addressing the theme of a consistent ethic of life for Church and society. The convergence of themes concerning civil rights, human rights, and family life with the abortion issue is simply an indication of deeper bonds which exist along the full range of pro-life issues.

The proposals I have made on the linkage of issues are, I submit, a systematic attempt to state the vision which has always been implicit in a Catholic conception of "pro-life." A Catholic view of the meaning of pro-life stresses the interdependence of life in a social setting, the way in which each of us relies upon the premise that others respect my life, and that society exists to guarantee that respect for each person. The interdependence of human life points toward the interrelationship of pro-life issues.

This interrelationship can be illustrated in precise, detailed moral arguments, but that is not my purpose in this address. I would simply appeal to a principle which I suspect is also an element of your own experience. It is the need to cultivate within society an attitude of respect for life on a series of issues, if the actions of individuals or groups are to reflect respect for life in specific choices. The linkage theme of a consistent ethic of life is designed to highlight the common interest and reciprocal need which exist among groups interested in specific issues—peace, abortion, civil rights, justice for the dispossessed or disabled—each of which depends upon a basic attitude of respect for life. The linkage theme provides us with an opportunity to win "friends" for the life issues. Just as we insist on the principle of the right to life, so too we must recognize the responsibility that our commitment places on us. Building bridges to people working on specific life issues demands respect and kindness toward these potential allies. An atmosphere of trust and understanding can do a great deal to promote the goals of the pro-life movement.

The consistent ethic seeks to build a bridge of common interest and common insight on a range of social and moral questions. It is designed to highlight the intrinsic ties which exist between public attitudes and personal actions on one side, and public policy on the other. Effective defense of life requires a coordinated approach to attitude, action, and policy. The consistent ethic theme seeks to engage the moral imagination and political insight of diverse groups and to build a network of mutual concern for defense of life at every stage in the policies and practices of our society.

The need for such a common approach is dictated by the objective interrelationship among the life issues. The strength of the Catholic contribution to such an approach lies in the long and rich tradition of moral and social analysis which has provided us with both detailed guidance on individual moral issues and a framework for relating several issues in a coherent fashion.

If we pursue a consistent ethic systematically, it will become clear that abortion is not a "single issue," because it is not even a single kind of issue. It is an issue about the nature and future of the family, both in its own right and as a basic unit of society. It is an issue about equality under law for all human beings. And it is an issue of life or death. For this reason, developments in all these areas may not always be the direct responsibility of each person in the right-to-life movement, but they should always be of intense interest to all. Whatever makes our society more human, more loving, more respectful of the life and dignity of others, is a contribution to your struggle; for the more committed society becomes to justice and compassion, the more incongruous will be its toleration of the killing of the unborn child. And whatever promotes respect for that child cannot help but promote respect for all humanity. With that in mind, I urge you to recommit yourselves with renewed energy to this cause. Where humanity is threatened at its most defenseless, we have no choice. We must stand up on its behalf.

4.

THE DEATH PENALTY

An International Human Rights Issue

GENERAL ANNUAL MEETING OF AMNESTY INTERNATIONAL,
LOYOLA UNIVERSITY CHICAGO, JUNE 23, 1984

I first want to express my appreciation for the opportunity to address this annual meeting of Amnesty International. The objectives of Amnesty International and your work throughout the world are well known in the Catholic Church. Indeed, as you know, in the United States many members of Amnesty International are Catholics who find in your organization a particularly effective way to express their moral concern about leading questions in international relations, so many of which affect the welfare of the human person.

As a way of addressing the topic of this morning's session—the death penalty as an international human rights issue—I will offer my reflections on the larger context of the issue. That is, I plan to illustrate the common ground we share on a wide range of issues and to examine some common objectives which both the Church and Amnesty International should pursue in a world that is still too violent, still too unaware of the dignity of the human person. Accordingly, I will focus on three topics: (1) protecting the person in a world composed of independent states; (2) the issues shaping a shared agenda; and (3) capital punishment in the international arena.

First, protecting the person in a world of nation-states. The genius of Amnesty International has been that it has found a way to concretize a major concern of international relations, and to do so in a way that has caught the imagination of large numbers of people. International politics is a very complex subject. The foreign policy of our own nation, for example, is at times so complex that people cannot deal with it personally. They feel that it is so far removed from them that they cannot really influence it. Amnesty International's method, however, helps people to cut through the complexity of governments, institutions, laws, rules, and conflicts. By adopting a prisoner of conscience, for example, you can become concerned about a specific individual in a specific country whose life and welfare are in danger. By identifying one human being for whom you feel a personal responsibility, a human being you know needs help, you concretize the meaning of international politics. The genius of this approach is demonstrated and proven in the way in which Amnesty International has become a major force in world politics.

I assure you that I do not make this assertion lightly. Amnesty International is known the world over. You are known both for the wide geographical scope of your concern—that is, the global range of your interest in protecting people from the reach of arbitrary power—and for your ability to form local, grassroots constituencies which can make and have made an impact on larger transnational problems. I hasten to add that the genius of your approach is not simply the result of an organizational technique. Rather, it is rooted in your ability to lift up the question of the protection of the individual person in the complex and often violent world of international affairs in a way that people can understand and act on.

I cite this accomplishment not only because you should be commended for the way in which you have protected and saved individuals whose lives and welfare were directly threatened, but also because you have engaged large numbers of people, who otherwise might never have taken an interest in foreign policy, in the task of protecting human rights the world over. My other reason for highlighting the way in which you have focused on the protection of the person in international relations is that the person is the foundation of the Catholic Church's concern in its entire social ministry. The Catholic Church, as a worldwide institution, is involved in a broad range of social questions at the international, national, and local levels. Indeed, if one were to list them all, it would be quite long because the concerns vary so much in the different countries and continents.

There is, however, a common element which links the many concerns of the Church's social ministry, namely, its conviction about the unique dignity of each human person. The person is the clearest reflection of the presence of God among us. To lay violent hands on the person—which is precisely the thing that Amnesty International seeks to prevent—is to come as close as we can to laying violent hands on God. Every social system—east or west, north or south, communist or capitalist—should be judged by the way in which it reverences, or fails to reverence, the unique and equal dignity of every person.

The person, then, is the key to the entire social presence and outreach of the Church. But the protection of the human person requires a broader view than simply the conviction that the person has a unique dignity. Protection of the person in a social setting requires that we have a clear conception of a doctrine of human rights. For rights are moral claims that persons make in light of their human dignity; they are moral claims that people can make against other persons and against the state. We protect the dignity of the human person in a social setting by surrounding each person with a spectrum of rights and responsibilities. These rights ensure that the individual's worth is rooted in his or her personhood, that the individual's worth is not swallowed up in a faceless collectivity. Those moral claims, in other words, provide a kind of space within which the fragile dignity of the human person is to be protected.

Catholic teaching argues that political relationships within and among states must be seen and developed within the context of human rights. This was the theme of Pope John Paul II when he visited the United Nations in 1979. He sought to examine problems as diverse as war and peace and economic justice from the perspective of the human rights of the person.

The affirmation that the person's human rights are to be respected both within and among states is fundamental and is critically important for our world today. It is a principle that Amnesty International puts into practice all the time. It affirms that in a world of states, the nation-state has real but only relative value; it is the dignity of the human person that has transcendent value and must be respected at all times. The nation-states do not have the right to so isolate themselves that they can ignore the moral concern of the rest of the world when, within their boundaries, there are serious allegations about human rights violations.

This relativization of the role of the state has implications for the way we view international relations. Indeed, one point of convergence between Amnesty International and the Catholic Church—even though our starting points may be different—is our affirmation of the primacy of the person in international affairs, the need to protect the person in a world of states, and the need to judge every state by the way it reverences and enhances, or fails to reverence and enhance, the dignity of each person.

A second point of convergence between Amnesty International and the Catholic Church is that we are both transnational actors in today's increasingly interdependent world. Interdependence, first of all, is simply a factual condition. It arises from the growing exchange of information, ideas, contacts, and political and economic ties among nations. All of these ties illustrate our mutual vulnerability; they show how we are influenced by each other, how we can touch each other, for good or for ill, across national boundaries by our policies, our practices, our concern for what happens within other states.

Now, of special importance in an increasingly interdependent world is the growing role of transnational actors. The world is still composed of states, and states are a unique organizing force in international politics. But they are no longer the only organizing force.

Transnational actors have the following characteristics: they are based in one place but are present in several places; they have a trained corps of personnel, a single guiding philosophy, and a sophisticated communication system. There are a handful of organizations that possess these characteristics. We readily identify corporate actors who have those characteristics and who exert enormous influence. But other organizations, perhaps to a less visible degree, also have the characteristics of transnational actors. The Catholic Church is clearly such an actor in the world today. In a less visible but real way, Amnesty International has become a recognized transnational actor which focuses on the protection of the person in a world of nation-states. Both in terms of the vision which motivates and guides our action in international politics and in terms of our organized presence in an increasingly interdependent world, the Church and Amnesty International have shared concerns and a capability to cooperate to the benefit of both.

Indeed, the second topic I would like to address is precisely our shared concerns, the issues shaping our shared agenda. Amnesty International is known today primarily for its protection and promotion of human rights. And here again, our shared vision of what we mean by human rights provides a common meeting ground. Both Amnesty International and the Catholic Church have a view of human rights which cuts across political and civil rights on the one hand, and socioeconomic rights on the other. And this view shapes one's perspective relative to international affairs.

This seems self-evident, as it has been affirmed in United Nations' declarations and documents, as well as scholarly literature. But it is not universally accepted, even in our own country. The dominant view in the West, for example, is often to stress political and civil rights and to regard social, economic, and cultural concerns as something less than rights. The dominant view in the East, on the other hand, is to stress socioeconomic and cultural rights and to pass off political and civil rights as peripheral or unnecessary, or even a hindrance in the organization of society. But if one adopts the view that the protection of the dignity of the person requires a spectrum of rights which extends from the right to life itself, to the right to basic nutrition, social welfare, housing, education, and a job, to the right of freedom of conscience and religion, freedom of association, and the right to know the truth—then one has a broader perspective on the relevant issues in a given country or in relationships among countries. My point is not to outline a whole doctrine of human rights but to emphasize the fact that when one sees the full spectrum of human rights, this influences the way one interprets issues in international relations. It should be evident to all of us how a shared vision of the full range of human rights provides the basis for a shared agenda of issues that are our concern.

Let me press this idea of a shared view of issues one step further, this time concentrating more on what goes on in my own faith community. However, it is a theme and a tendency that is relevant to the topic you have asked me to address.

Just as we see a linkage among human rights in the protection of the person, increasingly in the Catholic Church today we see a linkage among what I would call "life issues." Precisely because we reverence the dignity of the human person as a unique being, unlike any other creature in the world, the question of the protection of human life from attack becomes for us a central theme in our whole social ministry. I suspect we would not have difficulty sharing views on why human life is sacred and how important it is in the organization of a society, whether nationally or internationally, to give primacy to the sacredness of human life. But it is not enough simply to say why we believe life is sacred. It is also necessary to examine the challenges to the unique dignity and sacredness of human life today.

Human life has always been sacred and there have always been threats to it, but we live in a period of history when we have produced, sometimes with the best of intentions, a technology and a capacity to threaten human life which previous generations could not imagine.

The threat to life today can be illustrated by examining our technology. Technologically, we can do almost anything. In its effort to understand and shape our world, to push back the boundaries and barriers of our knowledge so that we can use the world well in all its dimensions, science has produced many marvelous and commendable inventions. It is simply a fact of life, however, that as we do one thing with science and technology, there are often side effects or unexpected effects, or even things we planned to do, that go far beyond what we expected would happen. The result is that life is often threatened. Today, for example, in areas as diverse as medical ethics and nuclear strategy, the challenge to human life is very great. When we cracked the atom and the genetic code—both tributes to human genius—we penetrated the recesses of the secrets of nature. In itself, this is good; we were created to do this. The consequences of these breakthroughs of knowledge present us with a complicated and sometimes problematic set of questions. For example, how do we control and direct the power we have created, whether it be in laboratories and hospitals or in arsenals? My point is that, if we begin by affirming the sacredness of all life, and then move to an examination of the threats to life, we soon realize that, if we want to protect the sacredness of life, we must do it in a number of places; there is no one place where the entire threat to life is lodged.

Certainly the nuclear question on which I have spent a substantial amount of time over the past four years represents in a unique way a threat to the sacredness of life which the Church and others in society must take with utmost seriousness. We must be convinced that only by concerted, sustained action can we move away from the perilous condition in which we find ourselves today because of the nuclear arms race. But as serious as it is, the arms race is not the only threat to life.

As you so well know, the Catholic bishops have been deeply involved in the effort to stem the increasing number of abortions in our society. I am fully aware that some who agree with us on the position we have taken on nuclear questions do not agree with us on abortion, and vice versa. But we are convinced that the same principle is at stake in both issues. That is not to say that the issues are identical. What we do say is that the protection of innocent human life from direct attack is a principle underlying both issues and it is this linkage, which goes far beyond nuclear warfare and abortion, that makes it necessary for us to examine a broad range of threats to life.

Indeed, our conviction that life is threatened at a number of points on the life spectrum prompts us to think more explicitly about how we relate one life issue to another. It has certainly influenced our view on capital punishment. The Catholic Church for many centuries has taught that in extreme circumstances the state has the right to take life, either to defend its people against external threats through what is called the "just war," or to defend society against threats from within through the use of capital punishment. That statement of Catholic moral teaching still prevails at the level of principle. Principles, however, must be applied. Each age must exercise its capacity for critical moral discernment in its particular circumstances. So, as the bishops became more involved in the questions of abortion and nuclear war, their convictions about the death penalty also came under review. Basically, we have taken the position that, while in principle the state has the right to use capital punishment, that right should not be used in the United States. In other words, we have not reversed our traditional teaching on this point; what we have said is that there are other ways— more appropriate and effective than capital punishment—for the state to defend its people. For example, through a carefully considered process of moral discernment, the bishops of Kentucky in a recent pastoral letter concluded "that under the circumstances prevailing in society today, the death penalty as punishment for reasons of deterrence, retribution, or the protection of society cannot be justified." Their conclusion comes after an examination of the death penalty in itself and in relationship to American society today.

Another reason why the American bishops have concluded that the death penalty is inappropriate is their vision of the linkage among life issues; that is, the linkage among the life issues convinces us that one must foster a positive attitude toward life in society if life's sacredness is to be cherished and protected. While the state has the obligation to defend its people against attacks on their lives and to protect them against forces that threaten key societal values, we believe that the exercise of the right to capital punishment does not foster the kind of reverence for life that is needed to deal creatively and effectively with the whole range of life questions we face in our society today. In a complex, sophisticated democracy like ours, means other than the death penalty are available and can be used to protect society. Moreover, we recognize the need of society to move beyond mere justice in dealing with the victims of crime and their families. We must offer people afflicted by violence our deepest compassion, understanding, and support.

When we move to the question that you are particularly concerned about—the death penalty in the international arena—there are new problems: the diversity of legal systems in each country; the diversity of cultural traditions; the diversity of capabilities of states to maintain order and to protect their people. There is, in other words, a range of problems in the international sphere that does not confront us in precisely the same way in the United States. But I welcome this opportunity to come before you to affirm my support for your goal to eliminate the death penalty, especially as a means of dealing with political prisoners. I am convinced that this is a step which needs to be taken.

Pope John Paul II has addressed this very question. In his address to the diplomatic corps at the Vatican on January 15, 1983, he stated:

[T]he Holy See, in its humanitarian concern, is prompted to recommend clemency and mercy for those condemned to death, especially those who have been condemned for political reasons, which can be changeable, linked as they are to the personalities of the authorities of the moment.

The Church likewise takes to heart the plight of all those who are subjected to torture, whatever the political regime may be, for in her eyes nothing can justify that debasement which unfortunately often accompanies barbaric, repugnant cruelties. Likewise she cannot remain silent about the criminal action which consists in causing a certain number of people to disappear without trial, leaving their families in a cruel state of uncertainty.

It should be noted that this statement from Pope John Paul II is in line with the thinking of his predecessor, Pope Paul VI. Pope Paul never made such a clear statement of principle or call for prohibiting capital punishment as a way of dealing with political prisoners although he intervened in a number of specific cases where political prisoners were sentenced to death. Both the practice of Pope Paul VI and the teaching of Pope John Paul II, I believe, support and affirm Amnesty International's position and objective on this question.

I should like to add that the papal concern is humanitarian, as is yours. But the significance of what you are trying to do is in the fact that your efforts also seek to embody that human concern in political and legal measures which would restrain the power of a state in dealing with the question of political prisoners.

There are reasons to pursue this objective in spite of the difficulties which exist in the international system. Precisely because of the variety of governments and legal systems involved, there is a need for a common movement—one that cuts across states—seeking to ban capital punishment as a means of dealing with political prisoners.

It does seem to me that one way to pursue this objective is precisely to speak to states about their role in the world today. In a world marked by violence and often a disregard for the dignity of the person, the state must protect its people and the key values of its society, but it should do so in a way that promotes reverence for the life of each person. Forswearing the right to execute those it has declared to be political prisoners would be a remarkably useful public declaration by the state of its concern about the protection and enhancement of human life.

There is need for an organization not in the governmental sector to raise this question and to argue for its inclusion on the agenda of nation-states. You have proved your capability of doing just that. I wish to affirm the value of the task you have undertaken and to wish you Godspeed in the work you have undertaken.

5.

WORKING TOGETHER TO HEAL THE HUMAN PERSON

UNIVERSITY OF ILLINOIS MEDICAL SCHOOL,
JUNE 27, 1984

I am delighted to be with you today. I thank Dr. Hyman Muslin for the gracious invitation. And I thank all of you for your participation. The topic suggested to me, one which I gladly accepted, is: how we can work together for the healing of the human person. It is an extremely challenging subject. It admits a number of possible approaches. Perhaps it would be helpful if I share with you the kind of concern which generated its formulation.

I would like to quote from Dr. Muslin's letter to me:

I now wish to tell you, as I indicated in my original invitation, why I thought it would be important for us to have you come to talk to the physicians, medical students and nurses. We are distressed in medicine about our difficulties and our failures in being of service in the development of man. Specifically, we see eruptions of hatred and violence on all levels of the local, national, and international scene, and do not see that our teachings and ministrations have had sufficient impact on the capacity of man to advance in his empathy toward his fellowman and thus be able to experience other people's distresses. This developmental accomplishment, in our view, would be of greater service towards the acquisition of operational restraints against hatred and violence. Our wish to have man develop an operational humanism is, of course, shared by you as we know, and our failures are the failures of us all. We would like, if at all possible, for you to include in your remarks to us, your views on our mutual dilemma, what direction we might be taking, or what views we might entertain that would sustain us in our mission?"

As you are well aware, Dr. Muslin's questions are critically important. They are, in fact, vital; that is to say, central to our lives together. For when we dwell on the issues he raises, a core pattern emerges. The many questions begin to center on two challenges: How can we live in peace? How can we contribute to a peaceful climate in this world?

There seems to be a certain brokenness or woundedness within us that keeps us from living peacefully. If we could engage in a healing process, it would undoubtedly be better.

Although we can state the challenges simply—how to live in peace, how to contribute to peace, how to contribute toward the healing of people to bring about peace—the questions are not so simply solved. With no pretensions of claiming a complete response, I would like to offer some ideas for reflection and dialogue. I hope that these ideas—indications, as it were, of how we might approach the theme—will contribute to the wider dialogue in which we must be engaged.

Before I begin, I want to make a disclaimer and I want to clarify the intent of my comments.

The disclaimer is simply this. I am *not* an academician. In fact, you should know that the university is not my regular terrain of activity. I value theory, follow it as much as I am able; perhaps I have even been able to make modest contributions to its advancement. Overall, however, I am not a theoretician of peace and healing. I am, first and foremost, a pastor, and, therefore, engaged in the *practice* of making peace and promoting healing. It is as a pastor practitioner that I wish to speak with you.

In other words, what I want to offer you is not a theory. Much more simply, I want to share with you how I work for the kind of healing that brings about peace. As I offer you these reflections on "my practice," I think that certain points of convergence will emerge between your work in medicine and mine as a representative of the Church. At that point, we can, through our dialogue, discover ways of deeper collaboration rooted in a common purpose.

By way of an overview of my remarks, let me note that I will share four areas of activity on different levels of life: my concern for global peace, my initiatives on behalf of a consistent ethic of life, my service to Chicago, and, finally, my own inner life and personal quest for healing and peace. So let me begin these remarks, which I would categorize as "reflective sharings."

World Peace Initiatives

I am deeply concerned, as no doubt you are also, about the survival of the human race, the survival of our planet. Our survival is threatened by the ever-increasing arsenal of nuclear weapons, by an arms race which seems to be out of control. Together with the other Catholic bishops in the United States, I was involved in the development and dissemination of a pastoral letter entitled, *The Challenge of Peace: God's Promise and Our Response.* Because we represent a voice for the Roman Catholic Church in our nation, because we passionately emphasized the urgency of coming to terms with the questions posed by the nuclear age, because we strongly encouraged both our own Catholic people and other citizens to see the questions of war and peace as crucial moral issues—because of all this, there has been a great deal of media coverage and publicity. Although many people have been involved, as chairman of the committee that drafted the letter, I have personally received quite a bit of attention. In itself, that attention or recognition is, of course, quite secondary when dealing with issues of survival. But from that experience, I have developed two insights: the first is in regard to the way I must look at the world; the second, the role I must play.

I have come to learn that I must look at the world and its problems of survival and achieving peace in a particular way. By instinct, I would have tended to look at particular problems as single and specific concerns. However, through study, prayer, and analysis, I have come to appreciate the perspective of the "total system." I may not be able to grasp all the parts of our world's woundedness and brokenness that lead us to the brink of international disaster. But I have come to appreciate how the parts are interconnected and need to be addressed in a more comprehensive fashion. There are links, for example, between the build-up of arms and the continued poverty of large parts of the world. There are links between diminished or reduced understandings of the true dignity of the human person, reduced perhaps to a functional component of the state, and the propensity to international violence. These are just two examples of the linkage that exists among the various issues confronting us in our contemporary society. If I want to grasp these issues more fully, I must see them as part of a larger picture, as part of a totality.

A second personal insight which came to me through my work on the peace pastoral was a deeper understanding of the role I am to play. I came to understand that my role, quite simply, is to be a voice. I am called, both by my position and my own inner sense, to be a voice—someone who articulates the concern. In our letter on the challenge of peace, for example, we did not offer detailed technical or political strategies. That would be beyond our competence. Our task, rather, was to voice the concern; to provide a moral vision, a framework within which people could make their own moral analysis of the issues. In an era of specialization, such as our own, it is perhaps unusual for one not to offer the solution to particular questions, but simply to raise the questions themselves and to do so in a way that makes other people take notice. I have come to understand my role in the healing and peacemaking process in this way. I am a voice.

Initiatives Concerning a Consistent Ethic of Life

In recent months, I have engaged in a dialogue—a debate, really—which has involved not only the Catholic community but the broader community as well. The specific theme of this debate is the need to promote what I have called a "consistent ethic of life."

At Fordham University last December and at St. Louis University this spring, I spoke of the various life issues confronting our society as constituting a "seamless garment." By that I mean that there is a linkage among such issues as abortion, war, hunger, human rights, euthanasia, and capital punishment; they belong in a common discussion, although the specific issues themselves are not identical and each requires its own moral analysis.

Reaction to the Fordham presentation, mainly within the Catholic Church but also others, was rapid and strong. Some of the responses stated that abortion and capital punishment are not identical issues. The principle which protects innocent life distinguishes the unborn child from the convicted murderer. Other letters stressed that, while nuclear war is a *threat* to life, abortion involves the actual *taking* of life, here and now. I accept both of these distinctions, of course, but I also find compelling the need to relate the cases while keeping them in distinct categories. Abortion, the direct taking of unborn life, is constantly increasing in our society. Those concerned about it, I believe, will find their case enhanced by taking note of the rapidly expanding use of capital punishment. In a similar way, those who are particularly concerned about these executions, even if the accused has taken another life, should recognize the elementary truth that a society which is indifferent to the life of an innocent, unborn child will not be easily stirred to concern for a convicted criminal. Aside from the moral considerations, there is, I maintain, a political and psychological linkage among the life issues from war to welfare concerns—which we ignore at our own peril: a comprehensive vision of life seeks to expand the moral horizon of society, not partition it into airtight categories.

I put it this way in my recent St. Louis lecture: "Each of the issues I have identified today—abortion, war, hunger and human rights, euthanasia, and capital punishment—is treated as a separate, self-contained topic in our public life. Each is distinct, but an *ad hoc* approach to each one fails to illustrate how our choices in one area can affect our decisions in other areas. There must be a public attitude of respect for all of life, if public actions are to respect it in concrete cases."

Our topic today is: working together toward the healing of the human person. From my reflections concerning a consistent ethic of life and my effort to get people to consider seriously the linkage among the many life issues, I have learned that working for the healing of the human person requires an integrated and unified vision of the underlying values which are at stake. Unless our understanding of the human person is rooted in a set of coherent, unified values, our attempts to promote healing and growth will accomplish little, given the diversity and complexity of the many issues which clamor for our attention today. We who are committed to serving human persons, our brothers and sisters, in a holistic fashion, will become fragmented and broken in our attempts to be of service.

As with the question of peace issues, so, too, with the consistent ethic of life, I have come to see a specific task for myself. With regard to peace issues, as I noted earlier, I see my role as that of being a "voice." From my concern and involvement in efforts to promote a consistent ethic of life by introducing it into our national dialogue, I have come to see my task as that of a connecting memory for my people. I feel called to help people remember the foundations of their values and to remember in such a way that they can connect the issues and deal with them creatively and effectively. The task of being a connecting memory for people is particularly important for me. For in providing this "service," I am able to help promote the healing of the human person, a task which is central to my ministry as a priest and bishop.

Service to Chicago

Another way in which I have invested myself in the ministry of healing is through my commitment to the people of Chicagoland, that is, the people of both the city and the metropolitan area. Chicago is an amazing mosaic of people who are different in color, in language, in culture—in a sense, different in everything except a common humanity and, I believe, a common potential for greatness and for mutual enrichment.

At the same time, it is quite evident that in many ways we are a divided city. We are divided racially, ethnically, socially, and economically. We are divided perhaps in as many ways as we are different. The divisions isolate us from each other and lead us to a climate which favors suspicion rather than trust, despair rather than hope, monotony rather than creativity; a climate which sometimes leads even to violence.

As the Roman Catholic Archbishop of Chicago, as a person who believes that we are destined to be together and find new life and wholeness through our different gifts, I seek in various ways to promote the unity of Chicago. This is no easy task. The woundedness and brokenness of the city have developed over a long period of time. For example, it was restrictive covenants in housing, developed in the early part of this century, that led to the stinging effects of racial segregation which we feel so sharply today. But I try not to let the magnitude of the difficulties discourage me or my collaborators. We are seeking something very simple. As a Church which is committed to being a healing agent in the community of Chicago, we seek to develop patterns of compassion which can be expressed in concrete ways.

The proclamation of an ideal, such as practical, concrete compassion —literally the specific ability to suffer with others and to celebrate with them—can be empty rhetoric. So often it is easy to convince oneself that *saying* something is the equivalent of *doing* something. So it has been the intent and the effort of the Church in Chicago to concretize in specific actions the compassion with which we hope to embrace all people. This has happened through our outreach to the entire community, especially through education, health care, and social services. We have tried to be as inclusive as possible. All of this is an attempt to specify in action the kind of compassion and tolerance we seek to call forth from the people of Chicago.

As I reflect on my task in this ministry of extending concrete compassion to the people in our city, I see myself primarily as an educator. I take that word "educator" in its Latin root sense as "one who draws out." A teacher is not merely one who lectures or talks about issues. A teacher can teach by doing, by indicating, by prodding, by accompanying those taught in certain directions. I see myself as a person who is learning both the ways of inclusion and compassion as I come to understand and serve the city better; I see myself as someone who is encouraging others to make connections. Through this sort of educational process, I hope that I am contributing in my own way to the healing of the divisions and woundedness that mar Chicago and cut short the greatness that is our possibility.

My Inner Life and Personal Quest for Healing and Peace

In these reflective sharings concerning my approach to healing and internal peace, I have spoken of my involvement in working for world peace, in working for a national consensus regarding the values which are at the heart of the life issues, and in working for a compassion and connection among the many diverse elements of the Chicago experience. I would like now to share still another level and dimension of my involvement in working for healing and for peace. This has to do with myself.

The questions of peace and healing are not simply issues "out there" on an international, national, or city scale. They are also issues that affect me in a deep and personal way. They are as much a part of me as they are of the world within which I live.

About seven years ago, I came to understand that the pace of my life and the direction of my activity were unfocused, uncentered in a significant way. I am not talking simply about the organization of time and energy for efficient work. The issues were really issues of the spirit; that is, I found myself unpeaceful and in need of healing. I came to understand, through the assistance of people who had already passed through this kind of personal journey toward healing, wholeness, and peace, that I, too, had to make changes.

It would be difficult for me to elaborate this set of changes in this context. So many elements—in fact, the core elements—are tied to my personal faith and belief system. Let me say this much, however. I found that the way to healing, peace, and wholeness meant that I had to have a centered life. I needed a renewal of prayer in my life.

Mention of prayer may evoke an image of "saying" prayers, of reciting formulas, of incantations of one sort or another. I mean something quite different. When I speak of the renewal of prayer in my life, I am speaking of reconnecting myself with the larger mystery of life and of my common existence with other people. This certainly involves a certain kind of discipline in the use of time; it requires, too, some exercise of centering. But the essential ingredient is a contemplative stance toward life. An attitude of openness that will be ready to receive what the larger mystery we call God has to offer me by way of insight, perspectives, feelings, sense of values, inspiration, and so forth.

This has been a remarkably rich, even if not always easy, path toward healing, wholeness, and a peaceful way of life. I have found myself called to be a contemplator in the widest and the narrowest sense of that word: one who gazes and looks beyond the surface, or, rather, one who allows the depth dimension of life to surface. I am not an expert in this. I am no guru. I am a learner, and I dialogue in a process we call spiritual direction about my prayer. The point I wish to make is simply this. The approach to healing, wholeness, and peace on the many levels of life that we have considered includes, in my experience, the decisive and crucial level of one's own personal self.

Conclusion

Dr. Muslin in his invitation spoke of the possibility of cooperation. I think that he meant the cooperation, collaboration, and the mutual re-enforcement that might take place between those in the Church who are concerned with healing and those in medicine who are also concerned and dedicated to the healing process. The overall view is one that goes much deeper than the physical, material level. While not ignoring that level, the question is how we might come to live a more peaceful life, and how a healing process might be promoted to that end.

What I have attempted to do is to offer you some reflective sharings of my own approach to healing and the search for a more peaceful life. I spoke of these in terms of the various levels of my involvement: the questions of international peace, the issues of life that face our nation, the move toward compassion and pluralism in our city, and, finally, my personal quest for healing and wholeness through a contemplative-prayerful attitude in life.

Are my own strivings so idiosyncratic as to preclude the possibility of others sharing them? I think not. I believe that if the question is a shared vision and a shared strategy in working for the healing—the integral healing—of the human person, then we can share many elements together and re-enforce our efforts.

When I spoke of my efforts for the cause of world peace, I spoke of my own insight into the need to deal with the larger systems and my own task in the process as that of being a voice that raises the issues and questions. Are these also not possible for people in the healing professions? That you would more clearly attend to the larger picture, the larger systems that give meaning to life, and voice your concern through whatever forum is available—is that not a real, viable, and effective kind of option?

When I spoke of my approach to life issues in the United States, I spoke of the linkage of the issues, how they are rooted in fundamental values which I consider it my task to recall and connect. Is this not also the task of people involved in medicine? Are you not also called to make the strenuous effort to understand the basic values that underlie so many disparate issues of human hurting, woundedness, and violence? Rather than moving in an *ad hoc* way on each of these issues, would it not be better to probe reflectively, philosophically, perhaps even religiously, into the underlying values that illuminate, give meaning to, and link together a broad spectrum of questions?

When I talked about my service to the city of Chicago, I spoke of a task of healing that involves bringing together many disparate parts, of creating a climate of tolerance, compassion, and inclusivity. I felt that my role was that of an educator, calling people to understand the need for compassion and what it means, in the concrete, to be compassionate. Is this not also a concern for the medical profession? For example, what are the implications of compassion in the delivery of health care services, in the distribution of skills and energy? The balancing of market values with human compassion in such a way that the public sees and recognizes in you a genuine commitment to contribute to the healing of human persons—that must be your goal and, if you realize it, it will make a great difference in you personally and in this community. Your success in this regard will truly have healing effects which will go far beyond yourselves.

Lastly, I spoke of my own journey and struggles toward wholeness, of being in touch with the larger mystery of life through a contemplative stance. Is this not the necessary path for all healers, that they themselves be in touch with their own need for healing, for making peace in their own hearts? From this, they can draw on reserves of experience and humanity which will serve their patients well.

I hope, through these reflections, that I have been able to communicate several things.

First, I hope you realize how important I find the topic that has been raised by this conference.

Second, I hope you appreciate how deeply I feel about your contribution to the healing of the human person and, indeed, the healing of human society.

Third, I hope you understand that the way to develop clearer insight into these deep and complex matters is not through abstract deductions but through a process of shared experience and wisdom, such as we are engaged in at this moment.

Finally, I hope and I pray that you will continue this quest on many different levels, that your involvements will not be limited to the treatment of specific diseases but that you will also search out the roots of our woundedness and apply the healing remedies there.

6.

CATHOLIC VISION AND VALUES

*Address to the National Consultation on Obscenity,
Pornography, and Indecency*

First let me express my gratitude for the invitation to address you this evening. It is always a pleasure to return to Cincinnati and my many friends here even if for only a few hours.

I would like also to commend the National Leadership Team for their dedicated work on behalf of the Consultation on Obscenity, Pornography, and Indecency. It is indeed gratifying to hear that many church and civic leaders have shown their deep concern about the challenges that face our society on these issues.

I want to be clear at the outset that I do not come before you as a politician or a legal expert, an art critic or a psychologist. I am a believer and a pastor in the Catholic Church. Although there are behavioral, aesthetic, legal and political dimensions to the issues this Consultation seeks to address, my concern is primarily theological and religious and will reflect the Catholic heritage.

I am aware that this year's Consultation is especially geared to action. I agree that sharing ideas without acting upon them can be an exercise in frustration and futility. Nonetheless, our experience suggests that before, during, and after taking action we need to continue reflection upon the basic vision and values that have motivated our actions. This helps ensure that we are clear about our purpose and that our actions are guided by our values.

That is why my reflections will seek to address the broader perspective of our vision and values and how these should shape our strategies for facing the problems of obscenity, pornography, and indecency in our society. My reflections are basically twofold: (1) the theological basis of our opposition to these problems, and (2) some guiding principles that relate to our strategies for action.

The Dignity of the Human Person

The theological foundation of our opposition to obscenity, pornography, and indecency is the dignity of the human person. Although we

41

include many concerns in our social ministry, the common element that links these concerns is our conviction about the unique dignity of each human person.

The very first chapter of Genesis states unequivocally that humanity represents the summit of the creative process. The Creator places all creation in our hands, giving us the awesome responsibility of stewardship over the earth's resources, including the gift of each human life. There is more to the human story: God makes each human person in his own image and likeness—not exactly a carbon copy, but, at least, a close resemblance. The person is the clearest reflection of the presence of God among us. To lay violent hands on the person is to come as close as we can to laying violent hands on God. To diminish the human person is to come as close as we can to diminishing God. Human dignity derives both from the creative act of God and from the constant care and concern that God shows toward all people.

This is the truth about the human person, a truth that makes us free. Unfortunately, there are many individuals, institutions, and systems in contemporary life which propagate as freedom what, in reality, is slavery. True human freedom is not illusory or superficial; it is found only when we face the truth about human life—the inherent dignity of each human being in all aspects and dimensions, including sexuality.

From our recognition of the worth of all people under God flow the responsibilities of a "social" morality. Catholic social doctrine is based on two truths about the human person: human life is both sacred and social. Because we esteem human life as sacred, we have a duty to protect and foster it at all stages of development, from conception to death, and in all circumstances. Because we acknowledge that human life is also social, we must develop the kind of societal environment that protects and fosters its development.

It is clearly inadequate simply to say that human life is sacred and to explain why this is so. It is also necessary to examine and respond to the challenges to the unique dignity and sacredness of human life today. Human life has always been sacred, and there have always been threats to it. However, we live in a period of history when we have produced, sometimes with the best of intentions, a technology and a capacity to threaten and diminish human life which previous generations could not even imagine.

In the first instance, there are *life-threatening* issues such as genetics, abortion, capital punishment, modern warfare, and euthanasia. These assaults on life cannot be collapsed into one problem; they are all distinct, enormously complicated, and deserving of individual treatment. No single answer and no simple response will solve them. Still, they must be confronted as pieces of a larger pattern.

That is why I have argued frequently during the past year for the need of developing a "consistent ethic of life" that seeks to build a bridge of common interest and common insight on a range of social and moral questions. Successful resolution of *any* of these issues is dependent upon the broader attitude within society regarding overall respect for life. Attitude is the place to root a consistent ethic of life. A change of attitude, in turn, can lead to a change of policies and practices in our society.

In sum, when human life under any circumstance is not held as sacred in a society, all human life in that society is threatened. When it is held as sacred in all circumstances, all human life is protected.

In the second instance, there are *life-diminishing* issues, such as prostitution, pornography, sexism, and racism. Again, each is a distinct problem, enormously complex, worthy of individual attention and action. Nonetheless, understanding that they all contribute in some way to a diminishment of human dignity provides a theological foundation for more specific reflection and concrete action.

At the same time, we need to face the fact that life-diminishing issues can become life-threatening. News reports frequently chronicle how prostitution, pornography, sexism, and racism can all too easily lead to violence and death in our society. With regard to pornography, psychological research appears to confirm this assertion. We can say then that, when human life is diminished in any circumstances in a society, it contributes to the devaluing of all human life in that society.

Each human person is a paradox. Each of us has the capacity for seeking and expressing what is true, good, and beautiful. Each of us also has the potential for embracing what is false, evil, and ugly. We can love and we can hate. We can serve and we can dominate. We can respect and we can diminish. We can protect human life and we can threaten it.

When I say "we," I do not mean simply each of us acting on his or her own. I also include our local communities, our nation, our entire society. Every social system—east or west, north or south—should be judged by the way in which it reverences, or fails to reverence, the unique and equal dignity of every person.

Our concern is not simply individual human rights but also the common good. Individual rights are to contribute to the good of society, not infringe upon other people's legitimate rights.

Human life is diminished when women or men, and especially children, are exploited in the production of pornography, whether in print, film, or television. A sacrilegious note is added when the sacred persons and symbols of religion are exploited. Diminishment of human dignity also occurs in the lives of those who purchase or use pornography. Even more serious diminishment can occur because pornography is not so much an outlet for the baser instincts of the human person, but a stimulant. Violence, degradation, and humiliation are simply not compatible with the true sexual nature of the human person.

It is relatively easy to make a case against certain kinds of sexual propaganda as corruptive of human freedom and dignity. They destroy or diminish rational freedom either by damaging the capacity for personal reflection or by exciting the passions to the extent where they interfere with rational control of thought and behavior. They diminish human dignity by reducing human persons to sex objects.

However, we must acknowledge that pornography like prostitution seems to have a permanent attraction for some people despite the fact that it perversely and sometimes viciously profanes the sacredness of sex and the dignity of human person.

What are we to do about such propaganda? When we ask that question we reach the threshold of the problem of social freedom, an issue that is as complex as it is essential for consultations such as this.

The Shaping of Action Strategies

I would like to address three topics in this section: (a) the distinction between morality and law, (b) the importance of striking a balance between freedom and restraint in society, and (c) the necessity of being faithful to our vision and values in whatever response we make to obscenity, pornography, and indecency in our society.

Distinction between Moral Principles and Law

Morality and law are clearly related but also need to be differentiated. Although the premises of law are found in moral principles, the scope of law is more limited and its purpose is not the moralization of society. Moral principles govern personal and social human conduct and cover as well interior acts and motivation. Civil statutes govern public order and concern only external acts and values that are formally social.

Hence it is not the function of law to enjoin or prohibit everything that moral principles enjoin or prohibit. History has shown over and over again that people can be coerced only into a minimum of moral actions. It would seem, therefore, that, when we pursue a legal course of action with regard to such matters as sexual morality, our expectations may have to be somewhat more limited than in other areas of human morality.

A further corollary of this is also demonstrable from our own American history. People obey good laws because they are good. When a law is held in contempt, it can defeat its own purpose and erode respect for law itself.

I am pointing this out not as an argument against a legal response to the problems we are addressing in this Consultation, but simply to put such a response in perspective, to make sure that it is sound and supportable.

Striking a Balance between Freedom and Restraint

Because human freedom is such an inalienable right, any constraint in society must be for the sake of freedom; that is, the constraint must create a freedom in another respect. This means that we must search for ways to strike a balance between freedom and restraint in society.

This is especially important when the restraint in question involves the area of communication within society. When we encounter sexual propaganda that is corruptive of human freedom, we need to ask ourselves whether the corruption is such that it requires attention by organized society. A second set of questions concerns whether public or private agencies in the society should attend to the corruptive influences. And, assuming that public order is the norm whose requirements are to be enforced in this action, we have to ask what requirements of public order can be applied validly against the claims of freedom.

The reason for ensuring that restraints against the claims of freedom are valid is that the limitation of freedom has many consequences—some of them identifiable only *after* the restraints have been imposed. One of the main consequences possible is that we may be taking the risk of damaging freedom in a third domain with consequences more dangerous to the community. At best the effect toward which we aim can only be foreseen with probability, not certainty. We are familiar with the biblical example of "the last state of the man becoming worse than the first."

Let me expand on this a bit to avoid misunderstanding. As the recipients of the Judeo-Christian heritage, we do not condemn every portrayal of vice. Not infrequently, the Bible itself portrays vice and violence. The biblical text not only records the history of salvation; it also wrestles with the problems associated with that history. The biblical authors did not avoid portraying the most vicious and violent components of human behavior. They confront this dimension of human life rather than escape from it.

Similarly, as Richard Griffiths has pointed out, "a refusal to experience art that often deals with eroticism and violence may be a refusal to face the world as it really is. But experience must lead to confrontation, not compromise." Overprotection can do almost as much harm as bad example in hindering young persons who are preparing to assume their rightful role in a human society which involves the experiences of eroticism and violence. Their proper role, of course, is one of confrontation rather than compromise when human life and dignity are threatened or diminished.

I want to make it clear that I am *not* suggesting that some pornography is legitimate. What I am saying is that we need a well-reasoned approach to the problems we are addressing with the express purpose of striking a balance between freedom and restraint. Only then will we find the broad base of support needed for effective action in the legal sphere. We may not find a simple formula that is applicable to all cases and similar for all segments of our society. The late Rev. John Courtney Murray, S.J., a respected authority on church-state matters, said that "in the United States we have constitutionally decided that the presumption is in favor of freedom, and that the advocate of constraint must make a convincing argument for its necessity or utility in the particular case." That is why the credibility of the argument is so essential to success in these matters.

Proceeding with great care and deliberation will help ensure an effective solution to the corruptive influences of obscenity, pornography, and indecency in our society. An uncritical approach runs the risk of grossly oversimplifying the problem and is inappropriate, given the importance of our primary concern: the worth and dignity of the human person. Public opinion can be changed regarding an issue like pornography to the extent that it encounters well-reasoned articles and oral communications as well as Christian witness on a personal level.

Having made these comments about the care with which we must proceed in addressing the problem of obscenity, pornography, and indecency in our society, I wish to reaffirm the urgency of the challenge confronting us and the need to face up to it creatively and decisively. We need to take legal action against these corruptive influences in our society. I accepted your invitation to address this Consultation because I want publicly to support your efforts. I mentioned earlier my conviction that we must approach the various life issues with a certain ethical consistency. It is precisely that consistency which brings me here this evening.

As I said in a lecture I gave at the University of St. Louis this past March, "A consistent ethic of life does not equate the problem of taking life with the problem of promoting human dignity. But a consistent ethic identifies both the protection of life and its promotion as moral questions. It argues for a continuum of life which must be sustained in the face of diverse and distinct threats. . . . Consistency rules out contradictory moral positions about the unique value (and dignity) of human life." The comprehensive moral vision, which the consistent ethic of life promotes, demands that we work together to eliminate the evils of obscenity, pornography, and indecency even as we address the other evils which threaten and diminish life in today's society.

Fidelity to Vision and Values

Christian witness includes fidelity to our vision and values as we carry out our social ministry. We know that pornography is primarily directed at the weaker members of our society: the immature and the inadequate, frequently children and teenagers. Our biblical tradition calls upon us to defend the rights of the weaker members of our society—today's widows, orphans, and resident aliens—who too easily can become the objects of oppression, degradation, and de-valuing. The Scriptures also tell us that it is a serious matter indeed to lead the little ones astray. Our ministry does not imply that we are superior to these brothers and sisters; neither does it signify that we have no base instincts within ourselves.

Fidelity to our mission means that we have to be careful that we do not contribute to the diminishment or devaluation of human persons as we combat the corruptive influences of obscenity, pornography, and indecency. Fidelity to our mission means not isolating these problems from other life-threatening or life-diminishing issues in the sense of neglecting anything that threatens human life or diminishes human dignity.

One further reflection: it is important that we portray beauty and not simply unmask ugliness. It is essential that we promote virtue and not simply scorn vice. It matters that we proclaim the truth of human dignity and freedom and not simply attack falsity and illusions. In a consumer-oriented society, we need to remind each person that our worth derives from who we are rather than what we own. In a society that prizes individualism, we need to promote the common good as well. In a society that is preoccupied with sexuality, we need to stress that human value consists in more than physical attractiveness, that the value of actors and writers and filmmakers is more than their ability to meet particular public demands.

The concerns that we are addressing in this Consultation are important, first of all, because they concern human life and dignity. They command our attention at this point in our history because there are so many influences in our society that seek to corrupt human life and cheapen human dignity. These are complex matters that do not allow for simple solutions. Thinking and reflecting and deliberating together, I am confident that we can arrive at solutions which will improve the societal environment in which we seek to protect and foster human life and dignity in all of its circumstances and in all its stages of development.

7.

RELIGION AND POLITICS

Stating the Principles and Sharpening the Issues

WOODSTOCK FORUM, GEORGETOWN UNIVERSITY,
OCTOBER 25, 1984

I am grateful to the Woodstock Theological Center at Georgetown University for sponsoring this forum dedicated to the memory of Father John Courtney Murray, S.J. His intellectual legacy to the Church in the United States needs to be recalled regularly lest we forget what he taught us. My lecture this evening will honor Father Murray's memory by drawing heavily on his theology.

My topic is religion and politics. Under this heading, I intend to speak to the issues of the day without being consumed by the problems of the moment. The theme of religion and politics has been part of Western culture since Christianity first appeared in the Roman world. The attention given the specific issues in this presidential election year sharpens the edge of the questions, but the problems themselves are not entirely new. I hope to keep a sense of both historical perspective and contemporary relevance as I address three questions: (1) the relationship of religion and politics; (2) the transition from theology to policy; and (3) public morality and personal choice.

Religion and Politics: Continuity and Change

From Washington's first inaugural to Lincoln's second inaugural, from the Declaration of Independence to the decisive issues of this election, the themes of religion, morality, and politics are woven through the American experience. Intellectually and politically, the key question in every stage of the American civil experiment has not been *whether* these themes should be discussed but *how* to structure the debate for the welfare of the Church and the state.

No single figure in American history has had a greater impact on how Catholics conceive of the relationship between religion and politics than John Courtney Murray. It is now almost a quarter of a century since he wrote *We Hold These Truths*, and it is exactly twenty years since his landmark essay, "The Problem of Religious Freedom," was published in *Theological Studies*. The intervening years have demonstrated the wisdom of his thinking.

48

Father Murray would be the first to warn theologians against the fallacy of "archaism"—his characteristically elegant way of describing how people keep repeating the formulae of the past when the need is to reverence the tradition by renewing it. As I look at the question of religion and politics in 1984, there are some truths Murray held which need to be reaffirmed today. There are also some issues in our present debate which he did *not* address.

Murray's lasting contribution was that he provided the Church with a theological understanding of its role in a democracy and offered society a philosophical grounding for religious pluralism.

Murray was convinced that the Catholic tradition could learn from and contribute to the American democratic experiment. To facilitate this exchange, he took on the task of being the "theologian of the First Amendment." "Separation of Church and State" is the phrase often invoked to explain religion and politics in the United States. Murray believed deeply in the political wisdom of the separation clause, but he resisted all efforts to transform the separation of Church and state into the division of religion and politics.

The separation clause has a crucial but limited meaning: it holds that religious institutions are to expect neither discrimination nor favoritism in the exercise of their civic and religious responsibilities. The separation intended is that of the Church as an institution from the state as an institution. It was never intended to separate the Church from the wider society or religion from culture.

The purpose of the First Amendment, Murray taught us, was not to silence the religious voice but to free religion from state control so that moral/religious values and principles could be taught and cultivated in the wider society. This left religious institutions with the kind of influence they should have in civil society—moral influence. We are not to be or to be seen as one more interest group, but we are free to teach and preach a moral vision designed to influence the laws and institutions of society. The First Amendment guaranteed religious institutions the right to be heard in the public debate. Their influence in the public arena would depend upon the quality of their contributions to the wider civil conversation.

In the United States civil discourse is structured by religious pluralism. The condition of pluralism, wrote Murray, is the coexistence in one society of groups holding divergent and incompatible views with regard to religious questions. The genius of American pluralism, in his view, was that it provided for the religious freedom of each citizen and every faith. However, it did not purchase tolerance at the price of expelling religious and moral values from the public life of the nation. The goal of the American system is to provide space for a religious substance in society but not a religious state.

Today, when our public debate on religion and politics is particularly intense and, at times, slightly unruly, Murray's writings remind us of the value of religious pluralism and the fragile framework which holds it together.

Murray would have welcomed the vocal debate in our nation about religion, morality, and politics. But he would have reminded politicians and preachers that the way we conduct our debate is as important as what we say. There is a legitimate secularity of the political process and there is a legitimate role for religious and moral discourse in our nation's life. The dialogue which keeps both alive must be a careful conversation which seeks neither to transform secularity into secularism nor to change the religious role into religiously dominated public discourse.

If he were with us tonight, Murray would find the context of the public debate different from that which existed when he wrote *We Hold These Truths*. That book appeared during the 1960 election year. That campaign surely had its share of religion and politics, but the 1980s have produced both new issues and new actors not experienced nor analyzed by Murray.

First, a central theme in Murray's work is the imperative of providing a moral foundation for public policy, law, and the institutions of democracy. Religious tolerance cannot be purchased at the price of a moral vacuum. A society stands in need of a public consensus which "furnishes the premise of a people's action in history and defines the larger aims which that action seeks in internal affairs and in external relations" (*We Hold These Truths*, p. 10).

Murray's writings ranged across the theory and practice of shaping a moral consensus in a pluralistic democracy. But he never once wrote about the abortion question—an issue which most dramatically symbolizes the encounter of religion, morality, and politics in American life today. I shall return to the subject of abortion later; here I only point out that, on this issue, Murray offers little concrete guidance.

Second, Murray never analyzed what is today called the "Religious Right" because it was not a factor in the 1960s. Today, the evangelical churches which comprise this phenomenon are central actors in the interaction of religion and politics. I use the phrase descriptively, not pejoratively. The premises of the movement are grounded in a particular scriptural interpretation of life. Moreover, its conclusions are solidly located on the right of the American political spectrum. If Murray had confronted the Religious Right, I think he would have done three things: defended its right to speak; differed with its doctrine of Church and state; and criticized its moral vision.

These points are worth pursuing. Some commentators associate the Catholic Bishops and the Religious Right because both oppose the *Roe v. Wade* decision of the Supreme Court on abortion. Both do oppose abortion, but they differ in both ecclesial style and moral substance on a range of issues. I specify these differences not to be contentious or divisive; indeed, I want to acknowledge that the issues of personal morality and family morality which have impelled evangelical churches into the public arena need attention. But specifying differences in approach and carefully distinguishing issues will highlight some crucial principles of religion and politics in the United States.

Murray spent a substantial amount of time and effort defending the Church's right to speak in the public arena. But he also stressed the limits of the religious role in that arena. Today religious institutions, I believe, must reaffirm their rights and recognize their limits. My intent is not, of course, to produce a passive Church or a purely private vision of faith. The limits relate not to whether we enter the public debate but *how* we advocate a public case. From Murray, I have learned to respect the *complexity* of public issues and recognize the legitimate *secularity* of the public debate.

While defending the right of the Religious Right to speak, I also think all of us in the religious community need to be tested and to test each other on how we address public questions.

The test of *complexity* is one we all must face; it is one the Religious Left has often failed and thereby paved the way for the Religious Right. From issues of defense policy through questions of medical ethics to issues of social policy, the moral dimensions of our public life are interwoven with empirical judgments where honest disagreement exists. I do not believe, however, that empirical complexity should silence or paralyze religious/moral analysis and advocacy of issues. But we owe the public a careful accounting of how we have come to our moral conclusions.

I sympathize with those voices who found the Catholic bishops' pastoral letter on the nuclear arms issue long and dense, but I could not agree to a shorter, simplified letter which failed to justify our criticism of the arms race and certain elements of U. S. policy.

The *secularity* of the public debate poses a different test. I stand with Murray in attributing a public role to religion and morality in our national life. But I also stand with him in the conviction that religiously rooted positions must somehow be translated into language, arguments, and categories which a religiously pluralistic society can agree on as the moral foundation of key policy positions.

In both their style of analysis and their mode of argument, the Religious Right, at times, fails to address the complexity of our policy agenda and the legitimate secular quality of our public discourse. On both counts, I find key differences between the Catholic view of religion and politics and the prevailing tenor of some of our contemporary debates.

Another difference is the framework of moral vision we use, even when we come to a conclusion similar to that of the Religious Right, such as our opposition to abortion. I have argued previously, and this evening will argue again, two points: the centrality of the abortion question in our national life and the need to situate a firm, unyielding opposition to abortion within a wider framework of respect for life on many fronts. This broader moral argument is different in tone, scope, and substance from the Religious Right's approach to public policy.

From Theology to Policy: The Logic of the Life Issues

Thus far, I have principally concentrated on *how* religion and politics should be related. But the issues of a religiously pluralistic society go beyond procedural questions. The *substance* of the religious/moral vision which the Church brings to the policy debate ultimately determines its impact in the public arena.

The sources of the contemporary interest in religion, morality, and politics lie in substantive questions. As a society, we are increasingly confronted with a range of issues which have undeniable moral dimensions. It is not possible to define, debate, or decide these policy issues without addressing explicitly their moral character. The issues span the spectrum of life from conception to death, and they bear upon major segments of our domestic and foreign policy.

Two characteristics of American society which intensify the moral urgency of this range of issues are the global impact of our policies and the technological character of our culture. The role of human rights in U.S. foreign policy, for example, has specific consequences each day for people from Eastern Europe through Southern Africa, from South America to Asia. But the formulation of a human rights policy is not a purely political or technical question. It requires sustained moral analysis from case to case.

Even more strikingly, the pervasive influence of technological change—transforming everything from medical science to military strategy—poses questions which are fundamental and moral in character, not merely technical or tactical. In the last two generations we have cracked the genetic code and smashed the atom. Neither event nor the revolution they symbolize can be understood apart from moral analysis.

It is significant, I think, that Pope John Paul II's approach to both medical ethics and nuclear policy is invariably placed in the larger context of the relationship of technology, politics, and ethics. The interaction of these three forces has, I believe, driven the question of religion and politics to the forefront of discussion. We have not simply chosen to discuss these themes; they have been forced upon us.

It is precisely this sense that human life can be threatened or enhanced along a broad spectrum of issues that moved me nearly a year ago at Fordham University to call for a "consistent ethic of life." I proposed a consistent ethic or "seamless garment" approach as a framework for dialogue within the Church and the wider society. My purpose was to highlight the diverse issues touching the dignity and quality of life today. I also wanted to indicate the resources of the Catholic theological vision which are available to address the wide range of moral issues in a systematic, sustained fashion. The discussion which I urged last year has been vigorously pursued within the Church as well as in the press and other circles.

A key concept in the formulation of a consistent ethic is an analogical understanding of issues which recognizes certain thematic ideas among them and is still capable of identifying the specific character of each problem along the spectrum of life. Such a vision pushes the moral, legal, and political debate beyond an *ad hoc* or "single issue" focus, setting our moral discussion in a broader context of concern for human life in diverse situations.

The purpose of this proposal, I wish to emphasize, has not been to downgrade the significance of a specific issue—whether it be abortion or nuclear arms—but to increase awareness of the multiple ways in which our attitudes or actions on a given problem can set a precedent or establish practices which influence other choices. The "seamless garment" does not equate all issues or subsume the moral problem of protecting and promoting life into one proposition. Rather, its objective is to sharpen our moral sensitivity and to expand the intellectual framework for debate of the life issues.

A year ago at Fordham, I invited a quest for consensus within the Church on the validity and logic of a consistent ethic. Tonight I am more convinced than ever that the ethic of the seamless garment is the best analytical setting in which to develop a posture in defense of human life. We obviously do not have a consensus on this point at present—even within the Church. But the framework of the consistent ethic does engage many who disagree on specific conclusions. John Courtney Murray once said that we can argue about an issue only on the basis of a certain agreement. I think the consistent ethic can provide the framework of Catholic moral teaching in light of which discussion about priorities, policies, and cases can occur. I have found such solid support for the idea of the seamless garment that I shall continue to pursue its development and implementation.

It is not sufficient in this lecture simply to state the purpose and intent of the consistent ethic of life. The specific relationship among the issues must also be explored. A consistent moral vision should begin with the initiation of life. The Catholic moral tradition anchors its ethic of life in its teaching on abortion.

Few moral questions have such a sustained and extensive history. The opposition to abortion reaches from the Didache in the first Christian century to the statements of Pope John Paul II and documents of our own Episcopal Conference in the 1980s. The antiquity of the tradition reflects the abiding concern of the Church for this question. Abortion anchors a consistent ethic because the unborn child symbolizes the fundamental challenge innocent life poses for individuals and society at every stage of human development. The very vulnerability of the unborn tests our moral vision, for the moral quality of any society is measured not by how it treats the powerful but how it respects the claims of the powerless.

Abortion violates two central tenets of the Christian moral vision. It is a direct attack on innocent life. It is also a failure to observe the command that we love the least among us. In the words of Pope John Paul II, abortion strikes "at the whole moral order." It attacks the moral order, not just one religious perspective about morality. Protecting innocent life from direct attack is a fundamental human and moral imperative, not an exclusively Catholic belief.

Many in our country wonder why the Catholic bishops have taken such a visible and vocal stand on abortion. We simply have no choice. In the face of 1.5 million abortions a year, as a nation we must acknowledge that the principle of protecting innocent life from direct attack is being systematically eroded. The moral order is threatened. We cannot be passive when the unborn die without anyone to speak on their behalf and without legal recourse. Nor can we allow the moral principle protecting innocent life to be subordinated to other claims because the consequences of such a process would not be confined to abortion.

To illustrate the stakes at work in this question, the seamless garment approach consciously connects the issues of war and abortion. The cases are not identical, but they are related. The Catholic moral tradition has allowed the taking of life as a last resort in well-defined circumstances of national defense, but it has never sanctioned the direct taking of innocent life in war. This remains true today. From the courageous article of Father John Ford, S.J., opposing the practice of obliteration bombing in World War II to the pastoral letter, *The Challenge of Peace*, which prohibits retaliatory strikes on civilian centers, the Catholic tradition has drawn an unyielding line against killing the innocent.

War and abortion are linked at the level of moral principle. They are also comparable questions in terms of national policy. As citizens of this nation, we face the responsibility of a policy of abortion on demand. We also face the reality of living in one of the two nations in the world which can initiate the nuclear cataclysm and perhaps the Nuclear Winter. I am convinced that the bishops and the Church as a whole must be equally engaged in both issues.

The policy of abortion on demand needs to be resisted and reversed. But this does not mean the nuclear question can be ignored or relegated to a subordinate status. The only "cure" for the nuclear threat is to prevent any use of nuclear weapons. We are not confronting a hypothetical or speculative future danger. The possibility of nuclear war is a clear and present danger. The dynamic of the arms race feeds the danger. The prevailing situation of both superpowers—proceeding with major weapons increases and no negotiations in progress—is a grave concern to all of us.

The value of the framework of a consistent ethic is that it forces us to face the full range of threats to life. It resists a "one issue" focus by the Church, even when the urgent issue is abortion or nuclear arms.

Indeed, the consistent ethic makes other connections among the life issues. It joins the duty to protect human life with the responsibility of promoting the dignity of each human person. The particular linkage which illustrates how these two duties relate is that of abortion and poverty. The Catholic position on abortion requires—by the law of logic and the law of love—a social vision which joins the right to life to the promotion of a range of other rights: nutrition, health care, employment, and housing. The defense of human life leads inexorably to respect for human rights, domestically and internationally.

In the past year, some have questioned whether the linkage of the right to life with other human rights may unintentionally dilute our stand against abortion. On both moral and social grounds, I believe precisely the opposite. The credibility of our advocacy of every unborn child's right to life will be enhanced by a consistent concern for the plight of the homeless, the hungry, and helpless in our nation, as well as the poor of the world.

Precisely because the unborn child represents the weakest member of our human community, there is an objective link to be made between unborn life and the lives of others who live defenseless at the margin of our society. A crucial challenge in raising awareness about abortion is that of enhancing the ability of people to "see" the fetus as a person deserving respect. A related challenge is that of helping us "see" all the other defenseless human beings who command our attention.

The statistics of our national life tell their story, but they are not easily seen. I hear the statistics of an increasing incidence of poverty, of 35 million people living below the poverty level. I hear the specific plight of women in poverty and of minorities, and it is like hearing the statistic of 1.5 million abortions. The statistics are *real*, and the people behind them are *real*! But if we do not "see" them as persons who lay claim on our consciences and our resources as a society, the reality has not penetrated our lives. The Church is called to help us "see" the different ways in which life is taken or threatened today. The Church needs to work with all others in a concerted effort to "see" the helpless among us. Here, I would point out that the media have a special responsibility in framing a correct vision of life in our society.

A consistent ethic is a social ethic; it joins the need for personal moral vision to the need for a just and compassionate social policy. We face today a curious paradox in our society: some groups assert a positive role for the state on a range of socioeconomic rights but want a neutral state on abortion. Others seemingly see the social role of the state exhausted when the child is born. A compassionate society must be capable of caring for the human person before and after birth. The state has responsibilities both to protect human life and to promote the dignity of each citizen, especially the least among us. We will not be a just society until civil law protects the right to life of each person, particularly the unborn child. We will not be a compassionate society until public policy and the private sector overcome the dangerous differences separating the rich and poor in our nation.

Public Morality and Personal Choice: Connection and Complexity

All three of these issues—abortion, war, and poverty—are questions of public morality. The phrase "public morality" is at the center of the debate on religion and politics, but it is not a concept which is well understood. The degree of confusion surrounding it in this political campaign is distressing.

The problem is partially due to the collapsing of two distinct questions into one argument. One question is how—in the objective order of law and policy—we determine which issues are *public* moral questions and which are best defined as *private* moral questions. A second question is the following: How, in the face of an issue of public morality, should a public official relate personal convictions about religion and moral truths to the fulfillment of public duty? Murray offered us some essential ideas on the first question; he did not address the second.

For Murray, an issue was one of public morality if it affected the public order of society. Public order, in turn, encompassed three goods: public peace, essential protection of human rights, and commonly accepted standards of moral behavior in a community. Whether a given question should be interpreted as one of public morality is not always self-evident. A rationally persuasive case has to be made that an action violates the rights of others or that the consequences of actions on a given issue are so important to society that the authority of the state and the civil law ought to be invoked to govern personal and group behavior.

Obviously, in a religiously pluralistic society, getting consensus on what constitutes a public moral question is never easy. But we have been able to do it—by a process of debate, decisions, then review of our decisions.

Two cases exemplify how we have struggled with public morality in the past. First, prohibition is an example of an attempt to legislate behavior in an area ultimately decided to be beyond the reach of civil law, and not sufficiently public in nature to affect the public order. Second, civil rights, particularly in areas of housing, education, employment, voting, and access to public facilities, were determined—after momentous struggles of war, politics, and law—to be so central to public order that the state could not be neutral on the question.

Today, we have a public consensus in law and policy which clearly defines civil rights as issues of public morality, and the decision to drink alcoholic beverages as clearly one of private morality. Neither decision was reached without struggle. There was not an automatic public consensus on either question. Philosophers, activists, politicians, preachers, judges, and ordinary citizens had to state a case, shape a consensus, and then find a way to give the consensus public standing in the life of the nation. The fact that a spontaneous public consensus is lacking at a given moment does not prohibit its being created. When he was told that the law could not legislate morality, Martin Luther King, Jr., used to say that the law could not make people love their neighbors but it could stop their lynching them. Law and policy can be instruments of shaping a public consensus; they are not simply the product of consensus.

The debate about public morality is inherent in a pluralistic society; it will never end. Today we struggle about the status of abortion. One of the valuable insights of my good and esteemed friend, Archbishop John O'Connor, articulated in his address on October 15, was that the *Roe v.*

Wade decision had undercut a solid prevailing consensus against abortion on demand. The need of the moment is to reformulate a public view of the meaning of abortion.

The Catholic bishops have consistently held that abortion is without question an issue of public morality because the unborn child's right to life is at stake. Precisely because the right to life is the foundation of other rights, we see the abortion issue in the same category as civil rights questions. This is not sectarian theology, but sound public moral philosophy. The Supreme Court decisions and its supporters have relegated abortion to the status of private morality—one in which society does not have an abiding interest. The entire logic of the seamless garment approach points the other way. By connecting abortion with other acknowledged human rights concerns, we seek to overcome the dangerous dichotomy which was introduced into our public life by the *Roe v. Wade* decision. We will not protect other rights securely, if we erode the right to life in our law.

The case the Catholic bishops have made is a moral case with direct legal consequences. In his October 14th statement, Bishop James Malone, President of the National Conference of Catholic Bishops, said: "We realize that citizens and public officials may agree with our moral arguments while disagreeing with us and among themselves on the most effective legal and policy remedies . . . In debating such matters there is much room for dialogue about what constitute effective workable responses; but the debate should not be about whether a response in the political order is needed."

Bishop Malone makes two central points which I want to endorse and expand upon. First, as a nation we must break through the present impasse in the abortion debate. The fact of 1.5 million abortions is a tragic reality. The very magnitude of the problem should be sufficient to establish a consensus that we have a *public problem* even if we recognize as a society that we differ about how to respond to it. As Bishop Malone said, the debate should not be *whether* a public response is needed.

Second, the distinction Bishop Malone makes between moral principle and political/legal strategies makes a significant contribution to the national debate and to the discussion within the Catholic community. On a series of questions from nuclear to social policy, the bishops advocate both moral principles and specific solutions. In the war and peace pastoral we called specific attention to the room for debate which exists at the level of particular strategies. We need the same kind of discussion in the Church and in the country on *how* to respond to the abortion problem in the legal sphere.

As an example of the kind of open discussion we need, I would endorse the suggestion of both Archbishop O'Connor and Father Theodore Hesburgh that we initiate a national dialogue on steps to restrict the present policy of abortion on demand. To enter—indeed, to initiate—a process of restricting abortion legally is not to change Catholic teaching on the morality of abortion. It is to recognize the different roles played by moral law and civil law in a pluralistic society. The civil law must be rooted in the moral law, but it may not at times incorporate the full range of the moral law. Along with Bishop Malone, Archbishop O'Connor, and all the bishops, I am committed to teaching the total moral law. But I am also committed to the search for what is possible and most effective in the civil arena.

This kind of careful distinguishing of the issues in the debate on public morality will set a better context in which to probe the second problem of personal conviction and public duty. It is an abiding problem of politics; every public figure faces the question. A few like Edmund Burke and Abraham Lincoln have put their thoughts in writing. To use a distinction I invoked earlier, the second question is not *whether* the deepest personal convictions of politicians should influence their public choices, but *how* the two should be related.

Clearly we do want people in public office whose deepest beliefs shape their character and determine the quality of their leadership. We choose public officials in part because we hope they will infuse public life with certain convictions. However, relating convictions to policy choices is a complex process. But it is precisely the complexity which should be debated.

As a theme for the debate, I find a sentence from Pope John Paul II's address to scientists and scholars at Hiroshima very suggestive. Speaking of the nuclear threat, he said: "From now on it is only through a conscious choice and through a deliberate policy that humanity can survive." This sentence spans the two dimensions of personal choice and public policy. Policy emerges as the result of conscious choices by individuals.

But the development of public policy requires a wider consensus than the personal conviction of any individual—even a public figure. Whether we look at the problem of how to reverse the arms race or how to reverse the policy of abortion on demand, the beginning of the process is a series of conscious choices that something different must be done. Then the search for deliberate policy can begin.

I would not want a candidate for public office today to be complacent, passive, or satisfied with the level or the dynamic of the arms race or the defense budget of our nation. I would look for the person who says, "What we have is unacceptable, and I will work for change." The process of change will surely not be simple, but the conscious choice and the willingness to change policy are the key. In the same vein, I would want candidates who are willing to say, "The fact of 1.5 million abortions a year is unacceptable, and I will work for a change in the public policy which encourages or permits this practice." In both areas—the arms race and abortion—it will take conscious decisions by citizens and public officials if we are to have deliberate policies which serve human life.

This address has gone on too long! I plead understanding based on the complexity and centrality of the problem I was asked to address. I shall test your endurance with one final thought. The issues of religion and politics, theology and policy, public morality and personal choice will be with us long after the current election is over. Elections are wonderful and necessary events in the democratic process. However, they are not well suited for producing reflective ideas or careful distinctions. The questions which have run through this election—about the role of religion in our public life, the relation of political responses to moral issues—are broader and deeper than election politics can handle. I recommend that we use the experiences of the moment to help set the agenda for the future.

The questions of public policy raised in this election year have been formulated in the political arena. Solid answers to them will require reaching beyond politics to universities, research centers, libraries, churches, and synagogues. I hope our Catholic universities will take the challenge seriously. I know the bishops will remain in the public debate, and we need help. Public officials will remain in the line of fire, and they need help. Citizens will ultimately make the difference, and they need the aid of institutions to advance the dialogue about conscious choices and deliberate policies on a range of issues.

As the debate proceeds, let us remember a favorite term of John Courtney Murray: the need for *civility*. We can keep our deepest convictions and still keep our civil courtesy. We can test others' arguments but not question their motives. We can presume good will even when we strenuously disagree. We can relate the best of religion to the best of politics in the service of each other and the wider society, national and human, to which we are bound in hope and love.

8.

THE FACT OF POVERTY TODAY

The Challenge for the Church

THE CATHOLIC UNIVERSITY OF AMERICA,
JANUARY 17, 1985

Let me begin by expressing my appreciation to Father Byron, President of Catholic University, for the invitation to deliver this address on the fact of poverty and the challenge it poses for the Church. Both the topic and the place of the lecture have special relevance.

The bishops of the United States are engaged in a major effort to help the Church in the U. S. in its analysis and response to the fact of poverty. The first draft of the pastoral letter, "Catholic Social Teaching and the U. S. Economy," is merely an initial step in an extended process. Its goal is to engage every level of the Church in study, discussion, and decisions about how the Church can and must respond to the cry of the poor.

The opportunity for me to address an audience at Catholic University as part of this process has both symbolic and substantive significance. The Church always acts with a sense of its history and its tradition. The tradition of the U. S. Church's social teaching on poverty has been profoundly influenced by this University. To come to the intellectual home of Msgr. John A. Ryan and Bishop Francis Haas, of Father Paul Hanley Furfey and Msgr. George Higgins is to acknowledge the U. S. Church's debt to this University. It also recognizes that the social tradition continues here, symbolized by Fr. Byron's own ministry and by the work of so many of your faculty.

My purpose this evening is to analyze the relationship of the Church to the fact of poverty in our time. I will examine where we stand as a Church, what we can bring to the struggle against poverty, and how we should proceed in this struggle precisely as the Church.

More specifically, I will address three questions: the nature of the problem we face, the role of the Church, and one aspect of the policy debate on poverty.

The Nature of the Problem: The Fact and The Faces of Poverty

Let me begin with two assertions: (1) much of the poverty in the world is hidden from us; (2) the poor usually live at the margin of society and too often at the margin of awareness of those who are not poor. Yet, in the world of the 1980s, although many of the poor are hidden, it is also impossible for the rest of us to hide from the poor.

The faces of poverty are all around us. Chicago and Washington are different cities, but I have lived in both of them long enough to know that the only way to hide from the poor is to stay in one's room or home. We cannot walk to work or to the bus stop, we cannot run a noontime errand without seeing the faces of poverty—on the heating grates, in the doorways, near the bus terminal, and huddled in the winter around the places which serve the cheapest cup of coffee.

After walking through the poverty of the city during the day, we are confronted with the faces of poverty on a wider scale in the nightly news. Ethiopia is an extreme case, but not as extreme as we might first think. The fact of poverty is the dominant social reality for over 100 countries of the world. Numbers can be numbing in their effect, but they can also crystallize a challenge.

The fact of global poverty means:

- 800 million people live in conditions of "absolute poverty," that is, "a condition of life so limited by malnutrition, illiteracy, disease, high infant mortality, and low life expectancy as to be beneath any rational definition of human decency" (Robert McNamara, Speech to Board of Governors of the World Bank);
- 2.26 billion people—half of the world's population—live in countries with a per capita income of less than $400 per year;
- 450 million people are malnourished.

Statistics illustrating the global reality of poverty could be given in much greater detail, of course. But statistics do not tell us all we need to know. The Gospel points out that these poor people are our brothers and sisters. The first draft of the pastoral letter wisely devotes a substantial section to the U. S. relationship with the rest of the world because the resources of this nation and its role in the world constitute a serious responsibility in responding to the absolute poverty of our 800 million brothers and sisters.

My specific concern this evening, however, is not the faces and figures of *global* poverty, but poverty in the United States. The fact of world poverty is so massive that it can overwhelm us. The fact of poverty in the United States is a part of our national life, but it is not recognized as a dominant fact of our existence. It can easily blend into a larger picture which stresses not poverty but the power and productivity of the nation.

Poverty is surely present but, in the dominant national perspective—provided by magazines, media, and movies—it is not a significant feature. Poverty is present but, when we plan for the future, the poor are not central to the planning. Poverty is present but, in the policy debates of the nation, the poor exercise little leverage.

The drafting of the pastoral letter on the economy is still in its early stages. However, it has already accomplished something which commentators have quickly noticed: The letter makes space in the policy debate for the fate of the poor in a way which has not been evident for some years now.

We need to make space for the faces of the poor in our personal consciences and in the public agenda because the facts tell us that poverty is not so marginal in this nation as we might think. At the end of 1983, by official government estimates, 35 million Americans were poor. That meant 15% of the nation was defined as poor. The hidden poor were another 20-30 million who lived just above the poverty line.

Who are the poor? They represent every race and religion in the nation. They are both men and women, and, so very often, they are children. The poor are a fluid population. People move in and out of poverty. With unemployment still affecting at least 7-8 million people, the condition of poverty touches millions for some part of their lives.

No group is immune from poverty, but not all share it equally. Some of the statistics in the pastoral letter are striking: blacks are 12% of the American population, but 62% of those persistently poor; women who head households constitute 19% of the family population, but 61% of persistently poor families. The very old and the very young know the reality of poverty in disproportionate numbers.

The causes of poverty are a subject of honest disagreement, but the fact of poverty, even in a nation of our resources, cannot be disputed. It is the Church's response to this fact which is my major concern this evening.

The Role of the Church

The role of the Church in this question or any other must be shaped by the perspective of the Scriptures as these are read in the Catholic tradition. The draft of the pastoral letter develops the Scriptural case in detail. Here I will simply indicate the lines of an argument which is self-evident to anyone who examines the biblical basis of our faith. The argument is quite simple: the poor have a special place in the care of God, and they place specific demands on the consciences of believers.

The biblical argument runs through both Testaments, as the draft of the pastoral letter has shown. The prophets, in particular, specify the theme. In spite of their different styles and personalities, the prophets converge on a single message: the quality of Israel's faith will be tested by the character of justice in Israel's life. For the prophets, the test cases for Israel are specific: the way widows, orphans, and resident aliens are treated measures the link between faith and justice.

Jesus himself continues the prophetic tradition. He clearly identifies his ministry with the preaching of the prophets as, for example, in the fourth chapter of St. Luke's Gospel. He consciously finds those on the edge of society—the "widows, orphans, and resident aliens" of his time—and lifts up their plight even as he responds to their needs. He identifies himself so concretely with the poor that the first letter of St. John can say that love of God is measured by love of neighbor.

The biblical mandate about the poor is richer and more powerful than I can convey in this address. I recommend further study of the pastoral letter because it concisely gathers these biblical themes in its first chapter. However, I can synthesize the lesson the Church is trying to learn from the biblical perspective. It is found in a phrase which runs throughout the letter: the Church must have a "preferential option for the poor." This concept, rooted in the Scriptures, developed with originality by the Church in Latin America, and now becoming a guide for ministry in the universal Church under the leadership of Pope John Paul II, illustrates how the Church learns anew from the Scriptures in every age.

The power of the phrase, "preferential option for the poor," is that it summarizes several biblical themes. As the pastoral letter states, it calls the Church to speak for the poor, to see the world from their perspective, and to empty itself so it may experience the power of God in the midst of poverty and powerlessness.

This, in all honesty, is an extraordinarily demanding view of what we should be as a Church. It is clear we have a distance to go in implementing this view of the Church's mission and ministry. Nevertheless, we have begun by taking the imperative seriously.

The option for the poor, I would suggest, will be realized in different ways according to the situation of the Church in different societies and cultures. Now we need to ask what the phrase means for the ministry of the Church in the United States.

I do not have a blueprint for determining the specific meaning of the "option for the poor" or integrating the concept into our ministry in this country. However, one dimension of the task especially interests me—the role of the Church as a social institution in our society. The Church as a social institution has made two distinct responses to the fact of poverty. The first has been to organize itself to carry out works of mercy. The fulfillment of the command to feed the hungry, clothe the naked, and care for the sick has found direct and immediate expression in the Church from the apostolic age until today. The methods of doing this work have varied, but all can be classified as direct, social service to the poor.

The manifestations of this dimension of ministry are well known in the United States. They include Catholic Charities and social services in every diocese, St. Vincent de Paul Societies in every parish, and institutions—such as orphanages, hospitals, and shelters for the homeless—established by communities of men and women religious and others throughout the country.

This form of social ministry is well known, but it is not the only way the Church addresses the fact of poverty. The second and complementary witness to the option for the poor is the Church's role as advocate and actor in the public life of society. The roots of this dimension of social ministry are found in the prophets who teach us to ask questions about how we organize our life as a society. The prophets asked questions in Israel about patterns of land ownership and wages, about the rules and customs used to design the social life of the nation. The prophets did not stop at formulating the norm that the quality of faith is tested by the character of social justice. They pressed specific questions about the social patterns in the life of Israel.

The conditions of twentieth-century industrial society are radically different from eighth-century-B.C. Israelite society. Nevertheless, the prophets' style of social questioning has been taken up in the Church's social teaching of this century. The purpose of this social teaching is to measure the social and economic life of society by the standards of social justice and social charity.

The leadership of the popes in this century has, in turn, produced a body of social teaching from the bishops. The best-known example was probably drafted in some faculty residence on this campus by John A. Ryan when he authored the 1919 pastoral letter of the U. S. bishops. The first draft of the 1984 pastoral letter on the economy stands in this tradition of social teaching.

These two dimensions of the Church's life—its ministry of direct social service and its role as an advocate for the poor in society—remain the principal channels for the Church's response to poverty. The challenge we face in making an effective option for the poor is how these two aspects of social ministry are integrated into the full life of the Church today.

In a large, complex, bureaucratic, secular society like the United States, the Church's social service role is more needed than ever. We should not try to duplicate what society does well in supplying social services, but, in particular, we should bring two dimensions to the system of social care. First, the delivery of some social services is best done in a decentralized local model. For many social services today, only the taxing power of the state can raise sufficient funds to meet human needs. But the state is often not the best agency to minister services to people in need. The Church and other voluntary agencies can often deliver, in a humane and compassionate way, services that only the state can fund.

Second, the Church's agencies of direct social service should be a source not only of compassion but also of creativity. Public bureaucracy is not known for creative innovation. Its size and complexity often prevent it from acting in anything but routine patterns. In every field from housing to health care to hospices, there is room for new creative methods of public-private cooperation to feed the hungry, shelter the homeless, and heal the sick. We can do better what we are already doing. With 35 million poor in our midst, we can reach beyond what we are doing!

In saying this, I want to be correctly understood. I am aware that Catholic Charities, the Catholic health care system, and other diocesan and national networks are already involved in significant efforts of creative and direct service. It is the very success of these efforts which will give us courage to extend our efforts.

There is another sense in which I want to be clearly understood. We cannot be consistent with Catholic tradition unless we accept the principle of subsidiarity. I fully support a pluralist social system in which the state is not the center of everything. Nevertheless, I do not want the principle of subsidiarity used in a way which subverts Catholic teaching on the collective responsibility of society for its poor. I am not endorsing a concept of decentralization or federalism which absolves the government from fulfilling its social responsibilities.

Both the Catholic and American traditions urge a pattern of public-private cooperation. This means the state has a positive social role, and we have social responsibilities as religious organizations. The churches alone cannot meet the social needs of this nation, and we should not try to do so. We should be prepared to play a major role, but part of our role is to enter the public debate and work for a compassionate, just social policy.

This is the second challenge which confronts the Church today: how to fulfill the role of advocate in the public debate. This is the role which the Bishops' Conference is seeking to fulfill in its pastoral letters, first on peace and now on social justice. It is the role Bishop Malone stressed in his presidential address to the bishops last November. He argued that, on issues as diverse as abortion, Central America, nuclear war, and poverty, failure of the bishops to speak would be a dereliction of civic responsibility and religious duty.

It is this role which puts the bishops in the midst of public controversy. Controversy is the companion of participation in public policy debate. That is why it should not be surprising that contributions of the scope and range of our two pastoral letters cause controversies.

At the same time, it is important to understand the purpose of the bishops' interventions. In the pastoral letters—and in many other documents, such as congressional testimonies, speeches, and letters of individual bishops—we speak at the level of both moral principles and the application of these principles to particular policies. We regularly assert that we understand and want others to understand that the moral principles we present have a different authority than our particular conclusions. We invite debate and discussion of our policy conclusions. We know they must be tested in the public arena, in the academic community, and in the professional community. We have been using the process of successive drafts to stimulate this discussion.

Since I was so directly involved in the pastoral letter on war and peace, I believe there is specific merit in joining principles and policy proposals in the same document. Its purpose is not to foreclose debate, but to foster it. The policy conclusions give a sense of how the moral principles take shape in the concrete situations our society faces. I think we would be mistaken as bishops if we did not distinguish principles from policy judgments. But I think we would fail to stimulate the public argument if we withdrew from the arena of policy choices.

Our role is not to design or legislate programs but to help shape the questions our society asks and to help set the right terms of debate on public policy.

We have an excellent example in the issue confronting the administration, the Congress, and the general public as we begin 1985—the deficit debate. It is the kind of highly technical and complex question which a modern state must face. The way the question is decided will shape the life of our society. The fact is that the deficit must be cut. The choices facing the administration and the Congress are *how* to cut spending to reduce the deficit.

The technical details are admittedly immense, but the general policy question is not purely technical. At the core of the deficit debate is the trade-off between military spending and social spending. How that trade-off is adjudicated requires moral discernment as well as economic competence.

In the 1980s virtually every program for the poor has been cut:
- more than 2 million poor children lost health care benefits;
- half a million disabled adults lost cash and medical assistance; and
- one million poor families lost food stamp benefits.

In general, spending for the poor is less than 10% of the federal budget, but it has sustained 33% of all budget cuts.

These cuts in social spending have been accompanied by significant, steady increases in military spending. It is the responsibility of the federal government to provide for the common defense *and* to promote the general welfare. Military spending will justifiably be part of the budget. But the deficit forces us as a nation to ask who will bear the burden of the deficit. Military spending should not be insulated when plans for reducing the deficit are formulated.

I have no misconceptions about bishops being competent to write a national budget. But it is not beyond our competence or role to say that the burden of reducing the deficit should not be borne by the most vulnerable among us. Programs for the poor have been cut enough! The burden must be shared by *all* sectors of the economy. The specifics of how to do it fall beyond my responsibility, but shaping the question of how we face the deficit is clearly part of what the Church should do as advocate in the social system.

The Poor and the Policy Debate—One Issue

In the deficit debate, the fate of many of the poor is at stake. This evening I would like to focus attention on a particular group by addressing a specific dimension of poverty: the feminization of poverty. This phrase has been coined by Dr. Diana Pierce, a Catholic University faculty member who has made a significant contribution to the study of poverty. She has focused her research on the plight of women who are divorced, widowed, or unmarried. She has surfaced data which have special relevance for the Church in the policy debate about poverty.

Dr. Pierce's pioneering work has helped many begin to understand the severe economic consequences of motherhood and sex discrimination in this country. Of course, men, especially minorities and youths, also suffer from unemployment and poverty, and millions of intact families have inadequate income. However, poverty is growing fastest among women and children.

As we look at this issue, it will be helpful to remember that nearly all (94%) women marry and nearly all of them (95%) have children. Reducing the economic price of motherhood should be a priority for our society. This disproportionate burden of poverty on women and children is appalling. Current statistics reflect some of this grim picture:
- two out of three poor adults are women;
- three out of four poor elderly are women;
- almost half of all poor families are headed by women, and half of the women raising children alone are poor;
- one in four children under six is poor;
- one in three black children under six is poor.

Even if poverty did not weigh so disproportionately on women, the growth of both the number and percentage of the poor would be cause for alarm and action. For those of us in the Church, this situation is profoundly disturbing. The fact that poverty is so concentrated among women and children should galvanize our energies and focus our attention on the conditions that create the situation.

A closer look at poverty among women reveals that it is strongly linked to two sets of factors: (1) job and wage discrimination, and (2) responsibility for the support and care of children.

Job and wage discrimination leave women concentrated in the lowest-paying jobs, with more problems finding full-time, year-round work. But, even when women overcome these obstacles, they still earn substantially less than men. Dr. Pierce's data indicate that women college graduates working full-time and year-round still make less than male high school dropouts! Of course, most women workers are not college graduates, and so the disparity in incomes is even greater for those in the lowest-paying jobs.

While this discrimination affects most women, those whose husbands are employed are partially insulated, at least temporarily, from its worst effects. For women raising children alone, of course, the situation is much worse because they are often financially responsible for most or all of their children's support. Despite some well-reported exceptions, child care and support fall mainly on women. The increased rates of divorce and out-ofwedlock births have left more women than ever solely responsible for the support of children.

Increasingly, it appears that it now takes the earnings of two adults to support a family in the United States. A single parent—widowed, divorced, or unmarried—finds it difficult to stay above the poverty line. When that parent faces additional obstacles, such as the cost of day care (which can easily take more than a fourth of an average woman's salary) and sex discrimination in employment, the cards are overwhelmingly stacked against her.

The job market often offers little hope to a single mother trying to escape poverty. Unfortunately, other potential sources of supplemental income are also very limited. Child support is paid regularly to only a very small proportion of eligible mothers. Welfare benefits are so low that, in most states, the combined value of Aid to Families with Dependent Children (AFDC) and food stamps doesn't even approach the poverty line. For the fifty states and the District of Columbia, the median benefit is 74% of the poverty threshold.

I cite these statistics and the case of women in poverty not because it is the only issue we must face as a Church in the policy debate but because it is one we should face with special emphasis. I am also aware that there are more fundamental remedies needed to address the feminization of poverty than the programs I have just mentioned. But I wanted to raise up these specific programs because they are so often criticized.

I have argued the case for a consistent ethic of life as the specific contribution which the Church can and should make in this nation's public debate. Central to a consistent ethic is the imperative that the Church stand for the protection and promotion of life from conception to death—that it stand against the drift toward nuclear war which has been so evident in recent years—and that it stand against the trend to have the most vulnerable among us carry the costs of our national indebtedness.

To stand for life is to stand for the needs of women and children who epitomize the sacredness of life. Standing for their rights is not merely a rhetorical task! The Church has its own specifically designed social services to protect and promote life. Through them we must counsel, support, and sustain women seeking to raise families alone and to provide their children with the basic necessities—necessities which the most well-endowed society in history surely should be able to muster.

But the Church cannot simply address the problem of the feminization of poverty through its own resources. It must also stand in the public debate for such programs as child care, food stamps, and aid to families with children. I do not contend that existing programs are without fault or should be immune from review. My point is that something like them is a fundamental requirement of a just society.

Whenever I speak about the consistent ethic, I am always forced by time limitations to omit or neglect crucial themes. In the past, I have stressed that our concern for life cannot stop at birth, that it cannot consist of a single issue—war or abortion or anything else. I have always considered that a substantial commitment to the poor is part of a consistent ethic and a concern for women in poverty a particularly pertinent aspect of this "seamless garment." This evening I am grateful for the opportunity to spell out why and how the Church should stand on these issues.

Ultimately, the pastoral letter on peace and the letter on the economy should help us as a Church develop the specific features of a consistent ethic. In the end, every social institution is known by what it stands for. I hope that the Catholic Church in this country will be known as a community which committed itself to the protection and promotion of life—that it helped this society fulfill these two tasks more adequately.

9.

MORALITY AND FOREIGN POLICY

Keynote Address, Conference on American Religion and International Relations

University of Missouri, Columbia, March 7, 1985

As a bishop who has long been involved in the public arena, I know the importance and influence of the media. I am aware of the daily demands you face and the impossibly wide range of issues you are expected to interpret for others. From personal experience and many years of study, I also acknowledge the complexity of religious belief and institutions. That is why I am particularly appreciative of this opportunity to dialogue on an intense and detailed basis with professional journalists. I have a profound respect for your vocation and for you.

My topic this evening is "Morality and Foreign Policy." As you know, I do not come to this podium as an expert in foreign affairs, but rather as a pastor and bishop in the Catholic Church. In the twentieth century, Catholic moral teaching has been particularly concerned with the moral dimensions of international relations. The involvement of the U. S. Catholic bishops in the public debates on war and peace, human rights, and other issues confronting our nation is a reflection and an extension of the teaching and practice of the Church throughout the world.

Basing my reflections on the experience which my brother bishops and I have had in the foreign policy debate, I wish to address three topics this evening: (1) establishing the links between moral analysis and foreign policy, (2) examining illustrative cases of moral discourse about policy, and (3) exploring the role of religious institutions in the debate about morality and policy.

Setting the Theme: Morality and Policy

The subject of moral purpose and American foreign policy has been a persistent topic in American history. The content of the debate has varied, from the idealism of Wilson to the realism of Morganthau, but the desire to provide moral direction for American policy has been a continuing theme of our national political life. There have always been critics of the theme. In the 1960s Dean Acheson quipped that there are two kinds of problems in foreign policy: *real* problems and *moral* problems. But Mr. Acheson took the subject seriously himself, and, if anything, the salience of moral argument in the policy debate has increased in recent years.

The 1970s saw a resurgence of interest in human rights issues, and the 1980s find much of the country involved in a spirited and serious discussion of morality and nuclear policy.

Both issues—human rights and nuclear policy—illustrate the complexity of moral debate about the ends and means of foreign policy. Both issues highlight, nonetheless, that the exclusion of moral factors from the policy debate is purchased at a high price not only for our values but also in terms of our interests. One of my purposes this evening is to argue the case for the *necessity* and the *possibility* of constructing a coherent linkage of moral principles and policy choices.

The *necessity* of moral analysis in policy debate is rooted in the character of the issues we face in the last two decades of this century. These major contemporary issues are not purely technical or tactical in nature. They are fundamental questions in which the moral dimension is a pervasive and persistent factor.

We live in a world which is interdependent in character and nuclear in context. Interdependence means we are locked together in a limited world. The factual interdependence of our economies raises key questions of access to resources for the industrial nations, but also justice in the economic system for the developing nations. The nuclear context of the age brings sharply into focus the problem of keeping the peace in an interdependent world governed by independent states.

The U. S. Catholic bishops in their pastoral letter, *The Challenge of Peace: God's Promise and Our Response*, spoke of today's dual challenge: building the peace in an interdependent world and keeping the peace in the nuclear age. Both tasks exemplify the necessity of shaping our factual view of the world in terms of the demands of the moral order. The absence of moral vision can erode both our values and our interests.

The *possibility* of meeting the moral challenge in our conception of foreign policy is rooted in two resources of our country and our culture. The first is the religiously pluralist character of the nation. The purpose of the separation of church and state in American society is not to exclude the voice of religion from public debate, but to provide a context of religious freedom where the insights of each religious tradition can be set forth and tested. The very testing of the religious voice opens the public debate to assessment by moral criteria.

The second resource is part of the constitutional tradition, itself a bearer of such moral values as respect for life, reverence for the law, a commitment to freedom, and a desire to relate liberty to justice. To ignore the moral dimension of foreign policy is to forsake both our religious and constitutional heritage.

The participation of the Catholic bishops in foreign policy discussion is rooted in our conviction that moral values and principles relate to public policy as well as to personal choices. It is also rooted in a belief that we honor our constitutional tradition of religious freedom precisely by exercising our right to participate in the public life of the nation. These convictions are shared by all major religious institutions in the United States. I am using the Catholic Church as an example because I know its involvement in detail.

If the linkage between morality and policy is both possible and necessary, it will be useful to move from a discussion of this general theme to specific analysis of issues where the moral analysis of policy has special relevance.

Examining the Cases: The Intersection of Morality and Policy

I have already argued that certain issues of foreign policy are so laden with moral content that wise policy must also be ethically correct policy. To ignore the moral dimensions of these questions is to miss crucial aspects of the policy challenge. Two cases where this proposition is well illustrated are the nuclear question and human rights.

The Nuclear Question

We are now in the fortieth year of the nuclear age. Nuclear arsenals and strategies of the superpowers present a political and moral problem of unique dimensions. Speaking at Hiroshima, Pope John Paul II specified the moral challenge of our age when he declared: "In the past it was possible to destroy a village, a town, a region, even a country. Now it is the whole planet that has come under threat."

The cosmic threat posed by nuclear weapons forces us to review our basic principles about war and politics. The classical formulations which guided foreign policy prior to the nuclear age came from Clausewitz and St. Augustine. Clausewitz, the preeminent theorist on war in the Western world, argued that war should be an extension of politics. War, for him, was a rational, purposeful activity which could be used to achieve political objectives. St. Augustine had argued that war could be, under certain restricted circumstances, a morally defensible activity.

Nuclear weapons challenge both of these propositions. The destructive capability of these arsenals threatens to destroy the very political values which are used to justify warfare. The same destructive capacity radically challenges the "just war ethics" contention that any *legitimate* use of force must be a *limited* application of force.

For four decades we have lived with this basic challenge facing us, and there are no signs that the dilemmas of the nuclear age will slip away. One of the characteristics of the 1980s, however, is an increased public awareness of the nuclear danger and a series of policy proposals—running from a "No First Use" policy to the Strategic Defense Initiative (SDI)—which challenge the accepted premises of U. S. policy for most of the past forty years.

Moral factors have played a major role in the public debate and policy discussions of this decade. The President defends his SDI proposal on moral grounds, and his critics launch moral as well as technical arguments against it. The Catholic bishops' pastoral letter has served as a framework of moral argument about a whole range of nuclear issues: from the strategy of deterrence to patterns of targeting to evaluations of arms control proposals. It is impossible to enter the nuclear debate in the United States today without some moral foundation for a proposed strategy. This visibility of moral argument in the policy debate has not always been so evident.

How does moral argument speak to the policy debate? Using themes from the bishops' pastoral letter, let me indicate some examples.

First, moral argument leads, in my view, to a basic proposition: the central moral and political truth of the nuclear age is the need to prevent any use of nuclear weapons under any circumstances. If this is really established as a primary goal of policy, then specific conclusions follow from it. There should be a conscious effort in both declaratory and deployment policies to build a political, strategic, technological, and moral barrier against resort to nuclear weapons.

It was in pursuit of this objective that the Catholic bishops supported a "No First Use" policy. It was also why we recommended against deploying weapons systems, like the MX, which can easily move either superpower in the direction of first strike nuclear policies in moments of extreme crisis. Each of these conclusions should be argued through on both political and moral grounds, but, in the brief compass of this address, I am merely trying to illustrate how the primary moral objective of preventing the use of nuclear weapons leads to a series of more specific policy proposals.

A second major theme in the bishops' pastoral letter is the relationship of technology, politics, and ethics in the nuclear age. Unfortunately, much evidence indicates that the technological drive of our age at key moments directs our political vision rather than having both political vision and moral assessment control technological development.

The decision to deploy MIRVed nuclear systems in the 1970s was a technological leap of enormous significance for our age.[1] Many have argued, persuasively I think, that MIRVing has mortgaged nuclear arms control in the 1970s and 1980s. But my point is that this momentous decision was made *without* sustained political or moral argument in the public debate.

Now we face a proposal—the SDI—to move in an entirely new technological direction. I mentioned earlier that it is both defended and opposed

---

[1] Editor's Note: MIRV is the acronym for " multiple independently targetable reentry vehicle," a term used to denote the addition of several warheads to a military rocket weapon.

on moral and strategic grounds. The fact that we are now having a major debate is a significant improvement over the MIRVing decision. Without attempting to resolve the SDI question here, I wish to express my profound misgivings about projecting the arms race on a new frontier in space even when the motivation for the proposal has entirely defensible moral intentions. Moral arguments are almost always multi-dimensional. One has to test not only the *intentions* of a policy but also its *consequences*. While I understand the motivation behind the SDI, I am very skeptical of its consequences on the arms race.

Human Rights

The tension between intentions and consequences is also visible in a second area of policy—human rights. If the moral debate of the 1980s has been focused on the nuclear question, the moral argument of the 1970s was cast principally around the topic of human rights and U. S. policy. First the United States Congress and then the Carter Administration gave new weight and significance to the human rights component of U. S. foreign policy.

But the intention to pursue a human rights policy and the specific steps needed to include human rights systematically in our policy are not identical. Looking at human rights policy of the 1980s, two comments seem appropriate. First, in the 1970s, it quickly became clear that trying to fuse the moral and empirical demands of a human rights policy was a more complex task than most believed at the time. Second, the dramatic decline in the priority of human rights during the 1980s illustrates a major problem: without sustained public and policy support for an objective as complicated as this, we will not make a difference in the long run.

We have, however, learned some valuable lessons from the 1970s, and these should be emphasized and kept alive for future use. Sustained moral argument about human rights and U. S. policy should, I submit, involve three steps.

First, we must make a commitment to include the human rights factor *at the outset* of policy making and recognize the need to sustain this factor *throughout* the development of policy in regard to a nation or a region. If we conceive of policy initially only in terms of our political, strategic, and economic interests in an area and *afterwards* attempt to factor in human rights, we will never give the latter sufficient leverage.

Second, although human rights should be systematically included in the policy equation, they have to be weighed against other factors. Foreign policy is too complex to have simply a human rights policy divorced from other considerations. This weighing of human rights objectives in a given region or case against other objectives is an exercise of moral reasoning as well as of political judgment. Our episcopal conference, for example, has been especially stringent in measuring *military assistance* to countries in light of human rights criteria. We have been less inclined to recommend cutting off *economic aid* for human rights violations.

Third, there should be some public understanding about the reason why a seriously pursued human rights policy will often seem as though we are criticizing our "friends" more than our "foes." Surely we should have and use human rights policies for Eastern Europe, Cambodia, or other communist-controlled states. But our relationship towards those governments is basically adversarial.

When we are considering a Latin American or East Asian country, with which the United States has close ties and which it is supplying with substantial amounts of military and economic assistance, human rights violations in these situations place us in a different setting. If the receiving government is an ally accused of human rights violations, there is a certain way in which we are implicated in the action by our support of that government. In this sense human rights criteria for U. S. policy speak as directly to the U. S. Government as to other governments. They tell us with what kinds of policies we should or should not be associated in another country.

Religious Institutions and Foreign Policy: The Moral Dimension

The advocacy of moral argument in the public policy of the nation is not uniquely a religious task. It is incumbent upon all citizens and every social institution to feel a sense of moral as well as political responsibility for national policies. But religious institutions would surely be culpable if they failed to provide leadership in fostering moral analysis of policy. They should bring their resources to the foreign policy debate: a disciplined moral tradition, a significant constituency, and a sense of transnational responsibility. I will comment briefly on each of these.

I have tried to illustrate above that joining moral and policy arguments is not a simple task. To take the moral dimensions of policy seriously is to be willing to take the discipline of moral argument as seriously as we do strategic theory or economic analysis. Religious traditions are schools of serious moral analysis. In both their formal teaching and their pastoral care, religious communities use moral analysis on a sustained basis.

I think the primary accomplishments of the bishops' pastoral letter were to create space in the public debate for moral analysis of nuclear policy and then to provide the concepts, principles, and arguments which could be used to debate the moral quality of policy. In this sense the tradition of moral argument which we offer the wider public is more important than the specific conclusions we draw from that tradition. Religious communities should facilitate moral argument about policy at least as much as they take specific positions on policies.

Second, religious institutions can facilitate this moral scrutiny very directly within their own constituencies. My panel presentation this morning stressed the importance of public opinion in the policy debate. Religious institutions have both the communities and the channels of access to press the moral questions of policy with a broad sector of the U. S. public. I do not think we should address ourselves *only* to our own communities, but I do think we should make a very special effort within them.

In a complex democracy like ours, public opinion will not dictate specific policy choices, but it can set certain directions for policy which elected officials will oppose only with much difficulty and at some risk. Setting a moral framework for policy direction should be a permanent part of the teaching of religious bodies.

Third, religious institutions, because of their teaching and, frequently, their structures, have a sense of transnational responsibility. In an interdependent world governed by independent states, this transnational perspective on what our policy should be can make a decisive difference. While this is true for any nation, it has a specific relevance for the United States. We remain the most significant single political, military, and economic power in the world. Our status is not that of the 1940s or 1950s, but it is still unique. This means, in moral terms, that we carry very specific responsibilities because of the decisive impact our policies have on the lives of others.

I have just returned from a visit to El Salvador and Nicaragua and from consultations with bishops from several Central American nations. Without entering the specifics of the Central American debate, let me simply say that one of the dominant impressions of the visit is the daily impact of U. S. policy on even the *most local* details of Central American life.

But our influence is not confined to that region. From nuclear strategy to monetary policies to food supplies in a hungry world, U. S. policies are life-and-death issues for many people. The role of moral argument in foreign policy is to call us to face our responsibilities squarely and to respond generously and wisely to them. Acknowledging this fact is a challenge which goes beyond religious institutions, but they should meet it in a way which calls the wider American community to the task of building the peace, shaping just relationships among nations, and enhancing the life of the people of this interdependent world.

10.

THE CONSISTENT ETHIC OF LIFE AND HEALTH CARE SYSTEMS

FOSTER MCGAW TRIENNIAL CONFERENCE,
CHICAGO, MAY 8, 1985

We meet on an auspicious day to explore more effective ways of preserving, protecting, and fostering human life—the 40th anniversary of the end of the war in Europe which claimed millions of lives, both European and American. It was also a war in which, tragically, the word Holocaust will be forever emblazoned in history. We must never forget!

This anniversary is a day not only for remembering victory over the forces of oppression which led to this savage destruction of life but also for recommitting ourselves to preserving and nurturing all human life.

Daily we encounter news headlines which reflect the growing complexity of contemporary life, the rapid development of science and technology, the global competition for limited natural resources, and the violence which is so rampant in parts of our nation and world. The problems of contemporary humanity are enormously complex, increasingly global, and ominously threatening to human life and human society. Each of them has moral and religious dimensions because they all impact human life.

At times we may feel helpless and powerless as we confront these issues. It is crucial that we develop a method of moral analysis which will be comprehensive enough to recognize the linkages among the issues, while respecting the individual nature and uniqueness of each. During the past year and a half, I have addressed this task through the development of a "consistent ethic of life"—popularly referred to as the "seamless garment" approach to the broad spectrum of life issues.

I come before you today as a *pastor*, not a health care professional or theoretician, not a philosopher, not a politician or a legal expert. As a pastor, I wish to share with you the teaching of the Catholic Church as it pertains to human life issues.

I am very grateful to Father Baumhart for the invitation to address you on "The Consistent Ethic of Life and Health Care Systems." I will first briefly describe the concept of a consistent ethic. Then I will explore the challenge it poses to health care systems both in terms of "classical" medical ethics questions and in regard to "contemporary" social justice issues.

The Consistent Ethic of Life

Although the consistent ethic of life needs to be finely tuned and carefully structured on the basis of values, principles, rules, and applications to specific cases, this is not my task this afternoon. I will simply highlight some of its basic components so that I can devote adequate attention to its application to health care systems and the issues they face today.

Catholic social teaching is based on two truths about the human person: human life is both sacred and social. Because we esteem human life as sacred, we have a duty to protect and foster it at all stages of development, from conception to death, and in all circumstances. Because we acknowledge that human life is also social, we must develop the kind of societal environment that protects and fosters its development.

Precisely because life is sacred, the taking of even one human life is a momentous event. While the presumption of traditional Catholic teaching has always been against taking human life, it has allowed the taking of human life in particular situations by way of exception—for example, in self-defense and capital punishment. In recent decades, however, the presumptions against taking human life have been strengthened and the exceptions made ever more restrictive.

Fundamental to this shift in emphasis is a more acute perception of the multiple ways in which life is threatened today. Obviously such questions as war, aggression, and capital punishment have been with us for centuries; they are not new. What is new is the *context* in which these ancient questions arise, and the way in which a new context shapes the *content* of our ethic of life.

One of the major cultural factors affecting human life today is technology. Because of nuclear weapons we now threaten life on a scale previously unimaginable—even after the horrible experience of World War II. Likewise, modern medical technology opens new opportunities for care, but it also poses potential new threats to the sanctity of life. Living, as we do, in an age of careening technological development means we face a qualitatively new range of moral problems.

The protection, defense, and nurture of human life involve the whole spectrum of life from conception to death, cutting across such issues as genetics, abortion, capital punishment, modern warfare, and the care of the terminally ill. Admittedly these are all distinct problems, enormously complex, and deserving individual treatment. No single answer and no simple response will solve them all. They cannot be collapsed into one problem, but they must be confronted as pieces of a *larger pattern*. The fact that we face new challenges in each of these areas reveals the need for a consistent ethic of life.

The pre-condition for sustaining a consistent ethic is a "respect life" attitude or atmosphere in society. Where human life is considered "cheap" and easily "wasted," eventually nothing is held as sacred and all lives are in jeopardy. The purpose of proposing a consistent ethic of life is to argue that success on any one of the issues threatening life requires a concern for the broader attitude in society about respect for life. Attitude is the place to root an ethic of life. Change of attitude, in turn, can lead to change of policies and practices in our society.

Besides rooting this ethic in societal attitude, I have demonstrated, in a number of recent addresses, that there is an inner relationship—a linkage—among the several issues at the more specific level of moral principle. It is not my intention to repeat these arguments today.

Nevertheless, I would like to examine briefly the relationship between "right to life" and "quality of life" issues. If one contends, as we do, that the right of every unborn child should be protected by civil law and supported by civil consensus, then our moral, political and economic responsibilities do not stop at the moment of birth! We must defend the *right to life* of the weakest among us; we must also be supportive of the *quality of life* of the powerless among us: the old and the young, the hungry and the homeless, the undocumented immigrant and the unemployed worker, the sick, the disabled, and the dying. I contend that the viability and credibility of the "seamless garment" principle depends upon the consistency of its application.

Such a quality-of-life posture translates into specific political and economic positions—for example, on tax policy, generation of employment, welfare policy, nutrition and feeding programs, and health care. Consistency means we cannot have it both ways: we cannot urge a compassionate society and vigorous public and private policy to protect the rights of the unborn and then argue that compassion and significant public and private programs on behalf of the needy undermine the moral fiber of society or that they are beyond the proper scope of governmental responsibility or that of the private sector. Neither can we do the opposite!

The inner relationship among the various life issues is far more intricate than I can sketch here this afternoon. I fully acknowledge this. My intention is merely to bring that basic linkage into focus so I can apply it to the issues facing health care systems today.

The Consistent Ethic and "Classical" Medical Ethics Questions

As I noted at the outset, the consistent ethic of life poses a challenge to two kinds of problems. The first are "classical" medical ethics questions which today include revolutionary techniques from genetics to the technologies of prolonging life. How do we define the problems and what does it mean to address them from a Catholic perspective?

The essential question in the technological challenge is this: In an age when we can do almost anything, how do we decide what we *should* do?

The even more demanding question is: In a time when we can do anything technologically, how do we decide morally what we should not do? My basic thesis is this: technology must not be allowed to hold the health of human beings as a hostage.

In an address in Toronto last September, Pope John Paul II outlined three temptations of pursuing technological development:

(1) pursuing development for its own sake, as if it were an autonomous force with built-in imperatives for expansion, instead of seeing it as a resource to be placed at the service of the human family;

(2) tying technological development to the logic of profit and constant economic expansion without due regard for the rights of workers or the needs of the poor and helpless;

(3) linking technological development to the pursuit or maintenance of power instead of using it as an instrument of freedom.

The response to these temptations, as the Holy Father pointed out, is not to renounce the technological application of scientific discoveries. We need science and technology to help solve the problems of humanity. We also need to subject technological application to moral analysis.

One of the most recent and most critical ethical questions which impacts the quality of human life is that of genetics, genetic counseling, and engineering. Perhaps no other discovery in medicine has the potential so radically to change the lives of individuals and, indeed, the human race itself.

As with most scientific achievements in medicine, there are advantages and disadvantages to the utilization of this theoretical knowledge and technological know-how. Many genetic diseases can now be diagnosed early, even in utero, and technology is also moving toward treatment in utero. Proper use of such information can serve to prepare parents for the arrival of a special infant or can allay the fears of the expectant parents if the delivery of a healthy infant can be anticipated. The accumulation of scientific data can lead to a better understanding of the marvels of creation and to the possible manipulation of genes to prevent disease or to effect a cure before the infant sustains a permanent disability.

On the other hand, people also use available diagnostic procedures to secure information for the sex selection of their children. Some may wish to use it to eliminate "undesirables" from society. Many believe that the provision of genetic information contributes to an increase in the number of abortions.

At the other end of life's spectrum is care of the elderly. Our marvelous progress in medical knowledge and technology has made it possible to preserve the lives of newborns who would have died of natural causes not too many years ago; to save the lives of children and adults who would formerly have succumbed to contagious diseases and traumatic injuries; to prolong the lives of the elderly as they experience the debilitating effects of chronic illness and old age. At the same time, some openly advocate euthanasia, implying that we have absolute dominion over life rather than stewardship. This directly attacks the sacredness of each human life.

Other new moral problems have been created by the extension of lives in Intensive Care Units and Neonatal Intensive Care Units as well as by surgical transplants and implants, artificial insemination and some forms of experimentation. Computers provide rapid, usually accurate, testing and treatment, but they also create problems of experimentation, confidentiality, and dehumanization. Intense debate is being waged about the extension of lives solely through extraordinary—mechanical or technological—means.

The consistent ethic of life, by taking into consideration the impact of technology on the full spectrum of life issues, provides additional insight to the new challenges which "classical" medical ethics questions face today. It enables us to define the problems in terms of their impact on human life and to clarify what it means to address them from a Catholic perspective.

The Consistent Ethic of Life and "Contemporary" Social Justice Issues

The second challenge which the consistent ethic poses concerns "contemporary" social justice issues related to health care systems. The primary question is: How does the evangelical option for the poor shape health care today?

Some regard the problem as basically financial: How do we effectively allocate limited resources? A serious problem today is the fact that many persons are left without basic health care while large sums of money are invested in the treatment of a few by means of exceptional, expensive measures. While technology has provided the industry with many diagnostic and therapeutic tools, their inaccessibility, cost, and sophistication often prevent their wide distribution and use.

Government regulations and restrictions, cut-backs in health programs, and the maldistribution of personnel to provide adequate services are but a few of the factors which contribute to the reality that many persons do not and probably will not receive the kind of basic care that nurtures life—unless we change attitudes, policies and programs.

Public health endeavors such as home care, immunization programs, health education, and other preventive measures to improve the environment and thus prevent disease, have all served as alternate means of providing care and improving the health of the poor and isolated populations. In the past, if patients from this sector of society needed hospitalization, institutions built with Hill-Burton funds were required to provide a designated amount of "charity care" to those in need.

In some instances, hospitals continue to follow this procedure.

However, access to these alternate, less expensive types of health care is becoming more difficult. Cuts in government support for health programs for the poor, for persons receiving Medicare or Medicaid benefits, are making it increasingly more difficult for people who need health care to receive it.

Today we seem to have three tiers of care: standard care for the insured, partial care for Medicaid patients, and emergency care only for the 35 million Americans who are uninsured. Do we nurture and protect life when there appears to be an unjust distribution of the goods entrusted to our stewardship? How can Catholic hospitals continue both to survive and to implement a preferential option for the poor?

This is not merely a theological or pastoral issue. Access to standard health care is largely non-existent for about half of the poor and very limited for the other half who are eligible for Medicaid or Medicare. The United States has the worst record on health care of any nation in the North Atlantic community and even worse than some underdeveloped nations.

Judith Feder and Jack Hadley, currently co-directors of the Center for Health Policy Studies at Georgetown University, have conducted research on uncompensated hospital care. Some of their findings are particularly disturbing. They concluded, for example, that *non-profit* hospitals—including Catholic facilities—do very little more for the poor than *for-profit* hospitals (which is very little, indeed). Free care provided by private, non-profit hospitals averaged only 3.85% of all charges (gross revenues) in 1982. I am aware that some dispute the accuracy of these findings in regard to Catholic hospitals, but I have not yet seen data which shows that, overall, these institutions provide substantially more free care than their counterparts.

I must also affirm, of course, that there are some inner city and other Catholic hospitals which do a great deal for the poor. Nonetheless, as the research seems to indicate, hospitals average less than 5% of patient charges for uncompensated care. Much of this is for deliveries to women who appear in heavy labor at our emergency rooms and the subsequent neonatal intensive care for their infants born with severe problems because of the lack of care given their mothers during pregnancy.

Our national resources are limited, but they are not scarce. As a nation we spend *more* per capita and a higher share of our Gross Domestic Product (GDP) on health than any other country in the world—nearly twice as much as Great Britain, for example. Yet our system still excludes at least half the poor. In 1982 the U. S. share of GDP devoted to health care was 10.6%, against 5.9% within the United Kingdom, which has universal access to health care and a lower infant mortality rate than the U. S.

The basic problem of health care in the U. S. is managerial: the effective allocation and control of resources. The key is the underlying philosophy and sense of mission which motivates and informs managerial decisions.

As a nation, we spend enormous amounts of money to prolong the lives of newborns and the dying while millions of people don't see a doctor until they are too ill to benefit from medical care. We allow the poor to die in our hospitals, but we don't provide for their treatment in the early stages of illness—much less make preventive care available to them.

These facts are disturbing to anyone who espouses the sacredness and value of human life. The fundamental human right is to life—from the moment of conception until death. It is the source of all other rights, including the right to health care. The consistent ethic of life poses a series of questions to Catholic health care facilities. Let me enumerate just a few.

Should a Catholic hospital transfer an indigent patient to another institution unless superior care is available there?

Should a Catholic nursing home require large cash deposits from applicants?

Should a Catholic nursing home transfer a patient to a state institution when his or her insurance runs out?

Should a Catholic hospital give staff privileges to a physician who won't accept Medicaid or uninsured patients?

If Catholic hospitals and other institutions take the consistent ethic seriously, then a number of responses follow. All Catholic hospitals will have outpatient programs to serve the needs of the poor. Catholic hospitals and other Church institutions will document the need for comprehensive prenatal programs and lead legislative efforts to get them enacted by state and national government. Catholic medical schools will teach students that medical ethics includes care for the poor—not merely an occasional charity case, but a commitment to see that adequate care is available.

If they take the consistent ethic seriously, Catholic institutions will lead efforts for adequate Medicaid coverage and reimbursement policies. They will lobby for preventive health programs for the poor. They will pay their staffs a just wage. Their staffs will receive training and formation to see God "hiding in the poor" and treat them with dignity.

I trust that each of you has an opinion about the importance or viability of responses to these challenges. My point in raising them is not to suggest simplistic answers to complex and difficult questions. I am a realist, and I know the difficulties faced by our Catholic institutions. Nonetheless, I do suggest that these questions arise out of a consistent ethic of life and present serious challenges to health care in this nation—and specifically to Catholic health care systems.

Medical ethics must include not only the "classical" questions but also contemporary social justice issues which affect health care. In a 1983 address to the World Medical Association, Pope John Paul II pointed out that developing an effective medical ethics—including the social justice dimension—"fundamentally depends on the concept one forms of medicine. It is a matter of learning definitely whether medicine truly is in service of the human person, his dignity, what he has of the unique and transcendent in him, or whether medicine is considered first of all as the agent of the collectivity, at the service of the interests of the healthy and well-off, to whom care for the sick is subordinated."

He went on to remind his listeners that the Hippocratic oath defines medical morality in terms of respect and protection of the human person.

The consistent ethic of life is primarily a theological concept, derived from biblical and ecclesial tradition about the sacredness of human life, about our responsibilities to protect, defend, nurture, and enhance God's gift of life. It provides a framework for moral analysis of the diverse impact of cultural factors—such as technology and contemporary distribution of resources—upon human life, both individual and collective.

The context in which we face new health care agendas generated both by technology and by poverty is that the Catholic health care system today confronts issues both of survival and of purpose. How shall we survive? For what purpose? The consistent ethic of life enables us to answer these questions by its comprehensiveness and the credibility which derives from its consistent application to the full spectrum of life issues.

11.

THE DEATH PENALTY IN OUR TIME

Address to the Criminal Law Committee

CRIMINAL COURT OF COOK COUNTY, ILLINOIS,
MAY 14, 1985

I wish to acknowledge with gratitude your considerable contribution to the quality of life among the people of Cook County as you preserve the value of justice and implement it each day. The court system is an indispensable part of our great American heritage of "justice for all under the law." I am aware that your dedicated work involves considerable frustration as you constantly encounter the seamier side of human behavior.

I am grateful for your invitation to meet with you this afternoon and to share my reflections on an issue of mutual concern: capital punishment. I come before you as a *pastor*—not a legal expert. It is my understanding that the constitutional principle of the separation of Church and state ensures religious organizations the right to engage in debate about public policy, expecting neither favoritism nor discrimination. At the same time, I firmly believe that they must earn the right to be heard by the quality of their arguments.

It has also been my longstanding conviction that civil law and social policy must always be subject to ongoing moral analysis. Simply because a civil law is in place does not mean it should be blindly supported. Encouraging reflective, informed assessment of civil law and policy keeps alive the capacity for moral criticism in society.

I also come before you as a *citizen* who cares deeply about the quality of life in our community.

I will address two dimensions of the topic this afternoon. First, I will situate the issue of capital punishment in the context of a consistent ethic of life and then examine the case for capital punishment in light of this ethic.

The Context: A Consistent Ethic of Life

Catholic social teaching is based on two truths about the human person: human life is both sacred and social. Because we esteem human life as sacred, we have a duty to protect and foster it at all stages of development, from conception to death, and in all circumstances. Because we acknowledge that human life is also social, society must protect and foster it.

Precisely because life is sacred, the taking of even one life is a momentous event. Traditional Catholic teaching has allowed the taking of human life in particular situations by way of exception, as, for example, in self-defense and capital punishment. In recent decades, however, the presumptions against taking human life have been strengthened and the exceptions made ever more restrictive.

Fundamental to this shift in emphasis is a more acute perception of the multiple ways in which life is threatened today. Obviously such questions as war, aggression and capital punishment have been with us for centuries; they are not new. What is new is the context in which these ancient questions arise, and the way in which a new context shapes the content of our ethic of life.

Within the Catholic Church, the Second Vatican Council acknowledged that "a sense of the dignity of the human person has been impressing itself more and more deeply on the consciousness of contemporary man" (*Declaration on Religious Freedom*, #1). This growing awareness of human dignity has been a dominant factor within Western culture. Within the United States, the struggle to appreciate human worth more fully is found in the civil rights movement and in the public debate about our foreign policy toward totalitarian regimes of both the right and the left.

This deepening awareness, as I intimated above, has been precipitated in part by a growing recognition of the frailty of human life today. Faced with the threat of nuclear war and escalating technological developments, the human family encounters a qualitatively new range of moral problems. Today, life is threatened on a scale previously unimaginable.

This is why the U. S. Catholic bishops and others have been so visible and vocal in the public debate this past decade or two, asserting belief in the sacredness of human life and the responsibilities we have, personally and as a society, to protect and preserve the sanctity of life.

Nonetheless, it is not enough merely to assert such an ethical principle. If it is to be acknowledged and implemented, it must impact all areas of human life. It must respond to all the moments, places, or conditions which either threaten the sanctity of life or cultivate an attitude of disrespect for it.

A consistent ethic of life is based on the need to ensure that the sacredness of human life, which is the ultimate source of human dignity, will be defended and fostered from womb to tomb, from the genetic laboratory to the cancer ward, from the ghetto to the prison.

Capital Punishment in Light of This Ethic

As you undoubtedly know, since the time of St. Augustine, great thinkers in the Roman Catholic tradition—St. Thomas Aquinas, for example—have struggled with such ethical questions as the right of the state to execute criminals. Through the centuries, as I noted above, the Church has acknowledged that the state *does* have the right to take the life of someone guilty of an extremely serious crime.

However, because such punishment involves the deliberate infliction of evil on another, it always needs justification. Usually this has consisted of indicating some good which would derive from the punishment, a good of such consequence that it justifies the taking of life.

As I understand the current discussion about capital punishment, the question is not whether the state still has the *right* to inflict capital punishment, but whether it should *exercise* this right. In present circumstances, are there sufficient reasons to justify the infliction of the evil of death on another human person?

This is the question which the U. S. Catholic bishops and others have been addressing recently—the United States Catholic Conference in 1980, the Massachusetts Catholic Conference Board of Governors in 1982, the Oklahoma Catholic bishops in 1983, the Tennessee bishops exactly one year ago today, and Florida church leaders last November. Although there are differences of presentation, basically the reasoning of these positions follows two lines of thought.

First, they review four traditional arguments justifying capital punishment: retribution, deterrence, reform, and protection of the state. Based on their review, the religious leaders have argued that these reasons no longer apply in our age.

I don't have time this afternoon to present the reasoning in regard to all four areas, but I would like to use the question of retribution as an example. The 1980 USCC statement states:

We grant that the need of retribution does indeed justify punishment. For the practice of punishment both presupposes a previous transgression against the law and involves the involuntary deprivation of certain goods. But we maintain that this good does not require nor does it justify the taking of the life of the criminal, even in cases of murder . . . It is morally unsatisfactory and socially destructive for criminals to go unpunished, but the limits of punishment must be determined by moral objectives which go beyond the mere infliction of injury on the guilty. Thus we would argue it is as barbarous and inhumane for a criminal who had tortured or maimed a victim to be tortured or maimed in return. Such punishment might satisfy certain vindictive desires that we or the victim might feel, but the satisfaction of such desires is not and cannot be an objective of a humane and Christian approach to punishment.

Basing their judgment on this and similar lines of reasoning, many religious leaders conclude that, under our present circumstances, the death penalty as punishment for reasons of deterrence, retribution, reform, or protection of society cannot be justified.

Nonetheless, our reflections on this issue do not stop at this level. As religious leaders we argue that there are gospel insights which bespeak the inappropriateness of capital punishment. First, there is the example of Jesus, offering forgiveness at the time of his own unfair death (Lk 23:24). [More than that, he offers the human family an alternative to the violence of the human heart, a violence which led to his own death. Jesus taught that, when one is faced with injury, the fully human response is "to turn the other cheek" (Mt 5:38-40).][1]

Another challenging gospel theme is that of "God's boundless love for every person, regardless of human merit or worthiness. This love was especially visible in Jesus' ministry to outcasts, in his acceptance of sinners" (Florida church leaders). Consistent with this theme and flowing from it is the biblical imperative of reconciliation. Wherever there is division between persons, Christ calls them to forgiveness and reconciliation.

While these themes are specifically grounded in the New Testament, I do not believe they are unique to the Christian vision. People of good will recognize that these values ennoble human experience and make it more complete. Commitment to these values changes one's perspective on the strengths and weaknesses of the human family.

This change in perspective seems to have been in mind when the ecumenical leaders of Florida stated that Jesus shifted the locus of judgment in this matter to a higher court: a court where there is absolute knowledge of the evidence, of good deeds and of evil, of faith and of works of faith, of things private and things public—a court in which there is both wrath and tenderness, both law and grace.

It is when we stand in this perspective of a "higher court"—that of God's judgment seat—and a more noble view of the human person, that we seriously question the appropriateness of capital punishment. We ask ourselves: Is the human family made more complete—is human personhood made more loving—in a society which demands life for life, eye for eye, tooth for tooth?

Let me acknowledge that your experience is probably quite different from mine. You have had to deal with heinous crimes, with persons so filled with hatred and violence as to chill the heart. You may be wondering whether my colleagues and I are naive or simplistic in our approach.

Perhaps I won't be able to dispel that perception with my response. Nevertheless, I want to affirm that the state does have the responsibility to protect its citizens. It deserves and merits the full support of all of us in the exercise of that responsibility. Although we don't have an adequate understanding of the causes of violent crime, society "has the right and the duty to prevent such behavior including, in some cases, the right to impose terms of lifetime imprisonment" (Florida ecumenical leaders).

---

[1]Editor's Note: Although these words appear in the written text, they apparently were not given in the address. The brackets were handwritten in the text, along with the word "omit."

I am not suggesting that society should be a prisoner of violence or violent crime. On the contrary, the consistent ethic of life requires that society struggle to eradicate poverty, racism, and other systemic forces which nurture and encourage violence. Similarly, the perpetrators of violence should be punished and given the opportunity to experience a change of heart and mind.

But, having said this, I also think that capital punishment is not an appropriate response to the problem of crime in our land. To take any human life, even that of someone who is not innocent, is awesome and tragic. It seems to me and to others that, in our culture today, there are not sufficient reasons to justify the state continuing to exercise its right in this matter. There are other, better ways of protecting the interests of society.

Recently the Gallup organization conducted a poll about capital punishment—something they had done on previous occasions. In 1966 42% of those polled favored capital punishment, in 1981 66% favored it, and this year the percentage was 72%.

Why has 24% of the population turned to favoring capital punishment in the last nineteen years? This question is even more urgent because that same poll reported that fully 51% of the respondents said "they would still support capital punishment even if studies showed conclusively it does not deter crime"! This is striking because people often use deterrence as a main argument to justify capital punishment. If it is not to deter crime, why do people support capital punishment? Thirty percent of those who favored capital punishment indicated their reason was simple: revenge!

One might argue that the cycle of violence has become so intense in our society that it is understandable and appropriate for people to support capital punishment. What alternative is there, some ask, in a violent society other than to meet violence with violence?

As a citizen in a democracy whose founding dream is of human dignity and as a disciple of Jesus, I must reject this alternative. In fact, as a citizen of this city which has recently been alarmed, saddened, and polarized by the senseless killing of a talented high school basketball star and a ten-year-old standing in front of his home, I assert that violence is *not* the answer—it is *not* the way to break the cycle of violence.

Pope John Paul II, speaking to Peruvians who were living in the midst of a rebel stronghold, told them: "The pitiless logic of violence leads to nothing. No good is obtained by helping to increase violence."

Capital punishment, to my mind, is an example of meeting violence with violence. What does it say about the quality of our life when people celebrate the death of another human being? What does it say about the human spirit when some suggest a return to public executions which only twenty years ago we would have considered barbaric?

We desperately need an attitude or atmosphere in society which will sustain a consistent defense and promotion of life. Where human life is considered "cheap" and easily "wasted," eventually nothing is held as sacred and all lives are in jeopardy. The purpose of proposing a consistent ethic of life is to argue that success on any one of the issues threatening life requires a concern for the broader attitude in society about respect for life. Attitude is the place to root an ethic of life.

Change of attitude, in turn, can lead to change of policies and practices in our society. We must find ways to break the cycle of violence which threatens to strangle our land. We must find effective means of protecting and enhancing human life.

12.

PASTORAL CONSTITUTION ON THE CHURCH IN THE MODERN WORLD

Its Impact on the Social Teaching of the U. S. Bishops

University of Notre Dame, October 1, 1985

I appreciate this opportunity to return again to the campus of Notre Dame University. Besides being a pleasant experience, it gives me another occasion to acknowledge the contribution of this University, and in a particular way, its President, Father Hesburgh, to the life of the Church in the United States. In providing Cardinal O'Connor and me a common platform to examine the social ministry of the Church in the post-conciliar era, Notre Dame continues its long history of service to the Church. This convocation is another in an already lengthy list of events in which the intellectual, spiritual, and physical resources of this campus have been used to help the Church in the United States, at every level, reflect upon the meaning and the challenge of being Catholic in the twentieth century.

Cardinal O'Connor and I will give two presentations which are designed to address a single theme. The setting for my lecture is the particular moment of ecclesial history in which we find ourselves: it is twenty-five years since the convocation of the Second Vatican Council and twenty years since the promulgation of one of the Council's major documents, the *Pastoral Constitution on the Church in the Modern World*. In this setting it is worthwhile to examine the role and impact of the *Pastoral Constitution* on the social ministry of the Church, and particularly on the bishops of the United States. My lecture will serve as a background for Cardinal O'Connor's examination of one example of the bishops' social teaching: the pastoral letter on Catholic social teaching and the U. S. economy.

In examining the content and consequences of the *Pastoral Constitution*, I will focus on three themes: first, Vatican II as the source of the *Pastoral Constitution*; second, the content and style of the *Pastoral Constitution*; and third, the post-conciliar consequences of this document in the ministry and teaching of the U. S. bishops.

The Conciliar Event: An Interpretation

By calling an Extraordinary Synod this November, Pope John Paul II has invited and urged the Church to reflect upon the meaning of Vatican II and its implications for the life of the Church and the world during the last fifteen years of this century. Ecumenical councils are powerful events in the life of the Church. In the two-thousand-year history of the Church only a few generations of Christians have experienced the event of a council, but every generation has been shaped by the work of the twenty ecumenical councils. There comes with the privilege of being a conciliar generation the responsibility to appropriate its meaning, interpret its content, and share its significance with future generations. The calling of the Synod helps to focus attention on the last twenty-five years since Pope John XXIII called us to a profound renewal of Christian life and witness for the world.

In the post-conciliar period there has appeared, of course, a voluminous corpus of commentary on Vatican II. Quite appropriately, most commentaries have focused upon one aspect or document of the Council and sought to explain its meaning and press forward its implications. In the last five years there has appeared another kind of commentary which I think is particularly helpful in preparation for the Synod and in evaluating any single aspect of Vatican II. It is an assessment which seeks to interpret the conciliar event in its totality, to evaluate its place in the historical and theological development of the Church.

Two examples of this kind of analysis are Karl Rahner's essay, "Toward a Fundamental Interpretation of Vatican II" (*Theological Studies,* 1979) and John W. O'Malley's essay, "Developments, Reforms and Two Great Reformations: Toward a Historical Assessment of Vatican II" (*Theological Studies*, 1983).

It is neither my purpose nor my role to provide a commentary on these extensive articles, much less to offer a systematic interpretation of my own. I cite them in an address on social ministry in the post-conciliar era because they provide the kind of broad framework we need to connect the conciliar and post-conciliar periods of Catholic life and ministry. Such a perspective helps us to dispel the popular notion that the Council suddenly dropped from heaven (or emerged from Hades!) in finished form. Interpreting the conciliar event means identifying its historical roots, evaluating its theological content, and recognizing that the implementation of the Council has been complex and even a bit untidy, but still a blessing. On several occasions recently the Holy Father has referred to the Council as a positive event in the life of the Church.

By examining the event of the Council we can show that it follows the law of development in Catholic thought—that is, the dynamic Father John Courtney Murray used to call "the growing edge of tradition." The Catholic style admits of change—indeed requires change, but it is change rooted in continuity. Anyone familiar with Catholic history knows that Vatican II was a surprise but not an aberration from the law of development.

In areas as diverse as liturgy, ecumenism, and social thought a basic pattern is visible in the Council. Everything said in the documents of the Council had a history in nineteenth- and twentieth-century Catholic authors and movements, but both the authors and movements had been relegated to the edge of the Church's life. The movements (in the fields of liturgy, ecumenism, and social action) and the authors (Congar, de Lubac, Chenu, Murray, and Rahner) had been in the Church but not at the center of attention. They had lived on the growing edge, saying and doing things which made some uncomfortable and others hostile. It was not a question of bad will, but the dynamic of a growing community and institution with its attendant tensions.

The significance of Vatican II, looked at through the history of these movements and authors, is not that it said brand-new things, but that it took these ideas from the edge of the Church's life and located them in the center. In the process the Council gave new legitimacy to the growing edge of the Catholic tradition and also added its own content to the ideas and movements. The Council authenticated and also created. Precisely because it followed the law of continuity and change, Vatican II was an event which summarized a previous process of development, becoming at the same time the starting point for a new process of growth. Once the growing edge had been taken into the center of Catholic thought, it was time for new growth at the edge.

This dynamic of receiving from the past, adding to it in the Council, and opening the road for new growth is particularly clear in the *Pastoral Constitution*. By examining this document we will see the dynamic of the Council at work.

The *Pastoral Constitution* of Vatican II: An Analysis

Many of the major themes of Vatican II had their roots in the previous one hundred years; one of them was the emphasis on social teaching and social ministry. Leo XIII had inaugurated the tradition of papal social encyclicals in 1891 and Pius XI had pressed the organizational dimension of social witness in his program of Catholic Social Action of the 1930s. The bishops of the U. S. had used this social teaching to address a broad range of issues, from labor questions to race relations to war and peace. In both teaching and development, therefore, the social dimension of the Church's life had a history in the twentieth century. This is why it is surprising to find that, in preparing for the Council, no provision was made for a document on the role of the Church in the world. When the first session of Vatican II opened in 1962, there was no thought of a document in the style of the *Pastoral Constitution*. There were social themes running through the draft documents on the liturgy and the Church, but no explicitly *theological* reflection on the Church's presence in the secular arena.

Assessing the Council from the perspective of 1985, it is clear that the *Pastoral Constitution*, along with the *Dogmatic Constitutions on the Church* and *on Divine Revelation,* stands as one of the key texts of the Council, yet no one thought so at the beginning. It is also significant that the call for a document on the Church in the world emerged directly from the experience of the Council. When the bishops addressed the task of defining the nature and mission of the Church, it became evident that an explicit, extensive interpretation of the role of the Church in the political, economic, cultural, and international arena was a theological fact which required expression. Few guessed, I think, how powerful a force such an expression would be in the post-conciliar ministry of the Church. In recognizing the impact of the *Pastoral Constitution*, it is important at Notre Dame to remember the contribution of Monsignor Joseph Gremillion to the development of this document.

The contribution of the *Pastoral Constitution* to the Church's social ministry has been a threefold gift: in *theological style, ecclesiological substance*, and *pastoral spirit*. I will comment briefly on each.

The theological style of the *Pastoral Constitution* is symbolized and represented by its use of the phrase "the signs of the times." Father Marie-Dominique Chenu, O.P., one of the great precursors of the Council, has said of this phrase that "it might well be considered as one of the three or four most important formulas used by the Council, one which served as a source of its inspiration and guided its progress."

The phrase implied both a principle of theological method and a basic posture of the Church toward the world. The method is that theological assessment of secular history and reality should begin with an evaluation of empirical data. In carrying out the social ministry, the Church is not to impose *a priori* solutions. Rather, it is to join with others, of all faiths and no faith, in seeking to understand the scope and depth of the secular challenge the world faces. When the empirical challenge has been honestly evaluated, it should then be "interpreted in the light of the Gospel." This methodological position does not simply equate theology with a secular discipline, nor does it imply moral relativism, but it does determine a pastoral posture for the Church. This posture respects the contributions of the scientific, social, and humanistic disciplines, and promises that the Church will have the humility and the seriousness to face the modern world in all its complexity and ambiguity.

The drafting of the pastoral *The Challenge of Peace* brought all the U. S. bishops face to face with this pastoral posture. The arcane complexity of deterrence had to be probed in all its dimensions before we could address its moral meaning. Now, after three years of work and the publication of the letter, we recognize that the danger of deterrence and the difficulty of containing the arms race mean that our moral surveillance is not finished. There has to be continual scrutiny of the technical "signs of the times" of the arms race and of the adequacy of the moral judgments we made in 1983.

The theological contribution of the *Pastoral Constitution* is not limited to methodology. The fundamental breakthrough of the conciliar text is that it provides an ecclesiological foundation for social ministry. Prior to the Council, the papal encyclicals had provided a solid philosophical and moral doctrine centered on human dignity and human rights and applied to problems as diverse as war, labor-management relations, and agriculture and trade policy. But this extensive moral teaching was often regarded as a secondary concern of the Church. Those who took the social teaching seriously often had to defend their work and ministry against charges that it secularized the Church or was devoid of truly religious content.

The *Pastoral Constitution* addresses these claims forthrightly. The document ties the entire Catholic tradition's defense of the human person directly to the very center of the Church's life. The vision of the Church which emerges from the Council is that of a community of faith committed to public defense of the person, to advocacy for the least and most vulnerable in society, and to the protection of human society in the face of the awesome technologies of war which this century has spawned. It is impossible to support the conciliar teaching and not support a socially engaged Church, for that is the theological mandate of the *Pastoral Constitution*.

The theological grounding of social ministry has produced a pastoral spirit of social leadership for the Church throughout the world. I hasten to add that my point here is hardly to be triumphal, for what remains undone is staggering. But a simple, descriptive account of the changes in the Church on social questions since Vatican II would force any observer to ask what is behind the change. From Soweto to Seoul, from San Salvador to Sao Paulo, from Warsaw to Washington—the Catholic Church is a major social force. The pressure of events in each place has called the Church into the public arena. However, we need to be honest enough to acknowledge that the Church has been challenged by injustice before and did not always respond. Today we still miss key moments, are timid about key choices, and do not see all the signs of the times acutely. But there has been a response which is worthy of note. I do not think it is because of random chance that the response has been made in all these places. It is the spirit of the *Pastoral Constitution* which has called forth the social resources of the Church. Today there is a consensus established by the Council that there can be no retreat from an engaged public ministry. The specific choices and challenges remain to be faced, but the premise of our ministry is clear: a socially active Church is not a distraction from gospel ministry; it is an essential component of that ministry.

The Social Implications of the Council: An Assessment

This conviction that social ministry is a central element of the Church's pastoral ministry is reflected in the post-conciliar record of the

U. S. episcopal conference. In his presidential report to the Holy See in preparation for the Extraordinary Synod, Bishop Malone expressed the strong conviction of the U. S. bishops that Vatican II has been a gift and a blessing for the Church in this country. One of the gifts of the Council is the consensus which has been created among our bishops about the significance of social ministry. We debate and disagree on specific choices, of course, but these debates about concrete issues never take the form of questioning *whether* we ought to be in social ministry. That point is now beyond dispute, and we have the *Pastoral Constitution* to thank for this consensus.

The same document has shaped the way in which the bishops have pursued social teaching and witness. A key passage in the *Pastoral Constitution* states: "And so the Council, as witness and guide to the faith of the whole people of God, gathered together by Christ, can find no more eloquent expression of its solidarity and respectful affection for the whole human family, to which it belongs, than to enter into dialogue with it about all these different problems" (#3).

The U. S. bishops have adopted this theme of dialogue with the world and sought to adapt it to the style of the democratic, pluralistic culture in which we minister. The dialogue theme is at work at two levels.

First, as a general principle, the bishops take positions on a wide range of social issues, from abortion to nuclear war to Central America. Moreover, they do so in forums which guarantee they will have to defend, explain, and argue their positions both inside and outside the Church. By taking concrete positions, rooted in religious and moral values, but applied to contingent realities, the bishops both state a position and stimulate the wider public dialogue.

The range of issues addressed is one of the distinguishing characteristics of the bishops' position. No other major institution in our society joins the defense of innocent human life in abortion with the defense of all life in the face of nuclear war in the way we have done. It is to highlight both the scope of our moral concern and the strength of Catholic social teaching that I have focused on the notion of a "consistent ethic of life" in a series of addresses I have given over the past two years.

Second, this method of dialogue has been at the core of both pastoral letters on peace and the economy. The subject matter of the letters demands that we be in dialogue with relevant disciplines. The process of publishing drafts requires that we listen and respond to a range of commentary on our work. Finally, the specificity of our conclusions requires that we make crucial distinctions in the pastorals between the moral authority of Catholic social and moral teaching and the less authoritative policy conclusions we draw, as bishops, from that teaching.

Committing the bishops to public dialogue in this way has been a demanding exercise in pastoral leadership. But I believe the vast majority of our bishops would agree with my view that it has been an effective method of presenting the social teaching, an important witness to the bishops' concerns about signs of our times, and a contribution to the wider civil dialogue in the United States.

I do not think we would have developed the method of the pastorals, nor do I believe we would have shaped the ecclesial consensus which is their foundation in the bishops' conference, if the Council had not occurred and the *Pastoral Constitution* not been written. I am convinced that we express our gratitude for both by continuing the dialogue with the world, solidifying the social ministry in the Church, and standing publicly in our society on a range of social issues which bear upon the human dignity of the person. The pastoral on the economy is one way we stand publicly today, and Cardinal O'Connor will now discuss it.

13.

HOMILY, PRO-LIFE MASS

NATIONAL SHRINE OF THE IMMACULATE CONCEPTION,
WASHINGTON, D.C., JANUARY 21, 1986

Her name is Lisa, and her story is typical, though nonetheless tragic for being so. Lisa is having trouble sleeping nights. Once upon a time, Lisa was in love. She gave away her heart and her soul the way teenagers have always done. But she was more in love with the *idea* of being in love than with the person she thought she loved, and she began to make some bad decisions. She chose to love in the easy ways but in none of the real. And soon Lisa found herself seventeen years old and pregnant.

Because commitment was not something taken to their bed, Lisa's boyfriend ran. Besides, he had a deeper interest—working on a football scholarship. And Lisa, all alone and pregnant, decided to take care of a problem that should never have happened.

One terrible afternoon, for $250, she bought what she thought would be a short-term solution. Instead, it became a long-term nightmare. You see, she is having trouble sleeping nights. Lisa sometimes wakes up to the sound of a baby crying, and she wonders how so much love could end in so much hurt. And God weeps in heaven. He weeps for his two precious children—for the baby that will never cry—and for Lisa who will always hear that silent cry.

My brothers and sisters in Christ: listen once again to the words of Jesus proclaimed in this evening's gospel: "I have come that they might have life and have it to the full." The Lord is talking about all the Lisa's of our land, about all the babies who will never cry, and all the babies yet to come. He is talking about us!

Life—life in all its fullness—is God's great and wonderful gift to us. Tonight we gather in this special church seeking to appropriate more deeply the preciousness of God's gift of life and the great responsibilities it entails.

Think of your favorite baby. Picture that son or daughter, that niece or nephew, that little child who is endlessly precious to you. The miracle of that little life is nothing less than sacred. The spontaneous love we have for our children affirms that fact.

Human life is not abstract. It is *real*! It is *tangible*! It is a source of inexpressible joy and awe. We feel this when we pick up a crying infant, when we share the joy of a baby at play, when we applaud the achievements of a growing child. We also know it, in a different way, when we experience the graciousness, vitality, and wisdom of the older members of our community.

For each of us, then, human life is our most precious gift but also, in many ways, our most fragile possession.

The fragility of human life lays claim upon us for nurturance, sustenance, protection. At best, our hold on life is rather tenuous. We are ever more aware of this in the contemporary world where the arms race is a constant threat to peace and security—indeed, even to human survival! We see it in the wake of famine, natural disasters, and diseases which quickly reach epidemic proportions.

The recognition that life is a precious, but also fragile, gift generates both a sense of responsibility and specific obligations. Human life is not meant to be lived in isolation from others. In our increasingly interdependent world, no one truly lives alone. Rather, we live on various levels of human community, called both to defend our brothers' and sisters' right to life and to work towards enhancing the quality of their lives.

Society expresses its esteem and respect for human life by protecting the life of each person through laws and social institutions. No life is of inferior value—beyond protection or sustenance. The law is the guardian of each person's life and rights, and it must apply equally to all of us.

But beyond the protection of the law, we must create an atmosphere within society, a climate in which the value and sanctity of human life are acknowledged, affirmed, and defended. Moreover, we must be consistent in our respect for and protection of human life at every stage and in every circumstance. A commitment to human dignity and human rights requires protection of human life from conception until natural death. It also requires a constant effort to assure every person a fullness of opportunity and a legitimate share in the material benefits and advantages of the modern world. This is a special challenge in the United States.

Our hold on life is only as strong as the most vulnerable member of our society. We can gauge our success in defending and respecting all human life by examining the plight of the most vulnerable in our midst—especially the unborn.

Human life usually begins quietly, almost mysteriously, in intimacy and love. Man and woman join in loving embrace, and God calls forth new life. This is the unending mystery of creation. In the earliest weeks and months after conception—quietly hidden in the mother's womb—the infant develops those physical characteristics by which each person is recognized: eyes, ears, head and limbs, heart and brain.

But the hold on this precious new life is tenuous, and the threats against it are frightening. Respect for the developing life of this newest member of the human family requires physical and emotional care of both mother and unborn infant. Nutrition, medical care, personal support and encouragement are necessary to enhance life and to create the atmosphere of hope and promise after birth when life will continue to develop through its various stages.

Unfortunately, at the very moment in human history when we have the greatest capacity to sustain unborn life and enrich the experience of pregnancy, we have also developed an attitude of callousness and the technological tools to destroy the life of the unborn. Since the 1973 Supreme Court abortion decisions, the unborn child's right to life is frequently ignored or denied.

The incidence of abortion grows annually and, in far too many cases, the reason is human convenience. We must not allow this to go unchallenged, just as we cannot acquiesce to any diminishment of the full range of human rights. To do so would be to fail in social responsibility and moral integrity.

We are here this evening to witness to the fact that the tragic 1973 Supreme Court abortion decisions will not be forgotten or allowed to settle comfortably into our societal subconsciousness. We come together at this time each year to remind the nation, and particularly our elected representatives, that there can be no silent acquiescence to the errors of the Court's opinions. We are here to proclaim to all that we will continue the struggle to have those errors erased from our juridical system and from our historic consciousness. There can be no acceptance or toleration of any erroneous reasoning that strikes at or undermines our understanding of the value and dignity of the human person.

Through the years many Americans who do not share our faith convictions have taken an increasingly active and visible role in their support and protection of the unborn. This is a hopeful and promising sign to the pro-life movement. It is also an added incentive for us Catholics to continue our pro-life efforts and to widen and deepen our perception of the sanctity and value of all human life.

Most of all, we gather in prayer during this vigil to beg of God a renewal of commitment, energy, and perseverance so that we may fulfill what the Second Vatican Council described as "the surpassing ministry of safeguarding life." We derive wisdom from praying together so that we might more effectively convince our governmental leaders that the constitutional protection of the right to life, liberty, and the pursuit of happiness must extend to every human being from conception to natural death.

And we derive our strength from praying *here*. It is no accident that we gather this evening in the National Shrine of the Immaculate Conception. There is no radar so finely tuned as the ears of a mother to the cries of her children. Mary, our mother, surely hears us, and in that hearing there is hope. She has known the pain and anxiety of bringing a child into the world. She has known the horror of the Holy Innocents' death. She has stood beneath her Son's cross. There is no pain we have encountered that Mary has not already withstood. Let us take our strength from her.

We gather this evening in love, not in hatred, for "love never wrongs the neighbor. Hence love is the fulfillment" of the gospel and the law. May the God of love, the creator of life, continue to show his care for us. May the Lord Jesus walk with us in our efforts for justice and peace. May he give us the very fullness of life. May our loving embrace of one another this evening reach out to include all our brothers and sisters in all stages of human development and in all circumstances.

14.

THE CHURCH'S WITNESS
TO LIFE

Seattle University, March 2, 1986

I wish to express my sincere appreciation to Seattle University, to its President Fr. William Sullivan, S.J., and to the Board of Trustees for the honor bestowed on me today. The relationship between centers of scholarship and learning and the episcopacy is one of the pre-eminent issues in the Church in the United States today. I accept your honorary degree with the pledge that I will do all I can to strengthen that relationship—to keep it based on standards of intellectual honesty, professional respect, and a shared concern for the welfare of the Church and its witness in society.

It is the Church's witness to life that I wish to address this afternoon. It is now over two years since I first proposed consideration of a "consistent ethic of life" in the Gannon Lecture at Fordham University. Since that time there has been a sustained process of reflection and analysis in the Church about the multiple issues which come under the umbrella of the consistent ethic.

Last November, the National Conference of Catholic Bishops adopted the consistent ethic theme in its revised *Plan for Pro-Life Activities*. Obviously, I find that step particularly significant, for it gives the consistent ethic the status of policy within the Episcopal Conference. Nevertheless, I believe the concept and consequences of the consistent ethic must be examined more deeply, its implications made clearer within the Church and in the wider civil society. So I am returning to the theme this afternoon at another Catholic university, seeking to press forward the dialogue of several disciplines in the quest for a comprehensive and consistent ethic of life.

During the past two years, as I have followed the commentary on the consistent ethic in journals and the media, and as I have carried on a wide-ranging personal correspondence with many bishops, theologians, philosophers, and social scientists, three topics emerged about the theme which I wish to address: its theological foundation, its ethical logic, and its political consequences.

The Theological Foundation: Systematic Defense of the Person

Some commentators, while very positive about the substance and structure of the call for a consistent ethic, have urged me to focus on its underlying theological foundations. I see the need for this and will comment here on two aspects of its theological substance, leaving for the next section some more detailed moral commentary.

The consistent ethic grows out of the very character of Catholic moral thought. By that I do not mean to imply that one has to be a Catholic to affirm the moral content of the consistent ethic. But I do think that this theme highlights both the systematic and analogical character of Catholic moral theology. The systematic nature of Catholic theology means it is grounded in a set of basic principles and then articulated in a fashion which draws out the meaning of each principle and the relationships among them. Precisely because of its systematic quality, Catholic theology refuses to treat moral issues in an *ad hoc* fashion. There is a continual process of testing the use of a principle in one case by its use in very different circumstances. The consistent ethic seeks only to illustrate how this testing goes on when dealing with issues involving the taking of life or the enhancement of life through social policy.

The analogical character of Catholic thought offers the potential to address a spectrum of issues which are not identical but have some common characteristics. Analogical reasoning identifies the unifying elements which link two or more issues, while at the same time it recognizes why similar issues cannot be reduced to a single problem.

The taking of life presents itself as a moral problem all along the spectrum of life, but there are distinguishing characteristics between abortion and war, as well as elements which radically differentiate war from decisions made about care of a terminally ill patient. The *differences* among these cases are universally acknowledged; a consistent ethic seeks to highlight the fact that differences do not destroy the elements of a *common moral challenge*.

A Catholic ethic which is both systematic in its argument and analogical in its perspective stands behind the proposal that, in the face of the multiple threats to life in our time, spanning every phase of existence, it is necessary to develop a moral vision which can address these several challenges in a coherent and comprehensive fashion.

If the theological style of the consistent ethic is captured by the two words, systematic and analogical, the theological rationale for the ethic is grounded in the respect we owe the human person. To defend human life is to protect the human person. The consistent ethic cuts across the diverse fields of social ethics, medical ethics, and sexual ethics. The unifying theme behind these three areas of moral analysis is the human person, the core reality in Catholic moral thought.

It is precisely the abiding conviction of Catholic ethics about the social nature of the person that ties together the emphasis—in the pastoral letter on the economy—on society's responsibility for the poor; the insistence of the bishops that abortion is a public not a purely private moral question; and the constant refrain of Catholic ethics that sexual issues are social in character.

The theological assertion that the person is the *imago Dei*, the philosophical affirmation of the dignity of the person, and the political principle that society and state exist to serve the person—all these themes stand behind the consistent ethic. They also sustain the positions that the U. S. Catholic bishops have taken on issues as diverse as nuclear policy, social policy, and abortion. These themes provide the basis for the moral perspective of the consistent ethic. It is the specifics of that moral perspective which now must be examined.

The Ethical Argument: The Logic of Linkage

The central assertion of the consistent ethic is that we will enhance our moral understanding of a number of "life issues" by carefully linking them in a framework which allows consideration of each issue on its own merits, but also highlights the connections among distinct issues. This is the moral logic of an analogical vision.

In essence the consistent ethic is a moral argument, and, therefore, its principles and perspective must be constantly measured and tested. The consistent ethic rejects collapsing all issues into one, and it rejects isolating our moral vision and insulating our social concern on one issue. What has been the response to the moral argument of the consistent ethic?

First, it has generated precisely the kind of substantive debate in the Catholic community and in the wider society which I believe is needed. The response began immediately after the Gannon Lecture in the press and weekly journals; it has now moved also to scholarly journals. Second, the range of the commentary has run from the ethical theory of the consistent ethic, to debate about its specific conclusions, to assessment of its contribution to the public witness of the Church in U. S. society.

A particularly extensive analysis of the theme appeared in the "Notes on Moral Theology" in *Theological Studies* last March. This annual review of scholarly writing on moral theology has been highly respected for many years. Among the many commentaries on the consistent ethic, I cite this one because it engages bishops and theologians in the kind of disciplined debate which is needed if our theology is to be authentically Catholic, intellectually responsive to contemporary moral challenges, and pastorally useful to the Catholic community and civil society.

In a time when continuing, respectful dialogue is urgently needed between bishops and theologians, I believe the kind of theological interest generated by the two pastoral letters of the U. S. bishops and the consistent ethic proposal is a healthy sign. The *Theological Studies* articles on the consistent ethic were a wide-ranging survey of several specific questions. On the whole, I found the commentary quite positive and very helpful. I lift it up for consideration by others even though I do not agree with every conclusion drawn by the authors.

One of the areas where I differ is the critique of the moral theory made by Fr. Richard McCormick, S.J. He supports the perspective of the consistent ethic, calling it "utterly essential," but he believes that I give the prohibition of direct killing of the innocent too high a status. Rather than calling it a basic principle of Catholic morality, Fr. McCormick would designate it as a moral rule, "developed as a result of our wrestling with concrete cases of conflict." Furthermore, he argues that the rule has been formulated in teleological fashion, by a balancing of values which yield some exceptions to the presumption against killing.

While I do not consider it my role to engage in a full review of the moral theory of the consistent ethic, I think the reduction of the prohibition against the intentional killing of the innocent to a status less than an absolute rule is not correct. As I argued in the Gannon lecture, the justification of the use of force and the taking of human life is based on a presumption against taking life, which then allows for a series of exceptions where the presumption is overridden. But within this general structure of reasoning, for example in the Just War doctrine, the direct killing of the innocent has not been regarded as a legitimate exception.

This means, as Fr. John Connery, S.J., and others have observed, that Catholic teaching has not ruled out the taking of life in all circumstances. There is a *presumption* against taking life, not an *absolute prohibition*. But the cutting edge of the Just War argument has been its capacity to place a double restraint on the use of force. One limit is based on the calculation of consequences (the principle of proportionality) and the other is based on an absolute prohibition of certain actions (the principle of non-combatant immunity).

As I read Fr. McCormick's proposal, both principles would become proportional judgments. My experience in addressing the nuclear question leads me to conclude that such an interpretation will weaken the moral strength of the ethic of war. In assessing the strategy of deterrence, having two distinct criteria of moral analysis provided the bishops with a perspective on the policy debate which was different from what a totally proportionalist view would have offered.

Because of my experience with this specific moral dilemma of deterrence and because I find the prohibition against the intentional killing of the innocent a crucial element across the spectrum of the consistent ethic, I find myself not persuaded by Fr. McCormick's recommendation, even though I appreciate the care with which he reviewed my lectures. I know adherence to the absolute prohibition creates very complex and difficult choices, not least in deterrence theory, but testing the absolute prohibition across the spectrum of life leads me to reaffirm it rather than reduce its status.

A very different objection to the consistent ethic arose primarily from persons active in the right-to-life movement immediately after the Gannon Lecture. The critique continues to this day. The objection is raised against the way I called for relating our defense of innocent life to support for social policies and programs designed to respond to the needs of the poor. The passage of the Gannon Lecture which attracted the most criticism read this way:

> *If one contends, as we do, that the right of every fetus to be born should be protected by civil law and supported by civil consensus, then our moral, political, and economic responsibilities do not stop at the moment of birth. Those who defend the right to life of the weakest among us must be equally visible in support of the quality of life of the powerless among us: the old and the young, the hungry and the homeless, the undocumented immigrant and the unemployed worker. Such a quality-of-life posture translates into specific political and economic positions on tax policy, employment generation, welfare policy, nutrition and feeding programs, and health care. Consistency means we cannot have it both ways: we cannot urge a compassionate society and vigorous public policy to protect the rights of the unborn and then argue that compassion and significant public programs on behalf of the needy undermine the moral fiber of the society or are beyond the proper scope of governmental responsibility.*

Reviewing those words in light of the criticisms of the last two years, I still find what I said to be morally correct and, if anything, politically more necessary to say than it was two years ago. In the first half of the 1980s we have seen many of the programs designed to meet basic needs of poor people systematically cut. Perhaps the prototypical example is what is happening to children—precisely those who first evoke our right-to-life defense. In the second draft of the pastoral letter on the economy the bishops graphically describe the situation of children in our country: "Today one in every four American children under the age of 6 and one in every two black children under 6 are poor. The number of children in poverty rose by 4 million over the decade between 1973-1983, with the result that there are now more poor children in the United States than at any time since 1965."

In a recent book of far-reaching significance, Senator Patrick Moynihan has made the point that children are the most vulnerable group in our society.

In the face of this evidence it is precisely the function of a consistent ethic to gather a constituency which stands against those social forces legitimating the taking of life before birth, and stands against other social forces legitimating policies which erode the dignity of life after birth by leaving children vulnerable to hunger, inadequate housing, and insufficient health care.

The criticism of my Gannon Lecture was twofold: that it confused two different moral issues and that it expected everyone to do everything. I have responded to this critique previously, but I wish to expand upon my response. Surely we can all agree that the taking of human life in abortion is not the same as failing to protect human dignity against hunger. But having made that distinction, let us not fail to make the point that both are moral issues requiring a response of the Catholic community and of our society as a whole.

The logic of a consistent ethic is to press the moral meaning of both issues. The consequence of a consistent ethic is to bring under review the position of every group in the Church which sees the moral meaning in one place but not the other. The ethic cuts *two* ways, not one: it challenges prolife groups, and it challenges justice and peace groups. The meaning of a consistent ethic is to say in the Catholic community that our moral tradition calls us beyond the split so evident in the wider society between moral witness to life before and after birth.

Does this mean that everyone must do everything? No! There are limits of time, energy, and competency. There is a shape to every individual vocation. People must specialize, groups must focus their energies. The consistent ethic does not deny this.

But it does say something to the Church: it calls us to a wider witness to life than we sometimes manifest in our separate activities. The consistent ethic challenges bishops to shape a comprehensive social agenda. It challenges priests and religious to teach the Catholic tradition with the breadth it deserves. And it challenges Catholics as citizens to go beyond the divided witness to life which is too much the pattern of politics and culture in our society. Responding to this multiple challenge requires consideration of the public consequences of the consistent ethic.

The Political Consequences: Shaping Public Choices

Some commentators on the consistent ethic saw it primarily as a political policy. They missed its primary meaning: it is a moral vision and an ethical argument sustaining the vision. But the moral vision does have political consequences. The consistent ethic is meant to shape the public witness of the Catholic Church in our society.

The first consequence is simply to highlight the unique place which Catholic teaching on a range of issues has given the Church in the public arena. As I have said before, no other major institution in the country brings together the positions the Catholic bishops presently hold on abortion, nuclear policy, and economic policy. Our positions cut across party lines, and they contradict conventional notions of liberal and conservative. I find that a healthy contribution to the public debate, and I believe we ought to stress the point.

The second public consequence of a consistent ethic is to establish a framework where we can test the moral vision of each part of the Church in a disciplined, systematic fashion. We will not shape an ecclesial consensus about the consistent ethic without the kind of vigorous public debate which has gone on in the Church in the last two years. But our debate will sharpen our ecclesial moral sense, and it can also be a public lesson to the wider society if it is marked by coherence, civility, and charity.

The third public consequence of a consistent ethic is that it provides a standard to test public policy, party platforms, and the posture of candidates for office. Here is where the challenge to moral reasoning, pastoral leadership, and political sensitivity reaches its most delicate level. But we should not shrink from the need to make specific the logic of the consistent ethic.

We are a multi-issue Church precisely because of the scope and structure of our moral teaching. But it is not enough to be interested in several issues. We need to point the way toward a public vision where issues can be understood as morally and politically interdependent. I propose the consistent ethic not as a finished product but as a framework in need of development. I invite more debate about it, precisely at this concrete level where specific choices on issues are made, where candidates take positions, and where citizens must evaluate them. I believe our moral vision is broader and richer than we have made it appear at this concrete, practical level of politics. Precisely because we are not yet in a national election year, we need to think about how a consistent ethic can be set forth in a convincing way. It will cut across conventional party lines, and it will not lead to crystal clear judgments on candidates, but it may give the Church, as an institution and a community, a better way to engage the attention of the nation regarding the intersection of moral vision, public policy, and political choices.

To think through the meaning of such a position, we need bishops who foster the debate, political leaders who enter the discussion, professors and policy analysts who can clarify categories, and members of the Church who exercise the supremely important role of citizens. It is my hope that we can have this kind of ecclesial and public debate in the months ahead.

15.

THE CONSISTENT ETHIC OF LIFE

*The Challenge and the Witness of
Catholic Health Care*

CATHOLIC MEDICAL CENTER, JAMAICA, NEW YORK,
MAY 18, 1986

The very mention of "Bhopal" or "Chernobyl" sends shudders through people everywhere. While the tragic deaths and injuries caused by the Bhopal disaster were confined to a particular area, its repercussions are still being felt worldwide. The Chernobyl incident, however, affects the planet in a more direct way through the spread of radioactivity. Its destructive potential is even more worrisome.

These two disasters highlight two important facts which have enormous significance for the future of the world community: the growing interdependence of contemporary life—an interdependence which has been accelerated by the rapid development of science and technology—and the worldwide competition for limited natural resources. The problems and challenges of the human family today are enormously complex, increasingly global, and ominously threatening to human life and society. Each of them has moral and religious dimensions because they all impact human life.

It is crucial that we develop a method of moral analysis which will be comprehensive enough to recognize the linkages among the issues confronting us, while respecting the individual nature and uniqueness of each. During the past few years, I have addressed this task through the development of a comprehensive approach to the broad spectrum of life issues which I have called the "consistent ethic of life."

I am very grateful to the Catholic Medical Center and St. John's University for the invitation to address you this evening on "The Consistent Ethic of Life: The Challenge and the Witness of Catholic Health Care." As you may know, I applied the consistent ethic concept to health care systems last year in an address to the Foster McGaw Triennial Conference in Chicago. I wish to follow a similar format this evening, applying the concept, however, to different, but related, issues.

More specifically, I will first briefly describe the concept of a consistent ethic. Then I will explore the challenge it poses to health care systems both in terms of "classical" medical ethics questions and "contemporary" social justice issues.

The Consistent Ethic of Life

The "consistent ethic of life" has become part of our ethical vocabulary in the past three years. No doubt you are already familiar with it—at least, to some extent. However, there are many misconceptions about it. That is why I want to ensure at the outset that the basic concept is correctly understood.

Although the consistent ethic needs to be finely tuned and carefully structured on the basis of values, principles, rules, and applications to specific cases, this is not my task this evening. I will simply highlight some of its fundamental components so that I can devote more attention to its application to health care systems and several of the issues they face today.

Catholic social teaching is based on two truths about the human person: human life is both *sacred* and *social*. Because God's gift of life is sacred, we have a duty to protect and foster it at all stages of development, from conception to natural death, and in all circumstances. Because we acknowledge that human life is also social, society must protect and preserve its sanctity.

Precisely because life is sacred, the taking of even one human life is a momentous event. Traditional Catholic teaching has allowed the taking of human life in particular situations by way of exception, as, for example, in self-defense and capital punishment. In recent decades, however, the presumptions against taking human life have been strengthened and the exceptions made ever more restrictive.

Fundamental to these shifts in emphasis is a more acute perception of the many ways in which life is threatened today. Obviously such questions as war, aggression, and capital punishment are not new; they have been with us for centuries. Life has always been threatened, but today there is a new *context* which we must take into consideration. And this new *context* shapes the *content* of our ethic of life.

The principal factor responsible for this new context is modern technology. Technology induces a sharper awareness of the fragility of human life. Speaking in Ravenna last Sunday, Pope John Paul II acknowledged that technical progress makes it possible "to transform the desert, to overcome drought and hunger, to lighten the burden of work, to resolve problems of underdevelopment, and to render a more just distribution of resources among people of the world." But he also warned that the same technology has brought us to see "the land uninhabitable, the sea unserviceable, the air dangerous and the sky something to fear."

The discovery of nuclear energy, for example, is one of the most important scientific developments of this century. Despite its benefits to the human family, however, we have become painfully aware of its potential to destroy life on a scale previously unimaginable. Likewise, while modern medical technology opens new opportunities for care, it also poses new threats to life, both immediate and potential. The extraordinary technological development of this century has brought with it a qualitatively new range of moral problems.

My basic thesis is this: technology must not be allowed to hold human beings as hostages. The essential questions we face are these: In an age when we *can* do almost anything, how do we decide what we *should* do? In a time when we can do almost anything *technologically*, how do we decide *morally* what we should not do?

Asking these questions along the whole spectrum of life from conception to natural death creates the need for a consistent ethic, for the spectrum cuts across such issues as genetics, abortion, capital punishment, modern warfare, and the care of the terminally ill. Admittedly these are all *distinct*, enormously complex problems, and they deserve individual treatment. No single answer and no simple response will solve them all. *But they are linked!* Moreover, we face new challenges in each of these areas. This combination of challenges is what cries out for a consistent ethic of life.

We desperately need an *attitude* or climate in society which will sustain a comprehensive, consistent defense and promotion of life. When human life is considered "cheap" or easily expendable in one area, eventually nothing is held as sacred and all lives are in jeopardy. The purpose of proposing the need for a consistent ethic of life is to argue that success on any one of the life-threatening issues is directly related to the attitude society has generally toward life. Attitude is the place to root an ethic of life, because, ultimately, it is society's attitude—whether of respect or nonrespect—that determines its policies and practices.

At the same time, I hasten to add that ethics concerns itself with principles which are supposed to guide the *actions* of individuals and institutions. That is why I have demonstrated, in a number of recent addresses, that there is also an inner relationship—a linkage—among the several issues at the more specific level of moral principle. It is not my intention to repeat these arguments this evening.

Nevertheless, I would like to examine briefly the relationship between "right to life" and "quality of life" issues. If one contends, as we do, that the right of every unborn child should be protected by civil law and supported by civil consensus, then our moral, political, and economic responsibilities do not stop at the moment of birth! We must defend the right to life of the weakest among us; we must also be supportive of the *quality of life* of the powerless among us: the old and the young, the hungry and the homeless, working mothers and single parents, the sick, the disabled, and the dying. The viability and credibility of the "consistent ethic" principle depend primarily upon the consistency of its application.

Such a quality-of-life posture translates into specific political and economic positions—for example, on tax policy, generation of employment, welfare policy, nutrition and feeding programs, and health care. Consistency means we cannot have it both ways: we cannot urge a compassionate society and vigorous public and private policy to protect the rights of the unborn and then argue that compassion and significant public and private programs on behalf of the needy undermine the moral fiber of society or that they are beyond the proper scope of governmental responsibility or that of the private sector. Neither can we do the opposite!

As I acknowledged earlier, the inner relationship among the various life issues is far more intricate than I can sketch here this evening. I fully acknowledge this. My intention is merely to bring that basic linkage into focus so I can apply it to some of the issues facing health care systems today.

Ordinary vs. Extraordinary Medical Procedures

As I noted earlier, the consistent ethic of life poses a challenge to two kinds of problems. The first are "classical" medical ethics questions which today include revolutionary techniques ranging from genetics to the prolonging of life. How do we define the problems, and what does it mean to address them from a Catholic perspective?

One of the most critical moral questions today is the appropriate use of ordinary and extraordinary medical procedures, especially in the care of the terminally ill. I would like to explore this issue with you in some detail.

Two fundamental principles guide the discussion. The *first* is the principle which underlies the consistent ethic: Life itself is of such importance that it is never to be attacked directly. That is why the Second Vatican Council taught: "All offenses against life itself, such as murder, genocide, abortion, euthanasia, or willful suicide. . . all these and the like are criminal; they poison civilization" (*Pastoral Constitution on the Church in the Modern World*, #31).

Consequently, even in those situations where a person has definitively entered the final stages of the process of dying or is in an irreversible coma, it is not permitted to act directly to end life. In other words, euthanasia—that is, the *intentional* causing of death whether by act or omission—is always morally unjustifiable.

The *second* guiding principle is this: Life on this earth is not an end in itself; its purpose is to prepare us for a life of eternal union with God. Consistent with this principle, Pope Pius XII, in 1957, gave magisterial approval to the traditional moral teaching of the distinction between ordinary and *extraordinary* forms of medical treatment. In effect, this means that a Catholic is not bound to initiate, and is free to suspend, any medical treatment that is extraordinary in nature.

But how does one distinguish between ordinary and extraordinary medical treatments? Before answering that question, I would like to point out that the Catholic heritage does not use these terms in the same way in which they might be used in the medical profession. That which is judged *ethically* as extraordinary for a given patient can, and often will, be viewed as ordinary from a *medical* perspective because it is ordinarily beneficial when administered to most patients. That being said, it is, nevertheless, possible to define, as Pope Pius XII did, what would *ethically* be considered as extraordinary medical action: namely, all "medicines, treatments, and operations which cannot be obtained or used without excessive expense, pain, or other inconvenience or which, if used, would not offer a reasonable hope of benefit."

This distinction was applied by the Congregation for the Doctrine of the Faith to the care of the terminally ill in its 1980 *Declaration on Euthanasia*, which states: "When inevitable death is imminent in spite of the means used, it is permitted in conscience to take the decision to refuse forms of treatment that would only secure a precarious and burdensome prolongation of life, so long as the normal care due the sick person in similar cases is not interrupted." In other words, while the Catholic tradition forcefully rejects euthanasia, it would also argue that there is no obligation, in regard to care of the terminally ill, to initiate or continue extraordinary medical treatments which would be ineffective in prolonging life or which, despite their effectiveness in this regard, would impose excessive burdens on the patient.

Recently the American Medical Association's Council on Ethical and Judicial Affairs adopted a policy statement on withholding or withdrawing life-prolonging medical treatment. Earlier this year the National Conference of Commissioners on Uniform State Laws adopted a "Uniform Rights of the Terminally Ill Act" for proposed enactment by state legislatures. While containing some helpful insights, this latter document raises serious moral questions which could result in ethically unsound legislative efforts that would further undermine the right to life and the respect for life in American society.

In addition, there has been a good deal of media attention given to certain cases involving seriously ill patients. In light of all this, there is need for serious reflection on the question of our ethical responsibilities with regard to the care of the dying.

Again, the consistent ethic of life will prove useful in such reflection. Here I will limit myself to two observations. First, an attitude of disregard for the sanctity and dignity of human life is present in our society both in relation to the end of life and its beginning. There are some who are more concerned about whether patients are dying fast enough than whether they are being treated with the respect and care demanded by our Judeo-Christian tradition.

To counteract this mentality and those who advocate so-called mercy killing, we must develop societal attitudes, policies, and practices that guarantee the right of the elderly and the chronically and terminally ill to the spiritual and human care they need. The process of dying is profoundly human and should not be allowed to be dominated by what, at times, can be purely utilitarian considerations or cost-benefit analyses.

Second, with regard to the manner in which we care for a terminally ill person, we must make our own the Christian belief that in death "life is changed, not ended." The integration of such a perspective into the practice of a medical profession whose avowed purpose is the preservation of life will not be easy. It also is difficult for a dying person's family and loved ones to accept the fact that someone they love is caught up in a process that is fundamentally good—the movement into eternal life.

In order that these and other concerns may be addressed in a reasoned, Christian manner, the dialogue must continue in forums like this. The consistent ethic, by insisting on the applicability of the principle of the dignity and sanctity of life to the full spectrum of life issues and by taking into consideration the impact of technology, provides additional insight to the new challenge which "classical" medical ethics questions face today. It enables us to define the problems in a broader, more credible context.

Adequate Health Care for the Poor?

The second challenge which the consistent ethic poses concerns "contemporary" social justice issues related to health care systems. The primary question is: How does the gospel's preferential option or love for the poor shape health care today?

Some regard the problem as basically financial: How do we effectively allocate limited resources? A serious difficulty today is the fact that many persons are left without basic health care while large sums of money are invested in the treatment of a few by means of exceptional, expensive measures. While technology has provided the industry with many diagnostic and therapeutic tools, their inaccessibility, cost, and sophistication often prevent their wide distribution and use.

Government regulations and restrictions, cut-backs in health programs, and the maldistribution of personnel to provide adequate services are but a few of the factors which contribute to the reality that—unless we change attitudes, policies, and programs—many persons probably will not receive the kind of basic care that nurtures life.

A significant factor impacting health in the U. S. today is the lack of medical insurance. The American Hospital Association estimates that nearly 33 million persons have no medical insurance. They include the 60% of low-income persons who are ineligible for Medicaid; nearly half of the "working poor;" the unemployed, seasonally employed, or self-employed; and middle-income individuals denied coverage because of chronic illnesses. They include disproportionate numbers of young adults, minorities, women, and children.

According to the most recent federal data, only one-third of the officially poor are eligible for the "safety net" of Medicaid. The Children's Defense Fund estimates that two-thirds of poor or near-poor children are never insured or insured for only part of the year. It is shocking, but not surprising in light of what I have just said, that the U. S. infant mortality rate is the same as that of Guatemala! Forty thousand infants die each year in the U. S. and others are kept alive by surgery and technology—only to die in their second year of life. The principal causes are well known: poverty and lack of adequate medical care. Moreover, many argue that the situation worsens as hospitals become more competitive and prospective pricing holds down the reimbursement rate.

I assume that we all share a deep concern in regard to adequate health care for the poor, but we also recognize that providing this is much easier said than done. Between 1980 and 1982 the number of poor and near-poor people without health insurance increased by 21%. During the same period, free hospital care increased by less than 4%.

A related concern is sometimes referred to as dumping. An article in a recent issue of the *New England Journal of Medicine* reported the results of a study of 467 patients transferred to Cook County Hospital in Chicago in a 42-day period in late 1983. The conclusions were disturbing for a number of reasons. First, the primary reason for a majority of the transfers was economic rather than medical. Second, at least one-fourth of these patients were judged to be in an unstable condition at the time of transfer.

In addition, only 6% of the patients had given written informed consent for transfer. Thirteen percent of the patients transferred were not informed beforehand about the transfer. When the reason for the transfer *was* given, there was, at times, a serious discrepancy between the reason given to the patient and that given to the resident physician at Cook County Hospital during the transfer-request phone call.

The problems facing Chicago hospitals are by no means unique. They can be found across the nation. Another article in the same issue of the journal described the Texas attempt to eliminate "dumping" of patients without valid medical reason. However, the same article summarized the ongoing dilemma which continues to face all segments of our society: "Who will pay for the medical care of the poor?"

Although each hospital must examine its own policies and practices in regard to uncompensated care of the poor, some recent studies suggest that such care of itself may not be an effective substitute for public insurance. Arizona, as you may know, is the only state without Medicaid. Recent studies reveal that the proportion of poor Arizona residents refused care for financial reasons was about *double* that in states with Medicaid programs. On the other hand, poor elderly Arizona residents—covered by Medicare—were found to have access to health care *comparable* to that of other states.

These facts are disturbing to anyone who espouses the sacredness and value of human life. The fundamental human right is to life—from the moment of conception until natural death. It is the source of all other rights, including the right to health care. The consistent ethic of life poses a series of questions and challenges to Catholic health care facilities. Let me enumerate just a few.

- Should a Catholic hospital transfer an indigent patient to another institution unless superior care is available there?

- Should a Catholic nursing home transfer a patient to a state institution when his or her insurance runs out?
- Should a Catholic hospital give staff privileges to a physician who won't accept Medicaid or uninsured patients?

If Catholic hospitals and other institutions take the consistent ethic seriously, then a number of responses follow. All Catholic hospitals will have outpatient programs to serve the needs of the poor. Catholic hospitals and other Church institutions will document the need for comprehensive prenatal programs and lead legislative efforts to get them enacted by state and national government. Catholic medical schools will teach students that medical ethics includes care for the poor—not merely an occasional charity case, but a commitment to see that adequate care is available.

If they take the consistent ethic seriously, Catholic institutions will lead efforts for adequate Medicaid coverage and reimbursement policies. They will lobby for preventive health programs for the poor.

My point in raising these issues is not to suggest simplistic answers to complex and difficult questions. I am a realist, and I know the difficulties faced by our Catholic institutions. Nonetheless, the consistent ethic does raise these questions which present serious challenges to health care in this nation—and specifically to Catholic health care systems.

To face these challenges successfully, Catholic health care institutions, together with the dioceses in which they are located, will have to cooperate with each other in new and creative ways—ways which might have been considered impossible or undesirable before. No longer can we all be "lone rangers." I know what you have done (and are doing) here in the Brooklyn diocese to maximize the effectiveness and outreach of your hospitals and other health care institutions. I commend you for this. In the very near future the Archdiocese of Chicago and its Catholic hospitals hope to announce the establishment of a new network which will provide a structure for joint action aimed at the hospitals' *market competitive position*, promoting *governance continuity*, and ensuring *maximum mission effectiveness*.

In short, today's *agenda* for Catholic health care facilities is new. The *context* in which we face this agenda is also new because, unlike the past, the Catholic health care system today confronts issues of survival and of purpose. How shall we survive? For what purpose? The consistent ethic helps us answer these questions. It is primarily a theological concept, derived from biblical and ecclesial tradition about the sacredness of human life, about our responsibilities to protect, defend, nurture, and enhance this gift of God. It provides us with a framework within which we can make a moral analysis of the various cultural and technological factors impacting human life. Its comprehensiveness and consistency in application will give us both guidance and credibility and win support for our efforts. The challenge to witness to the dignity and sacredness of human life is before us. With God's help and our own determination, I am confident that we will be equal to it.

16.

ADDRESS TO
THE CONSISTENT ETHIC OF LIFE
CONFERENCE

PORTLAND, OREGON, OCTOBER 4, 1986

I am deeply grateful for the invitation to address you on a topic to which I have devoted much time and energy during the past three years: the "consistent ethic of life."

This morning I will (1) give an overview of the concept, (2) explore the movement from moral analysis to public policy choices, and (3) identify issues needing further development: the implications of the consistent ethic for citizens, office seekers, and office holders.

The Consistent Ethic of Life: An Overview

The idea of the consistent ethic is both old and new. It is "old" in the sense that its substance has been the basis of many programs for years. For example, when the U. S. bishops inaugurated their Respect Life Program in 1972, they invited the Catholic community to focus on the "sanctity of human life and the many threats to human life in the modern world, including war, violence, hunger, and poverty" (NCCB Resolution, April 13, 1972).

Fourteen years later, the focus remains the same. As the 1986 Respect Life brochure states, "The *Pastoral Plan* is set in the context of a consistent ethic that links concern for the unborn with concern for all human life. The inviolability of innocent human life is a fundamental norm."

Moreover, the bishops' pastoral letter, *The Challenge of Peace: God's Promise and Our Response*, emphasized the sacredness of human life and the responsibility we have, personally and as a society, to protect and preserve its sanctity. In paragraph 285, it specifically linked the nuclear question with abortion and other life issues:

When we accept violence in any form as commonplace, our sensitivities become dulled. When we accept violence, war itself can be taken for granted. Violence has many faces: oppression of the poor, deprivation of basic human rights, economic exploitation, sexual exploitation and pornography, neglect or abuse of the

117

aged and the helpless, and innumerable other acts of inhumani-
ty. Abortion in particular blunts a sense of the sacredness of
human life. In a society where the innocent unborn are killed
wantonly, how can we expect people to feel righteous revulsion
at the act or threat of killing non-combatants in war?

However, the pastoral letter—while giving us a starting point for developing a consistent ethic of life—does not provide a fully articulated framework.

It was precisely to provide a more comprehensive theological and ethical basis for the Respect Life Program and for the linkage of war and abortion, as noted by the pastoral letter, that I developed the theme of the consistent ethic. Another important circumstance which prompted me to move in this direction was that I had just been asked to serve as Chairman of the Bishops' Pro-Life Committee. It was October of 1983, and I knew that both abortion and defense-related issues would undoubtedly play an important role in the upcoming presidential campaign.

It was urgent, I felt, that a well-developed theological and ethical framework be provided which would link the various life issues while, at the same time, pointing out that the issues are not all the same. It was my fear that, *without* such a framework or vision, the U. S. bishops would be severely pressured by those who wanted to push a particular issue with little or no concern for the rest. *With* such a theological basis, we would be able to argue convincingly on behalf of all the issues on which we had taken a position in recent years.

I first presented the theme in a talk at Fordham University in December 1983. At that time, I called for a public discussion of the concept, both in Catholic circles and the broader community. In all candor I must admit that the public response greatly exceeded my hopes and expectations.

Since that time there has been a lively exchange by both those who agree and disagree with the theme and its implications. By far, the majority of the reactions have been supportive. Nonetheless, it has been used and misused by those who have tried to push their own, narrower agendas. I myself have made further contributions to the discussion through subsequent talks and articles.

The concept itself is a *challenging* one. It requires us to broaden, substantively and creatively, our ways of thinking, our attitudes, our pastoral response. Many are not accustomed to thinking about all the life-threatening and life-diminishing issues with such consistency. The result is that they remain somewhat selective in their response. Although some of those who oppose the concept seem not to have understood it, I sometimes suspect that many who oppose it recognize its challenge. Quite frankly, I sometimes wonder whether those who embrace it quickly and wholeheartedly truly understand its implicit challenge.

Last November, when the U. S. bishops updated and reaffirmed the

Pastoral Plan for Pro-Life Activities, they explicitly adopted the "consistent ethic" for the first time as the theological context for the Plan.

In sum, to the delight of those who agree with its theological reasoning and to the dismay of the small minority who do not, the "consistent ethic" has entered into our theological vocabulary.

Let me now explain in greater depth the theological basis and strategic value of the "consistent ethic." Catholic teaching is based on two truths about the human person: human life is both sacred and social. Because we esteem human life as sacred, we have a duty to protect and foster it at all stages of development, from conception to natural death, and in all circumstances. Because we acknowledge that human life is also social, society must protect and foster it.

Precisely because life is sacred, the taking of even one life is a momentous event. Traditional Catholic teaching has allowed the taking of human life in particular situations by way of exception—for example, in self-defense and capital punishment. In recent decades, however, the presumptions against taking human life have been strengthened and the exceptions made ever more restrictive.

Fundamental to these shifts in emphasis is a more acute perception of the many ways in which life is threatened today. Obviously, such questions as war, aggression, and capital punishment are not new; they have been with us for centuries. Life has always been threatened, but today there is a new *context* that shapes the *content* of our ethic of life.

The principal factor responsible for this new context is modern *technology*, which induces a sharper awareness of the fragility of human life. War, for example, has always been a threat to life, but today the threat is qualitatively different because of nuclear and other sophisticated kinds of weapons. The weapons produced by modern technology now threaten life on a scale previously unimaginable. Living, as we do, therefore, in an age of extraordinary technological development means we face a qualitatively new range of moral problems.

The essential questions we face are these: In an age when we *can* do almost anything, how do we decide what we *should* do? In a time when we can do anything *technologically*, how do we decide *morally* what we should not do?

We face new technological challenges along the whole spectrum of life from conception to natural death. This creates the need for a consistent ethic, for the spectrum cuts across such issues as genetics, abortion, capital punishment, modern warfare, and the care of the terminally ill. Admittedly, these are all *distinct* problems, enormously complex, and deserve individual treatment. Each requires its own moral analysis. No single answer or solution applies to all. *But they are linked!*

Given this broad range of challenging issues, we desperately need a societal attitude or climate that will sustain a consistent defense and promotion of life. When human life is considered "cheap" or easily expendable in one area, eventually nothing is held as sacred and all lives are in jeopardy. Ultimately, it is society's attitude about life—whether of respect or non-respect—that determines its policies and practices.

The theological foundation of the consistent ethic, then, is defense of the person. The ethic grows out of the very character of Catholic moral thought. I do not mean to imply, of course, that one has to be a Catholic to affirm the moral content of the consistent ethic. But I do think that this theme highlights both the systematic and analogical character of Catholic moral theology.

The *systematic* nature of Catholic theology means it is grounded in a set of basic principles and then articulated in a fashion which draws out the meaning of each principle and the relationships among them. Precisely because of its systematic quality, Catholic theology refuses to treat moral issues in an *ad hoc* fashion. There is a continual process of testing the use of a principle in one case by its use in very different circumstances. The consistent ethic seeks only to illustrate how this testing goes on when dealing with issues involving the taking of life or the enhancement of life through social policy.

The *analogical* character of Catholic thought offers the potential to address a spectrum of issues which are not identical but have some common characteristics. Analogical reasoning identifies the unifying elements which link two or more issues, while at the same time recognizing why similar issues cannot be reduced to a single problem.

The taking of life presents itself as a moral problem all along the spectrum of life, but there are differences between abortion and war, just as there are elements that radically differentiate war from decisions made about the care of a terminally ill patient. The *differences* among these cases are universally acknowledged. A consistent ethic seeks to highlight the fact that differences do not destroy the elements of a *common moral challenge*.

A Catholic ethic which is both systematic in its argument and analogical in its perspective stands behind the proposal that, in the face of the multiple threats to life in our time, spanning every phase of existence, it is necessary to develop a moral vision which can address these several challenges in a coherent and comprehensive fashion.

The theological assertion that the human person is made in the image and likeness of God, the philosophical affirmation of the dignity of the person, and the political principle that society and state exist to serve the person—all these themes stand behind the consistent ethic. They also sustain the positions that the U. S. Catholic bishops have taken on issues as diverse as nuclear policy, social policy, and abortion. These themes provide the basis for the moral perspective of the consistent ethic.

From Moral Analysis to Public Policy Choices

Some commentators on the consistent ethic saw it primarily as a political policy. They missed its primary meaning: it is a moral vision and an ethical argument sustaining the vision. But the moral vision *does* have political consequences. The consistent ethic is meant to shape the public witness of the Catholic Church in our society.

Before exploring some of the political consequences, I would like to comment briefly on some related issues which provide a broader context for such a discussion. The movement from moral analysis to public policy choices is a complex process in a pluralistic society like ours.

First, civil discourse in the United States is influenced, widely shaped, by *religious pluralism*. The condition of pluralism, wrote John Courtney Murray, is the coexistence in one society of groups holding divergent and incompatible views with regard to religious questions. The genius of American pluralism, in his view, was that it provided for the religious freedom of each citizen and every faith. However, it did not purchase tolerance at the price of expelling religious and moral values from the public life of the nation. The goal of the American system is to provide space for a religious substance in society but not a religious state.

Second, there is a *legitimate secularity* of the political process, just as there is a legitimate role for religious and moral discourse in our nation's life. The dialogue which keeps both alive must be a careful exchange which seeks neither to transform secularity into secularism nor to change the religious role into religiously dominated public discourse.

John Courtney Murray spent a substantial amount of time and effort defending the Church's right to speak in the public arena. But he also stressed the *limits* of the religious role in that arena. Today religious institutions, I believe, must reaffirm their rights and recognize their limits. My intent is not, of course, to produce a passive Church or a purely private vision of faith. The limits relate not to *whether* we enter the public debate but *how* we advocate a public case. This implies, for example, that religiously rooted positions somehow must be translated into language, arguments, and categories which a religiously pluralistic society can agree on as the moral foundation of key policy positions.

Third, all participants in the public discourse must face the test of *complexity*. From issues of defense policy through questions of medical ethics to issues of social policy, the moral dimensions of our public life are interwoven with empirical judgments where honest disagreement exists. I do not believe, however, that empirical complexity should silence or paralyze religious or moral analysis and advocacy of issues. But we owe the public a careful accounting of how we have come to our moral conclusions.

Fourth, we must keep in mind the relationship between *civil law and morality*. Although the premises of civil law are rooted in moral principles, the scope of law is more limited and its purpose is not the moralization of society. Moral principles govern personal and social human conduct and cover as well interior acts and motivation. Civil statutes govern public order; they address primarily external acts and values that are formally social.

Hence it is not the function of civil law to enjoin or prohibit *every-*

thing that moral principles enjoin or prohibit. History has shown over and over again that people cherish freedom; they can be coerced only minimally. When we pursue a course of legal action, therefore, we must ask whether the requirements of public order are serious enough to take precedence over the claims of freedom.

Fifth, in the objective order of law and public policy, how do we determine which issues are *public* moral questions and which are best defined as *private* moral questions?

For Murray, an issue was one of public morality if it affected the *public order* of society. Public order, in turn, encompassed three goods: public peace, essential protection of human rights, and commonly accepted standards of moral behavior in a community. Whether a given question should be interpreted as one of public morality is not always self-evident. A rationally persuasive case has to be made that an action violates the rights of another or that the consequences of actions on a given issue are so important to society that the authority of the state and the civil law ought to be invoked to govern personal and group behavior.

Obviously, in a religiously pluralistic society, achieving consensus on what constitutes a public moral question is never easy. But we have been able to do it—by a process of debate, decision-making, then review of our decisions.

Two cases exemplify how we struggled with public morality in the past. First, Prohibition was an attempt to legislate behavior in an area ultimately decided to be beyond the reach of civil law because it was not sufficiently public in nature to affect the public order. Second, civil rights, particularly in areas of housing, education, employment, voting, and access to public facilities, were determined—after momentous struggles of war, politics, and law—to be so central to public order that the state could not be neutral on the question.

Today, we have a public consensus in law and policy which clearly defines civil rights as issues of public morality, and the decision to drink alcoholic beverages as clearly one of private morality. But neither decision was reached without struggle. The consensus was not automatic on either question. Philosophers, activists, politicians, preachers, judges, and ordinary citizens had to state a case, shape a consensus, and then find a way to give the consensus public standing in the life of the nation.

The fact that a spontaneous public consensus is lacking at a given moment does not prohibit its being created. When he was told that the law could not legislate morality, Dr. Martin Luther King, Jr., used to say that the law could not make people love their neighbors but it could stop their lynching them. Law and public policy can also be instruments of shaping a public consensus; they are not simply the product of consensus.

In sum, in charting the movement from moral analysis to public policy choices, we must take into account the facts that: (1) civil discourse in this nation is influenced and shaped by religious pluralism; (2) there is a legitimate secularity of the political process; (3) all participants in it must face the test of complexity; (4) there is a distinction between civil law and morality; and (5) some issues are questions of public morality, others of private morality.

This brings us to the third part of my address.

Implications of the Consistent Ethic for Citizens, Office Seekers and Office Holders

In light of the nearly three-year debate about the consistent ethic, questions have surfaced at the level of theological principle and ethical argument. As noted earlier, I have addressed these as they have arisen. The area that now needs attention is precisely how the framework of the consistent ethic takes shape (a) in the determination of public policy positions taken by the Church and (b) in the decisions that legislators and citizens take in light of the Church's positions.

Let me hasten to acknowledge that I do not have all the answers to the next set of questions. At this point in the dialogue I have chosen simply to identify questions which need further reflection and discussion. I also acknowledge that others have raised some of the questions; they are not all mine. Although I am not prepared to give answers to these questions, I do intend to address them at a later date.

What role does consensus play in the development of public policy and civil law? Earlier I suggested that its role is essential in the long run. But what about the short term? Moreover, what are the appropriate roles of civic and religious leaders in providing moral leadership in the public policy debate within a pluralistic community? What is the difference between a bishop's role and a politician's in the public debate about moral issues which the consistent ethic embraces? Should a politician wait until a consensus is developed before taking a stand or initiating legislation?

Must a Catholic office seeker or office holder work for all clearly identified Catholic concerns simultaneously and with the same vigor? Is that possible? If such a person need not work for all these concerns aggressively and at the same time, on what basis does one decide what to concentrate on and what not? Does theology provide the answer, or politics, or both? What guidelines does one use to determine which issues are so central to Catholic belief that they must be pursued legislatively regardless of the practical possibilities of passage? What are the consequences if a Catholic office seeker or office holder does not follow the Church's teaching in the campaign for or exercise of public office?

What is a Catholic office holder's responsibility in light of the Second Vatican Council's *Declaration on Religious Liberty* to protect the religious beliefs of non-Catholics? What is his or her responsibility under the Constitution? How are these responsibilities related?

How is the distinction between accepting a moral principle and making prudential judgments about applying it in particular circumstances—for example, in regard to specific legislation—worked out in the political order? What is the responsibility of a Catholic office holder or office seeker when the bishops have made a prudential judgment regarding specific legislation? How are Catholic voters to evaluate a Catholic office holder or office seeker who accepts a moral principle and not only disagrees with the bishops regarding specific legislation but supports its defeat?

Until questions like these are explored and ultimately answered, using the consistent ethic of life to test public policy, party platforms, and the posture of candidates for office will remain problematic and controversial. I firmly believe, however, that the consistent ethic, when pursued correctly and in depth, can make a genuine contribution. Solid, credible answers to the questions raised above will require an honest exchange of the best there is to offer in theological, political, and social thought.

I assure you that the Catholic bishops will remain in the public debate, and we need help. Public officials will remain in the line of fire, and they need help. Citizens will ultimately make the difference, and they, too, need help if the dialogue about how we are to respond to the broad range of contemporary issues is to proceed in a constructive fashion.

As the debate proceeds, we have a wonderful opportunity to bring together the best of our religious, political and social traditions in the service of each other and the wider society to which we are bound in hope and love.

17.

THE LORD OF LIFE

Reflections on a Consistent Ethic of Life

VISIT TO CHILE, NOVEMBER 24–28, 1986

My dear sisters and brothers:

My brother bishops, fellow priests, and I are very grateful for your warm hospitality during our pastoral visit to Chile. We bring you cordial greetings from your sisters and brothers in the Church in the United States. We know that these are very difficult times for you, and we want to assure you that the Church in the U. S. stands in solidarity with you as you seek to make an option in your country for the God of life.

I would like to address you today on the defense and promotion of human life. During the past three years I have articulated the need for developing—both conceptually and practically—a "consistent ethic of life" that seeks to build a bridge of common interest and insight on a broad range of social and moral questions.

Today I will, first, give an overview of the concept and, then, explore its applicability to the issues of human rights and poverty.

The Consistent Ethic of Life: An Overview

The idea of the consistent ethic is both old and new. It is "old" in the sense that its substance has been the basis of many Church programs for years. For example, when the U. S. bishops inaugurated a Respect Life Program in 1972, they invited the Catholic community to focus on the "sanctity of human life and the many threats to human life in the modern world, including war, violence, hunger, and poverty" (NCCB Resolution, April 13, 1972).

Their pastoral letter, *The Challenge of Peace: God's Promise and Our Response,* emphasized the sacredness of human life and the responsibility we have, personally and as a society, to protect and preserve its sanctity. The letter specifically linked the nuclear question with abortion and other life issues, stating:

> *When we accept violence in any form as commonplace, our sensitivities become dulled. When we accept violence, war itself can*

be taken for granted. Violence has many faces: oppression of the poor, deprivation of basic human rights, economic exploitation, sexual exploitation and pornography, neglect or abuse of the aged and the helpless, and innumerable other acts of inhumanity (#285).

I developed the theme of the consistent ethic precisely to provide a more comprehensive theological and ethical basis for the Respect Life Program and for the linkage of war and abortion and other human life issues.

What is the theological basis and strategic value of the "consistent ethic"? Catholic teaching is based on two truths about the human person: human life is both *sacred* and *social*. Because we esteem human life as sacred, we have a duty to protect and foster it at all stages of development, from conception to natural death, and in all circumstances. Because we acknowledge that human life is also social, society must protect and foster it.

Because life is sacred, the taking of even one life is a momentous event. Traditional Catholic teaching has allowed the taking of human life in particular situations by way of exception—for example, in self-defense and capital punishment. In recent decades, however, the presumptions against taking human life have been strengthened and the exceptions made ever more restrictive.

Fundamental to these shifts in emphasis is a more acute perception of the many ways in which life is threatened today. Obviously, such questions as war, violence, and capital punishment are not new; they have been with us for centuries. Life has always been threatened, but today there is a new *context* that shapes the *content* of our ethic of life.

The principal factor responsible for this new context is modern *technology*, which induces a sharper awareness of the fragility of human life. War, for example, has always been a threat to life, but today the threat is qualitatively different because of nuclear and other sophisticated kinds of weapons. Living, as we do, therefore, in an age of extraordinary technological development means we face a qualitatively new range of moral problems.

We face new technological challenges along the whole spectrum of life from conception to natural death. This creates the need for a consistent ethic, for the spectrum cuts across such issues as genetic manipulation, abortion, torture, capital punishment, modern warfare, and the care of the terminally ill. Admittedly, these are all *distinct* problems, enormously complex, and deserve individual treatment. Each requires its own moral analysis. No single answer or solution applies to all. But they are *linked* because of the impact they have upon the human person!

Given this broad range of challenging issues, we desperately need a societal *attitude* or climate that will sustain a consistent defense and promotion of life. When human life is considered "cheap" or easily expendable in one area, eventually nothing is held as sacred and all lives are in jeopardy.

Ultimately, it is society's attitude about life—whether of respect or non-respect—that determines or challenges its policies and practices.

The theological foundation of the consistent ethic, then, is defense of the person, the protection and promotion of human life. The theological assertion that the human person is made in the image and likeness of God, the philosophical affirmation of the dignity of the person, and the political principle that *society and state exist to serve the person*—all these themes stand behind the consistent ethic. They also sustain the position that the U. S. Catholic bishops have taken on issues as diverse as nuclear policy, social policy, economic policy, and abortion.

Application to Human Rights Issues

As I have intimated, the person is the clearest reflection of the presence of God among us. To lay violent hands on the person is to come as close as we can to laying violent hands on God. Every social system—east or west, north or south, communist or socialist or capitalist—should be judged by the way in which it reverences, or fails to reverence, the unique and equal dignity of every person.

Protection of the human person requires a broader view than simply the conviction that the person has a unique dignity. We protect that dignity and sacredness in a social setting by surrounding each person with a spectrum of rights and responsibilities. However, we must have a clear and correct understanding of human rights; that is, we must know their source and significance.

Human rights protect the individual's worth, which is rooted in his or her personhood. The individual's worth is not a negotiable privilege granted by the state. It is not swallowed up in a faceless collectivity. As Cardinal Fresno stated so clearly in his November 1984 message: "Human rights are the rights of God: that God's children be respected as God would have it."

Catholic teaching argues that political relationships within and among states must be seen and developed within the context of human rights. The affirmation that the person's human rights are to be respected both within and among states is fundamental and critically important today. It affirms that, in a world of states, the individual nation has real but only relative value. The dignity of the human person has transcendent value and must be respected at all times. Individual states do not have the right to so isolate themselves that they can ignore the moral concern of the rest of the world when, within their boundaries, there are serious allegations about human rights violations.

Pope John Paul II was very clear about all this when he stated during his 1981 visit to the Philippines: "Even in exceptional circumstances which sometimes may arise, violations of the human person's fundamental dignity or of the basic rights which safeguard that dignity can never be justified."

The protection of the dignity of the person requires a spectrum of rights that extends from the right to life itself, to the right to basic nutrition, social welfare, housing, education, and a job, to the right of freedom of conscience and religion, freedom of association, and the right to know the truth. This spectrum of rights provides an essential, broad perspective with which to assess the relevant issues in a given country or in relationships among nations.

Application to Issue of Poverty

The Second Vatican Council stated that, in the sphere of economics and social life, the dignity and vocation of the human person "have to be respected and fostered, for man is the source, the focus and the end of all economic and social life."

The bishops of Latin America, including the bishops of Chile, have rooted the Church's concern for the poor in the evangelical option for or love of the poor and youth. The results of their meetings at Medellin and Puebla have had an important impact on the Church throughout the world, especially in the United States. As I briefly develop the theme of the consistent ethic of life in terms of poverty, I want to acknowledge the debt of gratitude that the Church owes the Latin American hierarchy for their insight, courage, and perseverance in this matter.

The issue of consistency in the application of an ethic of life is tested in a different way when we examine the relationship between "right to life" and "quality of life" issues. If one contends, as the Church does, that the right of every unborn child should be protected by civil law and supported by civil consensus, then our moral, political, and economic responsibilities do not stop at the moment of birth! We must defend the right to life of the most vulnerable among us: the old and the young, the hungry and the homeless, the unemployed and the underemployed, women and children. And this means providing what is needed to make that right a reality, that is, providing what is needed to maintain a decent level of life.

Although the causes of poverty in a given nation or region may be a subject of honest disagreement, the *fact* of poverty cannot be disputed. As a Church, we are called to respond to this fact.

Who are the poor? As Cardinal Silva pointed out in a 1981 pastoral statement entitled, "Option for the Poor: Chile": "They are those actual faces, beaten down, of brothers and sisters in which we should recognize the imprint of Christ's suffering." They include children, young people, Indians, Negroes, mestizos, peasants, workers, the elderly, the marginalized, women, domestic employees. You know their faces. They live among you. You minister to them. Your hearts ache for their plight.

What is the Church's *role* in regard to the poor? There are at least *two* distinct responses. The first is to organize itself to carry out works of mercy.

The fulfillment of the command to feed the hungry, clothe the naked, and care for the sick has found direct and immediate expression in the Church from the apostolic age until today. The methods of doing this have varied, but all can be classified as direct, social service to the poor.

The second and complementary witness to the option for the poor is the Church's role as advocate and actor in the public life of society. The roots of this dimension of social ministry are found in the prophets who teach us to ask questions about how we organize our life as a society. When the prophets spoke on our behalf of the widow and orphans, they challenged us to provide for all members of the community. The purpose of the Church's social teaching is to measure the social and economic life of society by the standards of social justice and charity.

To stand for life, to make an option for the God of life, is to stand for the needs of poor people who epitomize the sacredness of life. Standing for their rights is not merely a rhetorical task! We must also act on their behalf!

My prayer for you and all the people of Chile is that this nation will be known as a community which committed itself to the protection and promotion of life. I pray that the Catholic Church will continue to help this society fulfill these two tasks with the assurance that, as you work to defend and foster human life, many Catholics throughout the world walk at your side. We are all children of the one Lord of life!

18.

SCIENCE AND THE CREATION OF LIFE

UNIVERSITY OF CHICAGO, APRIL 29, 1987

It is a pleasure to be here this afternoon and to participate in this forum co-sponsored by the Center for Clinical Medical Ethics and by Alpha Omega Alpha. I am aware of the work of the Center and applaud its study of day-to-day ethical and legal issues in medical practice. I also want to acknowledge the hard work and study of the distinguished members of the medical student honor society.

I come to this center of medical research and training to share with you some reflections on an Instruction recently issued by the Catholic Church's Congregation for the Doctrine of the Faith. The subject of that Instruction was "respect for human life in its origins and on the dignity of procreation."

The Instruction, as you know, received wide media coverage and mixed reviews. For example, a *New York Times* editorial said that "thoughtful people" can welcome this "considered set of views." In an Op-Ed piece in the *Chicago Tribune*, Kenneth Vaux of the University of Illinois wrote that the Instruction "affirms a much-threatened normative value of the natural goodness and sacred mystery of birth. Regrettably, in its desire to preserve the deeply human nature of procreation it plays down the salutary potential of science to ameliorate incapacity in the same procreative gift."

This afternoon I would like to pick up on what Dr. Vaux and others have said and highlight the Instruction's strengths and limits. I realize that not everyone will agree with all aspects of the document's teaching. Nonetheless, it would be helpful to the dialogue which should take place between science and a particular moral/ethical tradition to lay out clearly what the Instruction actually says and the rationale for the specific points it makes. Before doing that, however, I would like to situate the Instruction in the broader context of Roman Catholic thought.

Two Principles

In order to understand the Instruction, one must first attend to two principles which guide the development of Roman Catholic teaching in such matters.

The *first* principle is what has been called our "natural law" tradition.

130

According to this tradition we learn about God's will not only from the scriptures and the living tradition of the Church but also from what it means to be a human person. Our conviction is that there is an inner order or meaning to all that exists which was placed there by the Creator. We also believe that this meaning is accessible to all people of good will who reflect with care and wisdom on the experience of life.

This "natural law" tradition has served as the impetus for Roman Catholic involvement in many critical areas of human experience: war, peace, race relations, and the economy. Although Roman Catholics enter such discussions empowered by their faith, frequently the specific content of their reflections is devoid of strictly religious or sectarian premises. Rather, they are based on certain insights or principles about the meaning of human life that have been developed over the centuries and tested by time and experience.

This "natural law" tradition has also served as the basis for Roman Catholic involvement in the ethical dilemmas which you and your predecessors in the medical and health care professions have confronted for centuries. May I even suggest that much of what is taken for granted today by health care providers as the ethical "givens" of your profession had their origin in this "natural law" tradition. And this tradition continues to assist us today as we address critical issues such as patient rights and the withdrawal of nutrition and hydration.

While extolling the strengths and longevity of this tradition, I also must be candid and point out its limits. Human experience is not an unmixed blessing. Contemporary philosophical and sociological developments have made us more aware of the contextual nature of all knowledge. That is why it is possible that what appears to be a proper understanding or application of an ethical principle in one age may be found to be wanting or even incorrect in another. It is also possible to confuse the *application* of a principle for the *principle itself*. This possibility was not unknown to the medieval scholars who sought to distinguish between the unchanging primary principles of the natural law and other knowledge that is less certain.

This implies the possibility of error or misjudgment in our ethical reflections because of the limited nature of human knowledge and experience. Candor prompts me to acknowledge that some of those who read the Instruction will do so with some skepticism in light of some misjudgments which the teaching Church made in the past.

While I admit, as does the Instruction, that matters as complex as this require continuing study and dialogue, I do not believe that history will judge this Instruction to be in the same category as the Church's response to Galileo. In fact, my greater concern, because of the relativism that has come to mark so much of our contemporary culture, is that the Instruction will be rejected out of hand simply because it dares to assert that there are some normative principles which can and should guide our concrete choices—choices which are now possible because of technological advances.

The *second* principle which provides a context for the Instruction is the Roman Catholic understanding of human responsibility. The beginning point for this understanding is to be found in the First or Old Testament, the opening narratives of Genesis. There the human family is seen as made in the image and likeness of God and given the charge to be fertile and subdue the earth. In a sense, one can say that humanity has been given the charge to act as a co-creator with God, to assist in implementing the Divine Plan. This is an awesome and powerful responsibility. In addition to the capacity to love, the other agency of this co-responsibility is the human mind with its potential for creativity and insight.

The human potential for creativity is being fulfilled in our day in many ways. Human learning in general, the work of the laboratory, and technological advances in particular, are not to be feared but rather prized and celebrated as both gift and responsibility. We have and must continue to pursue our ability to lessen the blight of poverty and starvation, to bring healing to those who are ill, and to find ways to remedy the causes of human illness and suffering. In this perspective, the work of the scholar, the scientist, and the practitioner of medicine is not seen as merely human toil but a participation in a godly venture. Similarly, the effort to correct what would limit or eliminate the human response to the divine call to be fertile and multiply is a noble and worthy venture.

But this returns us to our starting point and brings our two principles into contact with each other.

While this may be difficult at times for us to admit, we are *not* God. The work of our minds and hands is not something unto itself. Rather, it is a participation in a power and a purpose greater than any one of us and therefore is accountable to that same divine plan or purpose. For that reason, all that the human mind or the scientific method is *capable* of doing is not necessarily *worth* doing. In fact, it might be something that should *not* be done.

In other words, all human activity, including scientific and medical research and practice, is subject to evaluation and review. But what principles do we use to guide that review? From a Roman Catholic perspective, it is those principles I mentioned earlier, garnered from our reflection on the nature and meaning of human life as we receive it from God's hands.

This, then, is the broader context in which the Instruction should be read: a belief in the dignity and goodness of human knowledge and creativity, together with the conviction that such creativity must always be evaluated in the light of perduring and normative human values.

Principles Found in the Instruction

Now I would like to turn to the Instruction itself. I will not detail all of its specific conclusions. They have been adequately reported by the media. Rather, I would like to examine those principles which inform or shape its ethical conclusions. I will highlight three of them.

The *first* principle concerns human life itself. Rooted in the natural law tradition, the Instruction insists on the inviolable dignity of every human life. Each person is viewed as having an inestimable worth as well as a right to exist that cannot be directly attacked; indeed, it must be respected and protected. I suspect that no person of good will would deny this principle. However, there is profound disagreement about both the breadth and the manner of its application.

As I enter into dialogue with people who, in good faith, disagree with the manner in which the Instruction applies this principle, I must be very clear about my own belief and that of the Church. Personal integrity requires this. I am confident that you respect this.

Our tradition teaches that, at the moment of conception, the process of becoming a human person begins, and, consequently, all of the rights of being human must be afforded the zygote, embryo, and fetus. I acknowledge the complexity of the scientific evidence in this matter. However, on a moral plane there is no way to distinguish the stages of the development of life that does not result in a type of relativism that would threaten the dignity and rights of all human life. I agree with Dr. Vaux when he says: "When the fetal diagnostics of amniocentesis and ultrasound are used to search, scan and destroy the imperfect fetus; when embryos and fetuses are used for experimentation . . . in such a world we realize that we are not so much engaged in medical therapy as a massive life denial, perhaps a death wish" (*Chicago Tribune*, March 20, 1987).

The intent, then, of the Instruction is not to oppose the pursuit of knowledge about the causes of genetic defects or the development of techniques that will remedy such defects but, rather, to ensure that in the pursuit of these goods a greater good—the inviolability of life—is not lost.

The *second* principle is the essential and necessary relationship between human sexuality, marriage, and parenthood.

There are several aspects of our humanity which set us apart from the rest of the life that populates the earth. We have the ability to engage in reflex thinking, the freedom to make choices, the capacity and the desire to enter into significant human relationships. This capacity for human relationships is also known as human intimacy. Intimacy bespeaks warmth, tenderness, love, fidelity, and generativity. Human intimacy specifies our sexuality and distinguishes it from the sexual activity of the animal world.

Human intimacy yearns for the interpersonal commitment and fidelity of heterosexual marriage and is celebrated in marital intercourse. Marital intimacy, in turn, has a natural propensity, a desire, to be generative of life for the couple and also of new life. In this perspective then, there is an essential unity between marital sexual intimacy and the generation of new life.

This unity is violated by surrogate parenthood, artificial donor insemination, extracorporeal fertilization using gametes other than those of husband and wife, "twin fission," cloning, and parthenogenesis. The Instruction speaks against these procedures not because it is opposed to the generation of life or to scientific knowledge and application, but because it seeks to protect what it sees as an essential connection between the creation of life and faithful, committed marital intimacy.

If I have correctly interpreted their reactions to these two principles, many people seem to think that they make common sense. Although some may argue for the right to an abortion in certain narrowly defined situations, many in this nation are deeply concerned about an erosion of respect and protection for human life. Although people sympathize with the desire of a couple or an individual to have a child, most are very uncomfortable with the separation of the generation of life from the stable context of married family life. That is why many who might otherwise ignore the teaching office of the Catholic Church have welcomed, as one commentator noted, "a coherent set of principles that encourages a rigorous assessment of new methods of creating and manipulating human life" (Joan Frawley, *Wall Street Journal*, April 7, 1987).

This leads to the third and most controversial principle.

The Nature of the Marital Act

This principle speaks of the nature of marital intercourse. It finds its origin in the understanding of marital intimacy I just spoke about. If the purpose of marriage is both love and life, then the act of intercourse which celebrates and incarnates the meaning of marriage also has two purposes: love-making and life-making. And just as these aspects cannot be separated in marriage, so too they cannot be separated in marital intercourse.

To say it another way, the making of love is always to be open to life when a couple celebrates marital intercourse, and the making of life is always to be the result of the making of love in the context of marital intercourse. There is an essential unity that cannot be broken. This teaching, admittedly, is not accepted by many people, Catholics included.

Because of this principle, the Instruction opposes artificial husband insemination and extracorporeal fertilization using husband and wife gametes. In keeping with this principle, however, it does support any technique which would assist but not replace marital intercourse.

Obviously, this part of the Instruction has received the most press attention. And for good reason, because of the significant number of loving couples who experience the pain of infertility and for whom one of the proscribed procedures might be their only possibility for the conception of new life. I am aware that for many such couples and for many scientists and doctors, this is a difficult principle to accept.

Some argue that the Church is being inconsistent when, on the one hand, it says that marriage is ordered toward the creation of new life and then, on the other hand, opposes the use of scientific technology to allow a loving but infertile couple to conceive. Similarly, some argue that this is a narrow biological or "act-centered" approach which fails to take into account the total context of marital love. They ask what is wrong with using human intelligence to assist the natural process of marital life-making.

Before responding to this objection, I wish to make one point very clear: I have heard the pain of loving couples, Catholic and non-Catholic, who desperately want the gift of a child. My heart reaches out to them. Theirs is a difficult burden, and I share their pain. We must offer them love, support, and understanding. And in the end, after prayerful and conscientious reflection on this teaching, they must make their own decision.

But what of the perceived inconsistency? If one views the question only in the narrow terms of intercourse and the creation of life, then it is difficult to understand what the Instruction is saying. It can appear to be opposed to both life and human creativity.

However, the Instruction and the Catholic heritage argue that the terms of evaluation must be greater than the act of intercourse and the desire for new life. We must be open to asking ourselves such questions as the following: is there a qualitative difference between the creation of life and other human activities? If there is, does this difference place limits or constraints on what might be technologically or scientifically possible?

What are the consequences for the human family if we are to replace the ecstatic union of two bodies becoming one-in-love as the source of life with the technology of artificial insemination or in *vitro* fertilization? We are already aware of the psychological and other difficulties faced by a child conceived through intercourse devoid of love. And this happens despite the natural instinct which is central to human experience—an instinct which says that intercourse and life-making should be loving actions. This instinct has placed both personal and societal restraints on when and who should make love and participate in the creation of life. How does contemporary reproductive technology relate to this human instinct? Could it be that we are tampering with something so fundamentally human that we are endangering the quality of future life?

And finally, if we remove the creation of life from the mystery and unpredictability of interpersonal marital communion and make it the prerogative of scientific planning, are there any restraints on other applications? Are we comfortable with making possible an attitude which would encourage a couple genetically planning a "perfect" child to resist or reject anything less than their "ideal"? If we are not comfortable with turning the creation of human life into an impersonal or "pick and choose" process, what principles exist to restrain such activity?

The Catholic "natural law" tradition provides answers to these questions. It reasons that there is a fundamental meaning to the natural process of life-making that should not be violated even though the intention is noble: the creation of new life. It argues that in the creation of life, as in few other human endeavors, we are co-responsible with the divine Creator for new life and, consequently, there are limits beyond which we should not proceed. This caution was expressed recently by the noted ethicist Sidney Callahan. Although she would disagree with some of what I have said today, her observations are very much on target when she writes: "as medical professionals and the society as a whole confront these innovative interventions, the ethical, psychological, and cultural dimensions of technological procedures cannot be discounted. Everything that can be done to satisfy individual reproductive desires should not be done. As Ghandi said, 'means are ends in the making'" (*Commonweal*, April 25, 1986).

Today I echo Sidney Callahan's caution about the means we choose lest the ends be ones our children and grandchildren will regret.

I am grateful for your courtesy in permitting me to share these reflections with you. As I conclude, I wish to reaffirm the great value my religious tradition places upon the power of the human mind, and its great respect for those who serve the human family in the medical profession. May we continue our dialogue in openness to the truth so that we might be instrumental in bringing together, in a harmonious synthesis, both moral principles and technology in defense of human life and in response to the deepest yearning of the people whom we serve.

19.

THE CONSISTENT ETHIC OF LIFE, STAGE TWO

Symposium on the Consistent Ethic of Life

LOYOLA UNIVERSITY, CHICAGO, NOVEMBER 7, 1987

On December 6, 1983, I gave an address at Fordham University entitled, "A Consistent Ethic of Life: An American-Catholic Dialogue." Although the specific occasion for this lecture was the U. S. Catholic Bishops' pastoral letter, *The Challenge of Peace: God's Promise and Our Response*, I used the occasion to discuss the broader relationship between the Catholic moral vision and American culture. That presentation in the Bronx four years ago marked the beginning of Stage One of the consistent ethic of life, although, in effect, I was simply articulating the moral vision underlying the U. S. Bishops' Respect Life program from its inception in 1972.

I cast the Fordham address as "an inquiry, an examination of the need for a consistent ethic of life and a probing of the problems and possibilities which exist within the Church and the wider society for developing such an ethic." I immediately added that I did not "underestimate the intrinsic intellectual difficulties of this exercise nor the delicacy of the question—ecclesially, ecumenically, and politically." I asked for a discussion, and I got one!

Four years ago I had no idea of the extent to which the inquiry which I was proposing would become a significant part of my pastoral ministry. Frankly, I am very pleased that my basic message has been heard so widely and supported by so many. Four years ago I did not imagine that it would be the subject of a symposium such as this. I am very grateful to Loyola University, its President, Father Raymond Baumhart, and all of the participants for making this possible.

In the time allotted to me this afternoon, I will (1) briefly explain why I decided to develop the consistent ethic theme, (2) point out the need for collaboration between pastors and theologians in its further development, and (3) respond to some of the issues raised by the major speakers. As with some of the other addresses at this symposium, my published text will be somewhat longer and more detailed than this oral presentation.

Why Develop the Consistent Ethic Theme?

During the past four years, many people have asked why I introduced this concept, why I invested so much precious reflective time and exerted so much limited energy in its development. The answer is as simple, and as complex, as my ministry as a bishop.

As a pastor, I have the responsibility to proclaim Jesus Christ and his gospel "in season and out." This means that I must present an evangelical vision of self-sacrificing love and profound respect for the dignity of all human life. And I must do this in a way that is faithful—to the Word of God and to the Spirit-guided tradition of the Church as taught by the Pope and the bishops.

Moreover, this proclamation of the gospel does not take place in a vacuum. It is situated in a particular historical moment and a specific place. That is why my pastoral responsibility includes searching for an ever-increasing understanding and penetration of Christ's message in light of current realities and critiquing the quality of life in contemporary society in light of the gospel. I do this as a co-disciple with all other members of the community of faith as, together, we seek to be "like a leaven" in the world and to transform our culture so that God's Kingdom might truly come.

Our engagement with the world is not superfluous or marginal either to our lives as believers or to the world in which we live. Rather, it is something desperately needed. The vision and the values which we proclaim and seek to develop in the form of principles and strategic choices can enrich and transform both our own lives and our world.

Each of us experiences the weaknesses and the limits of our own personhood and the world. We encounter forces that oppose what we affirm and tempt us, as individuals and as a society, to be less than we would like to be and can be. We know that sin and evil are real—not merely in ourselves, but in others and in the world around us. Nonetheless, we also acknowledge that we dream of becoming the full persons and the perfect community that God intends for his creation. And we believe that the Spirit of our loving God is with us to assist us in bringing this dream to reality.

The pursuit of this dream motivated me to develop the consistent ethic of life. I am convinced that such an ethic gives us and other people of good will a unique perspective on such matters as international justice and peace, economic justice and business ethics, civil and human rights, the family and interpersonal relationships, the protection and nurturing of human life, and stewardship of the environment. Such an ethic provides both the vision and the norms needed to guide and direct individual and communal behavior in a great variety of contexts.

The Need for Collaboration in Developing the Concept

While I believe deeply in the concept of a consistent ethic of life, I also know that there are limits to what I, as a pastor, can and should do in regard to its development. If the consistent ethic is to be adequately developed and truly engage our contemporary society, then it requires the expertise of theologians and other scholars to refine and flesh it out. As I have intimated, from the very beginning I have not underestimated the difficulties of developing such an ethic. That is why many of my major presentations about it have been deliberately addressed to Catholic university audiences. Such institutions of higher learning should engage in the tasks of enriching U. S. culture through the study and sharing of Catholic wisdom and enhancing our understanding of the Catholic faith by drawing on both the riches and the poverty of this culture.

From what I have just said, it should be obvious how fitting it is that this symposium should take place, and that it should occur here. Fitting because it takes place at Loyola University, an institution of higher learning that is faithful to its Catholic, Jesuit, and American roots. Fitting also because the symposium brings together scholars of national and international stature to engage the concept, test it, critique it, and further develop it.

I would like to indicate briefly how I see the distinct but complementary roles of pastor and theologian in this dialogue.

As I have indicated, I come to this discussion as a pastor, not as a theologian. Nonetheless, part of my pastoral ministry is to teach—to conserve the faith handed on to us by the apostles, to explain the teachings of the Church developed over the centuries, and to provide guidance for proper living to individuals and society.

To fulfill this ministry, I must rely on the assistance of others, especially theologians. As I have said on several other occasions, theologians are explorers. Their work implies searching, casting about for deeper understandings of the mysteries of the faith in light of contemporary life. They look to the past, they look to present realities, and they look to future possibilities in order to provide a deeper understanding of what God is saying to us. They do not create revelation, but they help us assimilate, make our own, and apply the mystery of God's saving love to our particular situation.

Because theologians are explorers, they search for new areas of understanding, new approaches to old realities. Because they are explorers, they must have an appropriate amount of freedom. And because they are explorers, we must expect that their searches will not always be successful, that there will be mistakes.

We have gathered here today with mutual, complementary responsibilities within the Church. The relationship between theologian and bishop should be characterized by complementary, mutual respect, and dialogue, even though the bishop's overseeing ministry determines what results of theological exploration can or should be accepted by the community of faith.

Responses to the Four Major Papers

In this spirit of a pastoral teacher who needs the help of theologians and has invited the exploration of the strengths and limits of the consistent ethic of life theme, I will now respond to some of what has been said here today. I trust that the manner of my response will be in accord with the appropriate relationship between pastor and theologian that I have just described. Just as all the participants have spoken with great conviction and respect, so will I.

It is not possible for me to respond in a detailed way to everything that has been said here today. Nor should I even attempt to do so, because it is proper that much of what has been said today should be seen as a dialogue between fellow explorers over a particular concept. It is my hope that this discussion will continue and in this way refine and enrich the concept of a consistent ethic of life.

I will briefly examine each major presentation in light of the others and offer two observations on it. My response will not follow the order of presentation but will begin with the more abstract or ontological concerns and then move to the more concrete or specific.

Professor Gustafson

I will begin with Professor Gustafson's paper. I tend to agree with his hypothetical suggestion that a different theological point of departure might give different weight to matters under discussion, leading to some different ethical conclusions. I also share his concern about what he describes as an "anthropocentrism and ultimately the individualism" that he finds in my addresses. Fr. McCormick also raised the issue of individualism in another context.

Professor Gustafson suggests that theology must be more theocentric. With that in mind he proposes his central ethical statement: "We are to seek to discern what God is enabling and requiring us to do as participants in the patterns and processes of interdependence of life in the world."

At first reading I agree with the intent of such an ethical statement. We *are* called to discern the on-going movement and action of the divine Spirit in the events of everyday existence. And we are responsible to do this in a way that respects the fact that we have intrapersonal relationships and interpersonal relationships, as well as relationships with society and the world around us. And within those relationships there must be a sense of the awesomeness of God who is their origin and their ultimate and.

Nonetheless, where Professor Gustafson and I might differ is in the manner in which we discover this divine pre-eminence. Roman Catholic natural law tradition has insisted that when one turns to the natural world, one can find God's plan and purpose. Consequently, divine pre-eminence can be mediated to us in and through our experience of our humanity and of the world.

However, such an inductive experience of the divine carries with it the danger of reducing the divine to the experience through which it is mediated. And that is why this so-called "natural" experience of divinity must always be enriched by and accountable to the face of God revealed in

Scripture and worship, and expressed in the Church's teaching. In them we encounter the *"mysterium tremendum"* that shatters our temptation to build our own golden calves. We must then maintain a proper balance between the "naturalness" of the Divine and Divine pre-eminence.

I would like to address another dimension of Professor Gustafson's central ethical statement: the relationship between the individual and the social. He is correct in his reading of the development of Catholic thinking when he suggests that a priority has been given to the individual "made in the image and likeness of God." It is no secret that the *social* dimensions of Catholic theology have been advanced, in large measure, only over the course of the last century, and primarily at the prompting of the great social encyclicals of recent popes. And the consequences of this expanded vision have been explored in recent discussions about the so-called European "Political Theology" and the "Liberation Theology" of developing countries in Latin America, Africa, and elsewhere.

I have sought to be attentive to the interrelationship of the personal and the social as I included in some of my addresses the distinction between private and public morality. Moreover, the U. S. Catholic bishops, in their pastoral letter on the economy, clearly acknowledged the ethical imperatives of economic policy just as they did other social imperatives in their pastoral letter on war and peace.

Although we have recognized this social dimension of theology and ethics, we have not fully addressed the tension between the personal and the social. When we do so, we undoubtedly will find the ambiguity which Professor Gustafson intimated. I affirm the need for greater work in this area and respect the challenge which this offers. At this time, however, it still seems to me that, in moments of conflict between the individual and the social, the individual must predominate, for it is here that the fullest presence of the Divine is to be encountered.

Father McCormick

This last point of Professor Gustafson serves as a bridge to my response to Father McCormick's presentation. He moves from the more theoretical question of the proper relationship between the individual and society to the specific methods used in social and personal ethics. Father McCormick is not the first to highlight what many perceive as an inconsistency between the two approaches as they are found in the documents of the ecclesiastical magisterium. And, as a pastor who searches for consistency in ethical discussions, I, too, at times experience some of the same difficulty.

In a sense, this brings us back to Professor Gustafson's point that, in fact, the Church's moral teaching has given a priority to individual or personal ethics and that its moral valence is stronger there than in the social realm. And consequently, apart from other concerns which I will mention later, the result is that there seems to be greater room for an inductive approach in regard to social ethics than in the area of personal ethics. This brings me to my next point.

Father McCormick also engages the consistent ethic in a critique that originates in his dedication to an ethical method known as proportionalism. As one of the most respected and eloquent proponents of that method, he correctly enters into a discussion of the maxim, "no direct killing of the innocent."

It would be inappropriate for me to engage in a point-by-point response to his cogent observations. However, I must point out, respectfully, that proportionalism has not been accepted by the ecclesiastical magisterium. While some aspects of this approach are commendable, it has led to some conclusions that have, in fact, not been approved by the magisterium. This is why the magisterium has not accepted this method as an equally valid alternative to the Church's traditional moral methodology.

I am not disclosing a secret when I say this. And Father McCormick is correct in saying that the current tension in the Church about this matter *does* soften the underbelly of the consistent ethic. But it also threatens to do much more than that. The debates over moral methodology and concrete moral imperatives is draining vital energy from the lives of individual believers and the Church as a whole. And, at times, I myself become frustrated because I do not see a way in which we can move beyond this debate.

This simply means that continuing dialogue is needed. It must take place among theologians and between theologians and bishops. It must be marked by a spirit of civility and mutual respect. There is no room for caricature that inhibits understanding and the search for truth. Similarly, there is nothing inherently wrong with theological debate about points which are in conflict. Historically, such debate has given life and purpose to the various theological schools which have enriched our understanding of the Christian faith.

At the same time, it is not proper to ignore the distinctive teaching charism of the ecclesiastical magisterium and its right to expect at least a religious assent of mind and heart to what it proposes, as described in *Lumen Gentium*. I hope that through such dialogue we can move beyond current divisions to agree upon an ethical methodology that will integrate the wisdom of both ethical perspectives.

Professor Finnis

Let me begin by expressing my appreciation for Professor Finnis' lengthy and detailed written paper, which is much longer than his oral presentation today. His three propositions and his analysis of them provide a scholarly overview of many of the criticisms directed at the consistent ethic by some in the Catholic Church.

In partial response I would like to discuss the manner in which we elect public officials. Professor Finnis says initially that he agrees with the principle enunciated by the National Conference of Catholic Bishops that one should not vote in terms of a single issue. Rather one should be concerned about the *character* of the candidates. But, in analyzing that character, he says, a different weight should be given to their position on infanticide than on affirmative moral responsibilities. In fact, he suggests that one may properly use candidates' positions on infanticide as litmus tests of their good or bad character and give little or no weight to their preferences on other public policies.

I agree that the character of a candidate for public office is an important consideration for the electorate. I also affirm the priority which should be given to candidates' positions on matters pertaining to the life of the unborn. I am uncomfortable, however, with seeing that position as a singular litmus test. My reason for saying this is *not* a lack of commitment to elimination of the crime of abortion in our land. Throughout the 35 years of my priestly and episcopal ministry, and especially since the 1973 Supreme Court abortion decisions, I have vigorously worked to eradicate this grave evil. Rather it has to do with the complexity of the political process in a pluralistic society.

To insist that the only person a Catholic may vote for must pass a litmus test based on how a person has or presumably would vote on a particular issue, apart from an evaluation of the overall political process and the position of the candidate on other pro-life issues, could eliminate us as a political reality in our society. What we must find is a way, without compromising our fundamental convictions and, in particular, our commitment to the life of the unborn, that we can credibly remain as participants in the development and transformation of public policy.

The second issue I wish to discuss is his view about the role of bishops in the development of public policy. It has been my experience, and I believe that of other bishops in the United States, that the Church's social and moral teaching can be effectively introduced into public discussion on a wide range of political issues. It is necessary to be very clear about what is meant here: the bishops should not be political partisans, but they can specify, examine, and press in the public debate the *moral* dimensions of issues as diverse as medical technology, capital punishment, human rights, economic policy, and military strategy.

The experience of our U. S. episcopal conference in addressing the issues of nuclear and economic policies has shown us the need to give high priority to this teaching task. Our critics have said we have entered too deeply into the political order, that we are too specific in our teaching, and that we are usurping the proper role of the laity in the secular and, particularly, the political order. I addressed this issue in my intervention during the recently concluded Synod of Bishops.

It is my conviction that this is a mistaken criticism. While attributing a lesser degree of authority to our applications, we have nonetheless thought it necessary to show how principles are to be applied in our contemporary circumstances so that the principles and their implications will be correctly understood. In the final analysis, moral teaching involves concrete choices.

In truth, the distinct teaching role of bishops in addressing the political order complements the indispensable role of the laity as participants in the political process. And for that teaching role to be fulfilled, the character of the moral teaching must meet three requirements. (1) It must be morally credible; that is, it must have the theoretical capacity to illuminate the human values and dimensions of political questions. (2) It must be empirically competent in its assessment of problems. (3) And as noted above, it must lead toward specific recommendations and conclusions which are realizable. Teaching which combines these characteristics is a permanent mode of the Church's contribution to the political process.

At the same time, both the theology of the lay vocation and the political requirements of effectiveness demand that the Church's direct engagement in the political order be through lay people. Nonetheless, if this crucial role is to be filled well, those who undertake it need solid grounding in the faith and the Church's social teaching, as well as political skill and empirical competence.

Endowed with these capacities, Catholic lay men and women who enter the political process, whether by election or appointment, should have the encouragement of the bishops in undertaking this vocation. They must be addressed and treated as professionals in their sphere of competence. While commentary and critique of public debate, public policy, and specific political choices are necessary parts of the Church's social ministry, the freedom to exercise professional judgment and the virtue of prudence must be accorded those in public life. It is the task of Catholic politicians, in cooperation with others of good will and a wide range of political coalitions, to grapple with how the moral teaching should be joined with the concrete choices of the political order and the requirements of building public support for needed policies.

When we fulfill our role as moral teachers and help prepare lay people for the political vocation, we exercise a ministry of co-discipleship.

Father Hehir

Finally, I will address Father Hehir's paper, focusing on two concrete issues facing the implementation of the consistent ethic.

Father Hehir suggests that, in debating public policy, the Church should not try to create a voting bloc or political organization. Rather it helps test other positions in the light of a consistent philosophical vision. However, because this vision encompasses the full range of human life issues from conception to natural death, it is difficult to create a stable constituency for it. So, as Father Hehir rightly pointed out, the consistent ethic "has created expectations that have not been realized in practice."

I am acutely aware of this. While the phrase "the consistent ethic" has become a part of the U. S. Catholic vocabulary and seems to resonate with the ethical instincts of many Catholics, its systematic and analogical nature makes it difficult for individuals to apply it consciously or reflexively in their civic and political choices.

At times this difficulty leads me to believe that we need to find better ways to communicate the principle. In some way we must take what is an abstract principle and make it more understandable in the concrete. And for that to happen, we will need the expertise of pastoral ministers and religious educators.

While acknowledging this need, I also know that, in the Catholic tradition, other principles, also complex in their theological explanation, have become both familiar and helpful to individuals in their everyday ethical decision-making. Why? Because the moral intuition behind the ethical theory may be absorbed and used without the sophistication of its theological articulation. If the acceptance and integration of the fundamental insight into linkage of life issues found in the consistent ethic of life were to become "second nature" to people, then it will have served a great purpose.

The second issue I would like to address is Father Hehir's reflection on the evaluation of candidates for public office. I agree with his guidelines that reject the legitimacy of a split between the public and the personal positions of a candidate but allow a legitimate range of prudential choice about how to move from moral conviction to legislation or policy.

Some will disagree with the second of these guidelines. And this issue could become a source of division during next year's national elections.

What seems to be at stake is the acceptance or non-acceptance of the teaching of the Second Vatican Council about the nature of the state and the role of civil law. It is clear that the Council shifted the criteria by which we evaluate and understand civil law. No longer is the law responsible for the full and complete realization of the common good and, consequently, the expression of all moral teaching. The law's scope is limited, and its development must be evaluated by the criteria of the freedom of the individual, the public order, equitability, and enforceability.

This implies that candidates who unequivocally subscribe to the consistent ethic of life in its full scope, as well as in its moral analysis of distinct issues, could sincerely disagree with others about strategies for the implementation of that principle, could oppose legislation supported by some, could support legislation opposed by others, or could decide that it is not in the best interests of the state to seek particular legislation or to enact it at a given historical moment. Although we might disagree with such candidates and might not vote for them because we disagree with their prudential judgments, in this context it would be inappropriate to say that such candidates or public officials are either acting immorally or that they should be otherwise castigated or ostracized.

Even if one were to disagree with this teaching of the Second Vatican Council, the history of our ethical reasoning on the making and enforcing of public law is more complex than some would suggest. From the time of

Augustine it has been recognized that law must be applied according to the human condition. In fact, it has even been possible to tolerate evil in certain situations. What has been required of the lawgiver was *prudence*. This remains an appropriate criterion to use in evaluating whether candidates or public officials are faithful to the consistent ethic: Are they acting prudently? Such a criterion is faithful to the nature of the consistent ethic as well as the legitimate role of pluralism in our society.

I am very pleased that the consistent ethic of life theme has been taken seriously by many people in the last four years—including our distinguished speakers and respondents at this symposium. This is not the end of a long process but simply the beginning of the second stage in the development of the theme. Thoughtful, complex questions have been raised, and I trust that I can count on all of you to continue this dialogue with me and my fellow bishops.

20.

THE CONSISTENT ETHIC OF LIFE AND PUBLIC POLICY

U. S. Catholic Conference
Social Action Directors' Conference,
Washington, D.C., February 10, 1988

When I was invited to give this address on "The Consistent Ethic of Life and Public Policy," my schedule for this month was already over-committed. But I was convinced that I should not miss this opportunity, and so I simply forced the event onto my calendar. The opportunity which this topic provides has two dimensions: first, to address a crucial but still undeveloped part of the consistent ethic—its public application; and second, to engage with you as social action directors in a joint reflection on how the policy implications of the consistent ethic may be advanced.

To initiate this reflection, I will first review the origins of the concept of the consistent ethic, then analyze its development in the Church, and, finally, examine its public policy potential in U. S. society.

The Origins of the Idea

One way to explain the origins of the consistent ethic is to see it as an expression of the model of social teaching found in the *Pastoral Constitution on the Church in the Modern World* of the Second Vatican Council. This conciliar document, which stands as the *magna carta* of social ministry since Vatican II, asserted that the social task of the Church in the modern world is to read the signs of the times and to interpret them in light of the gospel. The idea of the consistent ethic arose for me in precisely this way.

It is possible to distinguish three challenges in the contemporary signs of the times which pose different but interrelated questions for the Church's social ministry. There is the *technological* challenge, the *peace* challenge, and the *justice* challenge. The three must be interpreted in light of the gospel truth about the sacredness of human life and the obligations of Christians to stand for life.

The *technological* challenge arises from the unique capacities which contemporary science and its medical applications have produced in our generation. This challenge is most clearly visible at the beginning and the end of life. At both ends of the spectrum of life—the mystery of conception and the mystery of death—our generation has developed capacities to intervene in the natural order in ways which earlier generations would have thought belonged solely to God. Today, from genetics through embryology to the care of the aged and the terminally ill, we confront the potential of shaping the beginning of life, making choices about its development, and sustaining it by life support systems.

At both ends of the spectrum of life the technological challenge has been experienced as a blessing and a burden. Some discoveries help us to enhance life expectancy, to correct inherited genetic defects, and to relieve pain and suffering. But the new technologies have also placed in human hands decisions about life and death for which there is little human experience to guide our choices.

As Pope John Paul II has often noted, the danger of our day is that we will use our technological genius to erode human dignity rather than to enhance it. The danger is that our choices will be dominated by technology rather than directed by human wisdom and the light of faith. Precisely for this reason, the Congregation for the Doctrine of the Faith last year issued an "Instruction on Respect for Human Life in Its Origins and on the Dignity of Procreation," which addresses the moral implications of some of the biomedical techniques which now make it possible to intervene in the initial phase of the life of a human being and in the very processes of procreation.

These questions of technology, life, and death are not, however, limited to the world of science and medicine. The unique moral character of our day is demonstrated by the linkage between the "micro-questions" of medical ethics and the "macro-questions" of war and peace in the nuclear age. The link between these two quite different areas of human existence is the technological revolution which has unlocked the genetic code and unleashed the power of the atom within the space of a lifetime. The technological challenge is part of the peace challenge: how to keep the peace in an age when the instruments of war can threaten the very fabric of human existence as a whole.

Technology provides the material link between the "micro" and the "macro" threats to life in our time. The moral link is the unique value of human life. In very different settings—in the laboratory and in the life of nations—our generation is called to protect the fragile fabric of human dignity against unprecedented dangers. Seeing the relationship—the connection—between these two areas of contemporary life is what started my reflection on the consistent ethic. In a special way, my chairmanship of the bishops' committee which drafted *The Challenge of Peace* and the committee presently writing the report on the moral evaluation of deterrence policy, along with my chairmanship of the bishops' Pro-Life Committee, helped me to see the common challenge of technology for life and death in the two areas I have just described.

The *justice* challenge poses a different but related set of questions. It calls us to expand our moral concern beyond the question of protecting life from attack to promoting and enhancing the dignity of human life in society. The justice challenge is how to build a society which provides the necessary material and moral support for every human being to realize his or her God-given dignity. As Christians, aware of the limits of human nature and the impact of sin on human affairs, we know that this work of shaping a humane society is a never-ending task. But this sober conviction that perfect justice is a characteristic of the completed reign of God does not mean that progress toward the conditions of the Kingdom is impossible. The reign of God is present when human dignity is defended and human rights are protected. The justice challenge calls us to this effort.

In the late 1980s the justice challenge is evident on several fronts:

- twenty years after the death of Dr. Martin Luther King, Jr., there are very disturbing signs of increased racial tension in the land;
- after almost a decade of neglect our housing problem yields the tragedy of the homeless and the looming catastrophe of more homeless families (just last week the Holy See's Commission on Justice and Peace issued a document entitled, *What Have You Done to Your Homeless Brother? The Church and the Housing Problem,* which addresses this worldwide problem);
- on our farms and outside our factories, there is still too much evidence that a decade of economic growth and a lower rate of unemployment still have left too many vulnerable to economic devastation.

Each of these challenges—technology, peace, and justice—has its own inner complexity. Each must be addressed on its own terms by slow, patient work. No one can do everything, and I am sure that you feel closer, experientially and vocationally, to some of the issues I have described than to others.

The consistent ethic recognizes the need for specific approaches to concrete issues, but it also raises a broader question. Are the Church and society well served by keeping these questions in isolated sectors of life and ministry? Do we not learn something about the personal and social challenge of this moment in history by consciously connecting what is usually addressed separately?

The consistent ethic sees the convergence of these multiple and diverse challenges as a time of opportunity. The opportunity resides in the character of Catholic moral teaching and in the capacity of the Church to respond to multiple challenges under the guidance of a coherent moral vision.

The concept of the consistent ethic is based upon two characteristics of Catholic teaching: its scope and its structure. The scope of Catholic teaching is broad enough to encompass the three distinct challenges I have outlined. We are simultaneously committed to a diverse set of objectives which many individuals and institutions in U. S. society find irreconcilable. We are committed to reversing *Roe vs. Wade* and reversing the arms race. We are convinced that we cannot have a just and compassionate society unless our care extends to both sides of the line of birth: we must protect the basic right to life and, at the same time, promote the associated rights of nutrition, housing, and health care which enhance the lives we have saved.

The scope of a comprehensive ethic is matched by a systematic structure of moral argument. It is not sufficient to face these three challenges of technology, peace, and justice only with good intentions. The problems posed in each area are inherently complex, and, on a number of these issues—from the Strategic Defense Initiative to health insurance to amniocentesis—U. S. society is deeply divided. A broad moral concern must be based upon solid moral analysis. A systematic moral tradition is necessary to call the ecclesial community to a position and then to project a position in the civil debate.

The Catholic moral tradition is both *simple* and *sophisticated*. It is simple in terms of its basic purpose: the protection and promotion of human dignity, understood as a reflection of the image of God within us. Catholic social ethics, medical ethics, and sexual ethics are all rooted in the nature and dignity of the person. This is the simple but fundamental starting point, for example, for documents as different in content as the two pastoral letters of the U. S. bishops on social ethics (war and peace, and the economy) and the Holy See's instruction last year on medical ethics (to which I referred a moment ago). Obviously, this single starting point is then developed in a highly systematic and *sophisticated* fashion so as to address in a detailed way the technological, peace, and justice challenges of our day.

The idea of the consistent ethic is to draw upon the scope and structure of the Catholic moral vision to confront the full range of questions endangering human dignity today. The idea must be linked to a community—a constituency—which holds and embodies the vision. A vision without a community is not capable of influence. A vision tied to a committed community is the first prerequisite of serious social impact. Hence, it is necessary now to examine how the idea of the consistent ethic has engaged the life of the ecclesial community.

The Consistent Ethic in the Church

In proposing the consistent ethic concept in 1983, I said that I wished to begin a discussion, not end one. In the four years since that first lecture on the topic, my hope for careful consideration of the idea has been realized. The concept has acted as a catalyst; it started a process. And the product of that process has been a vigorous discussion within the Catholic community about the meaning of the consistent ethic of life and its potential in the Church and in civil society. The response, of course, has not meant unanimous agreement with the idea or its implications. But the process as a whole has produced a solid consensus in support of the idea, even though it is not yet a finished design in my mind or in the minds of its supporters. One may point to several levels of the life of the Church where the consistent ethic has had a useful impact.

First, the idea is a concept in moral theology, so the response of the theological community is very important. The attention given to explaining and refining the idea in theological journals and in a recent symposium at Loyola University in Chicago has been a crucial contribution to shaping an ecclesial consensus on the concept. As always, the doubts and reservations theologians have about an idea may be as helpful as their support, because an idea which is this far-reaching requires development.

Second, a most important step has been the explicit incorporation of the consistent ethic theme into the pro-life activities of the National Conference of Catholic Bishops. The use of this concept by the episcopal conference gives us a framework within which we may pursue the multifaceted agenda of the bishops at the national level.

Third, I am aware that the consistent ethic has been used creatively and extensively by you who labor in the Church's social ministry. The framework of the consistent ethic has made it possible to incorporate some of our key social themes in the Church's wider ministry. In some places it has served as a means of bridging pro-life and other social justice concerns. I am aware, here in the Washington and Baltimore Archdioceses, of the legislative network which has effectively pressed the case for the unborn, then successfully achieved a reallocation of the state budget on behalf of the poor, and also linked these concerns with national advocacy to restrain defense spending. Other such efforts at the level of dioceses, state Catholic conferences, and religious communities have demonstrated that the consistent ethic is an idea with a constituency.

Finally, I would like to call attention to two developments beyond the Catholic community which point to the as yet unrealized potential of the consistent ethic. First, an ecumenical organization *Justlife* has been formed by Catholics and Protestants to support the consistent ethic concept. Second, the recent *Times-Mirror* public attitude survey has shown a solid and intriguing pattern of a constituency which joins a liberal social justice consensus and opposition to liberalized abortion.

Both the ecumenical initiative and the secular trend create a context within which the consistent ethic can provide a viable social agenda. This is a potential yet to be realized; it is hardly a sure thing. But all these developments inside and outside the Church point to my final point: the public policy potential of the consistent ethic.

The Idea, the Community, and Public Policy

It is useful to note from the beginning of this discussion that a primary purpose of the consistent ethic theme has been to increase the Church's public policy effectiveness in the United States. The consistent ethic provides a framework within which a range of policy issues may be pursued in a coordinated fashion. It also provides a method for establishing priorities among these many issues. Finally, it provides a method for resolving conflicts at the tactical level when some issues are in conflict.

The consistent ethic's public policy focus expresses the strong social orientation of all Catholic moral theology. It is not the position of this tradition that all moral values and principles should be legislated. But every stream of moral thinking which feeds into the consistent ethic—social ethics, medical ethics, sexual ethics—is based on the conviction that some key values, principles, and practices must be protected and promoted by law and public policy.

That is why we believe it is inadequate merely to teach that cultural, sexual, and racial discrimination are wrong; it is also necessary to outlaw discrimination in civil law. We are morally convinced that a just wage is needed to protect human dignity; but we also know that minimum wage laws are absolutely necessary. We are convinced that protection for unborn children cannot rely only upon moral persuasion; their lives must be protected, as our lives are, by the civil law.

These issues I have just cited as examples are among the priority items on the episcopal conference's legislative agenda. To fill out the consistent ethic would require a detailed listing of issues, but I do not think that would be the best use of our time this evening.

It is wiser, I believe, to highlight the several roles which the consistent ethic can play in public advocacy. First, it may and should be used nationally and locally. Particularly in this meeting, the national and local possibilities are clear. You are being briefed on the USCC national legislative agenda which is set in terms of the consistent ethic. But the same framework may be given different content at the local or diocesan level. The consistent ethic is not a rigid set of specific issues. It is a method for coordinating a spectrum of issues; and there are local issues which belong in the consistent ethic.

Second, the consistent ethic provides a grid for assessing party platforms and the records of candidates for public office. It is a broad-based set of criteria. Properly used, the consistent ethic will refute decisively claims that we are a "one-issue" constituency. The essence of the consistent ethic argument is that no one issue can exhaust the moral significance of our public policy concerns.

Third, the consistent ethic provides the scope of moral vision which allows the Church to address broad policy issues embodying several distinct moral concerns. Perhaps the best example is the federal budget. The budget, in a very real sense, is a moral document; it puts a price tag on what we value as a nation. The budget is also, of course, a complex technical document which is at the center of our national life.

The battle over the budget, a perennially important political question, has taken on new moral intensity in a time of persistent deficits. The deficits impose a straitjacket on the budget process: to vote funds in one place is to take them away from other concerns. There is little spare change in the U. S. Treasury to adjudicate the conflict in the policy process.

Faced with this policy problem, the consistent ethic provides a framework for addressing the central budgetary trade-off—defense spending vs. social spending—and it also provides a basis for lifting up specific issues with high moral content.

A good example, in my judgment, of the kind of issues which may be effectively highlighted by the consistent ethic is the needs of children. In the last four years a series of studies have demonstrated that the most fragile members of our society, children, are also the least protected. From infant mortality statistics—which place us near the bottom of industrialized countries—to health care, to housing—children's lives are under assault in our culture.

A century ago Dostoevsky said that the death of an innocent child was enough to destroy belief in God. Less dramatically, the suffering of innocent children is enough to indict the social priorities of a wealthy society. There is a consensus developing from the business community, to politicians, to child advocacy groups that a major coordinated effort on behalf of children is both a moral imperative and a national political necessity. Spending on children is cost-effective in the long run. But it requires wisdom and courage to mount the effort to spend now—even with deficits—on this solid investment in our nation's future.

The consistent ethic is anchored in a concern for unborn children; it is shaped in terms of the strong Catholic commitment to the family; and it is directed toward a preferential concern for the poor. All of these themes may be placed in support of a coherent, coordinated strategy to enhance the life of children from conception through high school graduation.

This example has a moral priority and a strong political potential, but it is only part of the larger vision we are invited to pursue through the consistent ethic. I am committed to this moral vision and committed to building a constituency for it. Your positions in dioceses across the country make you uniquely valuable allies. I pledge my support to your work and, along with my fellow bishops, I know we can count on the continuing high quality and deep dedication of your work. Together, we have an opportunity to share the reality of the consistent ethic with the society we are called to serve.

21.

EUTHANASIA

Ethical and Legal Challenges

CENTER FOR CLINICAL MEDICAL ETHICS,
UNIVERSITY OF CHICAGO HOSPITAL,
MAY 26, 1988

It is a pleasure for me to return to the University of Chicago and, in particular, to this prestigious medical center. I am very grateful to the Center for Clinical Medical Ethics for inviting me to give this address. Dr. Mark Siegler contacted me at a time when I was already deeply concerned about recent efforts to legalize euthanasia. I have been eager to participate more actively in the public discussion about this new challenge in our society.

Since I accepted his invitation, the issue has become even more pressing, especially in the debate that has followed the publication of the article, "It's Over, Debbie," in the *Journal of the American Medical Association.* And so, I assure you that I look forward to the responses and the discussion which will follow my presentation, as well as the colloquium later this afternoon.

My reflections will have four parts. First, I will explore the pluralistic context of the discussion of the public policy dimensions of euthanasia. Second, I will trace some of the reasons why euthanasia or assisted suicide has become a matter of current debate. Third, I will outline a moral or ethical perspective on euthanasia. And fourth, I will suggest how we might best respond to this challenge.

Euthanasia: A Platter of Public Policy

One of the hallmarks of our democratic system of government and our social environment here in the United States is the fact that a plurality of views informs our public discourse regarding fundamental human questions. At times, these views flow from religious beliefs. At other times, they derive from philosophical or pragmatic judgments about the meaning and purpose of life.

This pluralism is the result of the free speech accorded by the Constitution to each citizen as well as the right both to freely exercise one's religion and to practice no religion. But this constitutionally protected pluralism has not been bought at the price of excluding religious or moral values from the public life of the nation. On the contrary, the goal of the American system has been to provide space for a moral or religious substance in our society.

Indeed, in our pluralistic society we must decide how those who have such beliefs or ethical principles may appropriately participate in the development of public policy. In my view, positions that are informed by particular religious beliefs or philosophical assumptions need to be translated into commonly agreed-upon language, arguments, and categories before they can become the moral or ethical foundations for key public policy choices.

I am speaking here of *public* policy decisions. Because of the nature of our government and our social order, we have determined that certain areas of human life—although they have important ethical or moral dimensions—are not immediately or necessarily appropriate subject matter for public policies. Although the premises or foundations for public policy and civil law ought to be rooted in an ethical perspective, the scope of law and public policy is limited, and its purpose is not the moralization of society. Public policy decisions and civil statutes address primarily external acts and values that affect the common good.

But how do we determine which aspects of our life—whether social or personal—are subject to public policy decisions? A leading Catholic theoretician in this area, the late Father John Courtney Murray, argued that an issue was related to public policy if it affected the public order of society. And public order, in turn, encompassed three goods: public peace, the essential protection of human rights, and commonly accepted standards of moral behavior in a community.

Whether a given issue should be interpreted as belonging to public morality is not always self-evident. A rationally persuasive case must be made that an action violates the rights of another or that the consequences of actions on a given issue are so important to society that the authority of the state ought to be invoked, through public policy or civil statute, to govern personal and group behavior. Obviously, in a pluralistic society, arriving at a consensus on what pertains to public policy is never easy. But we have been able to achieve such consensus in the past by a process of dialogue, decision-making, and review of our decisions.

Our nation has developed its public policy and civil law through dialogue—first of all, about what aspects of human behavior ought to be regulated by public policy decisions and, then, about which ethical or moral perspective should guide the development of such policies. As a society, our constitutional structure and our historical experience indicate that it is appropriate for persons with a religiously or philosophically informed perspective to participate in these discussions. Moreover, we have learned that the best way to facilitate this participation is by translating religious or philosophical views into a common language that can guide and inform public policy decisions.

In regard to euthanasia or assisted suicide, the kind of decision-making which I have just described has already taken place. Long ago our predecessors determined that the taking of innocent life was contrary to the public good—even if it is done to alleviate pain or suffering. And consequently, it has been judged as being in the best interest of society to stop a person who is trying to jump from a bridge, and to impose civil penalties on those who engage in euthanasia or assist a person in suicide.

This public policy decision, informed by an ethical or moral understanding of the nature and meaning of human life, is being challenged today on two fronts. First, does the state have any interest in this matter, or should it be left up to the individual? Second, is euthanasia truly contrary to the public good?

Why the Movement to Legalize Euthanasia?

I now wish to turn to my second area of concern: Why is there a movement today to change our public policy on this matter? In addressing this question, we are not merely dealing with the case of "Debbie" and her doctor. There is a growing debate in our land about euthanasia and assisted suicide. There has been, for example, a special television report about the case of a Florida husband who killed his wife who had Alzheimer's disease.

Moreover, there was the California initiative that sought not only to reaffirm the right to withdraw life-sustaining procedures but also to secure the right to provide "aid in dying" through any medical procedure that would terminate life "swiftly, painlessly, and humanely." While the sponsors lacked more than 100,000 signatures to get this issue on the November ballot, they attribute this to a lack of time to organize the drive rather than the opposition of citizens. And they have indicated they will try again.

But why are we hearing this call to alter what has been a fundamental tenet of our society? We may identify three sources, among others, for this advocacy of change. While these three sources or movements may not afford a total explanation for this phenomenon, they provide a way to begin to analyze it.

Medical

The first movement flows from the world of medicine and medical technology. For centuries, the physician and others in the health care professions have had, as an essential aspect of their identity and mission, the responsibility to heal and preserve life. That responsibility has entered a new era with the development of medicines and technologies that have given physicians previously unknown capabilities in this area. We are grateful, indeed, for the great good which these advancements have brought to the human family.

This good, however, has not been an unmixed blessing. We know that it is fairly easy for technology or medicine to become an end in itself, and for life to be preserved when, in fact, death should be allowed to happen. This possible domination of technology over the proper course of life has left many people fearful of being kept alive in an inhumane fashion. And this fear has led some to say to their loved ones: "Do whatever you must, but do not let me live that way." The fear, then, of the pain and discomfort of a life prolonged inappropriately has led to an erosion of the natural instinct to preserve one's own life.

Legal

The second cause of the movement towards euthanasia involves two aspects of the legal dimension of our society. First, we have become a "contentious" society. The right to redress a wrong done to a person by another is now being actualized as it has never been before in our society. As you know, the medical profession and the health care industry have experienced countless lawsuits and settlements that make them fearful of future damages.

The result has been that, in certain critical decisions involving living and dying, many perceive that the focus of concern may no longer be the good of the patient—as that has been traditionally understood by our Judeo-Christian moral tradition. Instead, the concern will be whatever will best protect the physician and the health care institution from legal action. Many point out that decisions, which formerly have been made by the physician and the patient or the patient's family, are now made by legal counsel or the court.

What has been the result? Not only have people come to fear technology, they also fear losing a fundamental right—the right to self-determination. The combination of these two fears—the fear of the inappropriate use of medical technology and the loss of self-determination—have joined another movement in our society: the expanding notion of the right of privacy.

There is not time in this presentation to elaborate upon what Robert Bellah and others have said recently—that we have lost a sense of community in our society and witnessed the rise of an exaggerated concept of individualism. My pastoral experience confirms that there is some truth in their observations. Translated into the world of law, this separation of the individual from a community context has been expressed in a growing number of legal decisions that have expanded the notion of the right to privacy to such an issue as the taking of prenatal life.

It is but a next logical step to conclude that the individual should be autonomous in determining matters pertaining to the *end* of life. In our contemporary society an exaggerated *individualism* replaces concern and responsibility for the *common good*. This, in turn, becomes a welcome environment to discuss the fear of technology and the loss of self-determination. And in the light of this momentum, it is understandable that persons who ask family or friends to keep them from an unseemly death would think that those fulfilling this wish should not be prosecuted for doing a "good deed."

Cultural

With this consideration of the rise of individualism, and its legal expression, we come face to face with the third movement—our culture itself. Again, I will only be able to use broad strokes to describe a complex phenomenon under three headings: our culture's fixation on youth, our loss of meaning and consequent fear of suffering and death, and our experience of diminishing resources.

It is no secret that our society has become fairly fixated on youth and health. We seek to delay the effects of aging, and the pursuit of being healthy has become a significant growth industry. It is striking that this is occurring when more and more of our citizens are becoming older and their health more fragile. This contrast between our idealized notions and real life can have two effects. Those who are older and not so healthy may question whether they ought to continue living. And those who are younger and supposedly healthy may reject those who remind them of their own human frailty.

Likewise, our society is raising profound questions about the ultimate meaning of life. While it had once been assumed that pain and sacrifice were part of the human experience and contributed to the meaning of life, many would question that assumption today. An ethos of instant gratification does not suffer pain or sacrifice easily. A world whose meaning is centered in a seemingly unlimited present moment may interpret death as a purely human event, devoid of any relationship to a divinity who sustains a truly endless eternity.

Finally, living in the shadow of the earlier oil embargo and the more recent Space Shuttle disaster, our society has come face to face with the constraints of physical and intellectual resources. The American myth of the ever-expanding horizon which can be conquered by determination and skill has been shattered. Wherever we turn, we are faced with hard choices about the allocation of resources and the setting of individual and national priorities.

These three aspects of our culture, and others, are the context of the current discussion of euthanasia. A culture that does not prize the wisdom of aging and feels intimidated by ill health will be less likely to oppose the ending of an aged or infirm life. A culture that is devoid of a vision of values that transcend time and individual choice will be more likely to feel no discomfort with an immediate solution. And a culture of youth and immediacy will be uncomfortable with the allocation of precious fiscal and health resources to those who are marginal or sick.

When this third movement encounters the first two, then we should not be surprised by the fact that some are calling for a change in our public policy—a change that would legalize euthanasia. But does this mean we must accept what is being proposed?

Why Oppose Euthanasia?

This leads me to my third subject: an ethical or moral perspective that can serve as the foundation for public policy development. I will discuss two issues here: the argument against euthanasia, and why this should be a matter for public policy.

The foundation of my position on euthanasia is to be found in what I have described as a consistent ethic of life. As you may know, over the last four and a half years I have articulated the need for a consistent ethic of life. I have proposed it as a comprehensive concept and a strategy which will help Catholics and other people of good will to influence more effectively the development of public policy in our nation.

The grounding principle for this ethic is found in the Judeo-Christian heritage which has played such an influential role in the formation of our national ethos. In this religious tradition, the meaning of human life is grounded in the fact that it is sacred because God is its origin and its destiny. Many other people of good will also accept the basic premise that human life has a distinctive dignity and meaning or purpose, and that innocent human life must not be directly attacked, threatened, or diminished. They, too, argue that, because of the privileged meaning of human life, we are responsible to steward, protect, and nurture it.

The second principle which informs the development of the consistent ethic is the belief that human life is also social in nature. We do not come into being to live alone, but to move from the dependency of prenatal existence and infancy to the interrelatedness of adulthood. To be human is to be social, and those relationships, structures, and institutions which support us as individuals and as a community are an essential aspect of human life.

If one accepts these two principles about human life, then one may argue that two precepts or obligations necessarily flow from them. The first is that, as individuals and as a society, we have the *positive* obligation to protect life. The second precept is that we have the *negative* obligation not to destroy or injure human life directly, especially the life of the innocent and vulnerable.

This perspective about life and the precepts just mentioned were, in effect, recognized by and incorporated into our Anglo-Saxon common law tradition. Consequently, it has been reasoned that the protection of innocent life—and, therefore, opposition to abortion, murder, suicide, and euthanasia—pertains to the common good of society. As social beings, we cannot violate one of the constitutive goods of life. Consequently, our legal tradition has developed statutes that outlaw murder and euthanasia. In other words, our tradition has held that euthanasia is wrong because it involves a direct attack on innocent human life. And it is a matter of public policy because it involves a violation of a fundamental human good.

Having laid out the principles, let us turn now to the arguments being advanced against this traditional perspective.

The first argument attacks the premise that the obligation to protect and nurture human life applies to life that is painful and unable to achieve its full human potential. Although I will elaborate on this in the last section of my presentation, I wish to mention here that our first response to this line of reasoning must be—to use an analogy from the teaching of grammar—to parse the question and make clear what we are saying when we uphold the obligation to protect and nurture human life, even when it is painful or dying.

We are saying that those whose lives have, in fact, entered the dying process should be helped to live the remainder of their lives with full human dignity and with as little pain as possible. We also are saying that those measures which we would consider to be ethically extraordinary need not be used to prolong life. We also are saying that, when considered on a case-by-case basis and in light of our ethical principles, there are situations when we can withdraw what have become useless or burdensome measures.

In this nuanced context, we are opposed to creating *a priori* categories of persons whose lives no longer need be protected, where life is no longer seen as being sacred and inviolable. Once we begin saying that a certain category of persons or a specific individual—for whatever reason, and whether the person is conscious or unconscious—no longer possesses human dignity, then we have assumed a prerogative which belongs only to God. Human rights may then be given or withdrawn as arbitrarily as they were in the Third Reich of yesterday or in South Africa today. The dignity of innocent life is absolute; it cannot be violated.

The second argument pertains to the development of public policy. Some argue that one may hold to this line of moral reasoning, but that the actual determination of how to end life should be left to the individual involved. The state has no interest in what is essentially a private decision.

As I indicated earlier, the perspective which supports this line of reasoning is fundamentally flawed. Human beings are meant to live in community. Social order is not an enemy but a necessary good that protects personal and social life. Kept in proper balance, the tension between personal rights and social goods can be healthy. And nowhere is this more evident than in matters pertaining to the defense and enhancement of life itself. Neither individuals nor society can long survive when respect for the inviolability of life is diminished. It is for this reason that the protection of innocent life must be understood as part of the public order of society. As such, it legitimately fits within the scope of civil law. The state has a moral and legal interest in protecting innocent life from the moment of conception to natural death.

We live in an age when violence has become part of our national fabric. We bury young people killed in gang violence. We read about persons who kill others in a dispute about which television program to watch. Is this *good* for us as individuals or as a society? No!

What would we be suggesting to one another and to our society, if, seemingly with the best of motives, we were to say that those who are sick, infirm, or unconscious may be killed? How could we allege that such actions would not affect us individually and collectively? We may never agree to this kind of privatization of life because, if we were to do so, we would undermine our ability to live in community. Life is both a private and a public good, and, therefore, social legislation to defend and protect it is both appropriate and necessary.

What Are We To Do Next?

Having argued against euthanasia and attempts to legalize it, what are we to do next?

We cannot pretend that "It's Over, Debbie" and the California initiative have not happened. Like it or not, the issue of euthanasia has become a question that will be answered, among other places, in the oncology wards and the legislatures of our land. And it will not be enough for those who oppose this movement merely to speak out against it. We should not yield the "high ground" of the language of compassion and personal rights to those whose views we oppose. On the contrary, in a manner faithful to our pluralistic heritage, we must engage this challenge forthrightly and persuasively. I would like to propose some of the ways in which we might do this.

First, it is important for us to address the sense of powerlessness which many people experience in regard to the contemporary practice of medicine. While the catchphrase "patient as person" is a helpful guide in this matter, we have to extend this concept more aggressively into the world of critical and terminal illness where the patient is frailest and most vulnerable. We must also face our own fear of death and learn to provide for those who are dying or critically ill in a way that preserves their dignity and ennobles them.

For example, in light of available medicines, is it conscionable that a dying patient should unwillingly suffer great pain today? I think not. Moreover, is it necessary for so many patients to die on a machine? Resolving such questions may require finding ways to provide the necessary funding, through the allocation of insurance and public monies, to establish and maintain hospice units in hospitals as well as to provide hospice programs in patients' homes. In this way we can eliminate many of the legitimate concerns that may motivate people to consider euthanasia—which otherwise would be unacceptable to them and society.

Second, we must face in a forthright manner the ethical and legal issues pertaining to the initiation and/or cessation of medical procedures that are ethically "extraordinary," and thus not morally obligatory. I refer to those procedures that have no reasonable hope of success, that are not likely to produce significant benefit for the patient, and that the Catholic tradition considers to be extremely burdensome, that is, extremely painful and costly. As citizens and leaders in our society, we must engage our legislatures and judicial system in a dialogue to find ways to ensure that appropriate medical decisions are made by patients or their surrogates, in consultation with the physician and others. If this process is improved, fewer physicians and health care institutions may feel a need to refer these decisions to the courts out of fear of legal liability.

Third, the controverted question of the artificial provision of nutrition and hydration for several categories of patients needs to be resolved. We cannot accept a policy that would open the door to euthanasia by creating categories of patients whose lives can be considered of no value merely because they are not conscious. We also may not develop a policy to keep alive those who should be allowed a natural death, that is, those who are terminally ill, or to preclude a decision—informed by our ethical principles and on a case-by-case basis—that the artificial provision of nutrition and hydration has become useless or unduly burdensome.

I know that this is a very complex issue. I am convinced that, from a moral point of view, the essential bond between food, water, and life argues convincingly for the presumption that nutrition and hydration should always be provided. But I am also convinced that we are not *morally* obliged to do everything that is *technically* possible. In other words, there are cases where we would not be obliged artificially to provide nutrition and hydration. The challenge is to develop a nuanced public policy to protect against an attitude that could erode respect for the inviolable dignity of human life. If we do not resolve this critical issue in a way that resonates with the common sense of people of good will, then we may contribute to the sense of desperation that will lead people to consider euthanasia as an alternative solution to the problem.

Fourth, we will have to assess the current allocation of medical resources. Significant funds are spent on the care of the elderly and the critically ill. At the same time our nation, especially in certain communities like Chicago, has a poor track record in prenatal care and infant mortality. Similarly, many people in our society do not have access to needed health care, whether it be curative or preventive, because they cannot afford health insurance.

In light of these facts, it is understandable that some argue that we should rearrange our health care priorities and reduce the amount of money spent on the elderly and certain categories of illness. Before we engage in a national debate on such a proposal, however, we must ask a prior question. Are we, in fact, spending too *much* on the elderly, or are we spending too *little* on all health care?

To say it another way, are we spending too much of our financial resources on certain patients, or are our overall allocations for health care too limited? In attempting to answer these questions, we encounter a more basic set of questions—our national priorities. I mention this, not to confuse the discussion about euthanasia, but to point out that the legalization of euthanasia is not the proper way to solve the problem of inadequate care for the poor and the unborn.

Fifth, as a society we will have to address the complex issue of the separation of the individual from the community. Religious leaders must initiate a dialogue with philosophers, anthropologists, and legal scholars to discern how we can preserve the rights of the individual without eroding or destroying our social nature. We need to find a new balance between these two dimensions of human life—a balance suitable to a society in which the population is more educated and mobile, but also more afraid and isolated.

Similarly, we will not successfully oppose the legalization of euthanasia if we cannot call forth from the depths of our national psyche those values which are constitutive of the American Dream. The interaction of our political heritage and our religious traditions can provide a response to the contemporary search for meaning—a response that will recognize the wisdom of the elderly and provide a broader perspective for the problem of pain and suffering.

Sixth, and finally, we must mobilize a common effort. In dialogues such as this, we need to confront the issue directly and help form a national consensus in favor of the presumption that the state has a compelling interest in opposing euthanasia. The basis for such a consensus is already present in our land. It is our task to bring it to the fore so that it truly can be said that, as citizens, we are entitled to life and need not fear that innocent life will ever be taken.

22.

THE CONSISTENT ETHIC AND ITS PUBLIC POLICY CONSEQUENCES

CONSISTENT ETHIC OF LIFE CONFERENCE,
CATHOLIC CONFERENCE OF OHIO,
JUNE 4, 1988

I am grateful for this opportunity to address you on "The Consistent Ethic and Its Public Policy Consequences," a topic of special interest during this year of a national election campaign. The opportunity which this topic provides has two dimensions: first, to address a crucial but still undeveloped part of the consistent ethic of life—its public application; and second, to engage with you in a joint reflection on how the policy implications of the consistent ethic may be advanced.

To initiate this reflection, I will first review the origins of the concept of the consistent ethic, then analyze its development in the Church, and, finally, examine its public policy potential in U. S. society.

The Origins of the Idea

One way to explain the origins of the consistent ethic is to see it as an expression of the model of social teaching found in the *Pastoral Constitution on the Church in the Modern World* of the Second Vatican Council. This conciliar document, which stands as the *magna carta* of social ministry since Vatican II, asserted that the social task of the Church in the modern world is to read the signs of the times and to interpret them in light of the gospel. The idea of the consistent ethic arose for me in precisely this way.

It is possible to distinguish three challenges in the contemporary signs of the times which pose different but interrelated questions for the Church's social ministry. There is the *technological* challenge, the *peace* challenge, and the *justice* challenge. The three must be interpreted in light of the gospel truth about the sacredness of human life and the obligations of Christians to stand for life.

The *technological* challenge arises from the unique capacities which contemporary science and its medical applications have produced in our generation. This challenge is most clearly visible at the beginning and the end of life. At both ends of the spectrum of life—the mystery of conception and the mystery of death—our generation has developed capacities to intervene in the natural order in ways which earlier generations would have thought belonged solely to God. Today, from genetics through embryology to the care of the aged and the terminally ill, we confront the potential of shaping the beginning of life, making choices about its development, and sustaining it by life support systems.

At both ends of the spectrum of life the technological challenge has been experienced as a blessing and a burden. Some discoveries help us to enhance life expectancy, to correct inherited genetic defects, and to relieve pain and suffering. But the new technologies have also placed in human hands decisions about life and death for which there is little human experience to guide our choices.

As Pope John Paul II has often noted, the danger of our day is that we will use our technological genius to erode human dignity rather than to enhance it. The danger is that our choices will be dominated by technology rather than directed by human wisdom and the light of faith. Precisely for this reason, the Congregation for the Doctrine of the Faith last year issued an "Instruction on Respect for Human Life in Its Origins and on the Dignity of Procreation," which addresses the moral implications of some of the biomedical techniques which now make it possible to intervene in the initial phase of the life of a human being and in the very processes of procreation.

These questions of technology, life, and death are not, however, limited to the world of science and medicine. The unique moral character of our day is demonstrated by the linkage between the "micro-questions" of medical ethics and the "macro-questions" of war and peace in the nuclear age. The link between these two quite different areas of human existence is the technological revolution which has unlocked the genetic code and unleashed the power of the atom within the space of a lifetime. The technological challenge is part of the peace challenge: how to keep the peace in an age when the instruments of war can threaten the very fabric of human existence as a whole.

Technology provides the material link between the "micro" and the "macro" threats to life in our time. The moral link is the unique value of human life. In very different settings—in the laboratory and in the life of nations—our generation is called to protect the fragile fabric of human dignity against unprecedented dangers. Seeing the relationship—the connection—between these two areas of contemporary life is what started my reflection on the consistent ethic. In a special way, my chairmanship of the bishops' committee which drafted *The Challenge of Peace* and the committee presently completing the report on the moral evaluation of deterrence policy, along with my chairmanship of the bishops' Pro-Life Committee, helped me to see the common challenge of technology for life and death in the two areas I have just described.

The justice challenge poses a different but related set of questions. It calls us to expand our moral concern beyond the question of protecting life from attack to promoting and enhancing the dignity of human life in society. The justice challenge is how to build a society which provides the necessary material and moral support for every human being to realize his or her God-given dignity. As Christians, aware of the limits of human nature and the impact of sin on human affairs, we know that this work of shaping a humane society is a never-ending task. But this sober conviction that perfect justice is a characteristic of the completed reign of God does not mean that progress toward the conditions of the Kingdom is impossible. The reign of God is present when human dignity is defended and human rights are protected. The justice challenge calls us to this effort.

In the late 1980s the justice challenge is evident on several fronts:
- twenty years after the death of Dr. Martin Luther King, Jr., there are very disturbing signs of increased racial tension in the land;
- after almost a decade of neglect our housing problem yields the tragedy of the homeless and the looming catastrophe of more homeless families (last February the Holy See's Commission on Justice and Peace issued a document entitled, *What Have You Done to Your Homeless Brother? The Church and the Housing Problem*, which addresses this worldwide problem);
- on our farms and outside our factories, there is still too much evidence that a decade of economic growth and a lower rate of unemployment still have left too many vulnerable to economic devastation.

Each of these challenges—technology, peace, and justice—has its own inner complexity. Each must be addressed on its own terms by slow, patient work. No one can do everything, and I am sure that you feel closer, experientially and vocationally, to some of the issues I have described than to others.

The consistent ethic of life recognizes the need for specific approaches to concrete issues, but it also raises a broader question. Are the Church and society well served by keeping these questions in isolated sectors of life and ministry? Do we not learn something about the personal and social challenge of this moment in history by consciously connecting what is usually addressed separately?

The consistent ethic sees the convergence of these multiple and diverse challenges as a time of opportunity. The opportunity resides in the character of Catholic moral teaching and in the capacity of the Church to respond to multiple challenges under the guidance of a coherent moral vision.

The concept of the consistent ethic is based upon two characteristics of Catholic teaching: its scope and its structure. The scope of Catholic teaching is broad enough to encompass the three distinct challenges I have outlined. We are simultaneously committed to a diverse set of objectives which many individuals and institutions in U. S. society find irreconcilable. We are committed to reversing *Roe vs. Wade* and reversing the arms race.

We are convinced that we cannot have a just and compassionate society unless our care extends to both sides of the line of birth: We must protect the basic right to life and, at the same time, promote the associated rights of nutrition, housing, and health care which enhance the lives we have saved.

The scope of a comprehensive ethic is matched by a systematic structure of moral argument. It is not sufficient to face these three challenges of technology, peace, and justice only with good intentions. The problems posed in each area are inherently complex, and, on a number of these issues—from the Strategic Defense Initiative to health insurance to amniocentesis—U. S. society is deeply divided. A broad moral concern must be based upon solid moral analysis. A systematic moral tradition is necessary to call the ecclesial community to a position and then to project a position in the civil debate.

The Catholic moral tradition is both *simple* and *sophisticated*. It is *simple* in terms of its basic purpose: the protection and promotion of human dignity, understood as a reflection of the image of God within us. Catholic social ethics, medical ethics, and sexual ethics are all rooted in the nature and dignity of the person. This is the simple but fundamental starting point, for example, for documents as different in content as the two pastoral letters of the U. S. bishops on social ethics (war and peace, and the economy) and the Holy See's Instruction last year on medical ethics (to which I referred a moment ago). Obviously, this single starting point is then developed in a highly systematic and *sophisticated* fashion so as to address in a detailed way the technological, peace, and justice challenges of our day.

The idea of the consistent ethic is to draw upon the scope and structure of the Catholic moral vision to confront the full range of questions endangering human dignity today. The idea must be linked to a community—a constituency—which holds and embodies the vision. A vision without a community is not capable of influence. A vision tied to a committed community is the first prerequisite of serious social impact. Hence, it is necessary now to examine how the idea of the consistent ethic has engaged the life of the ecclesial community.

The Consistent Ethic in the Church

In proposing the consistent ethic concept in 1983, I said that I wished to begin a discussion, not end one. In the four years since that first lecture on the topic, my hope for careful consideration of the idea has been realized. The concept has acted as a catalyst; it started a process. And the product of that process has been a vigorous discussion within the Catholic community about the meaning of the consistent ethic of life and its potential in the Church and in civil society. The response, of course, has not meant unanimous agreement with the idea or its implications. But the process as a whole has produced a solid consensus in support of the idea, even though it is not yet a finished design in my mind or in the minds of its supporters. One may point to several levels of the life of the Church where the consistent ethic has had a useful impact.

First, the idea is a concept in moral theology, so the response of the theological community is very important. The attention given to explaining and refining the idea in theological journals and in a symposium last November at Loyola University in Chicago has been a crucial contribution to shaping an ecclesial consensus on the concept. As always, the doubts and reservations theologians have about an idea may be as helpful as their support, because an idea which is this far-reaching requires development.

Second, a most important step has been the explicit incorporation of the consistent ethic theme into the pro-life activities of the National Conference of Catholic Bishops. The use of this concept by the episcopal conference gives us a framework within which we may pursue the multifaceted agenda of the bishops at the national level.

Third, I am aware that the consistent ethic has been used creatively and extensively by many who labor in the Church's social ministry. The framework of the consistent ethic has made it possible to incorporate some of our key social themes in the Church's wider ministry. In some places it has served as a means of bridging pro-life and other social justice concerns. Such efforts at the level of dioceses, state Catholic conferences, and religious communities have demonstrated that the consistent ethic is an idea with a constituency.

Finally, the consistent ethic has taken hold beyond the Catholic Church, creating a context within which the concept can provide a viable social agenda. This is a potential yet to be realized; it is hardly a certain thing. But all these developments inside and outside the Church point to my final point: the public policy potential of the consistent ethic.

The Idea, the Community, and Public Policy

It is useful to note from the beginning of this discussion that a primary purpose of the consistent ethic theme has been to increase the Church's public policy effectiveness in the United States. The consistent ethic provides a framework within which a range of policy issues may be pursued in a coordinated fashion. It also provides a method for establishing priorities among these many issues. Finally, it provides a method for resolving conflicts at the tactical level when some issues are in conflict.

The consistent ethic's public policy focus expresses the strong social orientation of all Catholic moral theology. It is not the position of this tradition that all moral values and principles should be legislated. But every stream of moral thinking which feeds into the consistent ethic—social ethics, medical ethics, sexual ethics—is based on the conviction that some key values, principles, and practices must be protected and promoted by law and public policy.

That is why the U. S. Catholic bishops believe it is inadequate merely to teach that cultural, sexual, and racial discrimination are wrong; it is also necessary to outlaw discrimination in civil law. We are morally convinced that a just wage is needed to protect human dignity; but we also know that minimum wage laws are absolutely necessary. We are convinced that protection for unborn children cannot rely only upon moral persuasion; their lives must be protected, as our lives are, by the civil law.

As I have intimated, the consistent ethic provides a framework for addressing *all* life issues as well as a broader context for taking action on any particular issue. The anguished cry of Jesus on Golgotha, "My God, my God, why have you forsaken me?," continues today in all those persons and situations where life is threatened, diminished, or destroyed—wherever the sanctity of human life is belittled or violated. Although they are not all the same, and they may not all be equally urgent at any given moment, *all life issues are linked*. And because of that linkage, no one of them may be eliminated from our overall vision of life and our responsibility toward this great gift.

But one in particular requires special attention at this moment in our history as a nation. The anguished cry of Jesus continues in a poignant way in the silent screams of unborn children who are denied their right to live. The scriptures tell us that, when Jesus died, a darkness covered the earth. This darkness now envelops our world. No matter how much we try to lift this darkness, we will not succeed unless we first decide, as individuals and as a nation, that we will protect the life of the unborn, that we will not deprive the most vulnerable of God's creatures of the gift of life which he has given them.

Even as I say this, another ominous cloud has developed, namely, the effort to legalize euthanasia and assisted suicide. The California initiative that sought not only to reaffirm the right to withdraw life-sustaining procedures but also to secure the right to provide "aid in dying" through any medical procedure that would terminate life "swiftly, painlessly and humanely" clearly indicates that the movement to legalize euthanasia will become more aggressive and pervasive. Although the effort failed in California this year, its proponents have indicated that it will be brought forward again in California, as well as other states. We must be firm in resisting, both in terms of public opinion and legislation, anything that would tolerate or encourage such an abomination.

As a bishop who worked very closely with the Catholic Conference of Ohio for ten years, I urge you to defend life at every stage of development and in all circumstances from the moment of conception to natural death. *The one issue is life* in all its manifestations. To ignore one life issue is to place all in jeopardy, and, so, we must be consistent in our support of all life issues. It is that very consistency, I submit, that demands that we be absolutely uncompromising in our defense of the life of the unborn, as well as in our opposition to the legalization of euthanasia and assisted suicide.

I will now highlight the several roles which the consistent ethic can play in public advocacy. First, it may and should be used nationally and locally. The consistent ethic is not a rigid set of specific issues. It is a method for coordinating a spectrum of issues; and there are local issues which belong in the consistent ethic.

Second, the consistent ethic provides a grid for assessing party platforms and the records of candidates for public office. It is a broad-based set of criteria. Properly used, the consistent ethic will refute decisively claims that we are a "one-issue" constituency. The essence of the consistent ethic argument is that no one issue can exhaust the moral significance of our public policy concerns, although at any given time some may be more important than others.

Third, the consistent ethic provides the scope of moral vision which allows the Church to address broad policy issues embodying several distinct moral concerns. Perhaps the best example is the federal budget. The budget, in a very real sense, is a moral document; it puts a price tag on what we value as a nation. The budget is also, of course, a complex technical document which is at the center of our national life.

The battle over the budget, a perennially important political question, has taken on new moral intensity in a time of persistent deficits. The deficits impose a straitjacket on the budget process: to vote funds in one place is to take them away from other concerns. There is little spare change in the U. S. Treasury to adjudicate the conflict in the policy process.

Faced with this policy problem, the consistent ethic provides a framework for addressing the central budgetary trade-off—defense spending vs. social spending—and it also provides a basis for lifting up specific issues with high moral content.

A good example, in my judgment, of the kind of issues which may be effectively highlighted by the consistent ethic is the needs of children. In the last four years a series of studies have demonstrated that the most fragile members of our society, children, are also the least protected. From infant mortality statistics—which place us near the bottom of industrialized countries—to health care, to housing—children's lives are under assault in our culture.

A century ago Dostoevsky said that the death of an innocent child was enough to destroy belief in God. Less dramatically, the suffering of innocent children is enough to indict the social priorities of a wealthy society. There is a consensus developing from the business community, to politicians, to child advocacy groups that a major coordinated effort on behalf of children is both a moral imperative and a national political necessity. Spending on children is cost-effective in the long run. But it requires wisdom and courage to mount the effort to spend now—even with deficits—on this solid investment in our nation's future.

The consistent ethic is anchored in a concern for unborn children; it is shaped in terms of the strong Catholic commitment to the family; and it is directed toward a preferential concern and love for the poor. All of these themes may be placed in support of a coherent, coordinated strategy to enhance the life of children from conception through high school graduation.

This example has a moral priority and a strong political potential, but it is only part of the larger vision we are invited to pursue through the consistent ethic. I am committed to this moral vision and committed to building a constituency for it. Your positions in dioceses across the state of Ohio make you uniquely valuable allies. I pledge my support to your work and, along with my fellow bishops, I know we can count on the continuing high quality and deep dedication of your work. Together, we have an opportunity to share the reality of the consistent ethic with the society we are called to serve.

23.

A CONSISTENT ETHIC FOR CHURCH AND SOCIETY

Annual Meeting, Diocesan Pro-Life Directors,
Denver, August 8, 1988

As you know, in the last four and a half years I have given many pre-sentations throughout the country and abroad about the need for a consis-tent ethic of life. I delivered most of the major addresses on the theme to university audiences, whom I challenged to reflect upon the richness of Catholic teaching and tradition about the dignity and sacredness of human life.

This afternoon I am especially grateful for this opportunity to speak with you about "A Consistent Ethic for Church and Society." The topic lies at the very heart of your efforts to carry out the Church's Respect Life Program. As a matter of fact, I developed the concept of the consistent ethic of life nearly five years ago precisely to place in sharper focus the theologi-cal foundations of the U. S. Bishops' Program which began in 1972.

Since my first address on the topic at Fordham University in December 1983, the consistent ethic of life has received both support and criticism. In recent months it has received both praise and blame from those who judge it primarily as a political strategy. To some extent, such debate is inevitable because this ethic has much to say about moral issues with political implications—and about political issues with moral implications. But, unfortunately, the concept may become too closely linked—by both its critics and its advocates—with particular interpretations or applications of it. The danger, particularly in a national election year, is that a moral vision which transcends party platforms may be perceived as one partisan option among others.

This afternoon I would like to place this debate in perspective by ask-ing: Why should we uphold a Consistent Ethic of Life?

The *first* and most basic answer to that question is this: we should uphold it because it is true. That truth is firmly rooted in our Christian tra-dition. As Michael Gorman has pointed out recently, some pagans also opposed abortion during the earliest centuries of Christianity. However, Christians, building on their Jewish heritage, were distinctive in seeing abortion in the context of other forms of violence. Gorman writes:

The same writers who opposed bloodshed in any other form

172

also condemned abortion. . . For these people the love which obliterated distinctions between adult and child, guilty and innocent, friend and enemy also demolished the distinction between born and unborn. Christ's life and teachings raised the fetus to the status of neighbor. Abortion manifested violence and injustice to that neighbor and thus became an example of blood-shed, or murder. Those who refused to kill in war refused to kill in the womb, and vice versa . . . In this earliest period, Christians were unable to separate abortion from violence in general. (Michael J. Gorman, Abortion and the Early Church: Christian, Jewish and Pagan Attitudes in the Greco-Roman World, *New York: Paulist Press, 1982, p. 89)*

Gorman and other Christian pacifists believe this witness was rendered less consistent and persuasive by the Church's later acceptance of the "just war" theory and other developments. However, the case may be made to view such developments as refining the application of principles while remaining faithful to them. The theory of the just war is best seen as establishing a strong presumption *against* war—a presumption to be overridden only as necessary to defend fundamental rights such as the right to life. Even within war, the inviolability of innocent human life was respected through the moral norm against attacks on civilian populations.

This same absolute norm against the direct killing of the innocent is at the core of the Church's opposition to abortion. The consistency of the early Church's witness is reflected in the Second Vatican Council's condemnation of both abortion and acts of war against civilian populations as crimes against human life. It is also reflected in the U. S. bishops' pastoral letter on peace, which called on "all who would work to end the scourge of war" to "begin by defending life at its most defenseless, the life of the unborn" (*The Challenge of Peace*, #289). My experience of helping to draft that letter was decisive in convincing me of the need to articulate a consistent ethic of life.

The credibility of the norm against the direct killing of the innocent relies on the consistency with which it is applied. For Christians, that specific norm is grounded in the conviction that every human person is made in the image and likeness of God and called to redemption in Jesus Christ. As creatures under God, and as brothers and sisters in Christ, we are called both to resist attacks on human life and to preserve and nurture life by serving one another's needs. Human life is inherently social and sacred, and our social responsibility is greatest when others are least able to protect themselves.

This concern for the weakest and most vulnerable members of the human family should move us to a special abhorrence of violence against the helpless, the frail elderly, the unborn, and the disabled. It should move us toward a preferential option or love for the poor, so that our efforts to reform society will always begin with love for those who suffer most from its injustices.

If it is to be comprehensive, then, the Church's program of respect for life must both defend the sanctity of life and enhance the quality of life, especially for the most powerless in our society. A consistent ethic is attentive to both efforts while recognizing that each issue requires its own moral analysis and its own response. Without in any way diminishing the importance of other issues, this ethic also highlights the importance of protecting life itself from attack.

As the U. S. bishops said in 1985 as they reaffirmed the *Pastoral Plan for Pro-Life Activities*, society's responsibility to ensure and protect human rights demands recognition and protection of the right to life as antecedent to all other rights and the necessary condition for their realization. It is unlikely that efforts to protect other rights will ultimately be successful if life itself is continually diminished in value.

As a guide to moral truth, then, a consistent ethic of life can help us clarify our priorities and assess the moral coherence of various proposals for social advancement. It is inconsistent to claim that one can improve human life by denying or undermining its inherent value. That is why the Church opposes proposals which would cut short the lives of mentally or physically disabled persons on the grounds that they lack a minimally acceptable "quality of life." As Pope John Paul II said recently about such proposals: "Quality of life must be sought, in so far as it is possible, by proportionate and appropriate treatment, but it presupposes life and the right to life for everyone, without discrimination and abandonment" (Pope John Paul II, Address to participants in the eleventh European Congress of Perinatal Medicine, April 14, 1988).

At the level of moral principle, then, a consistent ethic demands protection of life as a basic human good that is the condition for all others. It also supports efforts to enhance life by providing the material and spiritual assistance others may need to appreciate and enjoy life, and to live with dignity.

The *second* reason for upholding a consistent ethic of life is its value in building up our unity as a Church involved in diverse ministries. This "unity in the work of service," as you may recall, was the theme of the Holy Father's second pastoral visit to the United States. It is taken from St. Paul's Letter to the Ephesians: "And to some, his gift was that they should be apostles; to some, prophets; to some, evangelists; to some, pastors and teachers so that the saints together make a unity in the work of service, building up the body of Christ" (Eph 4:11-12).

The theme of unity is more important than ever in this age of specialization and diversity. The Church must respond to a bewildering array of issues and problems, but it must never become compartmentalized into a federation of separate interest groups, each attending to its own specific concern.

By teaching a consistent ethic, the Church emphasizes that its many efforts on behalf of suffering humanity constitute a coherent defense of human dignity wherever it is threatened, not a random list of unrelated projects. In this sense, we *are* a "single issue" Church, and the single issue is *life* in all its conditions and manifestations.

The practical consequence of this is not that pro-life directors, social action directors, coordinators for AIDS ministry, and others with specific ministries are expected to take responsibility for all the Church's concerns in regard to life issues. No one can do everything, and the complexity of the various issues demands some specialization. Even St. Paul's analogy of the Church as a body suggests this: Precisely because each part of the body is different and has a different role, the whole body can function harmoniously only when each part is doing what it was intended to do; each part, however, never functions in isolation from the rest. In the same way, each ministry within the Church, while having its own specific focus, should be aware of the work done by other ministries, appreciate and support that work as part of the same life-affirming agenda, and show a willingness to collaborate with the others on matters of common interest.

An attitude of solidarity with other defenders of life in the Church should help each of us to resist becoming mere adjuncts to partisan factions in the secular political arena. The Catholic Church is not a sect, nor does it maintain its identity by retreating from the world. But then it becomes all the more important to ensure that the Church's distinctive message is not swallowed up and lost by the world. We must see to it that the world does not change us in terms of our fundamental beliefs and heritage.

At the same time, it is our vocation, through word and deed, to do all we can to change the world for the better, and this brings me to the *third* reason for upholding a consistent ethic: its capacity to build a constituency for the protection of human life in our society. This necessarily entails involvement in politics in the broad sense of that word, for the actions of society as well as those of individuals, while formulated and implemented in the political arena, are subject to moral analysis and criticism. In this arena, the Church's insistence on the dignity of life in debates regarding issues as diverse as abortion, nuclear war, pornography, and economic justice makes its voice distinctive. It also makes it unusually appealing to many people at various points along the political spectrum.

That voice challenges people who accept the Church's witness on one issue to take seriously its arguments on other issues, because those arguments begin from the same basic premise and the same concern for human well-being. Moreover, because the consistent ethic relies on the principles of a "natural law" ethic, it can be defended persuasively in public forums where specifically religious arguments are not seen as convincing or appropriate.

I deliberately mention the political usefulness of the consistent ethic last because, while this dimension has received the most media attention, it should not be uppermost in our own minds. The consistent ethic is not first and foremost a political strategy to make the Church's message more popular. A message designed solely to achieve this purpose would not only be alien to the Church's mission but would also have a short life span even as a political strategy.

The potential appeal of the consistent ethic lies precisely in its ability to transcend considerations of political expediency and to ask where moral truth leads us. Thus, even if this message is inevitably misinterpreted, distorted, or abused in the political arena, in no way is the moral argument invalidated. At the same time, we need to minimize such distortions by explaining what the consistent ethic is *not*.

It is *not* a fully articulated political platform or an attempt to form a new voting bloc or political party. Still less is it a comprehensive system for rating candidates for public office. One organization that attempted to construct such a rating system this year has discovered some of its inherent drawbacks. In such a process, one inevitably ignores some important issues affecting the dignity of human life and may mislead others in regard to the distinctions and relative priorities among other issues.

Moreover, the consistent ethic of life is emphatically not a strategy for downplaying the issue of abortion in the Church or in society. As the U. S. bishops said in their 1985 reaffirmation of the *Pastoral Plan for Pro-Life Activities*: "Precisely *because* all issues involving human life are interdependent, a society which destroys human life by abortion under the mantle of law unavoidably undermines respect for life in all other contexts. Likewise, protection in law and practice of unborn human life will benefit all life, not only the lives of the unborn."

It follows from this that the consistent ethic should not discourage an emphasis on abortion in individual Catholics' political activity. This seems widely misunderstood. For example, some have suggested that Catholics for whom abortion is an issue of overriding political importance are somehow out of line with the policy of the Church's hierarchy. Such an opinion seems to be based on the USCC Administrative Board statements of 1984 and 1987, entitled "Political Responsibility: Choices for the '80s," which spoke against single-issue voting. Moreover, in the 1987 version, the Conference's Board explicitly adopted the concept of a "consistent ethic of life" as the moral framework within which issues in the political arena should be addressed.

However, the phrase "single-issue" voting requires clarification. The most recent version of the USCC statement on political responsibility says this:

> We urge citizens to avoid choosing candidates simply on the basis of narrow self-interest. We hope that voters will examine the positions of candidates on the full range of issues as well as on their personal integrity, philosophy and performance. We are convinced that a consistent ethic of life should be the moral framework from which we address all issues in the political arena. In this consistent ethic we address a spectrum of issues,

*seeking to protect human life and promote human dignity from
the inception of life to its final moment.*

Clearly, the statement's caution against voting on the basis of "narrow
self-interest" does not refer to voting on the basis of fundamental human
rights issues such as the right to life. This statement urges voters to examine the candidates on a full range of issues, but does not seek to answer *this*
complex question: Having examined positions on a range of issues as well
as a candidate's integrity, philosophy, and performance, may a voter decide
that the candidate should not receive support because he or she favors continued violation of the unborn child's right to life?

As I said recently in an interview with the *National Catholic Register,*
my own answer to that question is yes. Indeed, a commitment to a consistent ethic would support a conscientious decision of this kind. As the
Pastoral Plan for Pro-Life Activities says, "It is imperative that we, as
Christians called to serve the least among us, give urgent attention and priority to this issue of justice, [for] a policy and practice allowing over one
and a half million abortions annually cannot but diminish respect for life in
other areas."

Further than this, the Church cannot and should not go. Whatever
one's convictions about the importance of an issue, translating that conviction into an endorsement of an individual person is fraught with empirical
judgments and uncertain predictions that the Church must not identify with
its own principal message.

It is up to the individual citizen to make such a decision and, in the
process, several questions must be asked. For example, is a particular candidate truly committed to an issue as something more than a mere means
for attracting votes? Is he or she also committed to actions on other issues
that may undermine respect for life in other ways? Is the office in question
one that allows for decisive action on the issues? Will a national agenda
that is partly determined by forces beyond the candidate's control allow
for such action? These and other questions must be answered by individual voters to the best of their ability, and the Church can only hope, at
best, to inform correctly the consciences that make such difficult, complex
choices.

In explaining what the consistent ethic is *not* designed to achieve in
the political sphere, we must not ignore the vital contribution it *can* make
in addressing a wide range of life issues. That contribution is nowhere more
needed than in the current debate over euthanasia, which threatens to
assume the proportions which the abortion controversy took on two
decades ago.

While an initial attempt to legalize "assisted suicide" through a state
referendum failed in California this year, there is little doubt that such
efforts will continue there as well as in other states. Indeed, the campaign
for such legal changes is no surprise to us, for we have long said that acceptance of abortion would erode social and legal barriers against killing vul-

nerable persons already born. But simply restating our opposition to direct killing will not suffice in building effective barriers against this new assault on life.

This is true partly because the pressures toward euthanasia in our society include factors such as radical individualism, patients' fears of being over-treated against their will, the high cost of health care, and the inability of many Americans to see any meaning or value in a life that involves suffering. Moreover, euthanasia is often promoted not in terms of an active intervention to end life, but in terms of withholding or withdrawing the means needed to support life. And this renders the issue much more complex. The controversy about euthanasia also includes explicit debates regarding social spending and the allocation of scarce resources.

Formulating an effective response to this challenge, therefore, demands reflection on several aspects of the Church's consistent ethic regarding protection and preservation of life. That ethic opposes directly intended attacks on human life whether implemented by means of active intervention or withdrawal of the means for survival. It therefore views decisions on withdrawal of treatment as relevant to the issue of euthanasia. It upholds a moral obligation to take reasonable steps to preserve life—a teaching traditionally expressed in terms of the distinction between ordinary and extraordinary means.

That teaching remains pertinent, although some prefer to distinguish between "proportionate" and "disproportionate" means. Moreover, the Church insists that health care be provided justly in accordance with the transcendent dignity of human life regardless of mental or physical condition, and it calls on society to ensure that all persons have access to a basic level of health care.

Therefore, while opposing euthanasia carried out by act or omission, we should work to alleviate people's fears that questionable measures are needed to protect themselves from unwanted extraordinary interventions during the natural process of dying. We should cooperate with others committed to civil rights, especially those defending the rights of citizens with disabilities, so that elderly and disabled patients will not be singled out as having lives not worth living or preserving. We must add our voices to the increasingly complex debate about health insurance and the cost of health care, so that economic pressures will not lead our society to abandon helpless patients in need of long-term care.

A comprehensive effort will demand not only educational and public policy efforts but also a pastoral care dimension which meets the material and spiritual needs of people who might otherwise be prime targets of the campaign for euthanasia. In short, an effort by the Church even on this single issue will inevitably entail consideration of the Church's teaching on social and economic justice.

It is clear that no diocesan agency can carry out this mission alone. It will be an enormous challenge to the entire Church and to many other individuals and communities concerned about the defense of human life and dignity. But as with all other issues that concern us as defenders of human life, the broader context provided by a consistent ethic will help ensure that our message is convincing, comprehensive, and faithful to the richness of our moral tradition. Knowing that you will be among those helping the Church to confront this task gives me cause to welcome its challenge.

24.

POST-WEBSTER REFLECTIONS ON THE CONSISTENT ETHIC OF LIFE

FIRST FRIDAY CLUB, CHICAGO, OCTOBER 6, 1989

It is a pleasure to be with you this afternoon. It has been my privilege to speak in this forum before but never while the Cubs were playing for the National League Championship. I suspect that even the Sox fans present will cheer for a Cubs victory—although, perhaps, in a subdued fashion.

The baseball playoffs are not the only contests today in the state of Illinois. We have already entered a season of political playoff games—the primary elections. In this context, I would like to reflect with you about some of the implications of the consistent ethic of life for these elections. In doing so, I will highlight what I have said on earlier occasions about the significance of the consistent ethic of life for the political process.

My reflections will be divided into three sections: first, an overview of the consistent ethic of life; second, how we move from moral analysis to public policy choices; and finally, the implications of the consistent ethic for citizens, office seekers, and office holders, with particular reference to the abortion issue.

The Consistent Ethic of Life: An Overview

The idea of the consistent ethic is both old and new. It is "old" in the sense that its substance has been the basis of many programs for years. For example, when the U. S. bishops inaugurated their Respect Life Program in 1972, they invited the Catholic community to focus on the "sanctity of human life and the many threats to human life in the modern world, including war, violence, hunger, and poverty" (NCCB Resolution, April 13, 1972).

It was precisely to provide a more comprehensive theological and ethical basis for the Respect Life Program that I developed the theme of the consistent ethic. It was urgent, I felt, that a well-developed theological and ethical framework be provided which would link the various life issues while, at the same time, pointing out that the issues are not all the same.

The concept itself is a *challenging* one. It requires us to broaden, substantively and creatively, our way of thinking, our attitudes, our pastoral response. Many are not accustomed to thinking about all the life-threatening and life-diminishing issues in such an interrelated way. The result is that they remain somewhat selective in their response.

What is the theological basis of the "consistent ethic"? Catholic teaching is based on two truths about the human person: human life is both sacred and social. Because of its sacred character, we have a duty to protect and foster human life at all stages of development, from conception to natural death, and in all circumstances. Because human life is also part of the social fabric, society must protect and foster it.

Precisely because life is sacred, the taking of even one life is a momentous event. Traditional Catholic teaching has allowed the taking of human life in particular situations only by way of exception—for example, in self-defense and capital punishment. In recent decades, however, the presumptions against taking human life have been strengthened and the exceptions made ever more restrictive.

Fundamental to these shifts in emphasis is a more acute perception of the many ways in which life is threatened today. Obviously, such questions as war, aggression, and capital punishment are not new; they have been with us for centuries. Life has always been threatened, but today there is a new *context* that shapes our ethical analysis of life and the challenges it faces.

The principal factor responsible for this new context is modern *technology*, which induces a sharper awareness of the fragility of human life. War, for example, has always been a threat to life, but today the threat is qualitatively different because of nuclear and other sophisticated kinds of weapons. The weapons produced by modern technology now threaten life on a scale previously unimaginable. Therefore, living, as we do, in an age of extraordinary technological development means that we face a radically new range of moral problems.

The essential questions are these: In an age when we *can* do almost anything, how do we decide what we *should* do? In a time when we can do anything *technologically,* how do we decide *morally* what we should *not* do?

New technological challenges confront us along the whole spectrum of life from conception to natural death. This creates the need for a consistent ethic, for the spectrum cuts across such issues as genetics, abortion, capital punishment, modern warfare, and the care of the terminally ill. Admittedly, these are all *distinct* problems, enormously complex, and deserve individual treatment. Each requires its own moral analysis. No single answer or solution applies to all. *But they are linked!*

Given this broad range of challenging issues, we desperately need a societal *attitude* or climate that will sustain a consistent defense and promotion of life.

In sum, the theological assertion that the human person is made in the image and likeness of God, the philosophical affirmation of the dignity of the person, and the political principle that society and state exist to serve the person—all these themes stand behind the consistent ethic. They also sustain the positions that the U. S. Catholic bishops have taken on issues as diverse as nuclear policy, social policy, and abortion. These themes provide the basis for the moral perspective of the consistent ethic.

From Moral Analysis to Public Policy Choices

Some commentators on the consistent ethic have seen it primarily as a political policy. In doing so, they have missed its primary meaning. For it is basically a moral vision and an ethical argument sustaining the vision. But the moral vision *does* have political consequences. The consistent ethic is meant to shape the public witness of the Catholic Church in our society.

Before exploring some of the political consequences, I would like to mention five related issues which provide a broader context for such a discussion. The movement from moral analysis to public policy choices is a complex process in a pluralistic society like ours. Because of the restraints of time, however, I will merely list the first three issues and expand briefly on the final two.

First, civil discourse in the United States is influenced, indeed widely shaped, by *religious pluralism.*

Second, there is a *legitimate secularity* of the political process, just as there is a legitimate role for religious and moral discourse in our nation's life.

Third, all participants in the public discourse must face the test of *complexity.* The moral dimensions of our public life are interwoven with complex empirical judgments where honest disagreement exists, and, so, we owe one another a careful accounting of how we have come to our moral conclusions.

Fourth, we must keep in mind the relationship between *civil law* and *morality.* Although the premises of civil law are rooted in moral principles, the scope of law is more limited. Moral principles govern personal and social human conduct and cover as well interior acts and motivation. Civil statutes govern public order; they address primarily external acts and values that are formally social.

Hence it is not the function of civil law to enjoin or prohibit *everything* that moral principles enjoin or prohibit. When we pursue a course of legal action, therefore, we must ask whether the requirements of public order are serious enough to take precedence over the claims of freedom.

Fifth, in the objective order of law and public policy, how do we determine which issues are *public* moral questions and which are best defined as *private* moral questions?

For the late Father John Courtney Murray, S.J., an issue was one of public morality if it affected the *public order* of society. Public order, in turn, encompassed three goods: public peace, essential protection of human rights, and commonly accepted standards of moral behavior in a community. Whether a given question should be interpreted as one of public morality is not always self-evident. A rationally persuasive case has to be made that an action violates the rights of another or that the consequences of actions on a given issue are so important to society that the authority of the state and the civil law ought to be invoked to govern personal and group behavior.

Obviously, in a religiously pluralistic society, achieving consensus on what constitutes a public moral question is never easy. But we have been able to do it—by a process of debate, decision-making, then review of our decisions. For example, civil rights, particularly in the areas of housing, education, employment, voting, and access to public facilities, were determined—after momentous struggles of war, politics, and law—to be so central to public order that the state could not be neutral on the question. Today we have a public consensus in law and policy which clearly defines civil rights as issues of public morality. But the decision was not reached without struggle; the consensus was not automatic.

The fact, then, that a spontaneous public consensus is lacking at a given moment does not prohibit its being created. When he was told that the law could not legislate morality, Dr. Martin Luther King, Jr., used to reply that the law could not make people love their neighbors but it could stop their lynching them! Law and public policy can also be instruments of shaping a public consensus; they are not simply the product of consensus.

In sum, in charting the movement from moral analysis to public policy choices, we must take into account the facts that (1) civil discourse in this nation is influenced and shaped by religious pluralism; (2) there is a legitimate secularity of the political process; (3) all participants in it must face the test of complexity; (4) there is a distinction between civil law and morality; and (5) some issues are questions of public morality, others of private morality.

This brings us to the third part of my address.

Implications of the Consistent Ethic for Citizens, Office Seekers, and Office Holders

The recent decision of the Supreme Court in the *Webster* case, by giving the states some authority to limit abortions, has initiated a new era of public debate and legislative action. Therefore, it is important that we apply the criteria just outlined to the question of abortion.

The Catholic bishops have consistently held that abortion is without question an issue of public morality because the unborn child's right to life is at stake. Precisely because the right to life is the foundation of other rights, we see the abortion issue in the same category as civil rights questions.

The Supreme Court's *Roe v. Wade* decision and its supporters, however, have relegated abortion to the status of private morality in which society does not have an abiding interest. The entire logic of the consistent ethic of life points the other way. By connecting abortion with other acknowledged human rights concerns, we seek to overcome the dangerous dichotomy which was introduced into our public life by the *Roe v. Wade* decision. We will not protect other rights securely in our law if we erode the very right to life.

The moral case we make in this instance has direct legal consequences. As Bishop James Malone, then President of the National Conference of Catholic Bishops, said in October of 1984: "We realize that citizens and public officials may agree with our moral arguments while disagreeing with us and among themselves on the most effective legal and policy remedies . . . In debating such matters there is much room for dialogue about what constitute effective workable responses; but the debate should not be about whether a response in the political order is needed."

Bishop Malone makes two central points. First, as a nation, we must break through the continuing impasse in the abortion debate. The fact of 1.5 million abortions is a tragic reality. The very magnitude of the problem should be sufficient to establish a consensus that we have a *public problem* even if, as a society, we recognize that many of us differ about how to respond to it. The debate, in other words, should not be *whether* a public response is needed.

Second, the distinction between moral principles and political or legal strategies made a significant contribution to the national debate and to the discussion within the Catholic community. On a series of questions from nuclear to social policy, the bishops advocate both moral principles and specific solutions. But moral principles and practical strategies do not carry the same weight; there can be honest disagreement about the latter. In the pastoral letter on war and peace, for example, we called specific attention to the need for, and the legitimacy of, debate which exists at the level of particular strategies.

Today, in light of the *Webster* decision, we need the same kind of discussion in the Church and in the nation on *how* to restrict abortion in the legal sphere. As a bishop, I am committed to teaching the total moral law. But I am also committed to the search for what is possible and most effective in the civil arena.

This kind of careful distinction regarding the issues in the debate on public morality will provide a helpful context in which to probe another problem we face: the relationship between personal conviction and public duty. It is an abiding problem of politics; every public figure faces the question. To use a distinction I invoked earlier, the question is not *whether* the deepest personal convictions of politicians should influence their public choices, but *how* the two should be related.

Clearly, we do want people in public office whose deepest beliefs shape their character and determine the quality of their leadership. We choose public officials, in part, because we hope they will infuse public life with certain convictions. However, relating convictions to policy choices is a complex process. And it is precisely this complexity which should be explored and debated.

As a theme for the debate, I find a sentence from Pope John Paul II's address to scientists and scholars at Hiroshima very suggestive. Speaking of the nuclear threat, he said: "From now on, it is only through a conscious choice and through a deliberate policy that humanity can survive." This sentence spans the two dimensions of personal choice and public policy. Policy emerges as the result of conscious choices by individuals.

But the development of public policy requires a wider consensus than the personal conviction of any individual—even a public figure. Whether we look at the problem of how to reverse the arms race or how to reverse the policy of abortion on demand, the beginning of the process is a series of conscious choices that *something* different must be done. Then the search for a deliberate, specific policy can begin.

I would not want, for example, a candidate for public office today to be complacent, passive, or satisfied with the level or the dynamic of the arms race or our national defense budget. I would look for the person who says, "What we have is unacceptable, and I will work for change." The process of change will surely not be simple, but the conscious choice and the willingness to change policy are the key.

In the same vein, I would want candidates who are willing to say, "The fact of 1.5 million abortions a year is unacceptable, and I will work for a change in the public policy which encourages or permits this practice." In both areas—the arms race and abortion—it will take conscious decisions by citizens and public officials if we are to have specific policies which serve human life. Let us turn now to the question of what guidance the consistent ethic of life offers voters.

The consistent ethic is not first and foremost a political strategy to make the Church's message more popular. A message designed solely to achieve this purpose would not only be alien to the Church's mission but would also have a short lifespan even as a political strategy.

The potential appeal of the consistent ethic lies precisely in its ability to transcend considerations of political expediency and to ask where moral truth leads us. Thus, even if this message is inevitably misinterpreted, distorted, or abused in the political arena, in no way is the moral argument itself invalidated. At the same time, we need to minimize such distortions by explaining what the consistent ethic is *not*.

It is not a fully articulated political platform or an attempt to form a new voting bloc or political party. Still less is it a comprehensive system for rating candidates for public office. In such a process, one inevitably ignores some important issues affecting the dignity of human life and may mislead others in regard to the distinctions and relative priorities among other issues.

Moreover, the consistent ethic of life does not downplay abortion and should not discourage an emphasis on abortion in the political activity and electoral decisions of an individual Catholic when such an emphasis seems necessary. As the U. S. bishops said in their 1985 reaffirmation of the Pastoral Plan for Pro-Life Activities: "Precisely because all issues involving human life are interdependent, a society which destroys human life by abortion under the mantle of law unavoidably undermines respect for life in all other contexts. Likewise, protection in law and practice of unborn human life will benefit all life, not only the lives of the unborn."

It follows from this that the consistent ethic should not discourage an emphasis on abortion in an individual Catholic's political activity. This seems widely misunderstood. For example, some have suggested that Catholics for whom abortion is an issue of overriding political importance are somehow out of line with the policy of the Church's hierarchy. Such an opinion seems to be based on the USCC Administrative Board statements of 1984 and 1987, entitled "Political Responsibility: Choices for the '80s," which spoke against single-issue voting. Moreover, in the 1987 version, the Conference's Board explicitly adopted the concept of a "consistent ethic of life" as the moral framework within which issues in the political arena should be addressed.

However, the phrase "single-issue" voting requires clarification. The most recent version of the USCG statement on political responsibility says this:

> We urge citizens to avoid choosing candidates simply on the basis of narrow self-interest. We hope that voters will examine the positions of candidates on the full range of issues as well as on their personal integrity, philosophy and performance. We are convinced that a consistent ethic of life should be the moral framework from which we address all issues in the political arena. In this consistent ethic we address a spectrum of issues, seeking to protect human life and promote human dignity from the inception of life to its final moment.

Clearly, the statement's caution against voting on the basis of "narrow self-interest" does not refer to voting on the basis of fundamental human rights issues such as the right to life. This statement urges voters to examine the candidates on a full range of issues. However, it does *not* seek to answer this complex question: Having examined positions on a broad range of issues as well as a candidate's integrity, philosophy and performance, may a voter decide that the candidate should not receive support because he or she favors continued violation of the unborn child's right to life?

As I said last year in an interview with the *National Catholic Register*, my own answer to that question is yes. Indeed, a commitment to a consistent ethic would support a conscientious decision of this kind. However, beyond such guidance for conscientious decision-makers, the Church cannot and should not go. Whatever one's convictions about the importance of an issue, translating that conviction into an endorsement of an individual person is fraught with empirical judgments and uncertain predictions that the Church must not identify with its own principal message.

It is up to the individual citizen to make such a decision and, in the process, several questions must be asked. For example, is a particular candidate truly committed to an issue as something more than a mere means for attracting votes? Is he or she also committed to actions on other issues that may undermine respect for life in other ways? Is the office in question one that allows for decisive action on the issues? Will a national agenda that is partly determined by forces beyond the candidate's control allow for such action? These and other questions must be answered by individual voters to the best of their ability, and the Church can only hope, at best, to inform correctly the consciences that make such difficult, complex choices.

There is another very important point I wish to add before I conclude this presentation. The tragedy of abortion requires more of us than an informed legal or political response. Many of us—men, in particular—have not stepped back enough from the legal and political debate about abortion to be able to hear the real concerns, the trials, and the anguish of women who face life issues in a way that men never will. Many women make a decision about an unwanted pregnancy in relative isolation from those who should help and support them—their family, their husband or boyfriend, close friends, their pastor. Conception does not take place in isolation, and pregnancy should not be experienced in isolation. We must foster male responsibility. We must teach, insist on, and live out the reality that sexual activity carries with it significant and unavoidable responsibilities for men and women alike.

As I conclude, I simply wish to reaffirm again that the consistent ethic of life provides a useful framework for the public debate about abortion. It can help shape an attitude of respect in our society for human life across its full spectrum—from conception to natural death, and in all its circumstances. Admittedly, the abortion issue has divided our society. To prevent deeper divisions, all those participating in the public debate about abortion should speak and act in an honest, mutually respectful manner that can seek and find a common ground. And in order to attain such a common ground for the common good, we must, as I have already intimated, take into careful consideration both the right to life of the unborn and the concerns of women who face problem pregnancies.

25.

THE CONSISTENT ETHIC OF LIFE AFTER *WEBSTER*

WOODSTOCK THEOLOGICAL CENTER,
GEORGETOWN UNIVERSITY, MARCH 20, 1990

I wish to express my appreciation to Fathers O'Donovan and Connor for inviting me to return to Georgetown. It is always a pleasure to come, although I do not envy your students. At least in my case, you have a genius for assigning very difficult topics. In 1984, in the midst of the presidential campaign, you asked me to lecture on religion and politics. This time, you suggested the topic, "The Consistent Ethic of Life after *Webster*."

The title really contains two themes which I will not treat equally. On the one hand, it calls for assessment of the status and role of the consistent ethic of life. On the other, it focuses the discussion on one issue in the ethic, abortion, in light of the Supreme Court's decision of last July. I will explore the second topic at greater length, but in the context of the consistent ethic.

Specifically, I plan to (1) review the consistent ethic of life since 1983, (2) examine the abortion issue since Webster, and (3) close with a perspective on the future of the consistent ethic.

The Consistent Ethic Since 1983

The idea of the consistent ethic grew from a conviction I developed as chairman of both the committee which prepared *The Challenge of Peace* and the Committee on Pro-Life Activities. These two distinct efforts seemed to share a common goal. It struck me that the age-old task of the Church, to protect and promote human life as a gift and trust from God, faced in our time a series of threats and challenges of a different magnitude than the past. The new challenge was a product of "the signs of the times" in the sense that technological change, growing global interdependence, and the complexity of an advanced industrial society brought together in one large problematic several new challenges to life and some very old ones. I thought it would be useful to begin a discussion about the utility of relating problems without submerging one into another. How does the experience look after seven years? I will comment briefly on selected moral issues: where we stand, and what needs to be done.

The Nuclear Threat: The danger of nuclear war, perhaps more than any other single issue, symbolizes the new character of threats to life in the twentieth century. In the words of McGeorge Bundy's recent history, the Cold War has been played out between "danger and survival." Since political change was judged impossible, the best to be hoped for was strategic stability. In the pastoral letter on war and peace, our hope was for a mix of arms control measures and modest political changes to transform gradually the world we have known for almost fifty years.

However, the last two years have produced anything but modest change. Today, the possibility exists to reshape the U. S.-Soviet relationship in a fashion which would dramatically transform the nuclear relationship. There are still 50,000 nuclear weapons to be reduced, and a consistent ethic should contribute to the changing political and strategic drama we are experiencing. But the hope of the pastoral letter, radical reduction in the danger we have known and the possibility of a different political order in world affairs, is closer at hand than I would have ever guessed in 1983.

Capital Punishment: The consistent ethic's opposition to capital punishment is rooted in the conviction that an atmosphere of respect for life must pervade a society, and resort to capital punishment does not enhance this attitude. In contrast to the nuclear question, a brief report on this topic must be starkly negative. The number of men and women condemned to die grows each year; the general public does not share the conviction of the consistent ethic on capital punishment; and we have recently had the spectacle of people running for public office on the basis of whom they are prepared to kill.

Even though the Catholic tradition, in principle, allows states to resort to capital punishment, and in spite of the public consensus which presently exists, I am convinced that a consistent ethic cannot change on this question. But we must be prepared for a long, strenuous effort with no solid hope for early progress.

Euthanasia: Complementing a willingness to kill criminals to solve crime is the call to legalize euthanasia in our society. By no means do I wish to collapse these two different questions. I only want to point toward a troubling attitude which seems to hold that killing—whether done in an official act or even from a humanitarian motive—only affects the victim. A consistent ethic points out how killing can erode our societal reverence for human life, our bonds of trust, and our respect for one another. A society which is willing to make killing a normal solution for life's problems misunderstands its corrosive effect. Euthanasia may well be the abortion debate of the 1990s, dividing us again as a people over how life in its vulnerability is to be cared for. In 1983, euthanasia was a passing reference in the list of threats to life. It will be more central, I fear, in our future.

Social and Economic Justice: The consistent ethic joined the task of protecting life to that of promoting life. If life is to be respected in a society as a whole, it must be protected in its most vulnerable members. Centuries ago, the prophets taught Israel that the quality of its faith could be tested by how the widows and orphans were treated. These were the inhabitants on the edge of the circle of life in Israel. Jesus specified the message more dramatically. Those at the edge of the circle—the vulnerable and the broken—were very special to God, he said, and, indeed, God was found among them in a particular way.

Almost two millennia later, the prophetic message about the widows and orphans sounds starkly contemporary in our society. Today, women and children remain the most vulnerable members of U. S. society. Their lives reflect the persistent social problems of our society: health care, housing, and hunger. We have had a decade of remarkable economic growth, but the prophets would show us where to look, lest we be mesmerized by the illusion that everyone has shared equally in that growth. The consistent ethic of the 1990s will be tested by how the orphans and widows fare.

Abortion Since *Webster*

Having looked at a number of questions which the consistent ethic addresses, I turn now to the abortion issue as it stands after the Supreme Court decision *Webster vs. Reproductive Health Services* in July 1989. To evaluate the status of the abortion question since *Webster*, it is useful to look quickly at the larger picture of abortion since *Roe vs. Wade* and *Doe vs. Bolton* in 1973. Two characteristics stand out: the radical nature of the original decisions, and their divisive impact on our national life.

By the radical character of the 1973 decisions, I mean their profoundly damaging consequences for life and law in U. S. society; these were captured well by two legal scholars, John Noonan in 1973 and Mary Ann Glendon in 1989. Within weeks of the Court's decision, Noonan concisely summarized its impact. Examining how the Court, in its two sweeping decisions, had changed the prevailing consensus of both state law and recent public referenda, Noonan concluded: "By virtue of its opinions, human life has less protection in the United States today than at any time since the inception of the country. By virtue of its opinions, human life has less protection in the United States than in any country of the Western world."

His judgment, that the results of the *Roe* and *Doe* decisions would isolate the United States in the way it addresses abortion, has now been confirmed in the detailed study of Professor Glendon, *Abortion and Divorce in Western Law*. In an article written just prior to *Webster* in 1989, Professor Glendon observed that "no country in Europe has gone so far as our Supreme Court in permitting abortion on demand."

The radical character of the decision assured a profound and powerful social response. The response has taken shape in the emergence of a national grassroots pro-life/anti-abortion movement, committed to reversing *Roe* and *Doe*; it was born in the 1970s and has sustained the witness for life until today.

Also emergent in the 1970s was a pro-choice/pro-abortion constituency committed to maintaining U. S. law in the position of providing no effective protection to unborn life. The intensity of the public debate, the passions aroused, the positions taken, and the persistence of views cannot be understood without focusing squarely on the underlying issue. As Noonan observed in 1973, *Roe* and *Doe* were analogous to the Dred Scott decision. The aftermath of *Roe* and *Scott* in the Court's history forced this nation to debate and decide who was to be counted as legally protected and fully human.

In the nineteenth century, the debate centered on black slaves; in the twentieth century, on unborn life of every color and nationality. It is hard to conceive of a more fundamental challenge to the moral vision and character of a society: deciding who fits in the circle of the legally protected human community. If we cannot answer that question accurately, with clarity, compassion, and conviction, how can we hope to keep our moral integrity as a people and a nation?

The consistent ethic—both pre- and post-*Webster*—is helpful in that it illustrates the consequences of a range of issues when we fail as a society to protect the sacredness of every human life. A moral vision which does not have room in the circle of the human community for unborn children will inevitably draw the circle of life too narrowly in other decisions of social and economic policy.

Noonan and Glendon have illustrated how we failed in the 1970s to understand the humanity of life at its inception. Others in the 1980s—from the Congressional Budget Office to *America* and *Commonweal*—have documented how we have failed to protect children in terms of infant mortality, health care, nutrition, and housing. The combined judgment of the last twenty years is that both our constitutional policy on abortion and our social policies for women, children, and families have failed to meet minimum standards of justice. There must be a connection—logical, legal, and social—between our lack of moral vision in protecting unborn children and our lack of social vision in the provision of basic necessities for women and children.

The consistent ethic of life seeks to protect and enhance human life from conception to natural death. It is precisely in light of this larger perspective that I find unacceptable the contention that our society has given a responsible answer to the tragedy of abortion in the constitutional regime established by *Roe* and *Doe*. The view that *Roe* is satisfactory contends that its answer has a traditional American character to it: it protects freedom of choice. But this view reduces the compelling moral question—how do we recognize the human among us?—to a procedural problem. The *Roe* rationale asks, "Who decides?," but it does not focus on "What is being decided?" By ignoring the second question, it evades and eviscerates the heart of the moral challenge posed by abortion: not only who is human, but how do we respond to the human when it is vulnerable and voiceless?

As a bishop and a citizen, I cannot passively accept a definition of the fundamental human, moral, and social question posed by abortion which is cast in purely procedural terms. I find myself responding here as I have when the threat posed by the nuclear arms race is discussed solely in terms of the technical characteristics of missiles and warheads, with the human reality suppressed and ignored. The abortion question must be addressed within the Church and society in terms of its full human substance. There is more to this question than the mere phrase "freedom to choose" can capture. The substance of the issue must be argued at the moral, legal, and political levels.

The post-*Webster* period gives our society the opportunity to do precisely this. *Webster*'s significance is not that it reversed *Roe*, but that it returns the democratic process to the fifty states and gives them the opportunity to redress the faulty logic of *Roe*. It allows the public debate to focus on what is being decided in an atmosphere dominated by the question, who decides.

For the Church and for the consistent ethic, there are both *opportunities* and dangers in this post-*Webster* era.

We have the *opportunity*—by our witness, advocacy, persuasion, and arguments—to make a positive contribution to the national debate on abortion. We hope we can help our society turn away from abortion and save the lives of millions of our unborn sisters and brothers. We have the opportunity to be a consistent and constant defender of human life and dignity, a teacher of the truth that every life is precious—no matter how young or old, how rich or poor, no matter what race or sex or status in society.

But there is also the *danger* that we could make the mistake of some of the pro-abortion groups and narrow our public concern to a single issue, ignoring other threats to human life. There is the danger we might become increasingly shrill or strident, forgetting the importance of civility and charity in public discourse. There is the temptation simply to proclaim positions, forgetting that, in a pluralistic society, we must persuade, build coalitions, and reach out to shape public opinion to support human life. And there is the temptation to lose hope, to give up, to turn away in frustration, apathy, or discouragement.

I have been disappointed in the public dialogue since *Webster* because so much attention has been focused on protest and power, and so little on what is at stake substantively for our society. The basic question is the kind of society we want to be—one that destroys its unborn children, or one that commits itself to a decent life for the most vulnerable in our midst, especially women and children. This fundamental question must be addressed *morally*, *legally*, and *politically*.

At the *moral* level, the first challenge of the post-*Webster* period is to redress the consequences of *Roe*'s definition of the abortion issue. Redress means lifting up for evaluation the forgotten factor in *Roe*, the moral meaning of unborn life; in technical terms, the moral status of fetal life. This implies asking what moral claims the unborn child has on us. The claims cannot simply be on the mother of the unborn child, but on society as well. Catholic teaching has always seen in the abortion decision a personal and a social choice. The damage done in abortion is not simply to the unborn child, but also to the society which permits, sustains, or encourages abortion. Raising up the forgotten factor of *Roe* means reexamining publicly why life, which is demonstrably human in its genetic character and development, can be denied all legal protection for six months and any effective legal protection until birth.

The challenge for the consistent ethic in the post-*Webster* period is to make an effective case in our society for Pope John Paul II's assertion that the right to life is the fundamental human right. A consistent ethic will ask: What happens to other rights in a society when protection of the right to life is selective? What happens to our moral imagination and social vision if the right to life is not protected for those who do not look fully human at the beginning or end of life? What happens to the vulnerable along the full spectrum of life, if the right to life is denied to inherently vulnerable and dependent unborn life?

Precisely because of this forgotten factor in *Roe*'s definition of the abortion issue, a consistent ethic must assert with moral creativity and courage Vatican II's statement that "from the moment of conception life must be guarded with the greatest care."

It is my conviction that the strength of the Catholic moral tradition, its persistent defense of unborn life, responds directly to the needs of the post-*Webster* moment—redressing the exclusion of concern for the unborn in *Roe*. But I also want to face directly the critique which contends that, in our emphasis on the forgotten factor of *Roe*, we have ignored the problems faced by women.

Those who espouse a pro-life, consistent ethic—whether they be bishops or laity, authors or activists—need to address this critique very carefully. Our necessary—indeed, essential—public witness in providing a place in the public debate for the moral claims of unborn children can lead to a failure to address the situations faced by pregnant women. We can fail to consider the circumstances of conception—that it can be the result of coercion, ignorance, or abuse. We can seem to be unaware that women who want to bear their children are without the social and economic resources needed to sustain new life. We can appear to ignore the fact that pregnancy for some women is at least partly the experience of being left alone with the consequences of immoral, irresponsible male behavior—at the point of conception and afterwards. These issues, the circumstances surrounding conception and the resources needed to sustain a pregnancy and support children, are also part of the moral fabric of the abortion debate.

A pro-life, consistent ethic acknowledges the human and moral significance of these questions. It must respond to them at the levels of both moral analysis and social support. At the moral level, we should acknowledge the human complexity of many abortion decisions, but we should stress that the key to sound moral analysis is *how* the several moral elements of a complex situation are ranked and related to a decision. To acknowledge the moral weight of the circumstances of conception, and the challenge of sustaining a pregnancy, does not mean one has to accept the direct killing of innocent life as a solution. A consistent ethic challenges this conclusion and indicts it for its failure of social vision and moral courage.

The indictment is not directed in the first instance to the woman caught in these circumstances, but to a social policy and vision fostered since *Roe*, which presents abortion as the normal, natural response to the circumstances I have described. The consistent ethic must stand morally and socially against such a response. We should be second to none in our sensitivity to the problems pregnant women face. But we should offer a different moral response for individuals and society at large. Basing our position on Vatican II's judgment that abortion is an "unspeakable crime," we must combine moral wisdom with specific social policies of health care, housing, nutrition, and counseling programs in our own institutions. We must also support public programs which provide an alternative to the hard and narrow choices pregnant women often face.

But a moral position alone is inadequate for the post-*Webster* period. The essential challenge we face is that unborn life is deprived of even minimal legal protection. Another key post-*Webster* question is: By what civil law shall our society be guided?

I have argued earlier that Catholic teaching sees in abortion a double moral failure: a human life is taken, and a society allows or supports the killing. Both concerns, protecting life and protecting the society from the consequences of destroying lives, require attention. Both fall within the scope of civil law. Civil law, of course, is not co-extensive with the moral law, which is broader in its scope and concerns. But the two should not be separated: the civil law should be rooted in the moral law even if it should not try to translate all moral prohibitions and prescriptions into civil statutes.

When should the civil law incorporate key moral concerns? When the issue at stake poses a threat to the public order of society. But at the very heart of public order is the protection of human life and basic human rights. A society which fails in either or both of these functions is rightfully judged morally defective.

Neither the right to life nor other human rights can be protected in society without the civil law. To hold the moral position of the Catholic Church—that all directly intended abortion is morally wrong—and not to relate this moral position to civil law would be a grave abdication of moral responsibility. Precisely in a pluralistic society, where moral views differ, protection of fundamental rights is directly dependent upon the content of the civil law. In our society we cannot depend on moral agreement alone; the fact of our pluralism means that the content of civil law, what binds us all on essential social questions, is a major public concern.

But does this imply that we are imposing our religious beliefs on society as a whole? No, for two reasons. First, in making the case for a reversal of *Roe* and a legal order which protects the unborn, we present our views in terms of the dignity and equality of human life, the bond between human dignity and human rights, and the conviction that the right to life is the fundamental human right. Second, our objective, that the civil law recognize a basic obligation to protect human life, especially the lives of those vulnerable to attack or mistreatment, is not new in our society. The credibility of civil law has always been tested by the range of rights it defends, and the scope of the community it protects. To return to the analogy of civil rights: the struggle of the 1960s was precisely about extending the protection of the law to those unjustly deprived of protection. The people of the United States did not need a religious consensus to agree on this proposition then; they do not need religious agreement today to understand the argument that a part of the human community is without fundamental protection of the law.

The extent or kind of legal protection that can be achieved for unborn children is partly dependent on the degree of public consensus which can be built to sustain a legal norm. Since civil law does not incorporate the moral law *in toto*, to build such a consensus, a convincing case must be made that abortion is a public order issue.

Pro-life constituencies, including the Catholic bishops, but not limited to them, have pursued two approaches to the civil law. At the constitutional level, for example, the bishops have supported and continue to pursue a constitutional amendment which would protect the life of the unborn child. This is a response as fundamental and far-reaching in scope as the *Roe* decision was. While the effort continues, there is much work to be done in terms of public opinion. A second approach has been to seek limits on abortions, even with *Roe* in place. Obviously, the *Webster* decision offers a new range of possibilities at the state level for this strategy. Moreover, there are solid public opinion grounds for pursuing a regime of limitation on abortions.

This pursuit, however, moves the abortion debate from the moral and legal levels to the *political*. New questions arise for the Church at this level: Should the consistent ethic be pursued in the political process—in the world of party platforms, campaigns, specific legislation, and an examination of the positions of public officials and candidates for public office?

There are two reasons why the Church—keeping within proper theological and constitutional bounds—should engage the issues of the consistent ethic in the political process. First, using the abortion question, the democratic process is the arena where we may be able to close the gap between the consequences of the *Roe* decision and the consistently expressed views of U. S. citizens. In polling data, it is clear that the regime of permissive abortion established by *Roe* and expanded by later Court decisions does not reflect a consensus in the public. While public views on abortion are often described as ambiguous, the ambiguity does not diminish the dissatisfaction with 1.5 million abortions a year. Let me simply summarize some data:

- In Connecticut Mutual Life's extensive survey of American values in the 1980s, 65% of U. S. citizens considered abortion morally wrong. Particularly significant was the finding that women, racial minorities, and the poor opposed abortion more strongly than 65%.

- In a *Newsweek*/Gallup poll last fall, 88% of U. S. citizens favored informed consent for women seeking abortions; 75% favored parental notification for teenagers; 61% favored prohibitions on public funding of abortions except in life-threatening circumstances.

- In the *New York Times* a month after *Webster*, 71% favored parental consent laws and 60% favored testing for fetal viability.

In a debate as complex and emotional as abortion, statistics can be used and abused. I wish only to make a basic point: The status quo of permissive abortion does not fit the moral or legal convictions of a large majority of U. S. citizens. They may not be where the Catholic bishops are, but neither are they where *Roe* and *Doe* left us.

Webster offers an opportunity to use the democratic process to translate a significant consensus on key limits to abortion into law. To grasp the opportunity of a post-*Webster* period, we need to join firm convictions about what is right and wrong at the moral level with a capacity to build a consensus at the legal level that will significantly reduce the number of abortions. We should join others—believers and humanists, Christians and Jews—who share the view that 1.5 million abortions a year is unacceptable for even one more year.

I am convinced that a potential exists which has not yet been grasped; the potential lies in the 60% of Americans who do not identify themselves completely with either of the major voices in the abortion debate. Without forsaking our moral principles, we should seek to address this constituency in a way that invites them to join us in setting significant limits on abortion. To do so will require clarity of moral vision on our part; it will also demand a capacity for creative choices to build consensus at the level of law and policy. It will also require that we raise the quality of the public debate on abortion from rhetoric to rational dialogue even as we seek to reduce the quantity of abortions performed.

The second reason the Church should pursue the consistent ethic in the political process is that religious institutions in a democracy stand at the intersection of public opinion and public policy decisions. In a complex democracy like ours, public opinion seldom translates directly into policy decisions. But it does set a framework for policy decisions. It sets limits for policy choices and provides indications of policies desired by the public.

The Church influences this intersection of opinion and policy through its access to the conscience of citizens. In the first instance, this will be the conscience of Catholics, but the U. S. bishops' pastoral letters showed that it is possible to gain a hearing beyond the confines of the Church.

Within the Church, teaching on moral and social policy is addressed to the community as believers and as citizens. Within the community, some citizens will carry specific professional or vocational responsibilities on certain issues. When we wrote the pastoral letter on peace, we addressed it to the citizens of a nuclear nation, but we were conscious of the specific responsibilities and choices faced by Catholics in the military. When we wrote the letter on the economy, we held special meetings with labor and business leaders. On health care issues, physicians, nurses, and administrators have unique choices to face, and special witness to offer.

Finally, there is the position of Catholics holding public office. In a sense, all of the above issues and more are encompassed in the decisions public officials must make. As you know, the question of Catholic political leaders and the abortion question was included in a resolution from the General Meeting of the National Conference of Catholic Bishops last November. My purpose a moment ago was simply to put it in the context of professional choices made by others in the Church. Now I will apply it to Catholic political leaders, offering here my personal interpretation of these issues. The relevant text from the bishops reads: "At this particular time, abortion has become the fundamental human rights issue for all men and women of good will . . . No Catholic can responsibly take a 'pro-choice' stand when the 'choice' in question involves the taking of innocent human life." I wish to make ten points on this sensitive issue.

1. Note that the bishops' text is addressed to *all* Catholics, not only to political leaders.

2. Its basic purpose is to state clearly the Church's objective moral teaching. Because all directly intended abortions are judged immoral in Catholic teaching, a pro-choice public policy— which, in effect, is pro-abortion—collides directly with this moral teaching. In this specific judgment of moral and legal precepts, the bishops could hardly have stated their principles any differently.

3. While public officials are bound to fulfill their offices in light of a given constitutional framework, they obviously have some room for specific choices within that framework and can choose to emphasize some issues over others.

4. In accord with the bishops' statement, I am firmly committed to the position that public officials who recognize the evil of abortion have a responsibility to limit its extent, to work for its prevention, and to protect unborn life.

5. I am also firmly convinced that *all* Catholics are bound by the moral principle prohibiting directly intended abortion. However, many Catholics, politicians and ordinary citizens, will disagree on strategies of implementation to lessen and prevent

abortions. At the level of strategy and tactics, we bishops should express views as we did in the pastoral letters. By definition, these views are open to debate.

6. The relationship of moral principle, civil law, and public policy is complex. We should encourage and foster an ongoing conversation within the Church about strategies to address abortion.

7. While public consensus is needed to support law, consensus must be created by many voices, including public officials who can try to move the public toward a better moral consensus. Neither church leaders nor politicians should simply wait for consensus to form.

8. The position of a public figure who is personally opposed to abortion, but not publicly opposed in terms of any specific choices, is an unacceptable fulfillment of a public role. I do not pretend to know in every circumstance which tactics such a figure should use, but moral consistency requires that personal conviction be translated into some public actions in order to validate the personal view. Sometimes public officials may be faced with a dilemma, for example, when they must decide whether to support a law which may not be in total accord with their moral convictions, but would nonetheless decrease the number of abortions. In such a situation, they must ultimately decide which is the better course of action.

9. I have always believed dialogue with public officials—Catholics and others—is an essential part of the Church's social ministry. Moreover, all public officials should be held accountable for their positions. Indeed, there are times when criticism is called for. It is important, however, that we continue to engage them and not cut them off.

10. The Church's teaching authority is ultimately a moral authority, a wisdom to be shared with all its members. I believe that the Church can be most effective in the public debate on abortion through moral persuasion, not punitive measures.

The Future of the Consistent Ethic

I return now—all too briefly because of the length of my presentation—to the consistent ethic. In assessing its future role, I will speak to questions of both *substance* and *style*.

In terms of *substance*, I remain convinced after seven years of experience that its original premise remains valid. It was proposed to help and urge the Church to keep our moral perspective broadly designed, to address issues on their intrinsic merits, but also to recognize that the life issues today are not confined to one area of human activity. It was also designed to draw upon the systematic resources of the Catholic moral tradition. We are not a single-issue tradition or a single-issue Church; we enhance our treatment of each issue by illustrating its relationship to others.

This general conviction, that the substance of the consistent ethic complements both the signs of our times and the strength of the Catholic tradition, is reinforced by the topic I have addressed at length this evening. In the polarized setting of the abortion debate, it is still possible to locate the majority of Americans as the broad middle, generally opposed to abortion on demand, but ambiguous about how many restrictions to place upon it. Neither the pro-life nor the pro-choice positions have moved this middle toward a viable political and civil consensus.

To convince this sixty percent of the populace of the wisdom of at least limiting abortion would be a major advance for life. I am convinced that moving the middle depends upon projecting a broad-based vision which seeks to support and sustain life. It will not be enough to be against abortion; we need to show convincingly that we are *for life*—life for women and children; *for life* in support of the very old and the very young; *for life*, which enhances the chance for the next generation to come to adulthood well-educated, well-nourished, and well-founded in a value structure which provides a defense against the allure of drugs, violence, and despair.

I believe that the work of the Campaign for Human Development, Catholic Charities, Catholic Relief Services, and the many other initiatives we sponsor around the country give us a start, an opportunity to project this vision persuasively. The consistent ethic gives us a way both to propose the vision and to pursue it.

The substance of the consistent ethic yields a *style* of teaching it and witnessing to it. The style should be prophetic, but not sectarian. The word "prophetic" should be used sparingly and carefully, but a truly consistent ethic of word and deed, which protects life and promotes it, is truly a work of God, hence a prophetic word in our time. Such a vision and posture inevitably will meet resistance. But we should resist the sectarian tendency to retreat into a closed circle, convinced of our truth and the impossibility of sharing it with others. To be both prophetic and public, a countersign to much of the culture, but also a light and leaven for all of it, is the delicate balance to which we are called.

The style should be persuasive, not preachy. We should use the model of the Second Vatican Council's *Pastoral Constitution on the Church in the Modern World*. We should be convinced we have much to learn from the world and much to teach it. We should be confident but collegial with others who seek similar goals but may differ on means and methods. A confident Church will speak its mind, seek as a community to live its convictions, but leave space for others to speak to us, help us to grow from their perspective, and to collaborate with them. May my words this evening contribute to this confidence.

26.

AN UPDATE ON THE CONSISTENT ETHIC OF LIFE

NORTH AMERICAN COLLEGE, ROME, JANUARY 23, 1991

I am very grateful to Seminarians for Life here at the North American College for inviting me to address you this evening, and to Msgr. O'Brien, the Rector of the College, for his gracious hospitality.

While there are many essential dimensions of academic and formational preparation for the priesthood, a familiarity with life issues and the Church's pastoral response to them must rank high today. A significant part of my ministry as a priest and a bishop has focused on these issues. And future priests in the U. S. can expect the same involvement in their ministry.

During the past seven years I have given many presentations and written many articles on a variety of topics related to the Church's stand on life-issues. This evening I will synthesize several of these, especially two addresses at Georgetown University, an address at the USCC Diocesan Social Action Directors' Conference in Washington, D.C., an article for *U. S. Catholic,* and a 1989 insert for diocesan newspapers in the Province of Illinois, entitled "Women and the Unborn: The Need for Respect."

The topic is so vast that a full course would be needed merely to introduce the complexities of the diverse life issues. My purpose this evening is much more limited. First, I will briefly describe the contemporary context of these issues and indicate the need for a consistent ethic of life in the Church and society. Second, I will discuss the status of the abortion debate in the U. S. since the Supreme Court's 1989 *Webster* decision. Third, I will explore some implications of a consistent ethic of life for citizens, office seekers, and office holders.

Respecting Life Today

Gaudium et spes, the *magna carta* of the Church's social ministry since Vatican II, asserted that the social task of the Church in the modern world is to read the signs of the times and to interpret them in light of the gospel. In the contemporary signs of the times, three challenges pose different but interrelated questions for the Church's social ministry. There is a *technological* challenge, a *peace* challenge, and a *justice* challenge. The three must be interpreted in light of the gospel truth that human life, a gift from God, is sacred, and that everyone has an obligation to defend, protect, and nurture it.

The *technological* challenge arises from the unique capacities which contemporary science, especially its applications in the medical field, has produced in our generation. This challenge is most clearly visible at the beginning and the end of life. At both ends of the spectrum of life—the mystery of conception and the mystery of death—our generation has developed capacities to intervene in the natural order in ways which earlier generations would have thought belonged solely to God. Today, from genetics to embryology, to the care of the aged and the terminally ill, we have the capacity to shape the beginning of life, make choices about its development, and sustain it by life support systems.

At both ends of life's spectrum, the technological challenge has been both a blessing and a burden. Some discoveries help us to enhance life expectancy, to correct inherited genetic defects, and to relieve pain and suffering. But the new technologies have also placed in human hands decisions about life and death which were previously unknown to Catholic moralists and for which there is little human experience to guide our choices.

As Pope John Paul II has often noted, the danger of our day is that we will use our technological genius to erode human dignity rather than to enhance it. The danger is that our choices will be dominated by technology rather than directed by human wisdom and the light of faith.

These questions of technology, life, and death are not, of course, limited to the world of medicine. The unique moral character of our day is demonstrated by the linkage between the "micro-questions" of medical ethics and the "macro-questions" of war and peace in the nuclear age. The link between these two quite different areas of human existence is the technological revolution which has unlocked the genetic code and unleashed the power of the atom within the space of a lifetime. So, the technological challenge is also part of the *peace* challenge: how to keep the peace in an age when the instruments of war can threaten the very fabric of human existence as a whole.

Technology provides the material link between the "micro" and the "macro" threats to life in our time. The *moral* link is the unique value of human life. In very different settings—in the laboratory and in the life of nations—our generation is called to protect the fragile fabric of human life against unprecedented dangers.

The *justice* challenge poses a different but related set of questions. It calls us to expand our moral concern beyond the question of protecting life from attack to promoting and enhancing the dignity of human life in society. Justice challenges us to build a society which provides the necessary material and moral support for every human being to realize his or her God-given dignity. As Christians, aware of the limits of human nature and the impact of sin on human affairs, we know that this work of shaping a humane society is a never-ending task. But this sober conviction that perfect justice is a characteristic of the completed reign of God does not mean that progress toward the conditions of the Kingdom is impossible. The reign of God is present when human dignity is defended and human rights are protected. The justice challenge calls us to this effort.

Each of these challenges—technology, peace, and justice—has its own inner complexity. Each must be addressed on its own terms by slow, patient work. No one can do everything, and some may feel closer to some of the issues I have described; indeed, they may feel better able to address them than others.

But seeing the relationship, the connection, among the three challenges—technology, peace, and justice—is what started my reflection several years ago on the need for a consistent ethic of life. A consistent ethic recognizes the need for specific approaches to concrete issues, but it also raises a broader question. Are the Church and society well served by addressing these questions in isolation from each other? Do we not learn more about the personal and social challenge of this moment in history by consciously connecting it with what has gone before and with its present implications which often are addressed separately?

The consistent ethic sees the convergence of these multiple and diverse challenges as a time of opportunity. The opportunity resides in the very nature of Catholic moral teaching and in the Church's capacity to respond to multiple challenges under the guidance of an overall, coherent moral vision. The consistent ethic of life, a moral vision based on two principles regarding the sacredness of human life—the obligations to protect and nurture it, and not to bring direct harm to it—provides a framework for moral analysis across the full spectrum of life issues.

The concept of the consistent ethic is based upon two characteristics of Catholic teaching: its *scope* and its *structure*. Its scope is broad enough to encompass the three distinct challenges I have outlined. The Church in the U. S. is simultaneously committed to a diverse set of objectives which many individuals and institutions in U. S. society find irreconcilable. We are committed, for example, to reversing a public policy of abortion on demand and also reversing the arms race. We are convinced that we cannot have a just and compassionate society unless our care extends to both sides of the line of birth: we must protect the basic right of unborn children to live and, at the same time, promote the associated basic human rights of nutrition, housing, and health care which enhance the lives we have saved.

The scope of a comprehensive ethic is matched by a systematic *structure* of moral argument. A broad moral concern must be based upon solid moral analysis. No two "life" issues are identical; they cannot be collapsed into one. At a given time, one may have to be given a higher priority than others. The solution to one may not be applicable to others. In short, each requires its own moral analysis. A systematic moral tradition is necessary for such analyses which then enable the ecclesial community to take a position on a given issue and then project that position in the civil debate.

The consistent ethic draws upon the scope and structure of the Catholic moral vision to confront the full range of questions endangering human dignity today. However, the idea must be linked to a community—a constituency—which holds and embodies the vision. A vision without a community is not capable of influence. A vision tied to a committed community is the first prerequisite of serious social impact.

I will now describe the status of the abortion debate in the United States and the implications of the consistent ethic of life for this public policy discussion.

The Abortion Debate in the U. S. after *Webster*

In this section I will briefly outline the legal dimensions of the issue, explore some of its political aspects, and then explain the Church's pastoral response, especially its role in the public policy debate on abortion.

Legal Dimensions

In effect, the U. S. Supreme Court's controversial 1973 decision, *Roe v. Wade*, and another one issued on the same day—eighteen years ago yesterday—struck down the abortion laws of virtually all the states. There is considerable confusion about the decision in the minds of many Americans. Many people think that the Court said a woman has an *absolute* right, protected under the U. S. Constitution, to an abortion. Others presume that a woman has an unlimited right to do with her body whatever she pleases. Still others claim that a woman may terminate her pregnancy at whatever time, in whatever way, and for whatever reasons she herself chooses.

But that is not what the Court said in *Roe v. Wade*. Instead, the Justices explicitly rejected these notions and said that the right to an abortion is balanced by the state's "important and legitimate" interests in safeguarding the health of the mother, maintaining medical standards, and protecting "the potentiality of human life." Moreover, the Justices said, these interests grow "in substantiality as the woman approaches term and, at a point during pregnancy, each becomes 'compelling.'"

Since 1973, many state legislatures and some municipalities enacted new abortion laws in light of the Court's rulings, especially its holding that there are "important and legitimate" interests in safeguarding maternal health and protecting "potential" human life. Several of these statutes were subsequently challenged in the courts and eventually came up for review by the Supreme Court. While it upheld some provisions, it struck down many others.

Given the history of the Court's decisions on this issue since 1973, it is not surprising that many people have assumed that abortion on demand is an absolute right, despite the Court's assertions to the contrary. Meanwhile legal scholars and others—including four members of the Court itself—continue to point out the flimsy grounds on which *Roe v. Wade* was based and to question the Court's increasingly more restrictive grounds for evaluating the constitutionality of statutes regulating abortions.

Some expected the Court to overturn *Roe v. Wade* and its subsequent abortion decisions in the 1989 *Webster* case, but it did not. Instead, the Court gave a strong signal to state legislatures that it would "allow some governmental regulation of abortion that would have been prohibited" by earlier Court decisions. In effect, this means that we have finally turned a corner in regard to abortion on demand in the United States. Most, if not all, state legislatures have become arenas of public debate and the sources of new statutes restricting abortions. This brings us to the political aspects of the public policy debate.

Political Aspects

As might be expected, public discourse on a politically divisive, moral issue like abortion has been lively and heated. While dedicated advocates of the pro-life and the so-called "pro-choice" positions are poles apart, the majority of Americans seem to stand somewhere in the middle. There is great ambiguity and confusion among many about the various issues of the abortion controversy. And when public opinion is divided, it is difficult to make headway with thoughtful, effective legislation.

Let me explain the current dilemma. On the one hand, as has been true for many years, Americans remain overwhelmingly opposed to a permissive abortion policy on the model of *Roe v. Wade*. Exit polls during last November's elections found strong majorities agreeing that abortion should be legally available either "never" or "only in some circumstances." It has also become evident that many simply do not realize the scope and magnitude of legalized abortion in the U. S. According to a survey carried out by the Wirthlin Group last August, almost half of our citizens surmise that there are fewer than 500,000 abortions annually in the United States. The real total is more than three times as many: 1.6 million—some 4,400 a day!

Again, Americans tend grossly to overestimate the extent to which so-called "hard cases" make up the abortions which are performed. According to the Wirthlin survey, people typically believe that over 20% of all abortions occur in cases of rape and incest, and over 15% in cases where the woman's life is endangered. Because of these beliefs, many are reluctant to support legislation which would ban all abortions. However, according to the research arm of Planned Parenthood, the actual percentages are quite different from popular belief. Fewer than 1% of abortions are performed in rape or incest cases, and only 7% of the women having abortions even cite "health" as a reason. This means that the pro-life movement in the U. S.— including the Catholic Church—faces a significant challenge: educating people, who are opposed in principle to permissive abortion, to fundamental facts about the number of abortions, the reasons for which they are performed, and the moral values which are often neglected in the public debate.

Often the public debate on abortion is intertwined with the concerns of many in the feminist movement, especially those who insist upon a woman's *right* to choose an abortion. However, among others, Dr. Sidney Callahan, a lay theologian, has very persuasively argued the case for *pro-life* feminism. She argues that "women can never achieve the fulfillment of feminist goals in a society permissive toward abortion" (see *Commonweal*, April 25, 1986). She has also pointed out that "permissive abortion laws do not bring women reproductive freedom, social equality, sexual fulfillment, or full personal development. Pitting women against their own offspring is not only morally offensive, it is psychologically and politically destructive. Women will never climb to equality over mounds of dead fetuses, now in the millions." My point in raising this issue is simply this: if we are going to be effective in discussing abortion policy with many women, we will have to be aware of its implications for legitimate feminist goals and be ready and able to persuade them that being pro-life and a woman are not incompatible—indeed, they are intimately connected.

While the right of the unborn to live surely needs legal protection—and we must insist on this—have we stepped back from the legal debate enough so that we can really *hear* the issues, the struggles, and the anguish of women who face life issues in a way that we never will? I wonder whether we have adequately spoken a word of faith to them? I wonder whether we have inspired the community to help carry the burdens of our sisters in faith.

Sadly, many women make a decision about an unwanted pregnancy in relative isolation from those who should help and support them—their family, their husband or boyfriend, close friends, their pastor. Conception does not take place in isolation, and pregnancy should not be experienced in isolation. We must teach, insist on, and live out the reality that sexual activity carries with it significant and unavoidable social and moral responsibilities for men and women alike. Abortion harms both the mother and her unborn child. It also has tragically destructive effects on families and society as a whole. It erodes respect for human life across the board. These are all reasons why the Church must address the issue.

The Church's Pastoral Response

The Church's pastoral response to abortion is basically twofold: working for legal protection for the unborn and striving for economic justice for women and children. In the public debate on abortion, the Church has three important tasks. First, because we're committed to establishing constitutional protection for the unborn child to the maximum degree possible, we must carefully review abortion-related bills before state legislatures and the U. S. Congress. Second, we must urge federal and stage legislators to work for laws and public policies which are both pro-life and pro-family and which address the legitimate concerns of women. Third, we must continue to educate people about the moral dimension of the abortion issue.

Having said that, I also acknowledge that the movement from moral analysis to public policy choices is a complex process in a pluralistic society like the U. S. As you know, civil discourse in our nation is influenced, indeed widely shaped, by religious pluralism. Moreover, there is a legitimate secularity of the political process, just as there is a legitimate role for religious and moral discourse in our nation's life.

In a religiously pluralistic society, achieving consensus on a public moral question is never easy. But we have been able to do it before—by a process of debate, decision-making, then review of our decisions. For example, civil rights, particularly in the areas of housing, education, employment, voting, and access to public facilities, were determined—after momentous struggles of war, politics, and law—to be so central to public order that the state could not be neutral on the question. Today we have a public consensus in law and policy which clearly defines civil rights as an issue of public morality. But the decision was not reached without struggle; the consensus was not automatic. And the issue is not yet fully resolved.

The fact, then, that a spontaneous public consensus is lacking at a given moment does not prohibit its being created. When he was told that the law could not legislate morality, Dr. Martin Luther King, Jr., used to reply that the law could not make people love their neighbors but it could stop their lynching them! Law and public policy can also be instruments of *shaping* a public consensus; they are not simply the product of consensus.

When some accuse us of forcing a Catholic point of view in regard to abortion on others, I reply that the defense of innocent human life is, indeed, a cornerstone of Catholic social teaching. But it is not a specifically sectarian concern. Abortion is a human problem, not a narrowly Catholic one. While not all moral values and principles need be legislated, certain key values, principles, and practices must be protected and promoted by law and public policy. Protection for unborn children cannot rely only upon moral persuasion; their lives must be protected, as our lives are, by the civil law.

As I have indicated, a consistent ethic of life demonstrates that it is not enough merely to protect and promote the rights of unborn children; we must also extend such protection and promotion of basic human rights to women and children. And this means working for economic justice. Besides its advocacy, the Church can be proud of the many maternity-related services which we offer to women, such as free or low-cost prenatal and maternity care, adoption services, emotional and spiritual support, housing, and continuing education.

From this brief description of the Church's response to abortion—and poverty—one might get the impression that the consistent ethic of life is primarily for the Church's pastors and official agencies. But it has implications for every member of the Church, and, indeed, for all people of good will. In the final section of this address, I will explore this in some detail.

Implications of the Consistent Ethic of Life for Citizens, Office Seekers, and Office Holders

As I have intimated, the development of public policy requires a wider consensus than the personal conviction of any individual—including a public figure. Whether we are addressing the problem of how to reverse the arms race or how to reverse the policy of abortion on demand, the beginning of the process is a series of conscious choices that *something* different must be done. Then the search for a deliberate, specific policy can begin. This involves both ordinary citizens and elected officials, and the consistent ethic offers valuable guidance for reflection and discussion.

But first let me make it clear that the consistent ethic is not first and foremost a political strategy to make the Church's message more popular. A message designed solely to achieve this purpose would not only be alien to the Church's mission but would also have a short life span, even as a political strategy.

The value and appeal of the consistent ethic lies precisely in its ability to transcend considerations of political expediency and to ask where moral truth leads us. Thus, even if this message is inevitably misinterpreted, distorted, or abused in the political arena, in no way is the moral argument itself invalidated. At the same time, we need to minimize such distortions by explaining what the consistent ethic is *not*.

As I intimated a moment ago, it is *not* a fully articulated political platform or an attempt to form a new voting bloc or political party. Still less is it a comprehensive system for rating candidates for public office. In such a process, one inevitably ignores some important issues affecting the dignity of human life and may mislead others in regard to the distinctions and relative priorities among other issues.

Moreover, the consistent ethic does not downplay abortion and should not discourage an emphasis on abortion in the political activity and electoral decisions of an individual Catholic when such an emphasis seems necessary. As the U. S. bishops said in their 1985 reaffirmation of the *Pastoral Plan for Pro-Life Activities:* "Precisely *because* all issues involving human life are interdependent, a society which destroys human life by abortion under the mantle of law unavoidably undermines respect for life in all other contexts. Likewise, protection in law and practice of unborn life will benefit all life, not only the lives of the unborn." It follows from this that the consistent ethic should not discourage an emphasis on abortion in an individual Catholic's political activity when the situation calls for such emphasis.

It was precisely because the *Webster* decision introduced a new and urgent element in the abortion scene that the U. S. bishops, at their general assembly in November 1989, issued an unequivocal statement about abortion. They said, "At this particular time, abortion has become the fundamental human rights issue for all men and women of good will . . . No Catholic can responsibly take a 'pro-choice' stand when the 'choice' in question involves the taking of innocent human life."

This statement has caused considerable controversy and has been misunderstood by many, sometimes for less than honest motives. In any case, the statement has significant implications for Catholics, whether they hold public office or not. I wish to make ten points on this sensitive issue.

1. Note that the bishops' text is addressed to *all* Catholics, not only to political leaders.

2. Its basic purpose is to state clearly the Church's objective moral teaching. Because all directly intended abortions are judged immoral in Catholic teaching, a pro-abortion public policy collides directly with this moral teaching. In this specific judgment of moral and legal precepts, the bishops could hardly have stated their principles any differently.

3. While public officials are bound to fulfill their offices in light of a given constitutional framework, they obviously have some room for specific choices within that framework and can choose to emphasize some issues over others.

4. In accord with the bishops' statement, I am firmly committed to the position that public officials who recognize the evil of abortion have a responsibility to limit its extent, to work for its prevention, and to protect unborn life.

5. I am also firmly convinced that *all* Catholics are bound by the moral teaching prohibiting directly intended abortion. However, many Catholics, politicians and ordinary citizens, will disagree on strategies of implementation to lessen and prevent abortions. At the level of strategy and tactics, we bishops should express views as we did in our pastoral letters, where we distinguish between moral principles and strategies. While we address many concrete questions concerning the arms race, contemporary warfare, weapons systems, and negotiating strategies in the pastoral letter on war and peace, we did not intend that our treatment of each of these issues carry the same moral authority as our statement of universal moral principles and formal Church teaching. Developing strategies to apply moral principles to specific issues involves prudential judgments based on specific circumstances which can change or which can be interpreted differently by people of good will.

6. The relationship of moral principle, civil law, and public policy is complex. We should encourage and foster an ongoing conversation within the Church about strategies to address abortion.

7. While public consensus is needed to support law, consensus must be created by many voices, including public officials who can try to move the public toward a better moral consensus. Neither Church leaders nor politicians should simply wait for consensus to form.

8. The position of a public figure who is personally opposed to abortion, but not publicly opposed in terms of any specific choices, is an unacceptable fulfillment of a public role. I do not pretend to know in every circumstance which tactics such a figure should use, but moral consistency requires that personal conviction be translated into some public actions in order to validate the personal view. Sometimes public officials may be faced with a dilemma, for example, when they must decide whether to support a law which may not be in total accord with their moral convictions, but would nonetheless decrease the number of abortions. At other times, the restraints of existing law or extant interpretations of constitutional law may restrict public officials' freedom, but this should not preclude their ability to witness to their personal convictions. In such situations, they must ultimately decide which is the better course of action.

9. I have always believed dialogue with public officials—Catholics and others—is an essential part of the Church's social ministry. Moreover, all public officials should be held accountable for their positions. Indeed, there are times when criticism is called for. It is important, however, that we continue to engage them and not cut them off.

10. The Church's teaching authority is ultimately a moral authority, a wisdom to be shared with all its members. I believe that the Church can be most effective in the public debate on abortion through moral persuasion, not punitive measures. In this regard, I am faithful to the spirit of Pope Paul's eloquent words in his encyclical *Ecclesiam Suam* (#75), where he spoke about the Church's dialogue with the world in this way: "Although the truth we have to proclaim is certain and the salvation necessary, we dare not entertain any thoughts of external coercion. Instead we will use the legitimate means of human friendliness, interior persuasion, and ordinary conversation. We will offer the gift of salvation while respecting the personal and civic rights of the individual."

In conclusion, a consistent ethic of life seeks to defend and enhance human life across its full spectrum from conception to natural death, and in all its circumstances. As I stated earlier, the life issues may not always be of equal importance, and they cannot be collapsed into one. But they are linked. One cannot, with consistency, claim to be pro-life if one applies the principle of the sanctity of life to one or more life issues but rejects or ignores it in regard to abortion or nuclear war.

It is essential that the Church—its pastors, its priests, and all its members—continue to address this moral dimension of the life issues in the public debate.

To prevent deeper divisions in our society, all those participating in the specific public debate about abortion must speak and act in an honest, mutually respectful manner that can seek and find a common ground. In order to attain such a common ground for the common good of our society, we must take into consideration both the right of the unborn to life and the concerns of pregnant women. Ignoring either of these will not promote justice, which is one of the hallmarks of the reign of God.

27.

THE ABORTION DEBATE AND
THE CONSISTENT ETHIC

*Address to the University of Illinois Health Care
Community*

Chicago, February 16, 1993

Thank you for inviting me to address you on an issue of great importance and enduring controversy in our nation today: abortion. During the past ten years, as a pastor, I have given many presentations and written many articles on the Catholic Church's stand on life issues, including abortion. However, we are at a new moment in the public debate on abortion, and I am grateful for this opportunity to refine my own thinking on the issue. I speak, of course, from my perspective as a Catholic bishop. I realize that there are some who hold other views.

Three federal initiatives contribute to the newness of the moment. They help shape the context of today's public policy debate on abortion and call the Church and its pastors to re-examine their approach to the discussion. The first is the U. S. Supreme Court decision last June on *Planned Parenthood of Southeastern Pennsylvania v. Casey.* The second is a series of executive orders on abortion policy issued by President Clinton on January 22, reflecting the new administration's position on legalized abortion, which is quite different from that of the two previous administrations. The third is what is today called the Freedom of Choice Act currently before the U. S. Congress.

This afternoon, I will, first, briefly describe the broader contemporary context of these issues and indicate the need for a consistent ethic of life in the Church and society. Second, I will discuss the current status of the abortion debate in the U. S. in the light of the three federal initiatives I just mentioned. Third, I will explore how the Church might shape its pastoral response to the debate about, and the reality of, abortion in our society today.

Respecting Life Today

The Pastoral Constitution on the Church in the Modern World is the *magna carta* of the Catholic Church's social ministry since the Second Vatican Council. The document asserted that the social task of the Church in the modern world is to read the signs of the times and to interpret them in light of the gospel. In the contemporary signs of the times, three challenges pose different but interrelated questions for the Church's social ministry. There is a *technological* challenge, a *peace* challenge, and a *justice* challenge. The three must be interpreted in light of the biblical truth that human life, a gift from God, is sacred, and that everyone has an obligation to defend, protect, and nurture it.

The *technological* challenge arises from the unique capacities which contemporary science, especially its applications in the medical field, has produced in our generation. This challenge is most clearly visible at the beginning and the end of life. At both ends of the spectrum of life—the mystery of conception and the mystery of death—our generation has developed capacities to intervene in the natural order in ways which earlier generations would have thought belonged solely to God. Today, from genetics to embryology, to the care of the aged and the terminally ill, we have the capacity to shape the beginning of life, make choices about its development, and sustain it by life-support systems.

At both ends of life's spectrum, the technological challenge has been both a blessing and a burden. Some discoveries help us to enhance life expectancy, to correct inherited genetic defects, and to relieve pain and suffering. But the new technologies have also placed in human hands decisions about life and death which were previously unknown to ethicists and for which there is little human experience to guide our choices.

The danger of our day is that we will use our technological genius to erode human dignity rather than enhance it. Technology has its own logic, but it does not have its own ethic. The danger is that our choices will be dominated by technology rather than directed by human wisdom and the light of religious faith.

These questions of technology, life, and death are not, of course, limited to the world of medicine. The unique moral character of our day is demonstrated by the linkage between the "micro-questions" of medical ethics and the "macro-questions" of war and peace in an age with the capacity of atomic, biological, and chemical warfare. The link between these two quite different areas of human existence is the technological revolution which has unlocked the genetic code and unleashed the power of the atom within the space of a lifetime. So, the technological challenge is also part of the *peace* challenge: how to keep the peace in an age when the instruments of war can threaten the very fabric of human existence as a whole. Now that the Cold War has ended, the new threats to life are posed predominantly by nuclear proliferation and the various forms of instability we find in such areas as the Middle East, the former Soviet Union, and especially the Balkans.

Technology provides the material link between the "micro" and the "macro" threats to life in our time. The moral link is the unique value of human life. In very different settings—in the laboratory and in the life of nations—our generation is called to protect the fragile fabric of human life against unprecedented dangers.

The *justice* challenge poses a different but related set of questions. It calls us to expand our moral concern beyond the question of protecting life from attack to promoting and enhancing the dignity of human life in society. Justice challenges us to build a society which provides the necessary material and moral support for every human being to realize his or her God-given dignity. We are aware of the limits of human nature and the impact of sin on human affairs. We know that this work of shaping a humane society is a never-ending task. But this must not prevent us from defending human life and dignity and protecting human rights. The justice challenge calls us to this effort.

Each of these challenges—technology, peace, and justice—has its own inner complexity. Each must be addressed on its own terms by slow, patient work. No one can do everything, and some may feel closer to some of the issues I have described; indeed, they may consider themselves better able to address them than others.

But acknowledging the relationship, the connection, among the three challenges—technology, peace, and justice—is very important. And it was that conviction that started my reflection several years ago on the need for a consistent ethic of life. A consistent ethic recognizes the need for specific approaches to concrete issues, but it also raises a broader question. Are the Church and society well served by addressing these questions in isolation from each other? Do we not learn more about the personal and social challenge of this moment in history by consciously connecting it with what has gone before and with its present implications, which often are addressed separately?

The consistent ethic sees the convergence of these multiple and diverse challenges as a time of opportunity. It has seemed to me and others that the very nature of Catholic moral teaching offers us an opportunity to respond to multiple challenges under the guidance of an overall, coherent moral vision. The consistent ethic of life is a moral vision based on two principles regarding the sacredness of human life: the obligation to protect and nurture it, and not to bring direct harm to it. We hope the consistent ethic might provide, not only for us but also for others, a framework for moral analysis across the full spectrum of life issues, from conception to natural death.

The concept of the consistent ethic is based upon two characteristics of Catholic teaching: its *scope* and its *structure*. Its scope is broad enough to encompass the three distinct challenges I have outlined. In terms of abortion, for example, the Catholic Church in the U. S. is committed to reversing a public policy of abortion on demand. But we are also convinced that we cannot have a just and compassionate society unless our care extends to both sides of the line of birth: we must protect the basic right of unborn children to live and, at the same time, promote the associated basic human rights of adequate nutrition, housing, and health care which enhance the lives which are saved.

The scope of a comprehensive ethic is matched by a systematic *structure* of moral argument. A broad moral concern must be based upon solid moral analysis. No two "life" issues are identical; they cannot be collapsed into one. At a given time, one may have to be given a higher priority than others. The solution to one may not be applicable to others. In short, each requires its own moral analysis. A systematic moral tradition is necessary for such analyses which enable the ecclesial community to take a position on a given issue and then project that position in the civil debate.

The consistent ethic draws upon the scope and structure of the Catholic moral vision to confront the full range of questions endangering human dignity today—from abortion to euthanasia. However, the idea must be linked to a community . . . which holds and embodies the vision. Within our own Catholic tradition, we recognize that a vision without a community is not capable of influence. A vision tied to a committed community is the first prerequisite of serious social impact. This is why we try to build that community and invite others into this discussion.

Let us turn now to the status of the abortion debate in the United States today.

The Abortion Debate in the U. S. Today

I will briefly outline the legal dimensions of the issue after the U. S. Supreme Court decision on [*Planned Parenthood of Southeastern Pennsylvania v.*] *Casey* and, then, explore its political dimensions, including the new Administration's liberal approach to abortion and the Freedom of Choice Act.

Legal Dimensions

In effect, the U. S. Supreme Court's controversial 1973 decision, *Roe v. Wade,* and another one issued on the same day, prohibited states from completely protecting the unborn in our country. There is considerable confusion about these decisions in the minds of many Americans. Many people think that the Court said a woman has an *absolute* right, protected under the U. S. Constitution, to an abortion. Others presume that a woman has an unlimited right to do with her body whatever she pleases. Still others claim that a woman may terminate her pregnancy at whatever time, in whatever way, and for whatever reasons she herself chooses.

But that is not what the Court said in *Roe v. Wade.* Instead, the Justices explicitly rejected these notions and said that the woman's right to an abortion is balanced by the state's "important and legitimate" interests in safeguarding the health of the mother, maintaining medical standards, and protecting "the potentiality of human life." Moreover, the Justices said, these interests grow "in substantiality as the woman approaches term and, at a point during pregnancy, each becomes 'compelling.'"

Since 1973, many state legislatures and some municipalities have enacted new abortion laws in the light of the Court's rulings, especially its holding that the state has "important and legitimate" interests in the matter. Several of these statutes were subsequently challenged in the courts and eventually came up for review by the Supreme Court. While the Court upheld some provisions, it struck down many others.

Given the confusing history of the Court's decisions on this issue since 1973, it is not surprising that many people have assumed that abortion on demand is an absolute right, despite the Court's assertions to the contrary. Meanwhile, legal scholars and others—including four current members of the Court itself—continue to point out the inadequate reasoning on which *Roe v. Wade* was based.

Last June, the U. S. Supreme Court issued its decision on *Planned Parenthood of Southeastern Pennsylvania v. Casey*. By the narrow margin of 5-4, a majority of the Justices decided to reaffirm the essential holding of *Roe v. Wade*, which, as the Justices pointed out, has three parts: (1) "the right of the woman to choose to have an abortion before viability and to obtain it without undue interference from the state . . . ;" (2) "the state's power to restrict abortions after fetal viability, if the law contains exceptions for pregnancies which endanger a woman's life or health . . . ;" and (3) "the principle that the state has legitimate interests from the outset of the pregnancy in protecting the health of the woman and the life of the fetus that may become a child."

The majority opinion in *Casey* rejected *Roe*'s rigid trimester approach and substituted for it the concept of viability. While it also emphasized the state's "legitimate interests" in protecting both maternal health and protecting the life of the fetus, the majority opinion offered the new concept of "undue burden" as a guide for deciding which statutory provisions regarding the state's interests would be constitutional or not.

The four dissenting Justices, including Chief Justice Rehnquist, who wrote the minority opinion, argued, instead, "that *Roe* was wrongly decided, and that it can and should be overruled consistently with our traditional approach to *stare decisis* in constitutional cases." Chief Judge Rehnquist's dissenting opinion also points out that the "undue burden" standard "does not command the support of a majority of this court." (Only Justices O'Connor, Kennedy, and Souter supported the "undue burden" standard.) The sharp division within the Court reflects the divisiveness of the abortion debate in our society as a whole.

Pro-abortion forces rejoiced in the reaffirmation of the woman's constitutional right to an abortion but were much less happy with the Court's emphasis on the state's legitimate interests in the matter. They were most upset by the Court's declaration that several provisions of the Pennsylvania statute being challenged were, indeed, constitutional, and only one was deemed unconstitutional (and that by a single vote). The specific provisions of the Pennsylvania statute which were challenged are these:

1. The Pennsylvania statute required "that the woman be informed of the availability of information relating to fetal development and the assistance available should she decide to carry the pregnancy to full term." The Court upheld this informed-consent requirement by a vote of 7-2, judging that it is "a reasonable measure to ensure an informed choice."

2. A requirement that the woman's spouse be notified before an abortion was declared invalid by the simple majority of 5 of the 9 Justices, who argued that a spousal notification requirement is "likely to prevent a significant number of women from obtaining an abortion."

3. A requirement that a minor seeking an abortion obtain the consent of a parent or guardian, provided that there is an adequate judicial bypass procedure, was upheld by 7 of the 9 Justices;

4. The record-keeping and reporting requirements of the Pennsylvania statute were also upheld by 7 of the 9 Justices.

In short, while a narrow majority of the Justices reaffirmed the woman's right to an abortion articulated in *Roe*, they, in effect, overruled many of the Court's decisions on abortion cases in the last twenty years.

While those of us who are pro-life were understandably disappointed by the Court's reaffirmation of abortion on demand, we also saw new possibilities for legislation at the state level which would finally reflect the state's "legitimate interests" in maternal health and protecting "potential" human life.

Despite the fact that the Court remains divided on the validity of *Roe*, it appears that we will have to live with its interpretation in *Casey* for the foreseeable future. Let us now turn to the political dimensions of the current status of the abortion debate.

Political Dimensions

As might be expected, public discourse on a politically divisive, moral issue like abortion has been lively and heated. While dedicated advocates of the pro-life and the so-called "pro-choice" positions are poles apart, the majority of our citizens seem to stand somewhere in the middle. There is great ambiguity and confusion among many about the various issues of the abortion controversy. And when public opinion is divided, it is difficult to make headway with thoughtful, effective legislation.

Let me explain the current dilemma. On the one hand, as has been true for many years, Americans remain overwhelmingly opposed to a permissive abortion policy on the model of *Roe v. Wade*. A recent issue of the *Chicago Sun-Times* carried a graph based on a Gallup poll which found strong majorities (about 70%) agreeing that abortion should be legally available either "never" (15%) or "only in some circumstances" (55%). Fewer than one out of three Americans think that it should "always" be available.

It has also become evident that many simply do not realize the scope and magnitude of legalized abortion in the U. S. According to a survey carried out by the Wirthlin Group in 1990, almost half of our citizens surmised that there are fewer than 500,000 abortions annually in the United States. The real total, as you know, is more than three times as many: 1.6 million—some 4,400 a day!

Again, Americans tend grossly to overestimate the extent to which so-called "hard cases" make up the abortions which are performed. According to the Wirthlin survey, people typically believe that over 20% of all abortions occur in cases of rape and incest, and over 15% in cases where the woman's life is endangered. Because of these beliefs, many are reluctant to support legislation which would ban all abortions. However, according to the research arm of Planned Parenthood, the actual percentages are quite different from popular belief. Fewer than 1% of abortions are performed in rape or incest cases, and only 7% of the women having abortions even cite "health" as a reason.

This means that the pro-life movement in this country—including the Catholic Church—faces a double challenge: (a) We need to educate people, who are opposed in principle to abortion on demand, to fundamental facts about the number of abortions, the reason for which they are performed, and the moral values which are often neglected or simply dismissed in the public debate. (b) We need to make some strategic choices which I will say more about later.

Often the public debate on abortion is intertwined with the concerns of many in the feminist movement, especially those who insist upon a woman's absolute right to choose an abortion. However, among others, Dr. Sidney Callahan, a lay theologian, has very persuasively argued the case for *pro-life* feminism. She argues that "women can never achieve the fulfillment of feminist goals in a society permissive toward abortion" (see *Commonweal*, April 25, 1986). She has also pointed out that "permissive abortion laws do not bring women reproductive freedom, social equality, sexual fulfillment, or full personal development. Pitting women against their own offspring is not only morally offensive, it is psychologically and politically destructive. Women will never climb to equality over mounds of dead fetuses, now in the millions." My point in raising this issue is simply this: being pro-life and being a woman are not inconsistent or contradictory; indeed, they are naturally compatible.

Let me turn now to two specific political initiatives which, in my opinion, ignore the disagreement of the vast majority of Americans with the current policy of abortion on demand and create a new moment in the abortion debate.

The President's Executive Orders (January 22, 1993)

First, during the campaign President Clinton adopted a fairly aggressive platform embracing legalized abortion on demand, and, within 48 hours of his presidency, he reversed five executive orders of his predecessors in regard to abortion. Specifically, he lifted: a ban on privately funded abortions at military hospitals; a ban on abortion counseling in federally funded clinics; a moratorium on federal research using fetal tissue; a ban on the import of the French abortifacient pill RU 486 for personal use; the restriction of funds going to United Nation programs giving abortion advice.

President Clinton stated that he signed the executive orders as part of his efforts to keep abortion "safe, legal, and rare." As Cardinal Mahoney of Los Angeles noted, how one keeps abortion rare by promoting and expanding its availability is difficult to comprehend. It is unfortunate that the President chose a very symbolic day for the pro-life movement—the 20th anniversary of *Roe v. Wade*—on which to issue these directives. However, his actions were in accord with his campaign promises and not unexpected. At the same time, he has said that he is personally opposed to abortion and wants to limit the number of abortions in this country.

The media has engaged in considerable speculation about the relationship between the Catholic Church and the new administration. We clearly disagree with the administration's pro-choice position and the executive orders which the President issued. But we agree with many of the administration's other positions; for example, putting children and families first, making health care more accessible to all our citizens, and lessening the gap between the wealthy and the poor of this nation. On February 5, President Clinton signed into law the Family and Medical Leave Act, long backed by the U. S. Catholic bishops. We hope that, through ongoing dialogue, the administration will come to see the necessary logic linking the various life-issues, including the right to life of the unborn. Our challenge is to keep making that case in a persuasive way in the public arena.

The Freedom of Choice Act

Second, a much more threatening initiative, which has very serious implications for the current debate on abortion, is the proposed legislation known as the Freedom of Choice Act (FOCA), which is before the U. S. Congress. As I have pointed out, in *Casey*, the U. S. Supreme Court, in effect, abandoned many of the Court's earlier decisions in abortion cases as ill considered. The legislation now before the Congress would impose a strict scrutiny standard and resurrect the kind of thinking which the Supreme Court has just abandoned.

I have been advised that, if FOCA is passed, it would likely prohibit the following kinds of statutes, which *Casey* allows:

- laws designed merely to influence the woman's informed choice between abortion or childbirth;
- laws designed to inform pregnant women of the probable

anatomical and physiological characteristics of the unborn child;
- laws designed to inform pregnant women of the existence of public and private agencies to help them if they decide to carry their child to term;
- laws designed to inform pregnant women of the availability of medical assistance benefits;
- laws designed to inform pregnant women that the father of their child is responsible for financial assistance should they carry the child to term;
- laws designed to inform pregnant women of the medical risks, including the physical and psychological effects of abortion;
- laws designed to ensure that for post-viability abortions, the physician choose an abortion procedure that will provide the best opportunity for the unborn child to be aborted alive unless use of that procedure would present a significantly greater medical risk to the life or health of the pregnant woman than some other procedure;
- laws designed to ensure that, during any abortion procedure that may result in the child's survival, a second physician is present to care for the child born alive and to take reasonable steps to preserve its life;
- laws promoting maternal health or unborn life, if the law results in *any* increased cost;
- laws requiring a physician (or someone other than the minor) to inform the minor's parents of her intent to obtain an abortion ;
- laws requiring that physicians counsel their patients or provide them with relevant information before performing an abortion;
- laws requiring a 24-hour waiting period;
- laws protecting health care providers, like Catholic hospitals (as distinguished from unwilling individuals), from having to participate in abortion;
- laws designed to prevent public facilities from being used to perform abortions or to prevent public employees, in the course of their employment, from performing or assisting in abortions;
- laws requiring viability testing such as that upheld in *Webster.*

In effect, under the amended Senate bill, FOCA, with limited exceptions, would deny states their historic role in protecting unborn life and women's health—interests that the U. S. Supreme Court reaffirmed in *Casey.* In other words, FOCA is an attempt to overrule Supreme Court cases, like *Casey* and *Webster,* that permit state regulation of abortion. As the Justice Department pointed out in a letter to Representative Henry Hyde of Illinois, FOCA "represents an extraordinary and unprecedented act of constitutional revisionism that would raise grave questions concerning Congress's power under section 5 of the Fourteenth Amendment" (March 2, 1992).

The Freedom of Choice Act goes well beyond *Roe v. Wade* and all subsequent U. S. Supreme Court decisions on abortion since 1973 by absolutizing and isolating abortion. It is of doubtful constitutionality. It would make bad law and worse public policy.

The Church's Pastoral Response Today

How should the Church and its pastors respond to this new moment in the nation's debate on abortion? Our pastoral response is basically three-fold: (a) working for legal protection for the unborn, (b) striving for economic justice for women and children, and (c) educating people about the reality of abortion and its moral dimension.

Because we are committed to establishing constitutional protection for the unborn child to the maximum degree possible, we will vigorously oppose the enactment of FOCA. Moreover, the House bill does not protect health care providers other than individuals, even if those providers have serious moral or religious objections to abortion. Can you imagine the dire consequences of such legislation on Catholic hospitals and other health care facilities which, as institutions, are opposed to abortion? As you may know, 25% of the hospitals in the United States are under Catholic sponsorship. How could these Catholic hospitals survive?

We will continue to urge federal and state legislators to work for laws and public policies which are both pro-life and pro-family and which address the legitimate concerns of women. Sadly, many women make a decision about an unwanted pregnancy in relative isolation from those who should help and support them—their family, their husband or boyfriend, close friends, their pastor or rabbi. Conception does not take place in isolation, and pregnancy should not be experienced in isolation. We must teach, insist on, and live out the reality that sexual activity carries with it significant and unavoidable social and moral responsibilities for men and women alike. Abortion harms both the mother and her unborn child. It also has tragically destructive effects on families and society as a whole. It erodes respect for human life. These are all reasons why the Church must address the issue and work for legislation which is both pro-life and pro-family.

At this moment, the most important response of the Catholic Church will be to continue to educate people—our own constituency and all who are willing to listen—about the reality and moral dimension of the abortion issue. In particular, I am concerned about reaching out in an effective way to the majority of Americans who do not accept the current permissive policy on abortion but do not want to see all abortions outlawed. They have a right to know the number of abortions annually in this country, the reasons why women choose abortion over childbirth, and the moral dimension of the issue.

If the vast majority of Americans can agree that some restrictions are needed in regard to abortions, what are the limits which the majority of our citizens will support? Some refuse to accept the possibility of merely restricting abortions, because they are committed to eliminating all abortions. I understand their feelings and respect their conscience on this matter. I, too, am strongly opposed to all directly intended abortions, without exception. However, a public policy which would not allow abortions under any circumstances does not have the support of the majority of our citizens at this time. I, for one, cannot justify waiting until such a consensus is developed before I support measures that will save the lives of any unborn children.

In a religiously pluralistic society, achieving consensus on a public moral question is never easy. But we have been able to do it before—by a process of debate, decision-making, then review of our decisions. For example, civil rights, particularly in the areas of housing, education, employment, voting, and access to public facilities were determined—after momentous struggles of war, politics, and law—to be so central to public order that the state could not be neutral on the question. Today we have a public consensus in law and policy which clearly defines civil rights as an issue of public morality. But the decision was not reached without struggle; the consensus was not automatic. And the issue is not yet fully resolved. The fact, then, that a spontaneous public consensus is lacking at a given moment does not prohibit its being created. But, as I said earlier, even as we work toward such a consensus, we should do all we can to save the lives of as many unborn children as possible. This does not mean that I understand morality in incremental terms but that we must use available means to achieve the full realization of our moral vision.

When some accuse us of forcing a Catholic point of view in regard to abortion on others, I reply that the defense of innocent human life is, indeed, a cornerstone of Catholic social teaching. But it is not a specifically sectarian concern. Abortion is a human rights issue, not a narrowly Catholic one. While not all moral values and principles need be legislated, certain key values, principles, and practices must be protected and promoted by law and public policy. Protection for unborn children cannot rely only upon moral persuasion; their lives must be protected, as our lives are, by the civil law.

A consistent ethic of life demonstrates that it is not enough merely to protect and promote the rights of unborn children; we must also extend such protection and promotion of basic human rights to women and children. And this means working for economic justice. Besides advocacy and education, the Church offers many maternity-related services to women, such as free or low-cost prenatal and maternity care, adoption services, emotional and spiritual support, housing and continuing education. The Church also reaches out to console those women and men who have been victimized by abortion through our Project Rachel counseling network.

As I have intimated, the development of public policy requires a wider consensus than the personal conviction of any individual—including a public official. The beginning of the process is a series of conscious choices that something different must be done. Then the search for a deliberate, specific policy can begin, and the consistent ethic offers valuable guidance for reflection and discussion.

The value and appeal of the consistent ethic lies precisely in its ability to transcend considerations of mere political expediency and to ask where moral truth leads us. Thus, even if this message is inevitably misinterpreted, distorted, or abused in the political arena, in no way is the moral argument itself invalidated.

A consistent ethic of life seeks to defend and enhance human life across its full spectrum from conception to natural death, and in all its circumstances. As I stated earlier, the life issues may not always be of equal importance, and they cannot be collapsed into one. But they are linked. One cannot, with consistency, claim to be pro-life if one applies the principle of the sanctity of life to one or more life issues but rejects or ignores it in regard to others. It is essential that the Church—its pastors, its priests, and all its members—continue to address this moral dimension of the life issues in the public debate on abortion.

To prevent deeper divisions in our society, I call upon all who participate in the public debate about abortion to speak and act in an honest, mutually respectful manner that can seek the truth and find a common ground. In order to attain such a common ground for the common good of our society, we must take into consideration both the right of the unborn to life and the concerns of pregnant women. Ignoring either of these will not promote justice in our land.

28.

THE RIGHT TO HEALTH CARE

A Test and an Opportunity for the Catholic Community

Health Care Conference, Chicago, May 11, 1993

Introduction

I have been asked to address the social justice dimensions of the health care debate. As pastors, we see this question most clearly in human terms. The statistics cited this morning have names and faces for us. In Chicago, there are thousands of children without care, poor communities without adequate health services, and Catholic hospitals in neighborhoods where the option for the poor can lead to financial disaster.

Let me tell you the story of David Murillo, who is nearly 22 months old. More than two years ago, when David's parents discovered they were expecting a baby, they faced a crisis. They both worked, but had no health insurance. They were ineligible for public aid because of their income. Their values told them to seek life, not an abortion. Fortunately, they learned about the Maternity Fund—a wonderful partnership forged among Catholic hospitals, dedicated doctors, and the Archdiocese of Chicago. David's parents contacted the Fund and were sent to St. Mary of Nazareth Hospital, where his mother became a patient of Dr. Seong Soo Lee, a doctor who has taken care of more than forty similar cases. The doctor reduced his fees; the hospital contributed many of the other costs for prenatal care and delivery; and the Archdiocese provided the rest of the needed funding so that David could be born as a healthy child.

This story of a family in need is repeated many times over in every diocese in this country. David and his family deserved more than the ingenuity and charity provided by the Maternity Fund. They have a *right* to decent health care, and so does every individual, regardless of his or her circumstances.

As Catholic bishops, our pastoral urgency is re-enforced by a heritage of moral reasoning that guides our contribution to the health care debate. This debate is not only an issue of political, economic, and social significance for the nation; it is also a time of testing and a moment of opportunity for the Church. We will be tested on how our teaching contributes to the moral framework for reform. Our tradition can illuminate important aspects of the debate, illustrating the potential of the Catholic social vision on contemporary issues.

Framing the Argument: Health Care, Common Good, and Social Justice

The right to health care is the starting point of the moral argument in Catholic social teaching. Our teaching that human life must be protected and human dignity promoted leads us to insist that people have a right to health care since its absence can destroy the life and dignity of the human person. This right is explicitly affirmed in *Pacem in Terris,* but it is not defined in specific terms. In the U. S. debate, it is our task as teachers of the Church to fill out the meaning of Pope John XXIII's assertion, and, indeed, our episcopal conference has sought to do this over the years in a number of ways. We have used the consistent ethic of life to frame the larger discussion. More specifically, the Conference, in a letter last year from Bishop Malone to members of the U. S. Congress, outlined eight basic criteria for health care reform. Health care meets all of the essential criteria of a right, i.e., a moral claim to a good, essential for human dignity. We insist that a basic floor of health care must be available to all persons.

When over 37 million Americans are without health coverage, when rising costs threaten the coverage of millions more, when infant mortality remains shockingly high, the right to health care is seriously undermined, and our health care system is in need of serious reform.

Common Good: It is best to situate the need for health care reform in the context of the common good—that combination of spiritual, temporal, and material conditions needed if each person is to have the opportunity for full human development.

The right to health care is a constitutive element of the common good. Failure to secure this right leads not simply to declining protection of human dignity, but can lead to the loss of life—the basis of human dignity. For example, in one recent year 40,000 children died before their first birthday, in large part because of the lack of access to prenatal care. This link between health care and the common good is a critical need and an elusive challenge in a debate likely to be dominated by powerful, special-interest lobbies, political action committee (PAC) contributions, and partisan goals.

The duty to create the conditions for the common good rests upon society as a whole, but no single element of society has total responsibility for the common good or, in this case, for health care. The duties are manifold:

1. *The duties of individuals:* Every right presupposes a duty; the duty incumbent upon each individual is to exercise proper stewardship of one's health.
2. *The duties of the health care professions:* Using the principle of

subsidiary, Catholic teaching turns first to the health care professions as having a primary responsibility for meeting health care needs. It is now abundantly clear that the health care professions cannot meet this need alone, so both the principles of subsidiarity and the idea of socialization (cf. *Mater et Magistra*), require going beyond the professions.

3. *The duties of government:* The requirements of providing health care today demand a role for government. Subsidiarity *first* demands that other agencies be designated as the source of health care. The same principle (subsidiarity), supplemented by socialization and solidarity (cf. *Centesimus Annus*), demands the involvement of the state as the guarantor of basic health care for each person. In Catholic teaching, the state has positive moral responsibilities for the common good and particular responsibilities for those most in need in society.

Health care is a basic good which should be guaranteed (at some decent and defined level) for each member of society. The ultimate (but not sole) guarantor is the government. It can fulfill this responsibility in multiple ways (e.g. taxation, powers of regulation, establishment of standards of care and levels of eligibility, as well as assisting individuals in securing care.)

Health Care and Social Justice: Since society as a whole is responsible for meeting the health care needs of its citizens, health care must be justly ordered if rights are to be protected, duties appropriately allocated, and the demands of the common good met.

The existing patterns of health care in the United States do not meet the minimal standard of social justice. The substantial inequity of our health care system can no longer be ignored or explained away. The current health care system is so inequitable, the disparity—between rich and poor, between the sick and the well, and between those with access and those without—is so great, that it is clearly unjust. The principal defect is that a significant part of the society (37 million) does not have guaranteed access to basic health care. Others have some access, but their coverage is too limited or too costly to offer health security for their families.

Traditional Catholic doctrines on distributive justice and the common good, as well as more contemporary teaching on the option for the poor and the imperatives of solidarity, point to a special obligation to meet the health care needs of the poor and the unserved. In our pastoral letter on the economy, we insist that the poor have the single most urgent moral claim on the policies of the nation. Personal and institutional decisions, policies of private and public bodies, must be evaluated by their effects on those who lack the minimum necessities, including health care. When we enter the public arena, our judgments should be based primarily on what public policy will mean for the poorest and most vulnerable in society.

As has been already suggested, *discrimination* exacerbates the injustice within our health system. African Americans and Hispanics are disproportionately uninsured. Many of the 40,000 who die before their first birth-day are minority children. Black mothers are three times as likely to die of preventable complications of pregnancy as white mothers.

Since this system consumes a seventh of our national economic resources, a Catholic approach to reform should reflect the traditional virtue of *stewardship*. We call for cost controls, not only to eliminate dupli-cation and waste, but also to free up resources for other vital national needs.

In summary, the Catholic case for reform begins with the right to health care, focuses on the common good and social justice, and reflects the virtues of solidarity and stewardship. Our teaching tradition leads to the kind of criteria outlined by our Conference and the urgency for reform that brings us here today. We seek a system which will ensure access for all, con-tain costs, respect pluralism, and enhance human life and human dignity.

Other Essential Moral Issues in the Policy Debate

Our task will be made much more complex and challenging by the likelihood that the proposal presented to Congress will include abortion as one of the basic health care services to be provided all citizens. Depending on the actual design of the proposal, this can seriously affect the participa-tion of Catholic health care institutions in the new system and, indeed, their very survival.

So, the question arises, how do the social justice themes I just described relate to other moral principles? Catholic concerns about health care go beyond (but never away from) its character as an issue of justice, and these concerns should never be seen as being in conflict with, or con-tradicting, each other. Since there are moral demands in both areas, it is cru-cial that both be maintained in any final position we take as a Conference.

How will we respond, then, as a Conference, if the proposed plan includes abortion as a basic health care service?

We will be able to affirm the basic elements of the plan, while work-ing, as we have in the past, to exclude abortion from the mandated servic-es. We have more than enough arguments to sustain this position. Our pri-mary objective should be a policy which seeks justice across the spectrum of life: legislation which excludes abortion (justice for the unborn) and guarantees health care (justice from birth to natural death). The best method of securing both of these goals is a federal policy which meets both criteria. At the same time, we should also advocate the inclusion in any leg-islation of conscience clauses that will protect the beliefs and convictions of individual health care workers and health care institutions which, by cor-porate identity, are opposed to abortion.

If this proves impossible at the national level, a secondary method might be to replace a national mandate with provisions that permit states to decide whether abortion is included in a health care package. Since most states have chosen not to fund abortion, this may be an alternative to explore.

What if some of our objectives are met in a bill, but not others? Obviously the specifics of this case would have to be known in detail before one could make a clear moral judgment. We do not face these ethical challenges empty-handed. We have a religious and theological heritage of reflection on how we maintain our ethical identity in a world of conflicting values. The difficulty is that these principles were developed in a very different socioeconomic environment. In large measure, they were intended to guide the decisions of individuals. Today, the challenge is to relate these principles to institutions that are either an expression of the Church's official ministry or are related to that ministry in a complex social and economic environment. And, to be candid, we have found ourselves in disagreement about the application of these very same principles in recent years.

In our response to the proposed reform, we will also build coalitions with other people of good will in order to achieve our objective of a reformed health care system that protects the dignity of human life from conception to natural death. Some will agree with us in our efforts to protect the life of the unborn, but will not agree with our other commitments. As a Conference, we must continue to point out that a positive moral vision sustains our commitment to the poor, our commitment to the dignity of the human person (including the right to adequate health care), as well as our commitment to the life of the unborn. If we do not do this, we will give the pro-abortion movement ample grounds to cast us in a narrow, sectarian, and elitist perspective.

Conclusion

The current health care system is failing to nurture the full health of the American people and the common good of our society. The present moment presents a unique opportunity when true reform of this unjust and unsustainable health care system seems a realistic possibility. Under these circumstances, we have an obligation to work for fundamental reform of health care, to achieve a system which fosters respect for all human life and human dignity.

We will need both moral wisdom and political skill to advance our values in a political environment often hostile to both the unserved and the unborn. Some say the choice is clear: pursue health care reform without regard for the anti-life dimensions of possible legislation. Others say: oppose health care reform if it includes abortion. Both of these strategies are inadequate. Both groups are too ready to accept defeat and call it victory.

Attempts to link public funding of abortion with national health care do not serve the best interests of our nation and would be a tragic setback.

So, too, would the demise of genuine health care reform be a tragic outcome for tens of millions of Americans. If we work as hard as we can, but cannot prevail on the abortion issue in this political climate, are we morally compelled to help defeat much-needed health care for poor families and vulnerable children? Such an outcome would be not only a defeat for a piece of vital legislation, but a loss for our Church and a serious setback for our social tradition. I hope we can find in our community the political resources to avoid this nightmare, if at all possible. I pray we will find in our moral tradition the ethical principles to guide us through this terrible dilemma, if it proves necessary. In this regard, we need to involve in our deliberations theologians as well as the religious who sponsor and administer Catholic health care institutions.

What is really at stake in this case is not simply politics or principles, but the lives and dignity of millions of our sisters and brothers. Health care is a matter of fundamental justice, because, for so many, it is literally a matter of life and death, of lives cut short and dignity denied.

29.

EUTHANASIA AND A GLOBAL ETHIC

PARLIAMENT OF THE WORLD'S RELIGIONS,
CHICAGO, AUGUST 31, 1993

Most people were amazed at Chicago's rapid comeback after the Great Fire of 1871. The city of "big shoulders" also had some "big ideas"! In 1893, only twenty-two years after the fire, Chicago offered the world the spectacular Columbian Exposition and hosted the World Parliament of Religions, an historic first step in interreligious dialogue and understanding. Cardinal Gibbons attended the World Parliament, but, later, Pope Leo XIII forbade Catholic participation in such "dubious events."

Much has changed in the past century. In 1986, for example, Pope John Paul II invited the world's religious leaders to join him in Assisi to pray for peace. And metropolitan Chicago has undergone enormous changes. But one thing has not changed: the need to learn from one another and to work together to face the major issues which confront all of us. Indeed, in our increasingly shrinking and interdependent world, such collaboration is imperative. This is why I am so delighted to be a participant in this second Parliament of the World's Religions.

This morning, I will share with you some thoughts on an ethical issue that confronts us in the United States and in many other first-world nations. It is paradigmatic of broader cultural or societal movements that have already affected or will impact all of the world's religions. I am speaking of the movement to legalize euthanasia or assisted suicide.

The Movement to Legalize Euthanasia

In the United States, advocates of euthanasia, or "mercy killing" as it used to be called, have been around for decades. However, up to recently, they have had little impact on our society, its laws, and its public policies. Today, this seems to be rapidly changing—a cause of grave concern for many of us.

One of the reasons for this disconcerting change in attitude stems from the fact that the advocates of euthanasia no longer refer to it as "mercy killing." They now use such ambiguous euphemisms as "aid in dying," similar to the practice of pro-abortion forces in the United States who prefer to identify themselves simply as "pro-choice." This tactical change has accompanied a growing attention in this country to the plight of families when confronted with a loved one with a debilitating or painful fatal disease, as well as to the condition of those who are permanently unconscious, in what is known as a "persistent vegetative state."

As a result, initiatives have been introduced by way of state referendums, which, in addition to codifying laudable and appropriate clarifications of the law, also have sought to secure the right to provide "aid in dying" to patients. The goal of this legislation is not to legalize all euthanasia, but it would allow a doctor, upon the request of a patient, to administer or provide a legal drug that would bring about the patient's immediate death.

I am pleased to report that, to date, these efforts have failed. That is the good news. The bad news is that the margin of victory has not been great and has required the expenditure of significant amounts of money. Whether this expenditure can be sustained in the future is questionable. It is also possible that, having learned from their failures, the pro-euthanasia forces will be able to draft legislation that will achieve at least part of their objective and gain the support of a majority of voters.

This movement is not confined to the United States. In April of 1990 the Committee on the Environment, Public Health, and Consumer Protection of the European Parliament adopted a motion for a resolution concerning care for the terminally ill. Again, as in some of the proposed U. S. legislation, many of its recommendations were positive and quite acceptable. For example, reflecting widespread concerns about the inappropriateness of some aggressive, very burdensome treatments at times of terminal illness, the document acknowledges that "attempts to cure at all costs . . . must be avoided." It also urges that all health care personnel be trained to have a persistently caring attitude toward the dying.

The document further calls for "palliative care" units in all European hospitals to care for those who are terminally ill. Such care seeks to reduce the distressing symptoms of a disease without treating its cause. The goal of this care is to help the patient "fight against pain, discomfort and fear" in the face of incurable illness. Moreover, pointing to the importance of the loving presence of relatives and friends to the dying, the resolution proposes that the treatment of the terminally ill should take place in the familiarity of their home whenever possible.

Unfortunately, the resolution also went far beyond these recommendations. First, in a somewhat subtle manner it sought to redefine the meaning of the human person so that personhood could easily be identified with consciousness. Obviously such a change would have dire consequences for the unconscious, persons with serious mental disorders, and persons with certain disabilities. It is a change that must be resisted.

The document also recommended the use of euthanasia when (1) no cure is available for a terminal illness, (2) palliative care fails, (3) "a fully conscious patient insistently and repeatedly requests an end to an existence which has for him been robbed of all dignity," and (4) "a team of doctors created for that purpose establishes the impossibility of providing further specific care."

In other words, as Archbishop Charles Brand, President of the Commission of the Episcopates of the European Community, has pointed out, the resolution "claims to legitimate acts which terminate life when it is considered to be no longer dignified and human." Such a change not only violates the injunction, "You shall not kill," found in the Decalogue of the Hebrew Scriptures or Old Testament and other foundational religious documents, but also is a radical departure from the entire code of medical ethics as it has been handed on for over two millennia. This code was first expressed in the so-called Hippocratic Oath attributed to an ancient Greek physician. This oath is still used at some medical school graduations. Its second section includes a pledge to use only beneficial treatments and procedures and not to harm or hurt a patient. It includes promises not to break confidentiality, not to engage in sexual relations with patients or to dispense deadly drugs. It specifically says: "I will never give a deadly drug to anybody if asked for it, nor will I make a suggestion to this effect."

In a moment I will speak of the religious issues involved in the rejection of the injunction, "You shall not kill." For now, however, I will address the consequences of revising a traditional code of medical ethics which has been widely accepted and respected.

What would happen to the doctor-patient relationship if the proponents of euthanasia or assisted suicide are successful in legalizing these unethical, immoral activities? Would you trust a doctor who is licensed to kill? Would you entrust the life of your elderly mother or father, a seriously ill or disabled child—or your own life—to such a person?

Moreover, what added pressures would patients face? If euthanasia or assisted suicide were legal, might this not influence the decisions of elderly persons, for example, who do not want to be a burden to their families? Would not the poor be especially vulnerable to such pressure? Would they perhaps think that the best thing to do would be to ask their doctors to end their lives before their natural death? Moreover, when we are seriously ill, can we know clearly what we want? Would these be free choices?

These are significant, realistic issues which must be addressed. Some would respond by saying that they reflect unnecessary fears, that they are nothing but a "smoke screen" to cover up an attempt to perpetrate an outdated morality. In developing a response to this charge, let us consider what has happened in the Netherlands.

As you might know, the Netherlands has a unique position on the question of euthanasia. Technically euthanasia is still illegal. However, since 1973 a series of court cases has allowed the current practice to develop. In effect, these court decisions give doctors considerable latitude in deciding whether or not to resort to euthanasia in each case. A doctor is expected to report an act of euthanasia to a public prosecutor who must then decide whether or not to prosecute the doctor. Rather than claiming innocence, doctors are to justify their actions by pointing to mitigating circumstances. In effect, they are to prove that they had no alternative under the circumstances—when explicitly asked for "aid in dying" by mentally competent patients.

In such a context it is not a stretch of the imagination to surmise that many, if not most, acts of euthanasia are simply not reported. This means that few cases are actually investigated by public authorities. And this, in turn, means that it is difficult to get an accurate picture of precisely what is going on there. It is widely known, moreover, that Dutch doctors often misrepresent the cause of death on death certificates to avoid having to report acts of euthanasia and face the possibility of prosecution.

Several years ago, the Dutch government established a commission to study the practice of euthanasia in that country. Personally, I found the results of that study to be appalling, but not surprising. The so-called Remmelink Commission concluded that more than 1,000 patients underwent euthanasia without their consent. The lives of another 14,000 patients were shortened by pain-killing medication, also without their consent. The Dutch government has said that only about 200 cases of euthanasia are reported annually. However, according to Catholic News Service, the Remmelink Commission counted 2,340 cases of voluntary euthanasia, 390 cases of assisted suicide, and 1,040 cases of "life terminating acts without explicit and persistent requests" in 1990 alone!

In other words, the Dutch experiment justifies the concerns I mentioned earlier. There is no convincing evidence that active euthanasia can be regulated and managed. There is a valid reason to be concerned about the impact it would have on the doctor-patient relationship, not to mention the entire code of medical ethics. We may rightly question how safe our most vulnerable persons would be in any society that accepts euthanasia.

In the light of information like this, one might legitimately question why the euthanasia movement has become so popular. In the United States there are three possible explanations.

The first possible explanation relates to the world of medicine and medical technology. As I noted earlier, for centuries those in the health care professions have had, as an essential aspect of their identity and mission, the responsibility to heal and preserve life. That responsibility has entered a new era with the development of medicines and technologies that have given physicians previously unknown capabilities in this area. We are grateful, indeed, for the great good which these advancements have brought to the human family.

This good, however, has been a mixed blessing. It is fairly easy for technology or medicine to become an end in itself, and for life to be preserved when, in fact, death should be allowed to occur. This possible domination of technology over the proper course of life has left many people fearful of being kept alive in an inhumane fashion. And this fear has led some to say to their loved ones: "Do whatever you must, but do not let me live that way." The fear, then, of the pain and discomfort of a life prolonged inappropriately has led to an erosion of the natural instinct to preserve one's own life.

A second possible explanation is more particular to the United States and its legal system. Although recent years have seen the enactment of legislation that has alleviated many legal problems, a fear remains that sick persons or their families will be prevented from making the necessary medical decisions on their own and that they will have to become embroiled in a contentious legal process.

These two fears—being kept alive needlessly and losing autonomy to the complexity of the legal system—have been exploited by the pro-euthanasia forces in this country. Many people who now favor the legalization of euthanasia do so, not because they see euthanasia as a good in itself, but because they view it as the only avenue available to remedy these fears effectively.

This leads to the third explanation for the spread of pro-euthanasia attitudes. While this reason is present in the United States, it moves far beyond our borders and infects many parts of the world. It pertains to certain assumptions that have dominated, or are beginning to dominate, many of the world's cultures. For our discussion today I will note four such assumptions. In doing so, I am building on the work of Harvard University Professor Arthur J. Dyck.

First, there is a sense of human autonomy which asserts that an individual's life belongs entirely to the individual, and that each person is free to dispose of that life entirely as he or she wishes. Second, in addition to the absence of external restraint, there is an understanding of human freedom to make moral choices which says that one must also be free to take one's own life. In other words, there also are no internal restraints. Third, it is possible to identify times when life simply is not worth living. This can be because of illness or handicaps or even despair. Finally, the true dignity of being human is to be found in the ability to make conscious, rational choices that control life. In the absence of that capacity, human dignity is lessened.

While one might nuance these assumptions, they capture something of the ethos of the euthanasia movement. And to be candid, there is something to be said for these assumptions. For example, they remind us that there are values in addition to the value of physical survival. Also, death is not the worst evil a person can face.

But they also contain great weaknesses. For example, they contain neither limits nor controls. There is no reason to believe they cannot be extended in a fashion similar to that of the Nazi movement to conclusions that would be destructive to the human family in general and, in particular, to those who are the most vulnerable. Moreover, these assumptions self-evidently attack the basic notion of the human person as a member of a human community that is to be characterized by trust and care for one another. In other words, the movement to legalize euthanasia involves not only decisions at the end of life but also about the very nature of human life.

This means that, if one carefully analyzes the assumptions which would support the legalization of euthanasia, one finds a perspective that challenges the underpinnings of human civilization as we know it. This is why I have chosen this topic for our consideration this morning. As religious persons from around the world, we must attend to this threatening force with conviction and fervor. If we remain silent, the course of human history will be significantly altered.

A Consistent Ethic of Life

But how can we proceed in a meaningful fashion when we experience such diversity of belief and practice? How can a parliament of the world's religions, whose members' ancestors so often persecuted those of other religions, become a catalyst for human change? The obvious answer is that we must find a common ground which would unite us in responding to this challenge while respecting our religious diversity.

Over the past ten years I have sought to develop such a common ground within the Catholic tradition through what I have described as a consistent ethic of life. I have proposed it as a comprehensive concept and a strategy that will help Catholics and other people of good will to influence more effectively the development of public policy on life issues.

The grounding principle for this ethic is found in the Judeo-Christian heritage which has played such an influential role in the formation of the national ethos of this nation. In this religious tradition, the meaning of human life is grounded in the fact that it is *sacred* because God is its origin and its destiny. Many other people of good will also accept the basic premise that human life has a distinctive dignity and meaning or purpose and, as a result, that innocent human life must not be directly attacked, threatened, or diminished. They, too, argue that, because of the privileged meaning of human life, we have the responsibility for preserving, protecting, and nurturing it.

The second principle underlying the consistent ethic of life is the belief that human life is also *social* in nature. We are not born to live alone, but, rather, to move from the dependency of prenatal life and infancy to the interrelatedness of adulthood. To be human is to be social, and those relationships, structures, and institutions which support us, as individuals and as a community, are an essential aspect of human life.

If one accepts these two principles about human life, then one may argue that two precepts or obligations necessarily flow from them. First, as individuals and as a society, we have the positive obligation to protect life. Second, we have a negative obligation not to destroy or injure human life directly, especially the life of the innocent and the vulnerable.

These principles and the resulting precepts have served as the foundation for much of what is known as the Anglo-Saxon legal tradition. They are the context for laws which oppose abortion, murder, and euthanasia. This movement from religious insight to public policy is an important one. In the common law tradition these laws have been maintained, not because of religious insight, but because it is recognized that they pertain to the common good of society. In other words, the commonweal of public life and order would be destroyed if innocent human life could be directly attacked. In more recent years this same insight regarding the fundamental dignity of the human person has been given international recognition in the United Nations Charter of Human Rights.

I have addressed the need for a consistent ethic of life because new technological challenges confront us along the whole spectrum of life from conception to natural death. This creates the need for a consistent ethic, for the spectrum cuts across such life-threatening issues as abortion, capital punishment, modern warfare, and the care of the terminally ill. Admittedly, these are all *distinct* problems, enormously complex, and deserve individual treatment. Each requires its own moral analysis. No single answer or solution applies to all. At any given time, because of the circumstances, one may demand more attention than another. *But they are linked!*

Moreover, life-threatening issues are also linked with life-diminishing issues such as racism, sexism, pornography, prostitution, and child abuse. Wherever human life is considered "cheap" and easily exploited or wasted, respect for life dwindles and, eventually, every human life is in jeopardy.

The concept of a consistent ethic of life is challenging. It requires people to broaden, substantively and creatively, their way of thinking, their attitudes, their responses to life issues. Many are not accustomed to thinking about all the life-threatening and life-diminishing issues in such an interrelated way. As a result, they remain somewhat selective in their response. Some are very committed in their efforts to eradicate the evil of abortion in this nation, but neglect issues of poverty. Others work very hard to alleviate poverty, but neglect the basic right to life of unborn children.

Given this broad range of challenging life issues, we desperately need a societal *attitude* or climate that will sustain a consistent defense and promotion of life. In other words, it is not enough merely to assert an ethical principle like the consistent ethic of life. If it is to be acknowledged and implemented, it must impact all areas of human life. It must respond to all the moments, places, or conditions which either threaten the sanctity of life or cultivate an attitude of disrespect for it. A consistent ethic is based on the need to ensure that the sacredness of every human life, which is the ultimate source of human dignity, will be defended and fostered from the genetic laboratory to the cancer ward, from the ghetto to the prison.

The movement from moral analysis to public policy choices is a complex process in a pluralistic society like the United States. Moreover, there is a legitimate secularity of the political process, just as there is a legitimate role for religious and moral discourse in our nation's life. The moral dimensions of our public life are interwoven with complex empirical judgments where honest disagreement exists, and, so, we owe one another a careful accounting of how we have come to our moral conclusions.

Moreover, in accord with our tradition in the United States, it is not the function of civil law to enjoin or prohibit *everything* that moral principles enjoin or prohibit. When we pursue a course of legal action, we must ask whether the requirements of public order are serious enough to take precedence over the claims of freedom. In a religiously pluralistic society like the United States, achieving consensus on what constitutes a public moral question is never easy. But we have been able to do it—by a process of debate, decision-making, then review of our decisions and their impact on human lives, including the most vulnerable among us.

A Challenge to Address Euthanasia within a Global Ethic

My efforts to articulate the need for a consistent ethic of life have helped others in the U. S. to address a full range of life issues from conception to natural death. However, I am not so presumptuous as to propose it in its current formulation as being adequate for the tasks we face throughout our religiously pluralistic world. Rather, I propose it as a model of what I think needs to be done—namely, the drawing together of religious insight in a way that will provide for a comprehensive context or common ground for addressing the challenges we face with regard to the very nature and dignity of human life.

To that end I recommend that, as religious persons and leaders, we must engage three questions, in particular, in the light of our respective religious traditions:

First, is human life in its bodily form a thing to be used, an instrument, as it were, for the fulfillment of rational choices? Or does it have a meaning and a purpose that affirms the integrity of body and spirit, which is the origin of the dignity of the human person and which is more than human consciousness?

Second, what is the value and significance of human community? For example, is it true, as theologian Stanley Hauerwas has proposed, that an essential aspect of human experience is the need and the desire to be able to trust the community in which one is situated?

Third, what is the significance of individual human choices? Is there, as theologian Ron Hamel suggests, a cumulative effect of individual choices that, in time, influences the moral tone and character of a society—and, I would add, the entire human family?

As you may surmise, I believe that human life does have a meaning and a purpose that affirms the integrity of body and spirit. I affirm that all human persons do need and desire to be able to trust the community in which they abide. Moreover, I fully maintain that individual choices influence the moral tone and character of a community and the entire human family.

That is why I am opposed to the legalization of euthanasia. It compromises the fundamental dignity of the human person in its inordinate exaltation of rational consciousness and in its challenge to the belief that there can be any significance to human suffering. It does inconceivable violence to the trust that should exist between doctor and patient—and, indeed, among all human persons. And it naively pretends that individual human choices are isolated moments which have no impact on the lives and well-being of others.

I invite you to consider how *you* would answer these questions. Moreover, as we reflect upon the many threats to human life throughout the world, can we continue to develop a global ethic in such a manner that it will help us meet the challenge posed by efforts to legalize euthanasia? I believe this would enhance our efforts to defend and preserve the dignity of the human person in community and sustain our opposition to those who threaten or diminish human life.

Now, in the time remaining during this session, I am eager to hear your comments or reflections on what I have said in the light of your respective religious traditions.

30.

THE CONSISTENT ETHIC OF LIFE
AND HEALTH CARE REFORM

NATIONAL PRESS CLUB, WASHINGTON, D.C.,
MAY 26, 1994

As many of you may know, in the last year I have experienced a significant amount of press coverage for reasons that are happily behind me. There is a temptation in this prestigious forum to share some of my reactions and reflections based on that experience, but I am going to resist that temptation. At another time and after more reflection on my part, I might share some thoughts about what I learned about the news media and related topics. But today I address a more important and more timely topic—the moral dimensions of health care reform.

For the last decade as a pastor, a bishop, and a leader of our National Conference of Catholic Bishops, I have had the opportunity to address a series of vital moral challenges. I chaired the committee that produced the pastoral letter on war and peace a decade ago. I have served as chair of our bishops' committees on pro-life matters and family-life concerns. As a bishop, I have also seen the crime, injustice, and violence in our neighborhoods and the loss of roots and responsibility in our cities, the loss of the sense of family and caring in our communities that is undermining millions of lives.

I believe that at the heart of so many of our problems—in Chicago and Washington, in Bosnia and Rwanda—there is a fundamental lack of respect for human life and human dignity. Over the past ten years I have articulated a "Consistent Ethic of Life" as a moral framework to address the growing violence in our midst.

The purpose of the consistent life ethic is to provide a moral framework for analysis and motivation for action on a wide range of human life-issues with important ethical dimensions. The consistent life ethic, by design, provides for a public discourse that respects the separation of church and state, and also recognizes the proper role of religious perspectives and ethical convictions in the public life of a pluralistic society.

Over the past years I have addressed many issues in the light of the consistent ethic. In addition to the central question of abortion, I have spoken about euthanasia and assisted suicide, capital punishment, the newer technologies used to assist human reproduction, and war and peace, to

238

name a few. The foundation for all of these discussions is a deep conviction about the nature of human life, namely, that human life is sacred, which means that all human life has an inalienable dignity that must be protected and respected from conception to natural death. For the Christian believer and many others, the source of this dignity is the creative action of God in whose "image and likeness" we are made. Still others are aware that life is a precious gift which must be protected and nurtured.

For advocates of a consistent life ethic, the national debate about health care reform represents both an opportunity and a test. It is an opportunity to address issues and policies that are often matters of life and death, such as, who is covered and who is not; which services are included and which are not; will reform protect human life and enhance dignity, or will it threaten or undermine life and dignity? It is a test in the sense that we will be measured by the comprehensiveness of our concerns and the consistency of our principles in this area.

In this current debate, a consistent life ethic approach to health care requires us to stand up for both the unserved and the unborn, to insist on the inclusion of real universal coverage and the exclusion of abortion coverage, to support efforts to restrain rising health costs, and to oppose the denial of needed care to the poor and vulnerable. In standing with the unserved and the unborn, the uninsured and the undocumented, we bring together our pro-life and social justice values. They are the starting points for a consistent life agenda for health care reform.

In these remarks I speak as a pastor of a diverse local church. In Chicago we see both the strengths and the difficulties of our current system. We experience the remarkable dedication, professionalism, and caring of the people and the amazing contributions of the institutions that make up our health care system. I also see the children without care, the sick without options, the communities without adequate health services, the families and businesses strained and broken by health care costs. We see the hurts and pick up the pieces of a failing system—in our hospitals and clinics, our shelters and agencies, our parishes and schools. We look at health care reform from the bottom up, not who wins or loses politically, not how it impacts powerful institutions and professions, but how it touches the poor and vulnerable, the unserved and the unborn, the very young and the very old.

As I indicated earlier, I am also a member of the National Conference of Catholic Bishops, an organization deeply involved in this debate. Our principles and priorities are summarized in a resolution unanimously adopted by the Conference last year. A unanimous vote of our bishops is an unusual accomplishment, as those of you who have ever seen us discuss holy days or liturgical texts can attest! But we found unity in embracing a consistent life ethic approach to health care reform.

The broader health care debate is driven by many factors. For the sake of time, I will list only five without discussing them at any length.

1. The amount of money spent on health care is escalating at an unsustainable rate. It surpassed 14% of the gross domestic product (GDP) last year, and it is reasonable to assume that, without effective intervention, it could reach 18% of the GDP by the year 2000.
2. This uncontrolled growth is creating economic hardships for many of our fellow citizens, especially working families.
3. Private insurance programs are deteriorating through risk segmentation into programs that more and more serve those who have the least need for health insurance—the healthy.
4. Cost shifting—that is, the passing on of unreimbursed expenses by health providers to employer premiums—has become a "hidden tax" that no longer is sustainable.
5. Finally, and most significantly, the number of uninsured in the United States continues, now approaching nearly 40 million, a large portion of whom are people who work. Ten million are children. This lack of coverage touches African-American and Hispanic families most directly.

I join the many who have concluded that the United States needs profound systemic change in its health care system. We cannot rely on the system to correct itself. Without intervention, things are getting worse, not better.

I hasten to add that my advocacy is not partisan. Neither do I argue on behalf of any particular proposal before the Congress. I do, however, take exception with those who say that there is no serious systemic problem or that what we merely face is an insurance or a health care delivery problem. On the contrary, there is a fundamental health care problem in our nation today. I share this judgment with many leaders of the Catholic community whose outlook and convictions have been shaped:

- by the experience of Catholic religious communities and dioceses that operate 600 hospitals and 300 long-term care facilities, constituting the largest non-profit group of health care providers in the United States;
- by the experience of the Catholic Church in the United States, which purchases health coverage for hundreds of thousands of employees and their families;
- by the experience of Catholic Charities, the largest private deliverer of social services in the nation;
- by our experience as a community of faith, caring for those who "fall through the cracks" of our current system.

It is this broad range of experience that led the U. S. Catholic bishops to say last June:

> *Now is the time for real health care reform. It is a matter of fundamental justice. For so many it is literally a matter of life and death, of lives cut short and dignity denied. We urge our national leaders to look beyond special interest claims and partisan dif-*

*ferences to unite our nation in a new commitment to meet the
health care needs of our people, especially the poor and the vulnerable. This is a major political task, a significant policy challenge and a moral imperative.*

Before addressing some of the more specific issues associated with
health care reform, it is important that we consider some even more profound issues. I say this because President Clinton's health care reform proposal and the alternatives to it, like any significant government initiatives
that would reorder social relationships and responsibilities, have drawn us
into a discussion of fundamental values and social convictions. Several
important convictions, which serve as a kind of bedrock for the consistent
life ethic, can assist us in this broader discussion. They are:

- There are *basic goods and values* which we human beings share
  because we share the gift of human life; these goods and values
  serve as the common ground for a public morality that guides
  our actions as a nation and as a society.
- Within the individual, these common goods and values express
  themselves in an inalienable human dignity, with consequent
  rights and *duties*.
- One of the ways these rights and duties are expressed in the
  human community is through the recognition and *pursuit of the
  common good*; or, to say it differently, through a good that is to
  be pursued in common with all of society; a good that ultimately is more important than the good of any individual.
- This common good is realized in the context of a *living community,* which is nurtured by the virtues and shared values of individuals. Such a community protects the basic rights of individuals.
- As part of this community, both individuals and institutions
  (including government, business, education, labor, and other
  mediating structures) have an *obligation*, which is rooted in distributive justice, to *work to secure this common good*; this is
  how we go about meeting the reasonable claims of citizens striving to realize and experience their fundamental human dignity.

These convictions find their origin in a vision of the human person as
someone who is grounded in community, and in an understanding of society and government as being largely responsible for the realization of the
common good. As Catholics we share this vision with many others. It is
consistent with fundamental American values, though grounded differently.
For example, our Declaration of Independence and our Constitution reflect
a profound insight that has guided the development of our nation; namely,
that there are certain fundamental human rights that exist before the creation of any social contract (such as the constitution of a sovereign nation),
and that these must be protected by society and government. There is an
objective order to which we are held accountable and to which we, in turn,

hold others accountable in our many relationships and activities. The Catholic tradition also affirms such rights but sees them emerging from the organic relationship between the individual and the community.

As a nation, we also have had a sense of a common good which is greater than the agenda of any individual. Alexis de Tocqueville noted this when he commented on the American penchant for volunteering. We also have been a nation of communities. Whether in the small towns of the Plains or the ethnic communities of the large cities, U. S. citizens had a sense of being bonded together and being mutually responsible. We also recognized that our individual and collective existence is best protected by virtuous living—balancing the demands of personhood and social responsibility. In more recent years, as our social order has become more complex, we have come to see that a proper sense of mutual responsibility requires a greater presence of the state in helping individuals to realize their human potential and social responsibility. Public education and social security are but two examples of this presence.

Without being overly pessimistic, I suggest that these fundamental convictions, which are essential both to a consistent life ethic and to our well-being as a nation and a society, are being challenged today. There is abroad a certain tendency which would suggest that law and public order are accountable only to the subjective convictions of individuals or pressure groups, not to any objective, albeit imperfectly perceived, moral order. Robert Bellah and his associates have convincingly shown how a sense of the common good, the role of community, and the value of virtuous living have been compromised, if not lost, in recent years. I am convinced that the violence that plagues our nation is a symptom of this loss of an overarching social order. We are a nation that is increasingly overly individualistic at the very time when the problems we face require greater common effort and collective responses.

All of this needs to be taken into consideration in any substantive discussion of health care reform. If we are not attentive to issues such as these, then our dialogues and debates will go nowhere because of disagreements—unknown and unacknowledged—on basic principles.

First, there is the issue of *universal access*. In the June 1993 statement I cited earlier, the U. S. Catholic bishops outlined key principles and priorities for initiating and executing reform. Our third principle was universal access to comprehensive health care for every person living in the United States.

We believe that health care—including preventive and primary care—is not only a commodity; it is an essential safeguard of human life and dignity. In 1981, the bishops spoke of health care as a basic human right which flows from the sanctity of human life. In declaring this, the bishops were not saying that a person had a right to *health*, but that, since the common good is the sum of those conditions necessary to preserve human dignity, one must have a right of access, insofar as it is possible, to those goods and services which will allow a person to maintain or regain health. And if one views this right within the context of the convictions I have just discussed, then it is the responsibility of society as a whole and government to ensure that there is a common social order that makes the realization of this good possible. Whether we have health care should not depend on whom we work for, how much our parents earn, or where we live.

So far, so good. Most would agree, at least in theory. Where the disagreement comes is in regard to the last of the convictions I noted in discussing the consistent ethic. Allow me to rephrase it: "Under the title of distributive justice, society has the obligation to meet the reasonable claims of its citizens so that they can realize and exercise their fundamental human rights."

When many of us Americans think of justice, we tend to think of what we can claim from one another. This is an individualistic understanding of justice. But there is another American instinct which has a broader understanding of justice. It has been summarized by Father Philip Keane, a moral theologian, who wrote: "Justice shifts our thinking from what we claim from each other to what we owe to each other. Justice is about duties and responsibilities, about building the good community." In this perspective, distributive justice is the obligation which falls upon society to meet the reasonable expectations of its citizens so that they can realize and exercise their fundamental human rights. And, in this instance, the right is that of access to those goods and services that make it possible for persons to maintain their health and thus broaden health care beyond what is provided by a hospital, a clinic, or a physician.

So far I have argued that health care is an essential safeguard of human life and dignity and that there is an obligation for society to ensure that a person be able to realize this right. I now want to go a step further. I believe that the only way this obligation can be effectively met by society is for our nation to make *universal health care coverage* a reality. Universal *access* is not enough. We can no longer tolerate being the only Western nation that leaves millions of persons uncovered. For many, this will be a "hard saying." The cry of political expediency and the maneuvering of special interest groups already are working either to provide a program of access that maintains a two-tiered health care system (which marginalizes large portions of our society) or to limit coverage. When I speak of universal coverage, I do not mean a vague promise or a rhetorical preamble to legislation, but the *practical means* and *sufficient investment* to permit all to obtain decent health care on a regular basis.

If justice is a hallmark of our national community, then we must fulfill our obligations in justice to the poor and the unserved *first* and not last. Similarly, we cannot ignore the millions of undocumented immigrants. Even if the demands of justice were set aside, reasons of public health would necessitate their being included. The undocumented will continue to need medical assistance, and hospitals will continue to be required to provide medical care for those who present themselves for treatment. In a reformed system, which should contain, if not eliminate, the cost-shifting that previously had paid for their care, the medical expenses of the undocumented must be covered for both policy and moral reasons.

Unfortunately, as the national debate on health care reform has evolved, and as legislation has been proposed, an important fact has been lost: namely, that it is not enough simply to expand coverage. If real reform is to be achieved—that is, reform that will ensure quality and cost-effective care—then we must do what is necessary in order to ensure that our health care delivery system is person-centered and has a community focus. Health care cannot be successfully reformed if it is considered only an economic matter. This reform will be morally blighted if the nature of care—something profoundly human, not easily measured, yet that which, far more than technology, remains the heart and breath of the art of healing—is not preserved and expanded along with health coverage itself. The challenge is to provide universal coverage without seriously disrupting the doctor/patient relationship which is so central to good medical care.

After a long period of research and discussion, the Catholic Health Association (CHA) developed a proposal for health care reform that seeks to meet this and other challenges. It is called "Setting Relationships Right." I hope that the values CHA has proposed and the strategies it has developed in this regard will not be lost sight of. Our objective must be a healthy nation where the mental and physical health of the individual is addressed through collaborative efforts at the local level.

Let me summarize my major points so far. First, we need a profound systemic reform of our health care system. Second, justice and the common good demand that this reform include universal coverage. Third, justice at this time requires a program of effective universal coverage that is person-centered and community-based. This leads us to two thorny questions: How is the program to be funded, and how are costs to be contained?

As you know, these two questions are essentially interrelated. It is clear that the rate of cost increases in health care cannot be sustained even if there is no systemic reform. It also is clear that the demands of a more fiscally responsible use of federal monies must be taken into account. We cannot spend what we do not have.

Our episcopal conference has insisted that health care reform must also include effective mechanisms to restrain rising health care costs. Without cost containment, we cannot make health care affordable and direct scarce national resources to other pressing national problems. Containing costs is crucial if we are to avoid dangerous pressures toward the kind of rationing that raises fundamental ethical and equity questions. The poor, vulnerable, and uninsured persons cannot be denied needed care because the health system refuses to eliminate waste, duplication, and bureaucratic costs.

But we may also have to consider other steps to restrain costs and distribute health care more justly. For example, we may have to recognize that basic and preventive care, and health care to preserve and protect life, should be a higher priority than purely elective procedures. This raises the often explosive concept of "rationing." I prefer a different word and a different concept—"stewardship." How do we best protect human life and enhance human dignity in a situation of limited health resources? How do we ensure that the lives and health of the poor and vulnerable are not less valuable or less a priority than the lives and health of the rest of us?

This is not an abstract discussion. Rationing health care is a regular, if unacknowledged, feature of our current health care system. Nearly 40 million are uninsured; 50 million more are underinsured. In 1992, nearly 10 million children were without medical coverage, 400,000 more than in 1991. In my own state of Illinois, 86,000 persons lose their health insurance each month. Being without insurance means being without care when you need it, delaying care until an illness or injury may require more costly intervention or be beyond any treatment.

We now have an insurance model that requires individuals to pay for the items and services which their health care needs require—some without limitations and others with enormous constraints. We have been rationing health care in recent years by squeezing people out of the system through insurance marketing techniques like medical underwriting, pre-existing condition exclusion, and insurance red-lining. Actuarial pricing designed to protect insurance company assets pits one group against another—the old against the young, the sick against the healthy—thus undermining the solidarity of the whole community. We can see this tension playing itself out in the disturbing debates around this country about assisted suicide.

In light of these concerns, the nation must undertake a broad-based and inclusive consideration of how we will choose to allocate and share our health care dollars. We are stewards, not sole owners, of all our resources, human and material; thus, goods and services must be shared. This is not a task for government alone. Institutions and individuals must be involved in reaching a shared moral consensus, which will allow us to reassert the essential value of the person as an individual and as a member of the community. From that moral consensus must come a process of decision-making and resource allocation which preserves the dignity of all persons, in particular the most vulnerable. It is proper for society to establish limits on what it can reasonably provide in one area of the commonweal so that it can address other legitimate responsibilities to the community. But in establishing such limits, the inalienable life and dignity of every person, in particular the vulnerable, must be protected.

The Catholic Health Association has addressed the ethics of rationing and offered some moral criteria. These demand that any acceptable plan must meet a demonstrable need, be oriented to the common good, apply to all, result from an open and participatory process, give priority to disadvantaged persons, be free of wrongful discrimination, and be monitored in its social and economic effects.

This kind of framework offers far better guidance than the moral bankruptcy of assisted suicide and the ethically unacceptable withholding of care based on "quality of life" criteria. We will measure any cost-containment initiative by two values: Does it distribute resources more justly? And does it protect the lives and dignity of the poor and vulnerable?

But the problem of rationed access to necessary medical care is only one aspect of the cost-containment debate. What of the issue of *funding*? Obviously I cannot offer a detailed analysis of the specific proposals which are on the table. But I can say this: If systemic reform addresses in a substantive manner issues of quality care and cost effectiveness, then justice will demand that all sectors of our society contribute to the support of these efforts. And this support takes two forms. First, each individual must assume appropriate responsibility for the costs associated with health care, and must assume responsibility to do all that is possible not to put his or her health at risk. Second, those segments of our economic order which have been able to avoid an appropriate level of responsibility for the health care of their employees, must begin to assume their fair share, just as the rest of society must. In other words, we all must be willing to help meet this demand of justice. We must share the sacrifices that will have to be made.

Thus far, I have insisted that a consistent life ethic requires a commitment to genuine universal coverage, because lack of coverage threatens the lives and diminishes the dignity of millions of men, women, and children. I must also say clearly and emphatically that a consistent life ethic requires us to lift the burden of mandated abortion coverage from needed health care reform. I say this for several important reasons:

1. It is morally wrong to coerce millions of people into paying for the destruction of unborn children against their consciences and convictions. How ironic it would be if advocates of "choice," as they call themselves, require me and millions like me to obtain and pay for abortion coverage, which we abhor. It is a denial of "choice," a violation of conscience, and a serious blow to the common good.

2. It is politically destructive. Needed national health care reform must not be burdened by abortion coverage, which neither the country nor the Congress supports. Public opinion polls and recent Congressional action clearly indicate that, whatever their views on the morality or legality of abortion, the American people and their representatives do not wish to coerce all citizens into paying for procedures that so divide our nation. A University of Cincinnati poll in January of this year indicated that only 30% favor the inclusion of abortion as a basic benefit even if it could be included at no cost at all. Only 14% wanted abortion coverage if it would add to the cost of health premiums.

3. Abortion mandates would undermine the participation of Catholic and other religious providers of health care, who now provide essential care in many of the nation's most underserved communities. I fear our hospitals will be unable to fulfill their mission and meet their responsibilities in a system where abortion is a mandated benefit. Strong conscience clauses are necessary to deal with a variety of medical/moral issues, but are not sufficient to protect Catholic and other providers who find abortion morally objectionable. The only remedy is not to link needed reform to abortion mandates.

The sooner the burden of abortion mandates is lifted, the better for the cause of reform. We continue to insist that it would be a grave moral tragedy, a serious policy mistake, and a major political error to link health care reform to abortion. An insistence on abortion coverage will turn millions of advocates of reform into adversaries of health care legislation.

We cannot and will not support reform that fails to offer universal coverage or that insists on abortion mandates. While this offers moral consistency, it can place us in conflicting political alliances. For example, we concur with the position of the President and Mrs. Clinton in calling real universal coverage essential. We concur with Representative Henry Hyde and the pro-life caucus in insisting that abortion coverage must be abandoned. We concur with the Hispanic Caucus in our commitment that universal coverage must be truly "universal coverage."

This is our consistent ethic message to the White House, the Congress, and the country. We are advocates of these key principles and priorities, not any particular plan. We will not choose between our key priorities. We will work with the leaders of our land to pass health care reform, reform that reflects a true commitment to human life and human dignity. As I noted above, the polls indicate that most Americans join us in support for both authentic universal coverage and the exclusion of abortion coverage in health care reform. We will carry this message forward with civility and consistency. We offer our moral convictions and practical experience, not political contributions and endorsements. We have no "attack ads" or PAC funds. But we can be a valuable partner for reform, and we will work tirelessly for real reform without abortion mandates.

For defenders of human life, there is no more important or timely task than offering an ethical and effective contribution to the health care debate. The discussions and decisions over the next months will tell us a lot about what kind of society we are and will become. We must ask ourselves: What are the choices, investments, and sacrifices we are willing to make in order to protect and enhance the life and dignity of all, especially the poor and vulnerable? In the nation's Capital, health care reform is seen primarily as a *political* challenge—the task of developing attractive and workable proposals, assembling supportive coalitions, and securing the votes needed to pass a bill. But fundamentally, health care reform is a *moral* challenge—

finding the values and vision to reshape a major part of national life to protect better the life and dignity of all.

Ultimately, this debate is not simply about politics—about which
party or interest group prevails. It is about *children*, who die because of the
lack of prenatal care or the violence of abortion. About *people* who have
no health care because of where they work or where they come from. About
communities without care, and workers without coverage.

Health care reform is both a *political* task and a *moral* test. As a religious community with much at stake and much to contribute to this debate,
we are working for health care reform that truly reaches out to the
unserved, protects the unborn, and advances the common good.

31.

EUTHANASIA IN THE CATHOLIC TRADITION

ROCKHURST COLLEGE, KANSAS CITY, MISSOURI, FEBRUARY 1, 1995

This evening, I will share with you some thoughts on an ethical issue that confronts us in the United States and in many other first-world nations. It is paradigmatic of broader cultural or societal movements that have already affected or will impact all of us. I am speaking of the movement to legalize euthanasia or assisted suicide.

I will (a) describe the movement to legalize euthanasia or assisted suicide, (b) offer some reasons why it has become so popular, and (c) examine the issue in the light of the Catholic tradition. Let me begin, however, by clarifying certain terms.

As the U. S. Catholic Bishops pointed out in their Ethical and Religious Directives for Catholic Health Services, approved last November 17, euthanasia "is an action or omission which of itself or by intention *causes* death, in order to alleviate suffering." In *assisted suicide* a third party provides the means for a person to kill him- or herself by lethal injection, a prescription for a lethal drug, or another means. To *cause* death, rather than to *allow* it to occur in the natural course of life, makes all the difference in deciding whether or not a given procedure is euthanasia or assisted suicide. To respect a patient's refusal of treatment or a request to cease treatment is *not* euthanasia. To withdraw or withhold treatment when the burdens are disproportionate to the benefits is *not* euthanasia. To administer medication to relieve pain, even if the foreseen but unintended effect may be to hasten death, is *not* euthanasia. The intention in euthanasia and assisted suicide is to *cause* death, not merely to allow it to happen.

The Movement to Legalize Euthanasia

In the United States, advocates of euthanasia, or "mercy killing" as it used to be called, have been around for decades. However, up to recently, they have had little impact on our society, its laws, and its public policies. Today, this is rapidly changing—a cause of grave concern for many of us.

One of the reasons for this disconcerting change in attitude stems from the fact that the advocates of euthanasia no longer refer to it as "mercy killing." They now use such ambiguous euphemisms as "aid in dying," similar to the practice of pro-abortion forces in the United States, who prefer to identify themselves simply as "pro-choice." This tactical change has accompanied a growing attention in this country to the plight of families when confronted with a loved one with a debilitating or painful fatal disease, as well as to the condition of those who are permanently unconscious, in what is known as a persistent vegetative state.

As a result, three kinds of initiatives have been introduced around the country: (1) state referendums, which, in addition to codifying laudable and appropriate clarifications of the law, have also sought to secure the right to provide "aid in dying" to patients; (2) court cases, which seek to have state legislation against euthanasia or assisted suicide declared unconstitutional; and (3) the provocative actions of Dr. Jack Kevorkian, a retired Michigan pathologist.

Let us first consider the state referendums. Initiatives to legalize euthanasia were defeated by voters in the state of Washington in 1991 and in California in 1992 by 54% to 46% margins. While these efforts failed, the bad news is that the margin of victory was not great and required the expenditure of significant amounts of money.

More recently, having learned from their failures in Washington and California, the pro-euthanasia forces drafted similar but revised proposals for a referendum in Oregon in order to achieve at least part of their objective and gain the support of a majority of voters. They modified their proposals to exclude lethal injections and to limit the role of physicians to prescribing lethal drugs. This apparently made Measure 16, as it was called, less objectionable to voters. Last November 8, the measure passed by a margin of 51% to 49%, and Oregon became the only state in our nation to decriminalize physician-assisted suicide for terminally ill patients; that is, those who are expected by their doctor to die within six months.

On December 27, 1994, U. S. District Judge Michael Hogan granted a preliminary injunction against implementation of Measure 16. In his opinion, he noted that the "law invokes profound questions of constitutional dimension." He concluded that "surely the first assisted-suicide law in this country deserves a considered, thoughtful constitutional analysis." He also noted the seriousness of the plaintiffs' objections to the Measure, including, for example, the possibility of misdiagnosis of terminal illness or that physicians and health care workers might be required by the new law to comply with procedures contrary to their religious and moral convictions.

A second set of initiatives has involved challenging state laws that prohibit physician-assisted suicide. Currently, 31 states have statutes banning assisted suicide, and almost all of them have homicide statutes under which it can be prosecuted. In a case in the state of Washington, concluded on May 3, 1994, U. S. District Judge Barbara Rothstein stated that a competent, terminally ill adult *does* have a constitutionally guaranteed right under the 14th Amendment to commit physician-assisted suicide. This ruling is the *first* judicial decision that alleges a constitutional right to assisted suicide. However, as its critics immediately pointed out, the judge's decision blurred the fundamental moral distinction between *allowing* someone to die and *causing* that person's death. Moreover, Judge Rothstein based her opinion, in large part, on alleged analogies with the U. S. Supreme Court decisions on abortion, especially the 1992 *Planned Parenthood v. Casey*. It comes as no surprise that Judge Rothstein's decision is under appeal.

On December 5, 1994, U. S. District Judge Thomas Griesa in New York came to the opposite conclusion in another case that tried to overturn New York's statute on assisted suicide. The plaintiffs had argued in terms similar to Judge Rothstein's, but Judge Griesa concluded that their attempt to apply Supreme Court abortion decisions on constitutional rights was "too broad." He also held that it is not "unreasonable or irrational for the state to recognize a difference" between "refusing treatment in the case of a terminally ill person and taking a dose of medication which leads to death."

The legal battles will continue, and we can expect that eventually, some cases will appear before the U. S. Supreme Court.

The third kind of initiative in support of assisted suicide is Dr. Jack Kevorkian's public flaunting of a Michigan statute by helping people commit suicide. Last spring, Dr. Kevorkian was tried under a law that banned assisted suicide, but a Detroit jury, quite surprisingly, found him not guilty even though he had admitted what he had done. The statute's constitutionality has been challenged before the Michigan Supreme Court, and the state legislature is working on another law. Meanwhile, last November Dr. Kevorkian helped another person commit suicide by supplying her with carbon monoxide gas. This was the 21st death in which he assisted since he began his activities in June 1990. We can expect that he will vigorously continue his efforts to legalize assisted suicide. Unfortunately, the extensive media coverage about his actions often ignore alternatives available to the elderly and the terminally ill—including, for example, living wills.

The movement to legalize euthanasia or assisted suicide is not confined to the United States. In April of 1990 the Committee on the Environment, Public Health, and Consumer Protection of the European Parliament adopted a motion for a resolution concerning care for the terminally ill. Again, as in some of the proposed U. S. legislation, many of its recommendations were positive and quite acceptable. For example, reflecting widespread concern about the inappropriateness of some aggressive, very burdensome treatments at times of terminal illness, the document acknowledges that "attempts to cure at all costs . . . must be avoided." It also urges that all health care personnel be trained to have a persistently caring attitude toward the dying.

The document further calls for "palliative care" units in all European hospitals to care for those who are terminally ill. Such care seeks to reduce the distressing symptoms of a disease without treating its cause. The goal of this care is to help the patient "fight against pain, discomfort and fear" in the face of incurable illness. Moreover, pointing to the importance of the loving presence of relatives and friends to the dying, the resolution proposes that the treatment of the terminally ill should take place in the familiarity of their home whenever possible.

Unfortunately, the resolution also went far beyond these recommendations. First, in a somewhat subtle manner it sought to redefine the meaning of the human person so that personhood could easily be identified with consciousness. Obviously such a change would have dire consequences for the unconscious, persons with serious mental disorders, and persons with certain disabilities. It is a change that must be resisted.

The document also recommended the use of euthanasia when (1) no cure is available for a terminal illness, (2) palliative care fails, (3) "a fully conscious patient insistently and repeatedly requests an end to an existence which has for him been robbed of all dignity," and (4) "a team of doctors created for that purpose establishes the impossibility of providing further specific care."

In other words, as Archbishop Charles Brand, President of the Commission of the Episcopates of the European Community, has pointed out, the resolution "claims to legitimate acts which terminate life when it is considered to be no longer dignified and human." Such a change not only violates the injunction, "You shall not kill," found in the Decalogue and other foundational religious documents, but also is a radical departure from the entire code of medical ethics as it has been handed on for over two millennia. This code was first expressed in the so-called Hippocratic Oath attributed to an ancient Greek physician. This oath is still used at some medical school graduations. Its second section includes a pledge to use only beneficial treatments and procedures and not to harm or hurt a patient. It includes promises not to break confidentiality, not to engage in sexual relations with patients or to dispense deadly drugs. It specifically says: "I will never give a deadly drug to anybody if asked for it, nor will I make a suggestion to this effect."

In a moment I will speak of the religious and moral issues involved in the rejection of the injunction, "You shall not kill." For now, however, I will address the consequences of revising a traditional code of medical ethics which has been widely accepted and respected.

What would happen to the doctor-patient relationship if the proponents of euthanasia or assisted suicide are successful in legalizing these unethical, immoral activities? Would you trust a doctor who is licensed to kill? Would you entrust the life of your elderly mother or father, a seriously ill or disabled child—or your own life—to such a person?

Moreover, what added pressures would patients face? If euthanasia or assisted suicide were legal, might this not influence the decisions of elderly persons, for example, who do not want to be a burden to their families?

Would not the poor be especially vulnerable to such pressure? Would they perhaps think that the best thing to do would be to ask their doctors to end their lives before their natural death? Moreover, when we are seriously ill, can we know clearly what we want? Would these truly be free choices?

These are significant, realistic issues which must be addressed. Some would respond by saying that they reflect unnecessary fears, that they are nothing but a "smoke screen" to cover up an attempt to perpetuate an outdated morality. In developing a response to this charge, let us consider what has happened in the Netherlands.

As you might know, the Netherlands has a unique position on the question of euthanasia. Technically, euthanasia is still illegal. However, since 1973, a series of court cases has allowed the current practice to develop. In effect, these court decisions give doctors considerable latitude in deciding whether or not to resort to euthanasia in each case. A doctor is expected to report an act of euthanasia to a public prosecutor who must then decide whether or not to prosecute the doctor. Rather than claiming innocence, doctors are to justify their actions by pointing to mitigating circumstances. In effect, they are to prove that they had no alternative under the circumstances—when explicitly asked for "aid in dying" by mentally competent patients.

In such a context it is not a stretch of the imagination to surmise that many, if not most, acts of euthanasia are simply not reported. This means that few cases are actually investigated by public authorities. And this, in turn, means that it is difficult to get an accurate picture of precisely what is going on there. It is widely known, moreover, that Dutch doctors often misrepresent the cause of death on death certificates to avoid having to report acts of euthanasia and face the possibility of prosecution.

Several years ago, the Dutch government established a commission to study the practice of euthanasia in that country. Personally, I found the results of that study to be appalling, but not surprising. The so-called Remmelink Commission concluded that more than 1,000 patients underwent euthanasia *without* their consent. The lives of another 14,000 patients were shortened by pain-killing medication, also *without* their consent. The Dutch government has said that only about 200 cases of euthanasia are reported annually. However, according to Catholic News Service, the Remmelink Commission counted 2,340 cases of voluntary euthanasia, 390 cases of assisted suicide, and 1,040 cases of "life terminating acts without explicit and persistent requests" in 1990 alone.

In other words, the Dutch experiment justifies the concerns I mentioned earlier. There is no convincing evidence that euthanasia or assisted suicide can be regulated and managed. There is a valid reason to be concerned about the impact it would have on the doctor-patient relationship, not to mention the entire code of medical ethics. We may rightly question how safe our most vulnerable persons would be in any society that accepts euthanasia or assisted suicide.

Why Is This Movement So Popular?

In the light of information like this, one might legitimately question why the euthanasia movement has become so popular. In the United States there are at least three possible explanations.

The first relates to the world of medicine and medical technology. As I noted earlier, for centuries those in the health care professions have had, as an essential aspect of their identity and mission, the responsibility to heal and preserve life. That responsibility has entered a new era with the development of medicines and technologies that have given physicians previously unknown capabilities in this area. We are grateful, indeed, for the great good which these advancements have brought to the human family.

This good, however, has been a mixed blessing. It is fairly easy for technology or medicine to become an end in itself, and for life to be preserved when, in fact, death should be allowed to occur. This possible domination of technology over the proper course of life has left many people fearful of being kept alive in an inhumane fashion. And this fear has led some to say to their loved ones: "Do whatever you must, but do not let me live that way." The fear, then, of the pain and discomfort of a life prolonged inappropriately has led to an erosion of the natural instinct to preserve one's own life.

A second possible explanation is more particular to the United States and its legal system. Although recent years have seen the enactment of legislation that has alleviated many legal problems, a fear remains that sick persons or their families will be prevented from making the necessary medical decisions on their own and that they will have to become embroiled in a contentious legal process.

These two fears—being kept alive needlessly and losing autonomy to the complexity of the legal system—have been exploited by the pro-euthanasia forces in this country. Many people who now favor the legalization of euthanasia or assisted suicide do so, not because they see this as a good in itself, but because they view it as the only avenue available to remedy these fears effectively.

This leads to the third explanation for the spread of pro-euthanasia attitudes. While this reason is present in the United States, it moves far beyond our borders and infects many parts of the world. It pertains to certain assumptions that have dominated, or are beginning to dominate, many of the world's cultures. For our discussion today I will note four such assumptions. In doing so, I am building on the work of Harvard University Professor Arthur J. Dyck.

First, there is a sense of human autonomy which asserts that an individual's life belongs entirely to the individual, and that each person is free to dispose of that life entirely as he or she wishes. Second, in addition to the absence of *external* restraint, there is an understanding of human freedom to make moral choices which says that one must also be free to take one's own life. In other words, there are no *internal* restraints. Third, it is possible to identify times when life simply is not worth living. This can be because of illness or handicaps or even despair. Finally, the true dignity of being human is to be found in the ability to make conscious, rational choices that control life. In the absence of that capacity, human dignity is lessened.

While one might nuance these assumptions, they capture something of the ethos of the euthanasia movement. And to be candid, there is something to be said for these assumptions. For example, they remind us that there are values in addition to the value of physical survival. Also, death is not the worst evil a person can face.

But they also contain great weaknesses. For example, they contain neither limits nor controls. There is no reason to believe they cannot be extended in a fashion similar to that of the Nazi movement to conclusions that would be destructive to the human family in general and, in particular, to those who are the most vulnerable. Moreover, these assumptions self-evidently attack the basic notion of the human person as a member of a human community that is to be characterized by trust and care for one another. In other words, the movement to legalize euthanasia or assisted suicide involves not only decisions at the end of life but also certain assertions or assumptions about the very *nature* of human life.

This means that, if one carefully analyzes the assumptions which would support the legalization of euthanasia, one finds a perspective that challenges the underpinnings of human civilization as we know it. This is why I have chosen this topic for our consideration this evening. As people of faith, we must attend to this threatening force with conviction and fervor. If we remain silent, the course of human history will be significantly altered.

A Consistent Ethic of Life

But how can we proceed in a meaningful fashion in a pluralistic society like our own? The obvious answer is that we must find a common ground that will unite us in responding to this challenge, while respecting the religious diversity of our society.

Over the past eleven years I have sought to develop such a common ground within the Catholic tradition through what I have described as a consistent ethic of life. I have proposed it as a comprehensive concept and a strategy that will help Catholics and, indeed, all people of good will to influence more effectively the development of public policy on life issues.

The grounding principle for this ethic is found in the Judeo-Christian heritage, which has played such an influential role in the formation of the national ethos of this nation. In this religious tradition, human life is considered *sacred* because God is its origin and its destiny.

Consequently, innocent human life must not be directly attacked, threatened, or diminished. Many other people of good will—not of this tradition—also accept the basic premise that human life has a distinctive dignity and meaning or purpose. They, too, argue that, because of the privileged meaning of human life, we have the responsibility for preserving, protecting, and nurturing it.

The second principle underlying the consistent ethic of life is the belief that human life is also social in nature. We are not born to live alone, but, rather, to move from the dependency of prenatal life and infancy to the interrelatedness of adulthood. To be human, then, is to be social, and those relationships, structures, and institutions which support us, as individuals and as a community, are an essential aspect of human life.

If one accepts these two principles about human life, then one may argue that two precepts or obligations necessarily flow from them. First, as individuals and as a society, we have the positive obligation to protect and nurture life. Second, we have a negative obligation not to destroy or injure human life directly, especially the life of the innocent and the vulnerable.

These principles and the resulting precepts have served as the foundation for much of what is known as the Anglo-Saxon legal tradition. They are the context for laws which oppose abortion, murder, and euthanasia or assisted suicide. This movement from religious insight to public policy is an important one. In the common law tradition these laws have been maintained, not because of religious insight, but because it is recognized that they pertain to the *common good* of society. In other words, the commonweal of public life and order would be destroyed if innocent human life could be directly attacked. In more recent years this same insight regarding the fundamental dignity of the human person has been given international recognition in the United Nations Charter of Human Rights.

I have addressed the need for a consistent ethic of life because new technological challenges confront us along the whole spectrum of life from conception to natural death. This creates the need for a consistent ethic, for the spectrum cuts across such life-threatening issues as abortion, capital punishment, modern warfare, and the care of the terminally ill. Admittedly, these are all *distinct*, complex problems which deserve individual treatment. Each requires its own moral analysis. No single answer or solution applies to all. At any given time, because of the circumstances, one may demand more attention than another. But they are linked!

Moreover, life-*threatening* issues are also linked with life-*diminishing* issues such as racism, sexism, pornography, prostitution, and child abuse. Wherever human life is considered "cheap" and easily exploited or wasted, respect for life dwindles and, eventually, every human life is in jeopardy.

The concept of a consistent ethic of life is challenging. It requires people to broaden, substantively and creatively, their way of thinking, their attitudes, their response to life issues. Many are not accustomed to thinking about all the life-threatening and life-diminishing issues in such an interrelated way. As a result, they remain somewhat selective in their response. Some, for example, are very committed in their efforts to eradicate the evil of abortion in this nation, but neglect issues of poverty. Others work very hard to alleviate poverty, but neglect the basic right to life of unborn children.

Given this broad range of challenging life issues, we desperately need a societal *attitude* or climate that will sustain a consistent defense and promotion of life. In other words, it is not enough merely to assert an ethical principle like the consistent ethic of life. It must also be implemented, and when it is, it necessarily impacts all areas of human life. It responds to all the moments, places, or conditions which either threaten the sanctity of life or cultivate an attitude of disrespect for it. A consistent ethic is based on the need to ensure that the sacredness of every human life, which is the ultimate source of human dignity, is defended and fostered, from the genetic laboratory to the cancer ward, from the ghetto to the prison.

The movement from moral analysis to public policy choices is a complex process in a pluralistic society like the United States. There is a legitimate secularity of the political process. But there is also a legitimate role for religious and moral discourse in our nation's life because nearly every important social issue has a moral or ethical dimension. Moreover, this ethical dimension usually does not exist apart from complex empirical judgments where honest disagreement may exist even among those who agree on the principles involved.

In the legal tradition of our country, however, it is not the function of civil law to enjoin or prohibit *everything* that moral principles enjoin or prohibit. So when dealing with law or public policy we must ask, in addition to the moral or ethical implications, whether the requirements of public order and the common good are serious enough to take precedence over the claims of freedom. Achieving a consensus on what constitutes a matter which is both moral or ethical and essential for public order and the common good is not easy. But we have been able to do it—by a process of debate, decision-making, then a review of our decisions and their impact on human lives, especially the most vulnerable.

My efforts to articulate the need for a consistent ethic of life have helped many people, both Catholic and non-Catholic, see the need for addressing in a consistent way a full range of life issues from conception to natural death. Moreover, I believe that human life has a meaning and a purpose that affirm the integrity and inherent value of body and spirit, even in the midst of suffering. I also affirm that all human persons need and desire to be able to trust the community in which they abide. And I am convinced that *individual* choices influence the moral tone and character of the *community* and, indeed, the entire human family.

That is why I am opposed to the legalization of euthanasia. It compromises the fundamental dignity of the human person in its inordinate exaltation of rational consciousness and in its challenge to the belief that there is significance to human suffering. It does inconceivable violence to the trust that should exist between doctor and patient—and, indeed, among all human persons. And it naively pretends that individual human choices are isolated moments which have no impact on the lives and well-being of others. Both my faith and experience tell me otherwise!

32.

THE CONSISTENT ETHIC OF LIFE

Annual Helder Camara Lecture

Melbourne, Australia, February 23, 1995

I am deeply grateful to Archbishop Little and all of you for your warm welcome and kind hospitality. I am delighted to have this opportunity to address you on a topic to which I have devoted much thought during the past eleven years: the consistent ethic of life. It was in December, 1983, at Fordham University in New York City, that I first presented the idea and the rationale for it.

This evening, I will (1) give an overview of the concept, (2) point out the distinct levels of the problem, and (3) assess the contribution of the consistent ethic to the Church and society.

The Consistent Ethic of Life: An Overview

The idea of the consistent ethic is both old and new. It is "old" in the sense that its substance has been around for years. For example, in a single sentence the Second Vatican Council condemned murder, abortion, euthanasia, suicide, mutilation, torture, subhuman living conditions, arbitrary imprisonment, deportation, slavery, prostitution, and disgraceful working conditions (*Gaudium et spes*, 27). Moreover, when the U. S. Catholic bishops inaugurated their Respect Life Program in 1972, they invited the Catholic community to focus on the "sanctity of human life and the many threats to human life in the modern world, including war, violence, hunger, and poverty."

The U. S. Catholic bishops' 1983 pastoral letter, *The Challenge of Peace: God's Promise and Our Response,* also emphasized the sacredness of human life and the responsibility we have, personally and as a society, to protect and preserve its sanctity. In paragraph 285, it specifically linked the nuclear question with abortion and other life issues:

> *When we accept violence in any form as commonplace, our sensitivities become dulled. When we accept violence, war itself can be taken for granted. Violence has many faces: oppression of the poor, deprivation of basic human rights, economic exploitation,*

sexual exploitation and pornography, neglect or abuse of the aged and the helpless, and innumerable other acts of inhumanity. Abortion in particular blunts a sense of the sacredness of human life. In a society where the innocent unborn are killed wantonly, how can we expect people to feel righteous revulsion at the act or threat of killing non-combatants in war?

However, the pastoral letter—while giving us a starting point for developing a consistent ethic of life—did not provide a fully articulated framework.

It was precisely to provide a more comprehensive theological and ethical basis for the Respect Life Program and for the linkage of war and abortion, as noted by the pastoral letter, that I developed the theme of the consistent ethic. Another important circumstance that prompted me to move in this direction was that I had just been asked to serve as Chairman of the U. S. bishops' Pro-Life Committee. It was October of 1983, and I knew that both abortion and defense-related issues would undoubtedly play an important role in the upcoming U. S. presidential campaign.

It was urgent, I felt, that a well-developed theological and ethical framework be provided that would link the various life issues while, at the same time, pointing out that the issues are not all the same. It was my fear that, *without* such a framework or vision, the bishops would be severely pressured by those who wanted to push a particular issue with little or no concern for the rest. *With* such a theological basis, we would be able to argue convincingly on behalf of all the issues on which we had taken a position in recent years.

I first presented the theme, as I noted, in an address at Fordham University in New York City in December 1983. At that time, I called for a public discussion of the concept, both in Catholic circles and the broader community. In all candor I must admit that the public response greatly exceeded my hopes and expectations.

Since that time there has been a lively exchange by both those who agree and disagree with the theme and its implications. By far, the majority of the reactions have been supportive. Nonetheless, it has been used and misused by those who have tried to push their own, more narrow agendas. I myself have made further contributions to the discussion through many subsequent addresses and writings.

The concept itself is a complex and challenging one. It requires us to broaden, substantively and creatively, our ways of thinking, our attitudes, our pastoral response. Many are not accustomed to thinking about all the life-threatening and life-diminishing issues with such consistency. The result is that they remain somewhat selective in their response. Although some of those who oppose the concept seem not to have understood it, I sometimes suspect that many who oppose it recognize its challenge. Quite frankly, I sometimes wonder whether those who embrace it quickly and wholeheartedly truly understand all its implications.

In November 1985, the U. S. bishops explicitly adopted the consistent ethic as the theological basis for their updated *Pastoral Plan for Pro-Life Activities.* In sum, to the delight of those who agree with its theological reasoning and to the dismay of the small minority who do not, the "consistent ethic" has entered into our theological vocabulary.

Let me now explain in greater depth the theological basis and strategic value of the "consistent ethic." Catholic teaching is based on two truths about the human person: human life is both *sacred* and *social.* Because we esteem human life as *sacred,* we have a duty to protect and foster it at all stages of development, from conception to natural death, and in all circumstances. Because we acknowledge that human life is also *social,* society must protect and foster it.

Precisely because life is sacred, the taking of even one life is a momentous event. Traditional Catholic teaching has allowed the taking of human life in particular situations by way of exception—for example, in self-defense and capital punishment. In recent decades, however, the presumptions against taking human life have been strengthened and the exceptions made ever more restrictive.

Fundamental to these shifts in emphasis is a more acute perception of the many ways in which life is threatened today. Obviously, such questions as war, aggression, and capital punishment are not new; they have been with us for centuries. Life has always been threatened, but today there is a new *context* that shapes the *content* of our ethic of life.

The principal factor responsible for this new context is modern *technology,* which induces a sharper awareness of the frailty of human life. War, for example, has always been a threat to life, but today the threat is qualitatively different because of nuclear and other sophisticated kinds of weapons. The weapons produced by modern technology now threaten life on a scale previously unimaginable. Living, as we do, therefore, in an age of extraordinary technological development means we face a qualitatively new range of moral problems. The essential questions we face are these: In an age when we *can* do almost anything, how do we decide what we should do? In a time when we can do almost anything technologically, how do we decide morally or ethically what we should *not* do?

We face new technological challenges along the whole spectrum of life from conception to natural death. This creates the need for a consistent ethic, for the spectrum cuts across such issues as genetic engineering, abortion, capital punishment, modern warfare, and the care of the terminally ill. Admittedly, these are all *distinct* problems, enormously complex. Each deserves individual treatment. Each requires its own moral analysis. No single answer or solution applies to all. *But they are linked!* While each of these assaults on life has its own meaning and morality, they must be confronted as pieces of a larger pattern.

Given this broad range of challenging issues, we desperately need a societal *attitude* or climate that will sustain a consistent defense and promotion of life. When human life is considered "cheap" or easily expendable in one area, eventually nothing is held as sacred, and all lives are in jeopardy. Ultimately, it is society's attitude about life—whether of respect or non-respect—that determines its policies and practices.

The theological foundation of the consistent ethic, then, is defense of the person. The ethic grows out of the very character of Catholic moral thought. I hasten to add that I do not mean to imply that one has to be a Catholic to affirm the moral content of the consistent ethic.

As I mentioned earlier, the concept of the consistent ethic is both complex and challenging. It joins the humanity of the unborn infant with the humanity of the hungry; it calls for positive legal action to prevent the killing of the unborn or the aged, and positive societal action to provide shelter for the homeless and education for the illiterate. A consistent ethic identifies both the problem of taking life and the challenge of promoting human dignity as moral questions.

The theological assertion that the human person is made in the "image and likeness" of God, the philosophical affirmation of the dignity of the person, and the political principle that society and state exist to serve the person—all these themes stand behind the consistent ethic. They provide the basis for its moral perspective.

A consistent ethic does not say everyone in the Church must do all things, but it does say that, as individuals and groups pursue one issue, whether it is opposing abortion or capital punishment, the way we oppose one threat should be related to support for a systemic vision of life. It is not necessary or possible for every person to engage each issue, but it is both possible and necessary for the Church as a whole to cultivate a conscious, explicit connection among the several issues. And it is very necessary for preserving a systemic vision that individuals and groups who seek to witness to life at one point of the spectrum of life not be seen as insensitive to or even opposed to other moral claims on the overall spectrum of life. Consistency does rule out contradictory moral positions about the unique value of human life. No one is called to do everything, but each of us can do something. And we can strive not to stand against each other when the protection *and* the promotion of life are at stake.

The Consistent Ethic of Life: The Levels of the Question

A consistent ethic of life should honor the complexity of the multiple issues it must address. It is necessary to distinguish several levels of the question. Without attempting to be comprehensive, allow me to explore *four* distinct dimensions of a consistent ethic.

First, at the level of general moral principles, it is possible to identify a single principle with diverse applications. In my Fordham address, for example, I used the prohibition against direct attacks on innocent life. This principle is both central to the Catholic moral vision and systemically related to a range of specific moral issues. It prohibits direct attacks on unborn life in the womb, direct attacks on civilians in warfare, and the direct killing of patients in nursing homes.

Each of these topics has a constituency in society concerned with the morality of abortion, war, and care of the aged and dying. A consistent ethic of life encourages the specific concerns of each constituency, but also calls them to see the interrelatedness of their efforts. The need to defend the *integrity of the moral principle in the full range of its application* is a responsibility of each distinct constituency. If the principle is eroded in the public mind, all lose.

A *second* level of a consistent ethic stresses the distinction among cases rather than their similarities. We need different moral principles to apply to diverse cases. The classical distinction between ordinary and extraordinary means has applicability in the care of the dying but no relevance in the case of warfare. Not all moral principles have relevance across the whole range of life issues. Moreover, sometimes a systemic vision of the life issues requires a combination of moral insights to provide direction on one issue.

In my Fordham address I cited the classical teaching on capital punishment, which gives the state the right to take life in defense of key social values. But I also pointed out how a concern for promoting a *public attitude* of respect for life has led the Catholic bishops of the United States to oppose the exercise of that right.

Abortion is taking innocent human life in ever-growing numbers in our society. Those concerned about it, I believe, will find their case enhanced by taking note of the rapidly expanding use of public execution. In a similar way, those who are particularly concerned about these executions, even if the accused has taken another life, should recognize the elementary truth that a society which can be indifferent to the innocent life of an unborn child will not be easily stirred to concern for a convicted criminal. There is, I maintain, a political and psychological linkage among the life issues—from war to welfare concerns—which we ignore at our own peril. A systemic vision of life seeks to expand the moral imagination of a society, not partition it into airtight categories.

A *third* level of the question before us involves how we relate a commitment to principles to our public witness of life. As I have said, no one can do everything. There are limits to both competency and energy: both point to the wisdom of setting priorities and defining distinct functions. The Church, however, must be credible across a wide range of issues; the very scope of our moral vision requires a commitment to a multiplicity of questions. In this way the teaching of the Church will sustain a variety of individual commitments.

My addresses on the consistent ethic have not been intended to constrain wise and vigorous effort to protect and promote life through specific, precise forms of action. They *do* seek to cultivate a dialogue within the Church and in the wider society among individuals and groups that draw on common principles (e.g. the prohibition against killing the innocent) but seem convinced that they do not share common ground. The appeal here is not for anyone to do everything, but to recognize points of *interdependence* which should be stressed, not denied.

A *fourth* level, one where dialogue is sorely needed, is the relationship between moral principles and concrete political choices. The moral questions of abortion, the arms race, the fate of social programs for the poor, and the role of human rights in foreign policy are *public* moral issues. The arena in which they are ultimately decided is *not* the academy or the Church but the political process. A consistent ethic of life seeks to present a coherent linkage among a diverse set of issues. It can and should be used to test party platforms, public policies, and political candidates. The Church legitimately fulfills a public role by articulating a framework for political choices, by relating that framework to specific issues, and by calling for systemic moral analysis of all areas of public policy.

This is the role our episcopal conference has sought to fulfill by publishing a "Statement on Political Responsibility" during each of the presidential and congressional election years in the past two decades. The purpose is surely not to tell citizens how to vote, but to help shape the public debate and form personal conscience so that every citizen will vote thoughtfully and responsibly. Our "Statement on Political Responsibility" has always been, like our "Respect Life Program," a multi-issue approach to public morality. The fact that this Statement sets forth a spectrum of issues of current concern to the Church and society should not be understood, as I have already indicated, as implying that all issues are qualitatively equal from a moral perspective.

Both the Statements and the Respect Life program have direct relevance to the political order, but they are applied concretely by the choice of citizens. This is as it should be. In the political order the Church is primarily a teacher; it possesses a carefully cultivated tradition of moral analysis of personal and public issues. It makes that tradition available in a special manner for the community of the Church, but it offers it also to all who find meaning and guidance in its moral teaching.

The Consistent Ethic: Its Pastoral and Public Contribution

The Church's moral teaching has both pastoral and public significance. Pastorally, a consistent ethic of life is a contribution to the witness of the Church's defense of the human person. Publicly, a consistent ethic fills a void in our public policy debate today.

Pastorally, I submit that a Church standing forth on the entire range of issues, which the logic of our moral vision bids us to confront, will be a

Church in the style both of Vatican II's *Gaudium et spes* and Pope John Paul II's consistent witness to life. The pastoral life of the Church should not be guided by a simplistic criterion of relevance. The capacity of faith to shed light on the concrete questions of personal and public life today is one way in which the value of the Gospel is assessed.

Certainly the serious, sustained interest manifested throughout U. S. society in the bishops' letter on war and peace provided a unique *pastoral* opportunity for the Church. Demonstrating how the teaching on war and peace is supported by a wider concern for all of life led others to see for the first time what our tradition has affirmed for a very long time: the linkage among the life issues.

The *public* value of a consistent ethic of life is directly connected to its pastoral role. In the public arena we should always speak and act like a Church. But the unique public possibility for a consistent ethic is provided precisely by the unstructured character of the public debate on the life questions. Each of the issues I have referred to this evening—abortion, war, hunger and human rights, euthanasia and physician-assisted suicide, and capital punishment—is usually treated as a separate, self-contained topic in our public life. Each is indeed distinct, but an *ad hoc* approach to each one fails to illustrate how our choices in one area can affect our decisions in other areas. There must be a public attitude of respect for all of life, if public actions are to respect life in concrete cases.

Eleven years ago, the pastoral letter on war and peace spoke of a "new moment" in the nuclear age. The letter has been widely studied and applauded because it caught the spirit of the "new moment" and spoke with moral substance to the issues of the "new moment." I am convinced there is an "open moment" before us on the agenda of life issues. It is a significant opportunity for the Church to demonstrate the strength of a sustained moral vision. I submit that a clear witness to a consistent ethic of life will allow us to grasp the opportunity of this "open moment" and serve both the sacredness of every human life and the God of Life who is the origin and support of our common humanity.

But to take advantage of this new, "open moment," we must learn how to *work together* as a community of faith. Unfortunately, a great deal of polarization exists within the Church today. This has created at times a mood of suspicion, even acrimony. A candid discussion of important issues—and a common witness to them—is often inhibited, so that we are not always able to come to grips effectively with the problems that confront us. So what do we do?

As I conclude, I would like to suggest how we might *begin* to answer that question.

The reality is that those who take extreme positions are often the most noisy—they get most of the attention. Those in the middle—the majority—are often quiet. I submit that we must make a greater effort to engage those in the middle and, in the process, establish a common ground—a new space for dialogue—that will make it possible for us to reach those who are alienated or disillusioned or uninformed for whatever reason.

To establish this common ground—this space for authentic dialogue—a broad range of the Church's leadership, both clerical and lay, must recommit themselves to the basic truths of our Catholic faith. The chief of those truths is that we must be accountable to our Catholic tradition and to the Spirit-filled, living Church that brings to us the revelation of God in Christ Jesus. Jesus who is present in sacrament, word, and community is central to all we do. So our focus must constantly be on *him*, not ourselves.

This rules out petty criticisms and jealousy; cynicism; sound-bite theology; inaccurate, unhistorical assertions; flippant dismissals. It rules out a narrow, myopic appeal to our personal or contemporary experience as if no other were valid. It acknowledges that our discussions must take place within certain boundaries because the Church, for all its humanness, is not merely a human organization. It is rather a chosen people, a mysterious communion, a foreshadowing of the Kingdom, a spiritual family, the Body of Christ. When we understand the Church in this way, we will be able to see the full beauty and relevance of our heritage as it has developed under the influence of the Holy Spirit from the apostolic age to the present. It will also help us to become more tolerant of one another.

In sum, what we need in the Church today is a realization that there is room for considerable diversity among us. When there is a breakdown of civility, dialogue, trust, and tolerance, we must redouble our efforts to restore and build up the unity of the one Body of Christ.

Dealing with each other in a *consistent, gospel-inspired* way will add greatly—I would say it is indispensable—to our public, collective witness to the consistent life ethic which is so desperately needed in today's world.

33.

RENEWING THE COVENANT
WITH PATIENTS AND SOCIETY

Address to American Medical Association
House of Delegates

WASHINGTON, D.C., DECEMBER 5, 1995

Thank you for your invitation to speak with you this afternoon. These are turbulent times for medicine and health care, especially for physicians, and Dr. Todd and Dr. Bristow may have felt that, as a pastor, I could give some comfort to you who daily navigate these powerful currents of change. I am not sure how much comfort I can offer, but I can offer some observations that may help guide your own conduct and that of the medical profession as the pace of change accelerates in the coming years.

Such an offer may sound presumptuous, coming as it does from a priest, rather than a physician. So, before going further, let me share some of the experience that led me to this seemingly brash venture.

My many pastoral roles often intersect with doctors, institutions of health care, and health care policy. I am responsible, for example, for the spiritual care of the sick of the Archdiocese of Chicago. Within the diocese there are more than 100 health care agencies, including 20 hospitals and 28 nursing homes. As a member of the Administrative Committee of the National Conference of Catholic Bishops, I have helped to articulate the Conference's views on national health policy and other social issues. I am also a member of the Board of the Catholic Health Association of the United States, which represents about 900 Catholic health care providers nationwide.

In these roles I have the opportunity to converse and consult with some of the best minds in medicine and health care administration. And I have had the chance to write and speak frequently on the nature of health care and its significance in human life, with a particular focus on the importance of not-for-profit institutions. In all of this I have seen access to health care as a fundamental human right and discussed the ethical dimensions of health care within the framework of the consistent ethic of life, which I have articulated and developed over the past twelve years.

I also stand before you as someone recently diagnosed and treated for pancreatic cancer. I am the beneficiary of the best care your profession has to offer. This experience has shaped and deepened my reflections on the challenges you face as individuals and as a profession.

Your profession and mine have much in common—the universal human need for healing and wholeness. What special qualities do ministry and medicine share?

First, we both are engaged in something more than a profession—a vocation. In its truest sense, it means a life to which we are called. In my own case I was called to both professions. As an undergraduate, I had decided to become a doctor and followed a pre-med curriculum. But long before I graduated, I heard a stronger call to the priesthood.

Second, we both are centered on promoting and restoring wholeness of life. The key words in our professions—heal, health, holy, and whole—share common roots in old English.

Third, and most fundamentally, we both are engaged in a moral enterprise. We both respond to those who are in need, who ask us for help, who expose to us their vulnerabilities, and who place their trust in us.

As someone who has cared for others and who has been cared for by you and your colleagues, I hope you will allow me to speak frankly about the moral crisis that I believe currently grips the medical profession generally and physicians individually.

In speaking of a "moral crisis" I realize that I am assuming a position with which some within your profession would disagree. They would assert that the marketplace is the only valid reference point for evaluating medical practice. I respectfully, though forcefully, disagree with such an assertion. I believe that medicine, like other professions—such as teaching, law, and ministry—does have a moral center, even though this center is under attack. And I think you believe deep down as I do that such a moral center exists and that it must not be lost. Dr. Bristow's priority on medical standards as a hallmark of his administration reflects this concern.

What do I mean when I speak of a "moral crisis" in medicine? I mean that more and more members of the community of medicine no longer agree on the universal moral principles of medicine or on the appropriate means to realize those principles. Conscientious practitioners are often perplexed as to how they should act when they are caught up in a web of economics, politics, business practice, and social responsibility. The result is that the practice of medicine no longer has the surety of an accurate compass to guide it through these challenging and difficult times. In other words, medicine, along with other professions, including my own, is in need of a moral renewal.

My purpose today is not to dictate the details of medicine's moral renewal. Rather, it is to invite you to join me in a conversation that will lead to a restoration of medicine's first principles. I am convinced that, with good will and persistence, this process will benefit society, reinvigorate the medical profession, preserve its independence, and infuse your lives with a quality of meaning that has too often been missing.

How did we arrive at this situation? Medicine, like other professions, does not exist in a vacuum. The upheavals in our society, especially those of the past thirty years, have left their imprint on the practice and organization of medicine. Each of us has his or her own list of such upheavals. My list includes the shift from family and community to the individual as the primary unit of society, an overemphasis on individual self-interest to the neglect of the common good, the loss of a sense of personal responsibility and the unseemly flight to the refuge of "victimhood," the loss of confidence in established institutions, the decline in religious faith, the commercialization of our national existence, the growing reliance on the legal system to redress personal conflicts.

In addition to societal changes, there are causes specific to the medical enterprise that contribute to medicine's disconnection from its underlying moral foundation. For example, advances in medical science and technology have improved the prospect of cure but have de-emphasized medicine's traditional caring function. Other contributors include the commercialization of medical practice, the growing preoccupation of some physicians with monetary concerns, and the loss of a sense of humility and humanity by certain practitioners.

None of this, I am sure, is news to you. In surveys, newspaper articles, and personal conversations, many physicians report that they are increasingly concerned with the condition and direction of medical practice.

What may surprise you, however, is my contention that, to reverse these trends, you, as individuals and as a profession, must accept a major share of the responsibility for where you are today. Physicians have too often succumbed to the siren songs of scientific triumph, financial success, and political power. In the process medicine has grown increasingly mechanistic, commercial, and soulless. The age-old covenants between doctors and patient, between the profession and society, have been ignored or violated.

This dire view is tempered by hope. If the present predicament is the product of choices—explicit and implicit—made by members of your profession, then it is possible that you can choose to change it.

The change I have in mind is "renewing the covenant with patients and society." That covenant is grounded in the moral obligations that arise from the nature of the doctor-patient relationship. They are moral obligations—as opposed to legal or contractual obligations—because they are based on fundamental human concepts of right and wrong. While, as I noted earlier, it is not currently fashionable to think of medicine in terms of morality, morality is, in fact, the core of the doctor-patient relationship and the foundation of the medical profession. Why do I insist on a moral model as opposed to the economic and contractual models now in vogue?

Allow me to describe four key aspects of medicine that give it a moral status and establish a conventional relationship:

- First, the reliance of the patient on the doctor. Illness compels a patient to place his or her fate in the hands of a doctor. A patient relies, not only on the technical competence of a doctor, but also on his or her moral compass, on the doctor's commitment to put the interests of the patient first.

- Second, the holistic character of medical decisions. A physician is a scientist and a clinician, but as a doctor is and must be more. A doctor is and must be a caretaker of the patient's person, *integrating medical realities* into the whole of the patient's life. A patient looks to his or her doctor as a professional adviser, a guide through some of life's most difficult journeys.
- Third, the social investment in medicine. The power of modern medicine—of each and every doctor—is the result of centuries of science, clinical trials, and public and private investments. Above all, medical science has succeeded because of the faith of people in medicine and in doctors. This faith creates a social debt and is the basis of medicine's call—its vocation—to serve the common good.
- Fourth, the personal commitments of doctors. Relationship with a patient creates an immediate, personal, non-transferable fiduciary responsibility to protect that patient's best interests. Regardless of markets, government programs, or network managers, patients depend on doctors for a personal commitment and for advocacy through an increasingly complex and impersonal system.

This moral center of the doctor-patient relationship is the very essence of being a doctor. It also defines the outlines of the covenant that exists between physicians and their patients, their profession, and their society. The covenant is a promise that the profession makes—a solemn promise—that it is and will remain true to its moral center. In individual terms, the covenant is the basis on which patients trust their doctors. In social terms, the covenant is the grounds for the public's continued respect and reliance on the profession of medicine.

The first dimension of this covenant deals with the physician's responsibilities to his or her patients. They include:

- Placing the good of the patient over the interests—financial or otherwise—of the physician, insurance company, the hospital, or system of care. This issue is rarely overt; rather, it springs from a growing web of pressures and incentives to substitute someone else's judgment for your own.
- Ensuring that the use of advanced medical science and technology does not come at the expense of real caring. A recent study in the *Journal of the American Medical Association* documented a continuing compulsion to spare nothing for the dying patient, without regard for the patient's dignity, comfort, or peace of mind.
- Upholding the sanctity and dignity of life from conception to natural death. The consistent ethic of life calls on us to honor

and respect life at every stage and in all its circumstances. As a society, we must not lose our shared commitment to protect our vulnerable members: the unborn, persons with disabilities, the aged, and the terminally ill. We must not allow the public debates over the right to life of the unborn person and legalized euthanasia to deter us from our commitment.

- Attending to your own spiritual needs as healers. As a priest or a physician, we can only give from what we have. We must take care to nurture our own personal moral center. This is the sustenance of caring.

The responsibilities I just noted are not new to the practice to medicine. Almost 2,500 years ago, Plato summed up the differences between good and bad medicine in a way that illuminates many of the issues physicians face today in our increasingly bureaucratized medical system. In his description of bad medicine, which he called "slave medicine," Plato said, "The physician never gives the slave any account of his problem, nor asks for any. He gives some empiric treatment with an air of knowledge in the brusque fashion of a dictator, and then rushes off to the next ailing slave." Plato contrasted this bad medicine with the treatment of free men and women: "The physician treats the patient's disease by going into things thoroughly from the beginning in a scientific way and takes the patient and the family into confidence. In this way he learns something from the patient. The physician never gives prescriptions until he has won the patient's support, and when he has done so, he aims to produce complete restoration to health by persuading the patient to participate."

Similar ideas are reflected in the Hippocratic Oath attributed to an ancient Greek physician. This oath is still used at some medical school graduations. Its second section includes a pledge to use only beneficial treatments and procedures and not to harm or hurt a patient. It includes promises not to break confidentiality, not to engage in sexual relations with patients or to dispense deadly drugs. It specifically says: "I will never give a deadly drug to anybody if asked for it, nor will I make a suggestion to this effect."

There are plenty of pressures, some self-imposed and some externally imposed, that make it easy to practice bad medicine, just as there were two and one-half millennia ago. Sustaining your covenants requires a willingness to affirm and incorporate into your lives the ancient virtues of benevolence, compassion, competence, intellectual honesty, humility, and suspension of self-interest—virtues which many of you live quite admirably.

Let us move now from the covenantal obligations of the individual physician to the responsibilities of the profession. Medicine is a profession that has the freedom to accredit its educational institutions, set standards of practice, and determine who shall practice and who shall not. As such, it is a moral community subject to a set of moral obligations. First among these obligations is the requirement to enlist and train new members of the profession who befit the nature of the profession. Beyond intellectual ability, you must ask whether potential medical students have the potential to live up to the moral responsibilities of a physician; that is, will they be "good" doctors? In addition, those who teach and counsel medical students must be living models of the virtuous physician, living proof that the values we espouse are not romantic abstractions to be discarded when they enter the "real world" of medicine.

President Bristow has lamented the fact that one-fourth of our medical schools have no formal courses in medical ethics. Such courses should, of course, be required in every curriculum. Important as these courses are, however, they are not enough. Indeed, they run the risk of segregating these matters from the core of students' learning experience. If we do not infuse moral and ethical training into every class and practicum, in residencies, and in continuing education, we have not fulfilled our obligation to our students and the profession.

Finally, I would emphasize among medicine's professional obligations the setting and enforcing of the highest standards of behavior and competence. Although those who defraud government and private insurers, those who are incompetent or venal, those who look the other way at colleagues' wrongdoing are undoubtedly a minority, the profession is demeaned by them and must repudiate them. Your own Code of Medical Ethics speaks directly to this point.

Moreover, when physicians engage in sexual misconduct with patients, the "code of silence" that has protected physician and priest alike must be broken. I offer for your consideration what we have done in the Archdiocese of Chicago in matters of clerical sexual misconduct with minors. An independent review board, the majority of whom are not clerics, evaluates all allegations and presents to me recommendations for action. The participation of these dedicated individuals in this process has not diminished the priesthood, but enhanced it.

Failure to ground the profession in a strong set of moral values risks the loss of public respect and confidence, and with that the profession faces the further erosion of its independence. Society's stake in medical care is too great to sustain the present level of professional autonomy if confidence in the profession declines.

Although I am focusing on what I believe needs to be repaired, I do not overlook or take for granted the great and good works performed by physicians every day—the grueling work in hospital emergency rooms, the treatment of AIDS victims, the care for the poor and the homeless, the *pro bono* work—to name only a few.

Let me summarize my major points so far. First, the practice of medicine is by nature a moral endeavor that takes the form of a covenant. Second, that covenant involves moral obligations to patients, to the profession, and to society. Third, the moral compass that guides physicians in meeting those obligations needs to be fully restored so that the covenant can be renewed. I have discussed the covenantal obligations to patients and the profession and suggested some guideposts. I turn now to the obligations to society.

Physicians and the profession have a covenant with society to be advocates for the health needs of their communities and the nation. This function is not as immediate or obvious as the others I have discussed, and in some respects its successful exercise depends on fulfilling those obligations that are more intimate to medical practice. The nature of these obligations may also be more controversial, but let me outline the primary elements of the social obligation.

- First, the establishment of health care as a basic human right. This right flows from the sanctity of life and is a necessary condition for the preservation of human dignity. Dr. Bristow has indicated that the opportunity for comprehensive reform of our health care system is "at least two administrations from now." I trust that the medical profession will take this prediction as a challenge, not as an inevitability.

- Second, the promotion of public health in the widest possible sense. In addition to the traditional public health agenda—clean water, sanitation, infectious diseases—we must include the health implications of inadequate nutrition, housing, and education. In addition, our public health horizons must include the "behavioral epidemics" engulfing our society—drug and alcohol abuse, violence, children raising children.

- Finally, leadership on the question of how best to protect human life and enhance human dignity in a situation of limited health resources. Although this issue is often framed in terms of rationing, I prefer a different word and a different concept: "stewardship." As a profession, you must take the lead in advising policy makers. This is a matter too important to be left to the government and the insurance companies.

If you sense an urgency in my voice today, it is because I believe we cannot afford to wait to renew the covenant with patients and society until some indefinite time in the future. The future is about to inundate us. If we do not reset the moral compass before the flood arrives, our opportunity may be washed away. Let me suggest only a few of the overarching issues we are already contending with: the aging of our society and of the industrialized world, the explosion of genetic knowledge and the potential for the manipulation of human life itself, the revolution in information and the attendant privacy issues. Confronting each of these issues will require our moral compass to be crystal clear and firmly set.

It is my hope that today will mark the beginning of a conversation among all of us concerned with the moral framework of health care in the United States, but especially among those of you within the medical profession. If current trends continue, the moral authority at the basis of medicine is in danger of being lost, perhaps irrevocably. You are closest to these issues, and, in the end, your choices will determine our course as a nation and community. Recommitting yourselves to medicine's inherent moral center will give you the strength and wisdom to renew the covenant and provide the leadership your patients, your profession, and your nation need and expect from you.

34.

MANAGING MANAGED CARE

International Association of Catholic Medical Schools

Loyola University, Chicago, May 13, 1996

Introduction

It is an honor to be with this distinguished international assembly of medical educators this morning. I trust that those of you who are not from this country will indulge me as I share some reflections on the transformation of the United States' health care system. Although these reflections are couched in the specifics of our experience, many of the issues involved are universal and are the subject of debate in other countries as well.

The next class of Catholic medical school graduates will begin their careers in the coming millennium. We are inclined to think of such chronological watersheds as defining epochal shifts in human behavior and institutions. In the remaining years of the twentieth century we are likely to be barraged with predictions and prophecies of what the new century, and the millennium it ushers in, will bring.

In the field of health care, however, history has had a head start. The new epoch has not waited for the new millennium; it is already well under way. Among the significant forces for twenty-first-century health care that have defined themselves in the past decade are the following: the explosion of genetic information that brings new hope and new ethical challenges seemingly each week; the aging of our society and of the industrialized world; and the revolution in information that expands our horizons and jeopardizes our privacy.

This morning, I will address the phenomenon that will inform the organization and delivery of health care in the next century. You do not have to be a futurist or a prophet to know that this is the phenomenon known as managed care. In the United States, with more than half of our insured population in some form of managed care, we have already entered the era of managed care. Our challenge for the coming years is in *managing* managed care to ensure that it contributes to the purposes of health care for each person, as well as the common good.

I come to this discussion as a pastor, a bishop, a leader of our National Conference of Catholic Bishops, and a member of the Board of the

Catholic Health Care Association of the United States. In these capacities I
have, with my colleagues, wrestled with the issues raised by managed care
and sought to develop responses compatible with our Catholic heritage and
health care mission. I have pursued this within the context of the consistent
ethic of life which I have articulated over the past twelve years.

The purpose of the consistent life ethic is to provide a moral framework
for analysis and motivation for action on a wide range of human life-issues
with important ethical dimensions. The foundation for this framework is a
deep conviction about the nature of human life, namely, that human life is
sacred, which means that all human life has an inalienable dignity that must
be protected and respected from conception to death. It is from this vantage
point that we consider the nature and value of managed care. In its relatively
brief history, managed care has become many things to many people:

- To some federal policy-makers, it is a way to assure the solven-
  cy of the Medicare program and to stretch Medicaid dollars further.
- To teaching hospitals and medical schools, it is a danger to
  broad-based support for medical research and education.
- To some patients, it is the loss of choice of a provider; to other
  patients, it is a greater array of benefits, including preventive
  services.
- To some ethicists, it is a back-door rationing scheme; to others,
  it is a prudent use of scarce social resources.

Managed care appears to be so many different things, in part, because
it is a broad term that covers many different health care financing and
delivery arrangements. In this discussion, I use the term "managed care" to
describe an insurance or delivery mechanism that involves one or more of
the following elements:

- limiting the number of providers serving a covered population,
  either through direct ownership or employment, or through
  selective contracting, or through some combination of these elements;
- adherence by providers to utilization management controls;
- incentives for patients to use only the providers designated by
  the managed care plan;
- some degree of financial risk for providers, ranging from HMOs
  that assume full risk for the cost of care to contractual arrangements under which carriers and providers share risk.

The diversity of views on managed care stems in part from the great
variety of ways in which the elements of managed care are applied. It is also
true, however, that part of the controversy about managed care results from
its impact on the health care system. Many of the traditional health care
relationships—between doctors and patients, between insurers and doctors,
between hospitals and doctors, between patients and insurers, to name a
few—are being dramatically affected by the transition to managed care. In

some cases, entirely new entities are being created that replace or restructure existing relationships.

In these times of radical change in the U. S. health care system, we should not be surprised that there are many opinions and many public policy issues. Health care is intensely personal. Each of us and each of our family members has a direct, personal stake in the cost, availability, and quality of health care. In addition, since health care in this nation is a more than a one-trillion-dollar enterprise, the financial stakes for government, insurers, employers, hospitals, physicians, and others are also great, as managed care produces new winners and losers in the marketplace.

We must remember, however, that no system of health care is an end in itself. We must examine managed care in terms of the nature of health and purpose of health care and how it advances or detracts from those purposes. We may also look at managed care in historical terms: Has it brought improvements over the methods of financing and delivery it is replacing? Are there things of value that are being lost?

Health Care Values

What are the principles and values of health care against which managed care should be measured? The goal of health care is healing. To heal is to restore wholeness, "to make whole that which is impaired or less than whole." Achieving wholeness requires attention not only to the physical condition of the patient, but also to his or her spiritual and social well-being. Further, health care is focused not only on curing illness, but also on preventing it and building "wellness." Health care is not focused solely on the patient, but also attends to the overall health of the community. No person can be completely well if his or her community is unhealthy, and a community's health is dependent on that of its members. To fulfill these purposes, a health care system must embody the following values:

- Health care must be a service. Care of those who are ill and dying is an important measure of the moral character of a society. Health care is an essential social good, a service to persons in need; it cannot be a mere commodity exchanged for profit, to which access depends on financial resources. Each person's human dignity must be preserved. Because health care is critical to human dignity, all persons have a right to basic, comprehensive health care of the highest quality.
- The common good must be served. Dignity is realized only in association with others. Health care must serve the good of the nation and the community as well as the individual.
- The needs of the poor must have special priority. The wealthy and well must not ignore their obligation to help care for the poor and the sick. The health fate of the poor should be tied to

that of the average U. S. citizen.

- There must be responsible stewardship of resources. Our resources are not unlimited and must be managed wisely. The health care system must use economic discipline to hold health care spending within realistic limits.
- Health care should be provided at appropriate levels of organization. It should respect local diversity, preserve pluralism in delivery, protect a range of choice, and preserve the relationship between physician and patient.

In considering managed care and its significance for achieving the purposes and values of health care, it is important to recognize the context from which managed care springs. Many of the same forces driving the growth of managed care are also propelling changes in other areas of society. In the private sector, global competition has led companies to seek efficiencies through consolidations, downsizings, and reducing the cost of benefits. In the public sector, continuing federal deficits and resistance to tax increases have led to constraints on government expenditures at all levels for all purposes.

The Traditional System

Health care has not been immune from the impact of these forces. Indeed, it is regarded by many as a major contributor to excessive costs and inefficiencies of both the public and private sectors. So, the strengths and weaknesses of the health care system that existed before managed care are also part of the context of managed care. Before turning to a consideration of managed care, I will briefly describe the health care system that it appears to be on its way to replacing.

In this discussion I shall refer to managed care's predecessor as the "traditional" system, although in many respects that system has become prevalent only in the post-World War II years. In its full blossoming, between 1965 and 1985, the traditional system was characterized:

- by a proliferation of clinically and economically independent health care providers, such as doctors and hospitals;
- by employment-based health insurance for a majority, but by no means all, of the non-aged, non-poor population;
- by fee-for-service payment for medical services by the individual, employer, private insurance carrie or government program;
- by a growing government presence both as an insurer for selected populations and as a founder of health care research and education; and by health care institutions, particularly hospitals, and insurers that were predominantly locally based and not-for-profit.

Looking at the strengths and weaknesses of traditional health care in terms of the health care values I outlined earlier, we see a mixed picture. For those with adequate insurance or sufficient personal resources, traditional health care's strengths include maximizing the choice of providers for patients, and clinical freedom for physicians. Subject to broad categories of insurance coverage and general definitions of medical necessity, a patient and a physician had relatively few limitations on treatment options.

The traditional system also was characterized by pluralism in the delivery system and by a commitment to the highest quality medicine through public and private support for research and education. The view of health care as a service—as opposed to a commodity—was widespread among physicians and not-for-profit hospitals that provided charity care. Paradoxically, however, the advent of government health care programs may have eroded the private sector's commitment to health care as a service.

The traditional system's weaknesses include the absence of a right to health care for all and the lack of a strong commitment to public health. Although mitigated by community-rated health insurance plans and Medicaid, health care for the poor remained haphazard. The traditional system contributed little toward the responsible stewardship of resources. Indeed, for physicians and other providers, the traditional system offered financial incentives to provide unneeded services and no reason for insured patients not to seek additional care, regardless of its likelihood for success. It may be argued that the relentlessly rising costs of traditional care acted as a brake on expanding health care services to the poor and the elderly under existing programs as well as on efforts to achieve universal coverage as a matter of right.

Managed Care

Managed care is, in part, a response to the perceived problems of traditional health care. We are limited in assessing its strengths and weaknesses relative to our fundamental health care values because of its relative newness, its many forms, and its still-evolving nature. A key attraction of managed care is that it offers a vehicle for enhancing the value of stewardship. By emphasizing the efficient use of health care resources, managed care appears to have contributed to the recent moderation in health care cost increases for employers and governments. By extension, managed care offers the possibility, through containing costs, of broadening access to health care through stretching government budgets and encouraging more employers to offer coverage to their employees.

Many types of managed care plans, because they are financially responsible for all the health care a person may use, have a strong incentive to provide preventive health care and careful management of chronic conditions to avoid costly complications. At the same time, however, these incentives can encourage plans to try to limit their enrollment to healthier populations as a "preventive" technique. A final and important strength of many managed care plans is the promotion of quality by identifying, disseminating, and reinforcing the most effective medical practices to their physicians and other providers.

As I have noted, in some aspects, the features of managed care that promote certain health care values may threaten others. Financial incentives to conserve resources can lead to providing too few services even as the traditional system can lead to the provision of too many services. Implicit pressures—such as the linking of physician compensation to cost targets—or explicit practice guidelines can result in limitations on access to needed services. Managed care promotes the consolidation of health care services—the grouping of doctors, hospitals, and other providers through employment or contracting into networks. This offers economies of scale that contain costs, but also threaten the continued independence of health care institutions that contribute to pluralism in our system. I speak here of Catholic and other religiously affiliated or charitable institutions whose missions are explicitly and intimately bound to the poor and the vulnerable. Also, because managed care typically contributes less support for research and medical education than the traditional system, we must examine the needs of these programs, as well as appropriate funding mechanisms.

As I have expressed on other occasions, there can be little doubt that there are good reasons to change our health care system, among them to improve the stewardship of our resources. The rapid growth of managed care, however, has heightened concerns that the economics of health care may unduly predominate over other fundamental health care values. Economics have always played a role in health care, but managed care systems require exceptionally large infusions of capital, primarily to fund the databases and computer systems needed to monitor care and cut costs, and to fund the creation of networks through the purchase of physician practices. The need for such capital has led an increasing number of not-for-profit hospitals to convert to for-profit status or to enter into joint ventures with for-profit hospital companies. And, while the need to produce a return to stockholders may spur continuous efforts to improve efficiency, it also raises the concern that managed care plans may be tempted to achieve efficiencies by restricting needed care.

Rationing

Many of the concerns about managed care are related directly or indirectly to this fear: namely, that the economic imperatives of managed care will result in the inappropriate rationing of health care services. If we accept, as we must, that our resources are finite, then we must address this issue openly and clearly. The very concept of rationing is explosive. I prefer the concept of "stewardship." How do we best protect human life and enhance human dignity in a situation of limited health resources?

If we define rationing as the withholding of potentially beneficial health care services because policies and practices establish limits on the resources available for health care, rationing becomes an issue of balance between the individual and the community, both of which have acknowledged needs. Under this definition, we do not prejudge the issue of whether a specific proposal or method of rationing is good or evil; we leave open the possibility that withholding care may be justified by limits on resources.

This is not an abstract discussion. Rationing health care is a regular, if unacknowledged, feature of both our traditional health care system and of our system as modified by managed care. As a nation, we ration health care by choosing not to adopt a system of universal health care coverage. As a result, nearly 40 million are uninsured and some 50 million more are underinsured. Government programs, such as Medicare and Medicaid, ration access to care on the basis of age, income, and family composition. Private health care is rationed by a person's or an employer's ability and willingness to pay. It is also rationed through insurance marketing techniques such as medical underwriting, pre-existing condition exclusion, and red-lining.

In my own life, as a person diagnosed with pancreatic cancer, I could have been denied treatment on several different grounds:

- my age—if I had been under 65 (the Medicare qualifying age) and if I had been uninsured;
- the expected outcome for persons of my age and health; or
- lack of coverage by my health plan for a specific procedure.

I also could have been discouraged, directly or indirectly, from seeking treatment if my physician had incentives to inform me of only certain treatments, or incentives to provide needed treatments for my condition in a facility far from my home and loved ones. In my case, however, I was well insured through a combination of private coverage paid by my diocese and Medicare that allowed me and my physicians maximum flexibility in selecting a treatment regimen.

Two years ago, I called for national health reform that assured universal coverage for all Americans, that is, to end the rationing of access to health care through denial of insurance. In that context, I pointed out that we would have to undertake a broad-based and inclusive consideration of how to allocate and share our limited health care dollars. It is proper, based on a moral consensus, for society to establish limits on what it can reasonably provide in one area of the commonweal so that it can address other legitimate responsibilities. Although the national debate over universal access unfortunately has been stilled for the present, the Catholic Health Association has addressed the ethics of rationing and offered some moral criteria.

These criteria demand that any acceptable rationing plan must meet a demonstrable need, be oriented to the common good, result from an open and participatory process, apply to all, give priority to disadvantaged persons, be free of wrongful discrimination, and be monitored in its social effects. Although these criteria were conceived in the context of developing a universal health plan, most of them are still as appropriate to the rationing decisions of private health plans as they are to public programs and should be applied to managed care in both sectors.

For example, an employer purchasing a health care plan should look not only at price, but also at the policies of any plan that may limit needed care. The employer is obligated to consider whether its resources or those of its employees are so limited as to justify a health plan that relies on rationing. The employer must also be sure that access to any health plan offered is equitable. When employers contribute a greater share of the premium cost for employees earning lower wages, they reduce the potential for rationing based on ability to pay.

Likewise, some states may have a genuine problem raising tax money for their Medicaid programs. But others have simply decided, for political expedience, to maximize, that is, not to diminish some of their citizens' disposable incomes, regardless of the unmet health care needs among their poorer citizens. This is irresponsible. Health care rationing in this context is unfair.

As I have pointed out, such rationing is not unique to managed care. Indeed, it has been a staple in the traditional system. Under that system, however, rationing, although reprehensible, is relatively visible. Managed care may require greater scrutiny to ensure that rationing decisions are transparent to patients and the public.

Managing Managed Care

In terms of the health care values we uphold—human dignity, stewardship, the common good—managed care offers both *promise and peril*. By restraining costs, it offers the possibility of including more persons under public and private insurance. By explicitly addressing the appropriateness of care through practice guidelines and other means, it offers the possibility of improving the quality of health care and eliminating unnecessary care. By focusing on prevention, it offers the possibility of avoiding or mitigating many serious and disabling conditions.

As I have noted, however, the market forces and economic disciplines that are the engines of managed care can be socially insensitive and ethically blind. In managing managed care we must find ways to encourage and sustain its benefits and to constrain those tendencies which, if left unattended, could undermine important health care values.

Because managed care is not a single phenomenon, but, rather, a variety of organizations, practices, and techniques that share almost as many differences as commonalities, its deficiencies, present and potential, defy sweeping diagnosis and prescription. At the same time, it is clear that managed care raises issues that go right to the social and ethical core of our health care values. As managed care asserts itself as the health care paradigm for the next century, we are obligated to confront these issues and shape its development. I have organized my own reflections on managed care around three groupings of issues: (1) those dealing with the *common good*; (2) those affecting the *quality* of health care; and, finally, (3) issues relating to *stewardship* and *rationing*.

First, I will address the *common good*, the social dimension of managed care. The paramount health care issue of our time is the affront to human dignity that is occasioned by the lack of universal insurance coverage for even basic care. In addition to the fear, insecurity, and inadequate health care that afflict individuals, the existence of rural and inner city hospitals that care for the uninsured is threatened by competitive managed care. While in theory managed care should help free up resources to cover such persons, it is not clear, despite some innovative state experiments, that managed care savings from public programs will be recycled to expand coverage. On the private side, it is a troubling fact that, despite several years of moderation in the growth of employer health care costs, which many attribute in large part to the growth of managed care, the number of persons covered by employer insurance has declined, not increased. It is not enough to argue that, without managed care, more persons would lose their insurance. We must use the benefits of managed care to help achieve the broadest possible coverage of our population.

In this regard, we must also develop mechanisms to provide appropriate support for education and research from all participants in the health care system. In general, managed care plans avoid sending patients to hospitals and other institutions with primary responsibility for training health care professionals and conducting medical research—activities that provide broad public benefits. At the same time, our teaching priorities must be adjusted to produce an appropriate number and balance of specialists and primary care providers. Research must also give greater emphasis to public health issues and behavioral problems.

The last social issue I will comment on is not peculiar to managed care, but is one that could be compounded by the competitive environment in which managed care operates. We must develop and adopt methods to compensate health plans that enroll disproportionate numbers of sick people at the expense of plans that enroll disproportionate numbers of healthy people. If we do not, we will witness a morally repugnant system in which plans will compete to avoid caring for the sick, thus avoiding a central purpose of health care altogether. These methods, known as "risk adjustment," reduce incentives for managed care plans to compete based on enrolling only healthier populations.

I turn now to a set of issues relating to the *quality* of care. Responsible decisions about managing health care depend on good data regarding health outcomes. While increasing attention has been given to this issue by both public and private agencies, much remains to be done. We should take an expanded view of outcomes, going beyond death and illness rates to include functional outcomes, the quality of life from the patient's perspective, and the satisfaction of both patient and provider. Doctors and hospitals should be leaders in the effort to develop and put into use measures of successful care.

These measures should be available to all. Managed care networks should issue annual report cards to the public on their enrollees' demographic characteristics, their health status, the number and kinds of services rendered, and the outcomes of these services. Such report cards will help families choose plans more wisely and will provide the public with the information needed to manage managed care.

Ultimately, quality health care is more than the sum of statistical outcomes. The use of practice guidelines should be expanded to include a strong patient role in the decision process. Patient education and empowerment programs have demonstrated better outcomes and lower costs when patients are fully informed and active participants. Most importantly, the patient's active involvement in medical decisions is a critical ingredient in the preservation of human dignity.

Finally, let us consider the issues of *stewardship* and *rationing*. As I mentioned a moment ago, there remains the fundamental challenge of universally assuring access to health care. Until this is achieved, some of the rationing implications of managed care pose moral problems. The crux of this problem is that, while universal access creates a floor of benefits, rationing creates a ceiling. We find ourselves moving toward a morally untenable situation in which we are building health care ceilings without floors—a regime in which there will be no limits on how little care one might receive, only on how much.

In the absence of universal coverage, however, we must focus on how health care ceilings are built. For instance, the adoption of practice protocols and other explicit care-determining policies by managed care plans should include a formal role for physicians participating in the plan, as medical staffs at most hospitals participate in decisions with clinical implications. Plan enrollees should also be consulted and there should be provision for public oversight.

Even with such precautions, there remains the potential that economic incentives for doctors and other providers in managed care plans may lead to *ad hoc* rationing decisions that are designed to protect income, not the patient. Some reward for physicians' efforts to make care more economical is appropriate, but financial incentives to physicians to constrain care should be limited to avoid the potential for less than optimal care. One approach to this problem is contained in recent federal regulations that require Medicare HMOs to limit the financial risk of participating physicians to specified levels. This is intended to reduce possible conflicts between a physician's pocketbook and the patient's needs. In general, financial incentives should cover a group of doctors so that the focus is on promoting efficient practice patterns for all patients, not on rewarding individual physicians for denying care to individual patients.

Information on managed care plans' policies that limit care and physician financial incentives should be made available to all enrollees. Physicians must be free to discuss these issues directly with patients without fear of penalty. When controversies arise about the appropriateness of care, there must be clear guidelines for appeal within a plan, and physicians should have the explicit role of advocacy on behalf of their patients. These concerns go to the trust that must be at the heart of the doctor-patient relationship, a trust that in many ways is being challenged today and which we must work to strengthen, as I indicated in a recent address to the House of Delegates of the American Medical Association.

Conclusion

Managing managed care must involve both the public and private sectors, and there are many initiatives toward this end currently underway by individual health care systems and others. Large employer and employee coalitions can play an important role by demanding outcomes-based quality measures by plans that seek their business. Health care provider organizations, such as the American Medical Association, the National Committee for Quality Assurance, and the Joint Commission on the Accreditation of Hospitals and Other Health Care Organizations, also have a critical role to play in helping to ensure that managed care contributes to the values of human dignity and social good.

The Catholic Health Association, in its proposal for health care reform, entitled "Setting Relationships Right," has addressed many of these issues. And Catholic health providers, such as the several Mercy Health Systems, have developed explicit ethical guidelines for managed care contract negotiations.

By encouraging prudent use of our resources, managed care can help us achieve a broader and, ultimately, universal health care coverage. It can help improve quality standards and reduce unnecessary and dangerous medical care. It can promote preventive care and wellness. It can nurture comprehensive primary care relationships between patients and physicians.

Like most human endeavors, however, managed care contains within it the potential for creating as many problems as it solves. Without vigilance and thoughtful, constructive engagement, we could find that instead of expanding coverage, managed care might function primarily as an instrument to ensure that those who now enjoy health care coverage continue to do so. This is important—we do not wish to see an erosion of coverage—

but it is not enough. We could find that new, unacceptable means of rationing are added to those that already exist. We could find that economic goals supplant health goals. We could find that the trust that is so essential to the doctor-patient relationship might be undermined by financial incentives.

As we approach the new century, changes in the health care system will continue to accelerate. By evaluating and responding to those changes in terms of our consistent life ethic and our health care values, we have the opportunity and the obligation to manage managed care so that it advances the goals of human dignity and the common good.

35.

REFLECTIONS ON THE PUBLIC LIFE AND WITNESS OF THE CHURCH IN U. S. SOCIETY AND CULTURE

GEORGETOWN UNIVERSITY, SEPTEMBER 9, 1996

Let me begin by expressing my appreciation to Georgetown University, and particularly to Father Leo O'Donovan, for inviting me to return here to reflect upon the public life and witness of the Catholic Church in the context of U. S. society and culture. Each time I have come to Georgetown, it has been in a presidential election year, but I regard that as a secondary consideration. The Church must reflect continuously on its public witness. That witness is rooted in religious and moral convictions, so the reflection must be theological in its foundation and then related to the issues of policy that shape the life of our society.

This afternoon, I seek to provide a "broad" interpretation of the Church's public witness. It will be broad in two senses: First, I will address three large areas of intersection between the Catholic moral vision and U.S. society: (1) religion and politics, (2) economic choices and social justice, and (3) the sanctity of life and U. S. culture. Second, in each area—politics, economics, and culture—I propose to look not only at how Catholic teaching speaks to American society, but how these issues should be reflected upon in the internal life of the Church itself.

Building upon the premise that theological principles should ground our thinking about the Church's public life, I will rely principally upon a major teaching document for each area of my address, using Vatican II's *Declaration on Religious Liberty* for religion and politics, the U. S. Catholic bishops' pastoral letter on the economy *(Economic Justice for All)* for justice and the economy, and Pope John Paul II's *The Gospel of Life* to address life and culture.

Religion and Politics: The American Style

The relationship of religion and politics is as old as the U. S. constitutional tradition. The nation was founded in great part by those who had experienced religious discrimination or who were wary of any close connection of religion and politics. Religious pluralism has been for this nation

287

both a factual condition and a constitutionally protected characteristic of the society almost from its inception. Precisely because of its centrality to the U. S. political tradition, the issue of religion and politics requires constant intellectual attention. Commentators have often noted an apparent paradox: Religion is kept strictly separate from the institution of the state, yet the U. S. public overwhelmingly thinks of itself as a religious people, with a very high percentage consistently affirming their religious convictions. The paradox is apparent because an argument can be made that careful distinctions between religion and politics may be in fact our source of religious vitality. I suggest we think of the role of religion in our society in terms of three questions: church and state, church and civil society, and, finally, religion and politics.

The church-state question is the central structural element in understanding the role of religion in U. S. society. For all its centrality, however, it is actually a quite limited issue. It is best, I think, to try to keep it both limited in its significance and clear in its content. The church-state relationship governs how the institution of the state will relate to religiously based institutions in our society. To discuss, debate, or analyze church and state is not at all to engage the full range of religious conviction and commitment in our society. The church-state relationship is narrow, juridical, and institutional in character. Governed by the First Amendment to the U. S. Constitution, it essentially affirms that religious communities should expect neither special assistance from the state nor any discrimination in the exercise of their civil and religious activity in society. This description of the meaning of the First Amendment does not attempt to exegete the court decisions that address specific dimensions of the law. It is, rather, a political interpretation of this standard element of our constitutional life. From the perspective of Catholic teaching, embodied in the *Declaration on Religious Liberty,* the political meaning of the First Amendment is good law. It protects what the Second Vatican Council and Pope Paul VI asserted was the basic requirement of church-state relations in any culture: the freedom of the Church. Keeping secular and religious institutions distinct in purpose and function, in fact, creates space for the Church to teach, preach, and serve. Having the freedom to function guaranteed by law allows the Church—and any religious community in this society—to define its ministry, pursue its religious and civil objectives, and demonstrate the transforming power of faith, love, and grace in society.

It is precisely when the church-state relations are clearly defined in law, that the second dimension of the role of religion in society becomes centrally important: the relationships, networks, institutions, and associations that lie "beyond the state"; that is, they are neither created by the state nor are they controlled by the state. The concept of civil society is captured in the distinction between state and society that is pivotal in the Western liberal tradition of politics and that both Jacques Maritain and John Courtney

Murray used in building the case within Catholicism for the right of religious liberty.

Both external and internal events in the United States have refocused scholarly attention and policy debates on the role and function of civil society. The collapse of communism in Central Europe and the former Soviet Union has yielded proposals from the West on how "to shrink" the state and build the fabric of civil society. At the same time, troubling trends in the United States on issues as diverse as family life, education, citizen participation, and general standards of civility have concentrated attention on the quality and character of our own civil society. It is in the fabric of civil society that religious communities and institutions flourish. In terms of the U. S. political tradition, it is critically important to stress that the logic of church-state relations, which emphasizes legitimate separation of secular and sacral institutions, should not govern the logic of civil society. The logic of this relationship is engagement, not separation. In other words, to endorse a properly secular state, which has no established ties to any religious institution, does not imply or mean that we should support a secularized society, one in which religion is reduced to a purely private role.

Both Catholic social theory and U. S. constitutional principles support a substantive role and place for religion in the fabric of our society and culture. The state will not and should not be the agent for advancing a substantive conception of religious values and principles in the life of the nation, but the state should not be hostile to the enterprise. Precisely because of the pervasive role of religious convictions among the citizens of our society, there is a legitimate place in our national life for these convictions to find expression.

Civil society is a sphere of freedom; it provides political and legal space for a multiplicity of actors and institutions to help form and shape the fabric of our national life and culture. In this sphere of freedom, religious institutions can exercise the full range of their ministries of teaching and service. Religious witness will only be as effective and as persuasive as the religious communities render it through the lives and work of their leaders and members. This is the meaning of being "free to function." We can demand this right; then we must meet our responsibilities.

While the constitutional framework that generates our place in civil society is clear enough, it is also clear that one finds in the debate about civil society today some voices that are less than comfortable with a vigorous role for religious institutions in our public life and policy debates. This may in part be due to the way some religious witness is undertaken. But it is also the case that some versions of civil society are advanced, that carry the logic of separation to the point where the public life of our society would lose its religious content.

If this happened, I submit, we would be a poorer culture and society. There is clearly no place for religious coercion or proselytization in our public life, but there is a broad area in which religious ideas and institutions can contribute to issues as diverse as strengthening the family, humanizing the drive of economic competition, and defining our responsibilities as a nation in a very changed world.

To those who are skeptical or simply opposed to a public role for religion, and to the community of believers upon whom lies the responsibility for religious witness, I submit there are three ways in which religious traditions can enrich civil society. The first is through religious vision and discourse. The Hebrew scriptures tell us that where there is no vision, people perish. A constant responsibility of religious communities is to enrich our public vision through the resources of ideas, values, principles, and images that are the core of any great tradition.

In my own tradition, I have tried to take the theme of the sacredness of the human person and develop its implications through a consistent ethic of life. The ideas supporting the consistent ethic have been cultivated in the Catholic moral tradition for centuries. But the convergence of forces arising from contemporary society to threaten human life and sacredness creates a new context in which the ancient themes of an ethic of stewardship of life take on new relevance. Essentially, I have argued, as I will this afternoon, that we must systematically address a series of threats to life by building within civil society a shared vision of what human sacredness demands and how we install binding principles of restraint and respect in our personal codes of conduct and in our public policies.

The theme of "A Consistent Ethic" is only one way in which a religious tradition can enrich our public dialogue. I realize that part of the apprehension of some citizens, scholars, and analysts is that religious convictions that are not universally shared will be thrust into our policy debates. I understand the concern, and I will return to it in this address, but here I simply want to establish the point that a policy of excluding religious vision, discourse, and insights from our search for coherent, just, viable public policies is a price too high to pay. Without vision, people perish; we need all the resources we can muster today in developing an adequate vision for our society.

But religion is not exhausted by ideas and vision alone. A second crucial contribution it can make to civil society is through the ministry and work of religious institutions of education, health care, family service, and direct outreach to the poorest parts of our society. The web of religious institutions is a pervasive aspect of our social support system. I believe it is the time to think intensively about how a more extensive public-private pattern of collaboration could serve to extend the range of effectiveness of these institutions and at the same time use scarce public resources more efficiently in support of human needs.

Thirdly, perhaps the most effective, long-term contribution that religious communities make to civil society is the kind of citizens who are shaped, often decisively, by participation in a religious tradition. In Christian terms this is the link between discipleship and citizenship. Recent research, reflected in the work of Robert Putnam at Harvard University, as well as that of John Coleman and David Hollenbach in the Catholic community, points to the way in which religious affiliation has a decisive impact on the kind of civic engagement in which individuals participate, particularly engagement in the service of others.

In summary, my argument thus far has been in support of clear distinctions between church and state, in opposition to any exclusion of religion from civil society, and in advocacy of a broad, deep, activist role for religious institutions in shaping our public life.

There is a final piece of this argument, this one directed to the religious communities rather than civil society: the theme of religion and politics. My point here is that a proper understanding of both the logic of *separation* (church and state) and the logic of *engagement* (church and civil society) locates the church in the proper place for public witness. *How* religion engages the political order is a question of style, and style here carries major importance. *Style* refers to the way religious communities speak to the political process, and *style* also refers to the manner in which we engage others in debate and discussion. One reason why some have apprehension about religious involvement in public life is the style sometimes employed by religious institutions or communities. My proposal, therefore, is that effective religious witness depends, in part, on our style of participation. Engagement in civil society must be characterized by commitment and civility; witness must be a blend of advocacy and restraint. I am hardly pressing for a timid or feeble religious voice! My concern, rather, is to establish from within religious communities standards of participation that will shape our public witness.

Allow me to use two examples. First, while I know there is a healthy debate on this topic among scholars, I am inclined to the view that our style of arguing a social position ought to distinguish among how we speak within the church, how we participate in civil society, and how we address the state on law and policy. Within the church, the full range of biblical, theological themes that structure our belief should be used. Within civil society, I also think that explicit appeal to religious warrants and imperatives is both legitimate and needed if we are to address some of the profoundly human themes that are at the heart of our policy debates. But when we address the state, I believe we should be ascetic (sparing) in our use of explicitly religious appeals. Here we seek to shape law and policy that will obligate all in society. At this point we accept the responsibility of making our religiously grounded convictions intelligible to those who do not share the faith that yields these convictions.

Secondly, our style of religious witness should constantly be a testimony to the theological virtue of charity, which, in turn, produces the civic virtue of civility. Vigorous pursuit of our deepest convictions—even those involving life and death—should not involve questioning the motives of others, or their character. We should vigorously oppose conclusions we find unwise or immoral; we should vigorously pursue objectives that are essential for human life and dignity. But we should also be known for the way in which our witness leavens public life with a spirit of fairness, respect, restraint, and a search for common ground among contending positions. As you know, I have recently called for a Catholic Common Ground Project, a process of conversation and collaboration on issues that divide us within the Catholic Church. I do so not only because I believe we need such an initiative to enhance our own community but also because I believe that the style of our internal life is part of our public witness and contribution.

Justice and the Economy: A Catholic Perspective

One example of public religious witness, which attracted much attention a decade ago, was the pastoral letter on the U. S. economy, *Economic Justice for All*. The tenth anniversary of the letter is being observed by a series of symposia, commemorations, and efforts to reflect upon what the pastoral letter's teaching on justice says to us in the new conditions of the 1990s. Since its publication ten years ago, the U. S. economy has continued to experience deep and far-reaching change, generated by broader global patterns of economic interdependence. As bishops, we came to see in the 1980s that it was virtually impossible to isolate the U. S. economy for analysis apart from the global economy. Today, that truth is even more evident. Obviously many aspects of our economic life are quite positive: we are in a period of sustained economic growth, the competitiveness of American workers and industry has been demonstrated convincingly, the unemployment statistics are modest if not satisfactory, and inflation has been contained.

These "macro" indicators of our economic life are critically important, but they do not address crucial moral questions that must be part of our assessment of U. S. economic life. While we have demonstrated our ability to compete internationally, not all in our nation have survived the competition. Economic dislocation, downsizing of major industries and loss of jobs, threats to familial and personal economic security are experiences all too well known by significant sectors of our population. The dynamic of the global market does not address the human costs of global competition either here or in other countries. The dynamic of the market must be complemented by a broader framework of social policy that attends to the needs of those who lose in the economic lottery.

The pastoral letter, *Economic Justice for All,* sought to focus the attention of both church and civil society on those whom our economic life has left out, left behind, and left alone. Catholic social and economic teaching is always concerned for the welfare of society as a whole and for the human dignity and human rights of each person; this systemic concern is exemplified in the concept of the common good. Within the context of a concern for all, however, there is a basic obligation to attend to the needs of the vulnerable—old or young, black or white, male or female. This is the religious mandate specified by the Hebrew prophets' call to protect "the orphans, the widows, and the resident aliens." It is the contemporary theme in Catholic teaching embodied in "the option for the poor." The striking fact is how accurately the prophets of 2,700 years ago speak to our life today: Secular sources of analysis identify women and children as the most vulnerable groups in our society. Recent legislation—at the state and national level— effectively eliminates basic social support and services for "resident aliens" in our midst, whether they are legal or undocumented immigrants in our society. While pertinent *legal* distinctions exist among these two groups, the *moral* tradition of the prophets affirms moral obligations that we have to both, and uniquely to their children. The voices of the prophets are too accurate for us to be satisfied by "macro" indicators of economic health. The poor are still with us, and there is nothing in the Hebrew and Christian scriptures that tolerates complacency about their needs.

Two of our major socioeconomic policy debates of the 1990s should make us think deeply about our societal contract, or conception of moral obligation among the citizens of this nation. Both the health care debate of the early 1990s and the welfare debate of this past year point to deeper issues than either health or welfare policy. The health care debate, large and complex as it was, contained a core element of the need to extend the social safety net to the 40 million citizens without basic coverage. The welfare debate, also complex in its elements, forced to the surface the question of whether any social safety net would be preserved at all. I should be clear: in highlighting the complexity of both policy issues, I acknowledge that health care policy must address the exponential increase in health care costs, the need to restructure parts of our delivery system, and the need to strike a balance between competing objectives of quality of care and the kinds of care provided in the health care system. I also acknowledge that reform of the welfare system is required for the good of all concerned: recipients, taxpayers, and providers.

Even with these considerations squarely before us, however, both of the extended policy debates on these issues, in my view, failed to meet basic standards of responsible policy. The leading industrial democracy in the world failed to extend a minimum standard of health care to its citizenry as a whole, and it has effectively dismantled the most basic protection for children in our society. Both the prophets and the pastoral letter stand in judgment of these actions. If this society cannot protect its most vulnerable— our sick and our children—it must be because we cannot think and speak clearly to each other about fundamental moral imperatives. Even in a deficit-driven economic debate, the fate of the sick and the young holds primacy of moral standing. Yes, we have "changed" health care and welfare. But from the perspective of those for whom we bear moral responsibility, change does not equal reform. It looks more like abandonment.

The deeper issues behind health care and welfare involve not only our societal compact with each other; they also involve allocation of responsibility for social policy that meets both the standards of effectiveness and justice. On a range of issues—social policy, tax policy, the stability of families, the cultivation of key values in personal and public life—I fear we are carrying on fundamental debates in a style that does not match in depth the substance of the issues addressed.

Running through most of our social policy debates is the discussion of the appropriate role of the state in our common life as a society. Catholic social thought is hardly statist in its premises or principles. The concept of "subsidiarity," a staple of Catholic social theory, explicitly requires that responses to social needs not start with the state. But subsidiarity does not yield a conception of the state that removes from it basic moral obligations not only for "the general welfare" but also specific moral duties toward those afflicted by illness, hardship, unemployment, and the lack of adequate nutrition and housing. My point is that it is not sufficient to carry on a discussion of the appropriate role of the state purely in terms of efficiency or size or "intrusiveness." These criteria are important but not significant if we omit a conception of what the state's moral role is in society. To speak of the state's moral role is not only to address the cultivation of moral standards; it also involves specific duties, often of a socioeconomic nature, which the state has to its citizens.

Critics of this position will say I am making an abstract argument about the state's responsibility without acknowledging that the state does not generate the resources for its socioeconomic policies and programs; citizens do that. The critics are partially right; we cannot discuss the moral obligations of the state apart from a substantive analysis of the obligations we have to each other as members of civil society. To the critics I will grant their point because I am convinced the deeper issue beneath our policy debates is precisely this question: how we conceive of our social bonds of obligation and responsibility, within families, beyond families to neighborhoods, and ultimately to the national community of which we are a part. A purely "contractual" view of our relationships is inadequate; it quickly reduces our obligations to those freely chosen, with no wider fabric of accountability. Contractual relations serve useful, limited functions, but we need a stronger fabric of social ties to undergird our life as a society. We require a sense of obligation to those we do not know, will never meet, and yet bear a responsibility for, precisely because of their need and our capacity to share in meeting that need.

There are many ways to express this stronger sense of social responsibility; Pope John Paul II and the pastoral letter rely on the concept of "solidarity." Solidarity implies a fabric of moral bonds that exists among humans because of a shared sense of personhood. Solidarity precedes subsidiarity. The first defines our moral relationship; the second regulates how we will fulfill the duty of solidarity. Social solidarity finds expression in several ways. It sustains personal relationships; it binds families in a common life of love and support; it initiates and supports private efforts of charity and social service. But it also helps to define the moral responsibility of the state and its citizenry.

Solidarity points toward the neuralgic issue of U. S. politics: taxation. Taxes are one way in which the state facilitates our responsibilities to each other. Tax policy is a secular issue, but it is rooted in moral obligations we have to one another. A fair tax policy, one which obliges each of us to play a role in sustaining the human dignity of all in our society, is a requirement of distributive justice. In Catholic teaching, paying taxes is a virtue. Taxes help us to meet our pre-existing obligations to the poor.

In addition to establishing the basis for a just tax policy, Catholic teaching, I believe, has something critical to say to our contemporary debate about institutional responsibility and social policy. Over the last sixty years, three key ideas have characterized Catholic social teaching: subsidiarity, solidarity, and socialization. They need to be held in tandem: solidarity establishes the basis of common obligation; subsidiarity argues that private voluntary institutions are needed to fulfill our obligations; and socialization maintains that increased societal interdependence requires an activist state to meet the needs that private institutions cannot meet alone. I spoke earlier about the need for new patterns of public-private collaboration. To address the deeper issues of our social policy debate, we need to attend to these three concepts. We *do* have moral obligations to the vulnerable. So, we should have an adequate public policy to guarantee that the orphans, the widows, and the resident aliens are not left to the ravages of life.

As we seek to contribute to the societal debate about allocation of social responsibility, the role of our own social institutions becomes a crucial part of our public witness. Catholic schools, Catholic health care systems, and Catholic charities testify to our conviction that we have abiding social responsibilities. We live in a time of declining public resources and exploding public needs. Our institutions should not be used as an example that we do not need public engagement to meet social needs. But, as we argue for a strong fabric of social programs to meet human needs, our institutions can seek to demonstrate the quality of care for human life which a vision of human sacredness cultivates.

Precisely because we already support a broad range of social institutions, and because we are also committed in principle to an active if limited role for the state, the Catholic community should be a creative and articulate participant in the much-needed debate in this society about the comparative advantage that public institutions of the state have on some aspects of social policy and the severe liabilities they have on other issues. Seeking a new relationship of public and private agencies in our society is an imperative of the first order. Such a discussion involves constitutional issues of Church and state, societal issues of how best to structure civil society, and empirical issues of operational effectiveness. It is a far-reaching argument, but it must be undertaken because today too many suffer from the lack of an effective and humane policy vision.

The Sacredness of Life: Religion, Culture, and Politics

In this concluding section of my address, I return to the concept of the consistent ethic. Thus far this afternoon, in addressing religion and politics, justice and economics, I have sought to reflect upon how we care for life in our midst, both personally and through public policy. Caring for life, supporting it, and responding to basic human needs of nutrition, health care, housing, and education are an essential aspect of the consistent ethic. As I have indicated, I believe we have yet a substantial way to go in *caring* for the lives of the least among us. But, in the contemporary U. S. context, caring for life does not exhaust our moral obligations. We now face in the 1990s profoundly threatening public issues where life is being taken without moral justification.

In proposing the consistent ethic over a decade ago, my purpose was to help create a dialogue about the full range of threats to life which modern society poses. I recognize the difference between the obligation to care for life and that to defend life against attack. I recognize that the moral failure to care for life adequately is different from the moral crime of taking an innocent life. But I was convinced—and still am firmly convinced—that the overriding moral need in our society is to cultivate a conviction that we must face *all* the major threats to life, not only one or two. The "consistent ethic" precisely seeks to relate our moral analysis to *different* kinds of moral problems. It seeks to provide a framework within which individuals and groups, who begin with a concern for one moral dimension of life, can be brought to see the threat posed by other issues in our societies.

When we shift our focus in U. S. society from thinking about *caring* for life to *defending* life, there is hardly a better guide than Pope John Paul II's encyclical, *The Gospel of Life*. The Holy Father identified three issues—abortion, capital punishment, and euthanasia—in his sweeping critique of what he described as a creeping "culture of death." Here again, even within the Catholic tradition these three issues have not been simply collapsed into one question. Capital punishment has not in the past been regarded as "unjust killing" in the way abortion and euthanasia have been. But the power of the papal argument is that it helps us to see that, today, different kinds of taking life should be systematically related. Faced with a need to build a societal consensus that respects life, Catholic teaching has clearly moved to restrict the state's right to take life, even in instances previously approved.

There is an inner logic to an ethic that respects life and a contrary logic in quick, frequent resort to solving problems by taking life. While not seeking to simplify complex human problems, I suggest we think carefully about our society, which today sustains nearly 1.5 million abortions annually, which is overwhelmingly in favor of capital punishment, and which is now moving rapidly toward acceptance of assisted suicide. Each of these problems must be argued on its own terms. There are clearly distinctions among positions held across this spectrum of issues, but there is also a truth to be learned in relating these three questions. The truth is that respect for life will cost us something. To move beyond solutions and problems, which many would solve by taking life, will require a more expansive care for life—at its beginning and its end.

I cannot plunge at this point in my address into a detailed assessment of these three issues in our public life. But I do think that relating the experience we have had on abortion to the current debate about assisted suicide can be helpful. Once again, the deeper themes behind the specific choices are the most important ones. In both the abortion and the assisted-suicide debates, I am convinced that the basic picture one has of the social fabric of life is crucial to how one makes a moral judgment on the specific issues.

The abortion debate has been publicly framed as a "private choice." In both public debate and recent judicial decisions, assisted suicide has been argued in similarly "private" terms. Such a construction of these questions promotes the idea that social consequences are lacking in both cases. I am convinced that such a view is profoundly shortsighted. To use assisted suicide as an example, it is undoubtedly a deeply personal issue because it touches upon life and death, and a person's conception of whom they are accountable to in life and death. But it also directly affects the doctor-patient relationship and, through that, the wider role of doctors in our society. As has been noted by others, it threatens to introduce a deep ambiguity into the very definition of medical care, if care comes to involve killing. Beyond the physician, a move to assisted suicide and, perhaps beyond that, to euthanasia creates social ambiguity about the law. In civilized society the law exists to protect life. When it also begins to legitimate the taking of life as a policy, one has a right and a duty to ask what lies ahead for our life together as a society. There are deep psychological, social, and moral questions at stake in how we conceive our social relationship to each other and particularly to the most vulnerable in our society—again, the very young and the very sick become test cases.

After two decades of struggle over abortion, our society and our Church now face a double challenge to *defend* life even as we continue to pursue ways to *care* for and *nurture* it. I remain convinced that our witness will be more effective, more persuasive, and better equipped to address the moral challenge we face, if we witness to life across the spectrum of life from conception until natural death, calling our society to see the connection between caring for life and defending it.

Here again, there are implications for the internal life of the Church. It is urgently necessary that we remain a voice for life—vigorous, strong, consistent. In the recent case of partial birth abortion, the protest raised from within our Church and by others was absolutely necessary. The procedure should *not* be allowed; it *should* have been stopped; it *must* be stopped! There will undoubtedly be other cases, at both ends of life, when our voice, our advocacy, our legitimate efforts will be needed.

But we also must continue to witness by deed to a conception of caring for life that seeks to invite the wider society to see the linkage between *care for* and *defense of* life. So, I commend those who have been organized in support of single mothers, those who seek to provide a place for pregnant women of all ages to receive support and care, those who sponsor and serve in health care facilities and programs that care for the dying and sustain hope even in the face of a long, painful dying process. These efforts from within the Church are essential to match the public witness of the Church in society.

Conclusion

As you are well aware, this has been a long lecture. In bringing it to a close, I will consciously change its tone and tenor. When I accepted Father O'Donovan's invitation, I undertook the assignment of giving a policy lecture suited for an academic audience. I have tried to fulfill that task this afternoon. But I also thought at the time of the invitation that I would likely have several opportunities to contribute to the U. S. debate on religion and our public life, on the moral values of human dignity and the sacredness of human life.

As you are aware, I now face a very different horizon. In human terms, I have been advised my life span is now quite limited. This fact does not change any of the moral or social analyses that I have used in this address. But it does shape one's perspective decisively. I have already said that, as a person of faith—of resurrection faith—I see death as a friend, not a foe, and the experience of death is, I am convinced, a transition from earthly life to eternal life—from grace to glory, as St. Augustine said.

These are my deepest convictions of faith, which has been rooted in God's word and confirmed by the sacraments of the Church. But the experience I am now going through sheds new light on the moral order also. As a bishop, I have tried, in season and out of season, to shape and share a moral message about the unique value of human life and our common responsibilities for it. As my life now slowly ebbs away, as my temporal destiny becomes clearer each hour and each day, I am not anxious, but rather reconfirmed in my conviction about the wonder of human life, a gift that flows from the very being of God and is entrusted to each of us. It is easy in the rush of daily life or in its tedium to lose the sense of wonder that is appropriate to this gift. It is even easier at the level of our societal relations to count some lives as less valuable than others, especially when caring for them costs us—financially, emotionally, or in terms of time, effort, and struggle.

The truth is, of course, that each life is of infinite value. Protecting and promoting life—caring for it and defending it—is a complex task in social and policy terms. I have struggled with the specifics often and have sensed the limits of reason in the struggle to know the good and do the right. My final hope is that my efforts have been faithful to the truth of the gospel of life and that you and others like you will find in this gospel the vision and strength needed to promote and nurture the great gift of life God has shared with us.

INDEX